The Puerto Rican Movement

In the *Puerto Rican Studies* Series

edited by Luz del Alba Acevedo, Juan Flores, and Emilio Pantojas-García

The Puerto Rican *Movement*

Voices from the Diaspora

Edited by
ANDRÉS TORRES AND
JOSÉ E. VELÁZQUEZ

TEMPLE UNIVERSITY PRESS
Philadelphia

Temple University Press, Philadelphia 19122
Copyright © 1998 by Temple University, except Chapter 1 © 1998 by Andrés Torres,
Chapter 3 and 5 © 1998 by José E. Velázquez, and Chapter 12 © 1998 by Iris Morales
All rights reserved
Published 1998
Printed in the United States of America

⊗The paper used in this publication meets the requirements of the
American National Standard for Information Sciences—Permanence
of Paper for Printed Library Materials, ANSI Z39.48-1984

Library of Congress Cataloging-in-Publication Data

The Puerto Rican movement : voices from the diaspora / Andrés Torres
    and José E. Velázquez, editors.
        p.   cm.
    Includes bibliographical references (p. 000) and index.
    ISBN 1-56639-617-4 (cloth : alk. paper), — ISBN 1-56639-618-2
(pbk. : alk. paper)
    1. Puerto Ricans—United States—Politics and government.
2. Radicalism—United States—History—20th century.   I. Torres,
Andrés, 1947–   .   II. Velázquez, José E. (José Emiliano), 1952–   .
E184.P85P77   1998
973'.04687295—dc21   97-45189
                                                              CIP

For Rachel, Gabriel, Javier, Orlando,
and your generation

Contents

       Luis Aponte-Parés and Jorge B. Merced   296

18   An African American–Puerto Rican Connection
       James Early   316

19   Forging Solidarity: Politics, Protest, and the Vieques
       Solidarity Network
       Katherine McCaffrey   329

       Notes   341

       Bibliography   363

       Contributors   367

       Index   371

Preface

IN THE mid-nineteenth century Dr. Ramón Emeterio Betances, physician and abolitionist, emerged as the leader of Puerto Rico's struggle for independence from Spain. He was resolute in his conviction that the island could extract itself from colonial domination but became impatient with the pace of events. Exasperated that his homeland, along with Cuba, had yet to achieve liberation as did the rest of Latin America, he worried out loud, *"¿Qué hacen . . . que los puertorriqueños no se rebelan?"* "What's happening . . . that the Puerto Ricans don't rebel?" By the turn of the century Spain ceded her territory to the United States, victor of the Spanish-American War. Now Puerto Rico's fate was in the hands of the "Giant of the North," who refused to relinquish control. In the early to mid-twentieth century, another voice emerged challenging Puerto Ricans to overcome colonialism. Albizu Campos's great contribution was to revive the militant tradition of Betances who insisted that Puerto Rico be placed within the Caribbean and Latin American context and not retained as some appendix to the United States. By the 1960s the island was still a colony and a new revival in the independence movement took place, explicitly tracing its political lineage back to Campos and Betances. One of the most popular slogans of the era was *"¡Despierta Boricua! ¡Defiende lo tuyo!"* ("Wake up Puerto Rican, Defend what is yours!") Engaged in a century-old call and response with the venerable Betances, the new radical movement inscribed another chapter in Puerto Rico's political history.

However, an important development had occurred during the post–World War II period. As part of "Operation Bootstrap," the colony saw one-third of its population relocated to the great urban centers of the North through a state-sponsored mass migration. By the 1960s the Puerto Rican barrios of the United States stirred with Nationalist sentiment too, but here with a twist. Assimilating diverse influences from various social and political movements of the time, Puerto Rican radicalism merged island-oriented concerns with inequality and racism in U.S. barrios. Betances had spent much time in exile in New York City planning the end of Spanish domination in Puerto Rico. Not in his wildest dreams could he have imagined that a century later his descendants would be marching up and down the streets of this great metropolis, carrying his image on banners, responding to his call for an awakening. This book is the story of the movement—the Puerto Rican radical struggle in the United States. This movement started out in earnest during the late 1960s and continued throughout the 1970s and well into the 1980s. Although there has been a significant waning of radical political activism since the 1980s, there are important instances of organizing and educating still underway.

Combining autobiographical reflection, historical documentation, and political analysis, the chapters in this book provide the most comprehensive assessment yet of the experience of the Puerto Rican movement in the United States. Simultaneously contributing to the historical record of the island-based independence movement and U.S. radical struggles, this anthology is an effort to assert—proudly but without romantic naiveté—the importance of this movement in the history of Puerto Rico and the United States. It also augments the growing literature dealing with social movements within migrant communities. As globalization proceeds to break down national frontiers, we hope this work will be a reminder that the story of Puerto Rican radicalism is one of the foremost examples of political struggle in the diaspora of a colonized people. Almost all the writings were prepared explicitly for this publication, and practically all the authors are direct participants in this experience. It is to be regretted that important gaps remain in the recounting of this history. Time and space constraints prevented us from giving proper weight to some key dimensions of the movement's influence: labor, cultural and intellectual expressions, community organizing, and interactions with U.S. solidarity groups. Our geographic coverage was not fully representative, with omissions of such cities as Newark, New Haven, Gary, Ind., Cleveland, Los Angeles, and San Francisco. A large metropolis like Chicago certainly deserves more attention that it gets in this book. We hope these limitations will be addressed in the future by writers and researchers who see the need for a fuller documenting of our history.

This venture has connected us to many individuals who were protagonists of the movement. What is remarkable about this older generation is the extent to which they continue to be a force for liberation and self-determination, for social justice and human rights. Many are devoted to grassroots organizing, challenging police brutality and racial injustice, leading democratic-rights struggles, or opposing colonial domination of Puerto Rico. They include many who are active in the work to free the Puerto Rican political prisoners who are subject to outrageous jail terms and endure inhumane conditions. Without a doubt, the release of these men and women ranks as a primary objective in the social justice agenda of all persons, Puerto Rican or not, who have an ounce of compassion in them. (Note: in February 1998 one of the prisoners, Antonio Camacho Negrón, was released after having served eleven years in prison.)

Many participants now find themselves less involved in militant politics and direct action. Nevertheless they are a significant force in cultural, advocacy, electoral, and community-building strategies wherever there are concentrations of Latinos. They direct social service agencies, fighting off the next wave of government cutbacks. They teach in schools and colleges constantly threatened by retrenchment. As musicians, artists, and writers, they are leading a renaissance in the arts, highlighting the contributions of the Puerto Rican woman and recovering our African heritage, for example. They counsel youth and run health programs; fight the ravages of substance abuse, domestic violence, and the AIDS epidemic; operate cultural and educational programs that develop pride and self-esteem among young adults; and help to strengthen labor unions and organize for workers' rights. This is a generation that has produced leaders in civic, religious, and labor organizations and has even propelled a few elected officials into local and national government. And yes, some even have made their mark in the corporate world.

Furthermore Puerto Ricans in the United States continue to preserve cultural, political, and economic ties to Puerto Rico, which is reflected in recent demands by many Puerto Rican leaders for the right of mainland Puerto Ricans to participate in any plebescite or referendum to determine the future status of the island. Undoubtedly the views of Puerto Ricans on the mainland will have a significant impact on shaping U.S. policy toward Puerto Rico.

In sum this book is not a nostalgic exercise. Our generation continues to be concerned with the community's day-to-day struggle for survival and with the future of Puerto Rico. Let this anthology serve as a resource for those who follow in our footsteps. Let it be a marker of pitfalls and traps, a source of ideas for continued struggle, and above all, a wellspring of hope.

Acknowledgments

THIS PROJECT would not have been possible without the assistance of many people. From the beginning we strove to involve movement participants and observers in the chronicling and assessment of our experience. An unforeseen reward of this approach was the rekindling of old friendships as well as the making of new ones.

From the start, Carmen Vivian Rivera was our primary source of moral and intellectual support. She has been unfailingly available with her counsel and encouragement. We are also deeply grateful to each of the authors who contributed chapters to this anthology. For several of them, unaccustomed to the strange world of academic publishing, this has been a new venture, and we hope they will continue to produce other works. Many persons made themselves available for interviews by authors of the various chapters; their names are scattered about in the text and endnotes. We sincerely appreciate their willingness to reflect on their experiences.

Many individuals helped with documents, writings, interview material, advice, and other forms of assistance. Some submitted chapters that unfortunately could not be included in this volume. We take this moment to thank them all: Luis Aponte-Parés, Maritza Arrastía, Denis Berger, Dana Biberman, Alice Simon Berger, Rosa Borenstein, Elba Crespo, Gilberto Díaz, Angelo Falcón, Juan Flores, Laura Friedman, Iván Gutierrez, Jill Hamberg, Augustín Laó, Aurora Levins Morales, Melba Maldonado, Esperanza Martell, Nelson Merced, Iris Morales, Carlos Muñoz Jr., José Navarro, Nena Negrón, Palmira Ríos, Jaime Rodríguez, Plácido Rodríguez, Victor M. Rodríguez, José Rodríguez-Sellas, Olga Iris Sanabria, Paul Shneyer, José Soler, Jan Susler, Amilcar Tirado, Orlando Torres, David Traverzo Galarza, Sandra Trujillo, and Annette Walker. In 1994 and 1996, some of the chapter drafts were presented at panels of the Puerto Rican Studies Association (PRSA) conference. We are grateful to the participants in those discussions for their feedback. Thanks also to several anonymous reviewers for comments on earlier versions of the manuscript.

The photo selection is the result of a collaboration by several photographers. ¡Muchas grácias! to those who helped with this section: Michael Abramson, Maritza Arrastía, Claridad, the Center for Puerto Rican Studies, Máximo Colón, Eduardo "Pancho" Cruz, Eduardo "Chungo" Molina,

Bomexí Iztaccihuatl, the National Committee to Free Puerto Rican Prisoners of War and Political Prisoners, Carlos Ortíz, and Blanca Vázquez.

Copyeditor Kim Cretors did a thorough job of improving the original manuscript. Thanks go also to Fred Thompson of Book Production Resources, who steered the manuscript through the last stages of the editorial and production processes.

Finally, we are grateful to Doris Braendel and the staff at Temple University Press for supporting this project from the beginning.

Andrés Torres

1   Introduction

Political Radicalism in the Diaspora—
The Puerto Rican Experience

Then and Now: An Uncertain Future

Ask a group of students or young adults in any large city: What
are the defining characteristics of your generation? What are the unique
features of urban life in the nineties? The responses are likely to include
a catalog of social ills and concerns: the AIDS epidemic, "safe sex,"
drugs, violence in the streets and in the home, anxiety over employment
and career opportunities. White, Black, Latino, or Asian, they'll bemoan
the persistence of racial division, the conflict over affirmative action, and
the alleged apathy and cynicism of "Generation X."

If we poll *parents* about what it was like to be a young adult twenty or
thirty years ago, we are likely to come up with some interesting contrasts.
They remember an era of intense political and cultural upheaval as the
United States's "baby-boom" generation challenged the status quo: the
Civil Rights struggle, massive protests against the war in Vietnam, Woodstock, the sexual revolution, and a plethora of social movements. It was a
time of great turmoil, but one with an optimistic, hopeful spirit.

Fortunately, for those who were exposed to the social movements of the
time and for younger minds curious about those heady days, there has been
a growing effort to recover the history and meaning of that period. Many
books, dissertations, and documentaries have tried to come to terms with
the decade of the sixties. Sensing commercial possibilities, even Hollywood
has gotten into the act with such cinematic creations as "Born on the Fourth
of July," "Malcom X," "Panther," and "Ghosts of Mississippi."

This book represents another entry in the field of understanding the
sixties, but it deals with a movement that has received almost no coverage
or recognition. The old adage that "history is written by the victors"
seems acutely appropriate to the Puerto Rican movement in the United
States. The historical record on this experience is almost nonexistent. Even
within the "social movements" and "diversity" literature, we find barely
a mention of the Puerto Rican contribution to the insurgency that changed
the United States.

Why is this so? Is it an oversight attributable to the relatively small size of the Puerto Rican population in the United States—a population numbering fewer than three million people? Are Puerto Ricans rendered invisible by virtue of their being identified as "Latinos"? Perhaps, given the public ignorance regarding this country's major surviving colony, *Boricuas* are assumed to be foreigners and therefore not a proper object of analysis for those interested in U.S.-based social movements.[1] Another possibility has to do with timing. Because the Puerto Rican movement did not come into public view until the end of the 1960s, and because its "peak" years were during the early to mid-1970s, perhaps it is not seen by historians as an integral part of the political era of the sixties. Whatever the reason, the voices in this anthology are here to stake their claim in the historical record. Refusing to be ignored, they speak as representatives of an important chapter in the history of radical politics in the United States.

Two decades ago, in 1976, the federal government issued a report on the status of the U.S. Puerto Rican community. Based on extensive empirical and institutional analysis, *Puerto Ricans in the Continental United States: An Uncertain Future* detailed the perilous conditions of *Boricuas* who at that time numbered almost 1.7 million.[2] Suffering from substandard housing, high unemployment and low incomes, poor educational and health services, and frequent discrimination, these citizens had the dubious distinction of being among the poorest of the poor, ten years after the "War on Poverty" had been declared. To make matters worse, the study continued, Puerto Ricans were apparently being squeezed out of their fair share of antipoverty programs and resources. It was a dismal picture—one that lead the U.S. Commission on Civil Rights to declare, in its now-famous summary:

> The Commission's overall conclusion is that mainland Puerto Ricans generally continue mired in the poverty facing first generations of all immigrant or migrant groups. Expectations were that succeeding generations of mainland Puerto Ricans would have achieved upward mobility. One generation later, the essential fact of poverty remains little changed. Indeed, the economic situation of the mainland Puerto Ricans has worsened over the last decade.
>
> The United States has never before had a large migration of citizens from offshore, distinct in culture and language and also facing the problem of color prejudice. After thirty years of significant migration, contrary to conventional wisdom that once Puerto Ricans learned the language the second generation would move into the mainstream of American society, the future of this distinct community in the United States is still to be determined.[3]

This was the first official acknowledgment that "melting pot" assimilation might not be applicable to the Puerto Rican case. Already, reams of reports and several scholarly tomes had questioned its appropriateness for African Americans and Mexican Americans, not to speak of Native Americans, the first group to be left out of the mix. Now came confirmation that another population was in effect being marginalized from the mainstream.

The study was designed to increase public awareness about an invisible minority group. But the reality described by the report had long been known to *Boricuas*; it was one important ingredient that helped to give rise to the radical Puerto Rican insurgency of the sixties and seventies. *Objective* conditions—the constellation of daily experiences that shape the possibilities for political action—were pushing people toward unconventional measures. The other necessary factor—the *subjective* factor of political consciousness and organization—was what was provided by the new Puerto Rican movement.

EL NUEVO DESPERTAR

Sometime in the late 1960s a *"Nuevo Despertar"* of Puerto Rican radicalism took place in U.S. communities. This "New Awakening" drew on several sources. On the international scene, national liberation movements throughout Africa and Asia proved that European colonialism was coming to an end. And in 1959, the Cuban Revolution showed the United States that power in its backyard was not absolute. Not only that, the Cubans offered a model of socialism that appealed to the disenfranchised throughout the Americas. Domestically, there was the Civil Rights movement, the War on Poverty, and protests against the Vietnam War. Student unrest, growing labor militancy, feminism, Black power, Chicano and Native American militancy—these were all part of the political context within which the new Puerto Rican radicalism was to emerge.

Puerto Rico itself was in the throes of political contention, as the dormant independence movement underwent a revival.[4] Since the nineteenth century, the quest for Puerto Rican nationhood had been punctuated by key moments, each signifying turning points in the movement, each contributing various elements toward a collective memory of struggle. Certain years became associated with distinctive events. In a small mountain town in 1868, *independentistas* staged the first major armed revolt against Spanish colonialism—the famous *"Grito* [Cry] of Lares."* In 1898 the Spanish-American War led to a U.S. takeover. In 1917, Puerto Ricans were made U.S. citizens, an act that subjected them to the military draft for World War I. The Ponce Massacre occurred in 1937, when nineteen Puerto Rican Nationalists were killed by Puerto Rican police, and another two hundred were wounded during a peaceful demonstration.[5] The demonstration had been organized on Palm Sunday to protest the U.S. government's imprison-ment of Nationalist Party leader Albizu Campos on sedition charges. In July 1950 Pres. Harry S. Truman signed Public Law 600, which set the stage for permanent U.S. military and economic control in Puerto Rico. A new round of violent confrontations ensued, culminating in the Nationalist re-volt of October when the Nationalist Party organized military uprisings in several towns throughout the island. The revolt ultimately concluded with the attempt on Truman's life in Washington, D.C. The year 1954 saw an-other bold action—the attack on the U.S. Congress by four Nationalists; it was an act brought about by the establishment of Puerto Rico as a commonwealth and by the United States's success in getting the United Nations to declare Puerto Rico a noncolonial territory.

The 1960s represented another cycle of militancy rather than a new state of mind. The United States was coming under increasing criticism internationally for holding onto one of the world's last colonies. In re-sponse, such groups as the Puerto Rican Independence Party (PIP) and the Movement for Independence (MPI) surged, claiming a large following among a younger generation of islanders.

In mainland barrios, a similar process of radicalization began, fueled by developments in Puerto Rico as well as by the same forces that were feeding the social upheaval within the United States. Underlying these in-fluences was an important demographic factor—the growth and matura-tion of the second-generation Puerto Rican population, those who had been born in mainland communities. In 1950, out of a population of 300,000 Puerto Ricans in the United States, only 25 percent were U.S. born; by 1970, out of a population of almost 1.5 million, the proportion was 45 percent.[6] There were some perceptible signs of "assimilation" in the traditional sense: somewhat greater usage of English, marriage outside the ethnic group, higher employment and educational achievement. Yet there was nothing to indicate a socioeconomic breakthrough for Puerto Ricans born and bred in northern cities. Speaking English does not guar-antee equal opportunity, especially when one is stigmatized with "other-ness." The African American experience had already confirmed this situ-ation. Ghetto life was threatening to submerge a large segment of Puerto Rican families, and many young people were hanging on a thread; in other words they were feeling, as Piri Thomas so poignantly said, "I ain't got nothing but today and a whole lot of tomorrows."[7]

Mainland Puerto Ricans had a tradition of struggle dating back to the previous century, when they joined with Cubans to organize support for independence from Spain. Since the 1930s the Nationalist Party of Puerto Rico had organized support within U.S. communities, as did several U.S. leftist groups, such as the Communist Party, which established Puerto Rican "sections" whose responsibility was to win influence within the migrant barrios. Well-known community activists Bernardo Vega and Jesús Colón provided a link to an earlier generation of political radicalism.[8] Throughout the 1950s and 1960s, such New York activists as Gilberto Gerena Valentín, Evelina Antonnetti, and Antonia Pantoja led campaigns for political representation and built local organizations and institutions. Even the PIP maintained a presence, and in 1964, the MPI opened an office in New York City.

Through the early settlement period of the teens and twenties, through the depression years and early post–World War II era, *Boricuas* of a radical stripe had denounced the colonial despoliation of their homeland or the injustice and exploitation in the barrio. Usually, they denounced both. Perhaps the most significant prelude to the "New Awakening" was the large Puerto Rican mobilization for Martin Luther King Jr.'s Poor People's Campaign in 1968, which was organized by Gilberto Gerena Valentín.

Whether promoting the struggle for independence, organizing for social and economic rights in the United States, or blending all concerns, a long thread of political activism had been a feature of social life in the community. With the mass migrations of Puerto Ricans in the 1940s and 1950s, the social character of that population had been transformed thoroughly. The Puerto Rican presence was no longer just a network of tenuously linked enclaves in New York City. The migrant generation of the postwar era caused a metamorphosis in the character of this presence. By the late 1960s, it was time for the second generation to step onto the stage of history.[9]

THE CORE GROUPS

Who actually comprised the Puerto Rican Left? In general, the Left were those organizations that posited as a goal the independence of Puerto Rico.[10] Except for the Nationalist Party and the Puerto Rican Independence Party (PIP), most groups also promoted a radical transformation of U.S. society, seeing this as part and parcel of their mission. The organized nucleus of the movement was made up principally of eight organizations: the Young Lords Party (YLP), the Puerto Rican Socialist Party (PSP, its Spanish-language initials), El Comité–MINP (Puerto Rican National Left Movement), the Puerto Rican Student Union (PRSU), the Movement for National Liberation (MLN), the Armed Forces for National Liberation (FALN), the Nationalist Party, and the Puerto Rican Independence Party (PIP).[11]

Several factors distinguished these organizations from the myriad collectives, study groups, and networks that attracted militants of the day.[12]

First was their longevity and geographical reach. Unlike many other formations that burst into being only to disappear in a few months, each of these groups had an extended existence over several years or even decades.[13] With the Puerto Rican population expanding in dozens of cities, these groups endeavored to create a base throughout the diaspora, beyond the traditional strongholds of New York City and Chicago.

Also, each had articulated a *program* with which to attract adherents and guide their work. Typically, this program stipulated a set of *strategic* (long-term) objectives and *tactical* (short-term) proposals for action. Although Nationalist at their inception, by the early 1970s most of the groups employed some version of Marxism as the ideological framework for their program and as the theoretical tool for interpreting the economic and political situation in which they found themselves.

Consistent with their self-conception as integral components of a national liberation movement, each group also maintained an organic link to the struggle in Puerto Rico. There was a spectrum of relationships. The PSP in the United States was an important part of the structure of the national organization, which was based in San Juan, and it was accorded a certain autonomy.[14] El Comité–MINP and MLN had close ties with specific groups on the island but were not organizationally subordinate to them. The Young Lords inverted the historical pattern by creating affiliates in Puerto Rico with New York serving as the headquarters. The student activists of PRSU sustained a close relationship with the Proindependence University Federation (FUPI) and later collaborated with the Young Lords in their organizing drive in Puerto Rico.

Some groups also maintained connections with segments of the U.S. Left. The Young Lords began by cooperating with the Black Panther Party and later joined a Maoist coalition of groups seeking to construct a new, multiracial revolutionary party. In its various incarnations this coalition was referred to by adherents as the New Communist Movement. By the early 1970s, the Young Lords had transformed itself into the Puerto Rican Revolutionary Workers Organization (PRRWO). El Comité–MINP pursued a similar line, eventually aligning itself with the New Communist Movement. The PSP remained independent from the U.S. Left but worked within different coalitions, depending on the issue at hand.

The diversity of backgrounds and experiences that characterized the individuals and organizations who made up the movement are reflected by the many voices heard in this book. It would be wrong to assume that each group was uniquely identified in terms of its ideology and composition, that they were mutually exclusive. Indeed, sometimes political and personality differences *within* organizations appear to predominate over those *among* organizations. Yet the historical record, as well as the various writings and interviews that comprise this anthology, permit us to venture a brief portrayal of each group's distinctive nature. At the risk of oversimplifying the life stories of very complex entities, the following descriptions provide a starting point for a comparative analysis of five of the key organizations comprising the Puerto Rican independence movement.

A Comparative Perspective

Young Lords–PRRWO

The Young Lords experienced a shorter life span than the other organizations, but it was indisputably the main catalyst for the second generation's baptism into radical politics. Combining youthful exuberance, innovative direct action, and a revolutionary populism, the Lords charted new ground without mentors and without the benefit of a direct tie to the liberation movement in Puerto Rico. They had to win their legitimacy from scratch. Their heyday in terms of mass appeal covered the period from 1969 to 1972.[15] History will judge this a fleeting moment; but for those who were participants and witnesses, it will be remembered as a grand outburst of pride and courage.

In their initial stage, the Lords targeted street youth and the dispossessed, inspired by a belief in the revolutionary potential of the "most disenfranchised segment of our community" (chap. 12). Even when making interventions around workplace issues—as in the Young Lords' takeover of the detox unit at Lincoln Hospital—they employed direct action, infusing a community/labor perspective with a sixties-style militancy. The group's actions pioneered a breakthrough with the public, effectively bringing attention to the crisis in the Puerto Rican community. Youthful and English-speaking, they challenged the stereotype of Puerto Ricans as a community of rural immigrants. In this, the Lords were extremely effective in "working" the mass media. They created an alternative media, with a radio program and a bilingual newspaper, *Pa'lante*. As Juan González, a founding member and today a columnist with the *New York Daily News*, remarked in retrospect, "It was no accident that many of us in the leadership later chose permanent careers in the media."[16]

MPI-PSP

Known as the Movement for Independence (MPI) until 1971, the PSP, along with El Comité–MINP, stepped into the vacuum left by the Young Lords' decline. Although officially a presence in New York City since 1960, not until 1969 did the MPI begin to make that presence felt. The success of the Young Lords spurred the older, island-based members of the MPI to reconceptualize their mission in the United States. More attention had to be directed at day-to-day concerns of *Boricuas* on the mainland; otherwise the *independentistas* would be limited in their impact. Besides, the organization was already planning to transform itself into a socialist party, elevating the class aspects of its program. It would make no sense to ask U.S. Puerto Ricans—most of whom were here for good—to occupy themselves with poverty and injustice on the island without talking about the same problems in their own neighborhoods. By 1970 the MPI had made a strategic decision to go all out with an aggressive organizing strategy in U.S. communities. Winning independence was inconceivable without organizing the one-third of the nation that lived in the "belly of the beast." [17] And organizing this sector could not be done if the party was divorced from the community's struggles for economic and social justice.

The formula was not very different from what the Young Lords and other groups were espousing, but the PSP (by now the transition from the MPI was complete) on the mainland had the benefit of being an extension of a leading organization on the island. This appealed to a lot of young Puerto Ricans who were hungry for such a direct link (chap. 11). Until the late-1970s, the U.S. branch of the PSP displayed an impressive capacity for building active chapters throughout the diaspora, reaching as far as California. [18] All the while, it contended with a fundamental tension: how to operationalize the delicate relationship between support for independence and organizing for radical change in the United States (chaps. 3, 4, 5, 11).

El Comité–MINP

EL Comité (which in 1975 became MINP) was born on the West Side of Manhattan around 1970, originally as a militant community-based organization protesting so-called "urban renewal" programs that were replacing low-income housing with high-rise developments (chap. 5). It quickly evolved into a revolutionary cadre organization with links to other Latin American struggles and particularly with Dominicans who were then beginning to move into Manhattan areas *en masse*. Spreading to other areas in New York and to such cities as Boston, the group was largely responsible for reinvigorating the movement to free the five Nationalist prisoners, a campaign that came to fruition toward the end of the seventies. [19]

Much like the Lords and the MPI-PSP, El Comité sought to be a multi-issue organization, offering a comprehensive program for the community. Besides its community organizing, the group organized a student sector and a workers' organization and initiated a process that eventually led to the formation of the Latin Women's Collective. Through its publication *Unidad Latina*, it addressed the gamut of issues affecting the community, linking local issues to international forces. Years later, this notion, common to the Left, would be recycled in the slogan, "Think Globally, Act Locally." In the sixties and seventies, this was the normal mode of analysis for cadre organizations.

PRSU

The most important student group of the time was the Puerto Rican Student Union (PRSU). Its activists were found on campuses throughout the Northeast, especially in New York City. PRSU actually established a community office (first in the South Bronx, later in East Harlem), signaling that *Boricuas* fortunate to have access to a college education should use their skills in service of the community (chap. 7).

Along with the Young Lords, La Unión, as PRSU was often called, pulled together the first national conference of Puerto Rican students in 1970. It became a force throughout the U.S. student movement for building solidarity for Puerto Rican independence. Within the higher education system, PRSU promoted a culturally appropriate curriculum along with admissions and retention services for Puerto Rican and other Latinos, and the organization contributed to the creation and defense of Puerto Rican studies departments. PRSU members were critical in the founding of the Center for Puerto Rican Studies of the City University of New York, the first research institution devoted to the field (chap. 7). Although it always enjoyed a close relationship with the Young Lords, the PRSU was an autonomous group. For a while it played a unitary role, attempting to reconcile some of the differences among the cadre organizations. Later, PRSU decided to merge completely with the Lords' successor group, PRRWO. By the early 1970s, such groups as PSP and El Comité–MINP had also sponsored the creation of student federations.[20]

MLN

Sensing that a mood of defeatism had overtaken the Left and that the movement's turn toward Marxism had alienated the average Puerto Rican, the Movement for National Liberation (MLN) appeared on the scene in 1977. The initial core of activists emerged from community efforts in Chicago and had participated in educational struggles involving Latino students. Drawing on the traditional nationalism of the independence movement, the MLN adopted the position that the Puerto Rican community was an "internal colony" of the United States. The group stressed the right to armed struggle, which it believed had effectively been disregarded by the remaining leftist movement. Puerto Rico had the right to liberate itself by any means necessary, including revolutionary violence. International bodies, such as the United Nations, had acknowledged the right of colonized peoples to resort to extreme measures for self-determination, and the Puerto Rican experience—on the island and in the United States—still qualified as a case of suppressed freedom.

From its inception, the MLN organized public support for the clandestine Armed Forces of National Liberation (FALN). In the process, the MLN was harassed by the federal government and several of the group's members were arrested and imprisoned for refusing to cooperate with grand jury investigations in Chicago and New York City. Despite this continual persecution, MLN members managed to dedicate themselves to organizing efforts in a number of Puerto Rican barrios. In time, their activities expanded beyond the Second City, encompassing the building of cultural, social service, and day-care programs; by the late 1980s the MLN had chapters in New York, Philadelphia, Hartford, Boston, and San Francisco.[21] Like the Young Lords and other radicals before them, the MLN sought to establish a community base for their political ideology by servicing day-to-day needs of local constituents. Reformist programs could be a platform for advocacy, and beyond that, revolutionary politics.[22]

However, the organization could not avoid the fate of earlier groups. By the early 1990s, the combined strain of political repression and declining support for *independentista* goals took its toll. The MLN's political activity had declined from the earlier years, but the organization continues to organize campaigns to free Puerto Rican political prisoners and prisoners of war.[23]

COORDINATION AND COMPETITION

How closely did the various sections of the movement work with each other? Certain projects, such as the campaign to free five Nationalist prisoners, motivated a high degree of unity and coordination among the groups. Since the 1950s the *Nacionalistas*—Oscar Collazo, Lolita Lebrón, Irving Flores, Rafael Cancel Miranda, and Andrés Figueroa Cordero—had languished in federal penitentiaries. In 1970 the various Puerto Rican independence groups came together at a national conference, initiated primarily by El Comité–MINP, and all the principal organizations agreed to give top priority to freeing the prisoners. From then on, the campaign became a central issue—for the first time something that everyone could agree on, beyond differences in strategy and tactics, beyond disputes over what ideology or "line" to pursue on the question of independence.

By 1979, an intensive, decade-long public crusade secured the freedom of the five prisoners by way of a pardon from Pres. Jimmy Carter. Their release occasioned an emotional outpouring of joy and national pride—something of a cathartic release, as *Boricuas* everywhere saw these national heroes returned to their homeland. It was a momentous achievement, and the key to success was the massive popular support gained for the campaign from all sectors of the U.S. Puerto Rican population, as well as from U.S. progressives. Years earlier, similar efforts had led to the release of such patriots as Carlos Feliciano and Eduardo "Pancho" Cruz in New York City. Since then coordinated action has led to success in other campaigns, such as efforts to revive the case of Puerto Rico in the United Nations (chap. 18) and to stop the construction of a "super port" on Puerto Rico's northwestern coast, the crusade to stop strip mining on the island (chap. 7), and efforts to derail U.S. Navy bombing practice on the island of Vieques (chap. 9). A central ingredient of the large mobilizations that publicized the colonial status of Puerto Rico were North American solidarity organizations, such as the Puerto Rico Solidarity Committee and the Vieques Solidarity Network, groups that for years conducted educational and advocacy programs around the issue of Puerto Rican sovereignty. For much of the 1970s, the Puerto Rican movement was successful in keeping the colonial question at the top of the U.S. Left's agenda.

While the groups enjoyed a certain level of unity among themselves, their relationships were marked also by competition and ideological confrontations. After all, these were adversaries within a perilous environment, contending for disciples and testing theories under real-world, often dangerous conditions. Creating the Puerto Rican revolution does not fall into the category of "sandbox politics." Attracting and keeping a following meant having a distinctive agenda and an ability to win battles.

In the initial period, stereotypes abounded regarding the various factions: the Young Lords were seen as politicized street youth running social service programs, the MPI-PSP as exiled upper-class intellectuals absorbed in international politics, El Comité–MINP strictly as housing activists fighting urban renewal designs. But in reality, class composition and organizing strategy within the groups were much more nuanced, shifting over time as organizations changed in size and focus (chaps. 3, 5, 11, 12). Indeed the impetus for internal change often came from demographic changes—for example, the influx of U.S.-born cohorts into the MPI-PSP (chap. 3) and the incorporation of students into El Comité–MINP (chap. 10). To a greater or lesser extent, the Left's various member groups became a microcosm of the diversity and variation that was found in the community at large.

IDENTITY AND STRATEGY: The National Question

In addition to stresses arising from their differing origins, competition between groups was rooted in differences over strategy and tactics. The central theoretical dispute was over the so-called "national question."

From this debate—which lasted for years and was acted out in public forums, long ideological tracts, and heated personal confrontations— flowed many of the intergroup conflicts.[24] The national question essentially involved the relationship between *nation* and *class*. The following is one way of summarizing the argument.

Nation and Class

One group of activists argued that the primary reference point for Puerto Ricans is their status as a racial/ethnic minority. More than anything else, it is their nationality (nation) that defines them. This is what they are most aware of when *Boricuas* think about their position in U.S. society. This "otherness" has a peculiar origin because it arises from a very specific experience of U.S. colonialism in Puerto Rico. In this sense, the Puerto Rican case is similar to that of Native Americans, African Americans, and Mexican Americans, each of whose history is tied to an early period of U.S. settlement and imperialist expansion.

Born as U.S. citizens, many Puerto Ricans nevertheless feel ambivalent, even hostile, toward the United States. They are resentful that they were never given the chance to rule their own destiny and are indignant over their treatment in this country. This attitude is quite different from that of the great majority of those individuals who flocked to the United States during the great European migrations. Among Puerto Ricans, national pride is an instinctive response, and the anticolonial movement springs from this impulse.

Another point of reference, distinct from nationality, is class position. Class is determined by one's place in the material reproduction of society; where one fits into the grand cycle of production, exchange, and distribution. Simply stated, class status is determined by one's mode of survival in the world of work. Whether working for someone else (selling "labor power," as Marx put it), working for oneself, or employing others, each condition makes an enormous difference in an individual's life. It also colors one's world outlook, political and social views, and so forth.

The fact is that most people who call themselves Puerto Ricans happen to be working-class or are excluded from the world of work altogether. Could this mean that many Puerto Ricans have an identity that transcends their nationality, one that perhaps finds commonality with working people of other nationalities? Could this mean that *within* the Puerto Rican community, class differences are powerful enough to weaken if not dissolve the bonding agent of nation-consciousness? Those who argued strongly for the preeminence of class tended to adopt this view. Articulating the appropriate relation between nation and class became the litmus test for the movement. Is nationality more important to Puerto Ricans than class? Or vice versa? How an individual dealt with this connection had implications for issues of *identity* and *political strategy*.

Identity

Are *Boricuas* in the United States still part of the Puerto Rican nation, despite several decades of living here? This view was developed in the Young Lords' first phase with their "Divided Nation" thesis (chap. 12).

The Young Lords, through their Divided Nation thesis, explored many issues—including what was to be made of the increasing signs of assimilation within the U.S. Puerto Rican population: greater English-language usage, gradual adoption of U.S. customs and traditions, marriage with non–Puerto Ricans, increasing involvement in the political and civic institutions of the dominant society, including protest movements. The Lords determined at the time that to the extent this is true, the Puerto Rican community had in some way detached itself from its original roots on the island and had embarked on a distinctly new trajectory, formulating a new identity. It meant that Puerto Ricans in the United States constitute a "national minority." Even though racial and economic oppression condemned them to second-class citizenship, this does not negate the fact that they are part of the U.S. class structure (chaps. 3, 5, 10, 12).

On the other hand, it was obvious that Puerto Ricans suffered greatly from racism and poverty, from social and political isolation. A second generation was emerging that showed few signs of being incorporated into the dominant culture. This isolation could only mean that Puerto Ricans were *not* being assimilated—that, like other racial minorities, they were facing an atypical American experience. Not only that, but *Boricuas* were characterized by a high rate of "circular migration" wherein many residents were returning to the island for episodic stays, and many islanders continued to migrate to the United States, replenishing the barrios with nationalistic sentiment. Add all this up, and a vibrant nationhood in the diaspora emerged: sustained, on the one hand by an emotional attachment to the country of origin, and on the other by exclusion from the host country. "Nation" vs. "national minority"—this was the "national question" as Puerto Rican radicals understood the issue of identity at the time.

Political Strategy

This division was not a trivial debate over semantics. The nation/class dichotomy largely governed political strategy. The implications were clear: if one believed that Puerto Ricans in the United States were part of the nation, one argued that the prime political responsibility was to support the struggle for independence. Living "in the belly of the beast," *Boricuas* should see themselves as participants in a national liberation struggle, strategically located behind enemy lines. Other prescriptions followed. Organizing campaigns should privilege issues of cultural identity and national sovereignty: celebration of patriotic events and the denunciation of such U.S. military and corporate intrusions in Puerto Rican life as naval bombings of Vieques, environmental damage, sterilization abuse, and the harassment of proindependence political activists. Likewise with regard to local concerns, the focus should be on demands for racial equality and cultural autonomy. Campaigns demanding bilingual services and education and denouncing discriminatory practices and policies flowed logically from the nation-based concept of Puerto Rican identity. Finally, it was believed that activists should focus on getting North American anti-imperialists and progressives to pressure the U.S. government to abandon their Caribbean colony and on building international support for the liberation of the island.

If one was persuaded by the "national minority" thesis, on the other hand, then this dictated a focus on radical change of U.S. society. The political obligation facing Puerto Ricans was to participate in a revolutionary process, jointly with other forces, to bring about an end to poverty, discrimination, and class oppression. Only a postcapitalist society could deliver on this goal because the market economy is based on class divisions and inequality. An inevitable by-product of this process would be the weakening of colonial control over Puerto Rico. Therefore the greatest contribution that Puerto Ricans in the United States could make toward independence was to accelerate the advent of a socialist United States. From this perspective, organizing strategy should emphasize struggles over the day-to-day issues facing *Boricuas*, whether those issues had to do with their class condition or with their status as a racial/ethnic minority. The terminology associated with this concept was not always consistent or clear. Reforms, social and economic justice, democratic rights, civil rights—at one time or another each of these notions came to signify desired ends that all revolutionaries postulated. Though necessary, these goals were deemed insufficient as strategic goals because only a socialist system could permanently guarantee equality and freedom. But at least in striving for these goals, activists could raise the ideological challenge to capitalism.

In sum, the Nationalist outlook basically predetermined an anti-imperialist strategy; the class-based vision aimed for an anticapitalist approach. Both were revolutionary, but each ordered priorities differently and each assigned different roles to the Puerto Rican in the United States.

Complicating Caveats

The foregoing reconstructs the basic lines of the key debate within the Puerto Rican Left during its heyday. It is important to note, however, that rarely was the debate construed in terms of mutually exclusive strategies. Even the most "assimilated" of radical Puerto Ricans—those, for example, who were active in the New Left or in the Communist Party and other survivors of the Old Left—were ardent supporters of Puerto Rican independence and consistently advocated for this cause within their groups. Conversely, even among the most "nationalistic" of *Boricuas* one would find community activists involved in struggles for empowerment and social justice. And because most organizations were comprised of a membership reflecting elements of both views, each group contended with this challenge internally. Some groups, such as the Young Lords-PRRWO and the MPI-PSP, revised their positions over time.

The Young Lords dropped the "Divided Nation" thesis, substituting for it the notion of Puerto Ricans in the United States as an "oppressed national minority," eventually—as PRRWO—taking the position that *Boricuas* should merge with other U.S. radicals and form a new multinational (multiethnic) revolutionary party. The MPI-PSP always maintained the view of a single Puerto Rican nation, but in the early 1970s they revised the strategic implication of this position, allowing for the concept of a "dual priority" for Puerto Ricans in the United States. *Boricuas* should simultaneously fight for independence and participate in the revolutionary process here (chaps. 3, 5). As long as independence remained unattained, the MPI-PSP argued, Puerto Ricans should remain organically linked to the island Left.[25] El Comité–MINP came to share an outlook similar to that of PRRWO: Puerto Ricans are a national minority and have the duty to help reconstruct the U.S. Left. The MLN, consistent with its notion of an "internal colony," claimed that Puerto Ricans everywhere formed part of the same nation.[26]

Another distinction, the difference between strategy and tactics, needs to be kept in mind to avoid the impression that the national question uniquely determined the organizational practices of the various groups. For example, among those arguing from the purely Nationalist perspective, there were differences over the kinds of organizing methods and campaigns (tactics) that should be emphasized. Massive mobilizations to call public attention to the case of Puerto Rico at the United Nations? Work with North American progressives to lobby influential persons for support? Organize barrio residents for political and economic support? Freeing political prisoners? Direct action, in the form of civil disobedience or even clandestine armed struggle?

Similarly, a spectrum of tactical choices confronted activists and organizations predicating their strategy on a class-based analysis. Workplace and union organizing? Community control and empowerment? Advocacy or direct action around housing, education, health demands? Electoral politics?

A RETROSPECTIVE ASSESSMENT

What happened? Why did the movement fail to achieve its central objectives of independence for Puerto Rico and revolutionary transformation in the United States? Or perhaps the question should be posed from a more modest perspective: given the enormously ambitious goals, what *accomplishments* can we attribute to the movement?

Accounting for Decline

The contributors to this collection provide candid testimony concerning the flaws and limitations of the movement. Some, such as Guzmán and Rivera, point to the dogmatism and internal fighting that plague an organization when it loses its moorings in mass struggle. Democratic processes go by the wayside, alienating membership and supporters. Youthful inexperience leads to errors of judgement (chap. 12). In a paramilitary setting, the need to project an image of strength and vigilance can take extreme forms, including unsubstantiated accusations of treason (chap. 7).

Unclear priorities lead to member resentment. Groups that lack a precise hierarchy of goals and objectives, that say they stand for one thing but do another, send mixed messages to the very people they're trying to organize (chaps. 3, 5).

Almost unanimously, the authors inveigh against the Leninist type of party structure. By the 1970s, the Puerto Rican Left—here and in Puerto Rico—was swept up by the momentum of building revolutionary parties that operated as centralized, cadre-based formations. For the Puerto Rican movement—determined to make one last bid for independence before century's end—this was an appealing model. But toward the end of each group's life cycle, the disadvantages became obvious (chaps. 4, 11, 18).

Another casualty of this way of doing things was the lack of attention to what, in today's terminology, is referred to as the "politics of identity." Within the core organizations, gender questions were brought to the fore only after much internal pressure (chaps. 11, 12). While U.S.-based organizations, especially the Young Lords, were insistent on recognizing Puerto Rico's African heritage and dealing with internalized racism (chap. 9), these concerns were slow to permeate the independence movement in Puerto Rico. Homophobic attitudes marginalized many loyal and dedicated activists. In later years, gays and lesbians found it necessary to form autonomous organizations (chap. 17).

It would be a gross misreading of the movement's history to implicate internal practices as the central explanation for its demise. A balanced appraisal must necessarily take into account a host of external factors, largely beyond its immediate control. Primary among these is the sheer power differential between a small, stateless nation and a global super-power. Throughout the 1960s and 1970s, the U.S. government employed its vast power and influence to successfully withstand intense international and domestic pressure on the "Puerto Rican question." By the early 1980s the decline of socialist and communist ideologies and the collapse of real-world socialist "models" were already prefigured. The Mariel exodus of 1980 symbolized the stagnation of the Cuban model, traditionally the most appealing to the Puerto Rican Left. In the same year, Ronald Reagan's election inaugurated an era of conservatism.

U.S. government repression of the Puerto Rican independence struggle, in Puerto Rico and the United States, took its toll by intimidating many supporters and forcing organizations to privilege secrecy over openness and democracy. This intimidation was exercised through such covert programs as COINTELPRO, state-sanctioned assassinations, and the infiltration and sabotage that circumscribed the insurgency's domain of influence. Almost all the writings collected in this volume allude to these strategies.

In the final analysis, there is also the question of *political strategy*. In short, the movement failed to resolve the basic dilemma of how to sustain a long-term merger of socialist and Nationalist forces. On the one hand the effort to inculcate socialist and anticapitalist ideas among masses of Puerto Rican people fell victim to the worldwide offensive of capitalist ideology. On the other hand the attempt to persuade average Puerto Ricans of the viability of independence was unconvincing.[27] This is not to deny the lively *cultural nationalism* that runs deep within the consciousness and social institutions of the island and in the Puerto Rican diaspora. Neither can we ignore the existence of a broad *economic populism*, evidenced in multiple movements for social justice and equality. Indeed these forces—cultural nationalism and economic populism—may be the living inheritors of the movement.

Acknowledging Accomplishments

Mistakes and deficiencies notwithstanding, Puerto Rican radicalism made an indelible mark in the consciousness of the community and bequeathed a legacy of accomplishments that endures to the present.

True, independence has not been achieved; but without question, the movement successfully deterred its polar opposite, annexation. Utilizing the full range of political tactics, the movement sent a powerful message to circles within the U.S. and Puerto Rican governments who had been contriving to make Puerto Rico the fifty-first state. From throughout the diaspora was heard the response to that message: "We already know what statehood is; we have lived it." A popular chorus, internally generated, negated the latest colonial design. The independence movement, in all its manifestations—nationalists, socialists, communists, radicalized community and cultural activists—expressed its collective veto power on the annexationist initiative. That it required of the movement an almost two-decade effort indicates how resolutely the superpower that is the United States was working to advance its agenda. That the standoff attained came at such great sacrifice—including the incarceration of another generation of political prisoners—is testimony to the determination of the colonized. Nevertheless, the opposition to total assimilation of Puerto Rico was successful: this is the movement's greatest accomplishment of that time.

At the same time, the United States was forced to take notice of the Puerto Rican dilemma within its own cities. Refusing to be pigeonholed as an enclave in exile, the Puerto Rican community asserted its claim to full rights and equality. This was not the first time the voice of protest had been heard, but it was certainly the first time it reached a national audience. That this was done through a militant political activism is primarily attributable to the influence of the Left. This anthology offers case studies of the link between community struggles and the ideological Left, including the sometimes contentious nature of this relationship (chaps. 4, 16).[28]

There is an achievement of a more intangible nature as well. The movement became a vehicle for the political maturation of a significant sector of second-generation Puerto Ricans. Research has verified the link between *independentista* politics and community activism. Not surprisingly, the "activist stratum" of the 1970s stands farther to the left ideologically than the rest of the community, and its anticolonial sentiment is a key aspect of its politics.[29] In effect, the radical experience became a "school" to thousands of future leaders in all walks of life, people who went on to become figures in many areas: community organizing, labor, education, culture, and politics.

The institutional legacy of the movement is also remarkable. Numerous organizations and groups were spun out of the vortex of sixties and seventies activism, and they function to this day. The following examples—a limited, but representative, inventory—remind us of the continuing legacy of the *Nuevo Despertar* throughout the diaspora: the Puerto Rican Cultural Center and the Centro Cultural Segundo Ruiz Belvis (Chicago), Casa Don Pedro (Newark), Congreso Boricua (New Jersey), Taller Puertorriqueño (Philadelphia), Inquilinos Boricuas en Acción, (IBA; Boston), CATA (Committee in Support of Agricultural Workers, New Jersey), the Center for Puerto Rican Studies, Hostos Community College, Boricua College, El Puente, Institute for Puerto Rican Policy, Andrés Figueroa Cordero Foundation, El Museo del Barrio, the Caribbean Cultural Center, and the Association of Hispanic Arts. Across several states, such groups as the National Congress for Puerto Rican Rights continue their work around civil and human rights issues. The Puerto Rico Solidarity Network/ProLibertad and the National Committee to Free the Puerto Rican Political Prisoners and Prisoners of War press forward with their campaigns; a coterie of Puerto Rican/Latino/Caribbean studies departments still operates within academia.[30]

Radicals left their imprint on other important institutions that predated the movement but owed much of their vitality and commitment to activists who worked within them. United Bronx Parents, Lincoln Hospital, Aspira, the Puerto Rican Legal Defense and Education Fund are only a few of the groups found in New York. Each city, each community affords some examples.

This cataloging of accomplishments is a necessary task if we are to be left with a balanced assessment of radicalism in the Puerto Rican diaspora. Equally important is the need to assess the current state of political affairs in light of lessons past.

MOVEMENT POLITICS IN THE PUERTO RICO OF TODAY

Even if we accept the premise that developments in Puerto Rico have a significant influence on the community's political future in the United States, the current situation does not suggest in which direction the winds of change are blowing. One hundred years after the Spanish-American War, all indications point to a deadlock with regard to popular sentiment on the question of the island's political status. Each pole of the political spectrum, "statehooders" on one side and the *Autonomista-Independentista* forces on the other, appear to have a de facto veto power over the opposing option. This leaves the status quo of the commonwealth intact as the compromise solution, much as it has been for the past five decades.

Many among the independence forces argue that U.S. chauvinism and racism will never welcome among its ranks a Spanish-speaking, culturally distinct, multiracial, and largely poor population. A Puerto Rican state would actually result in a marginal loss of power for some states, as their representative share within the U.S. Congress would be decreased. Therein lies the strategy of the PIP, which favors the idea of putting the question directly to the U.S. public through another plebiscite in Puerto Rico. If statehooders win such a contest, it would finally elicit a clear statement of rejection from the colonizer, something that has never been done. Significant leaders within the PNP (the statehood party) itself have indicated that should this occur, they would then proceed to make the case for independence to the Puerto Rican people, thereby ending the three-way debate that has historically preserved the commonwealth status quo.

Needless to say, this is a high-stakes gamble. What if the U.S. Congress were to agree to *admit* the island on the basis of a plebiscite victory for statehooders? Barring an overwhelming triumph at the ballot box by pro-annexationist forces (for example, with a 70 to 80 percent vote), a move by Congress to make it the fifty-first state would undoubtedly thrust Puerto Rico into a period of violent confrontation.

An alternative route toward independence relies on international pressure to embarrass the U.S. government into finally agreeing to a process of decolonization. Independence movement leaders, such as the indefatigable Juan Mari Brás, believe this is a key to breaking the stalemate. In addition to escalating their traditional lobbying at United Nations forums, these leaders have recently embarked on a campaign to renounce their U.S. citizenship, hoping to focus the world's attention on the control of Puerto Rico by the United States. According to the veteran leader Mari Brás, this tactic, and not another plebiscite to measure Puerto Rican opinion, is the proper approach for anticolonial forces.[31]

Those who place less stock in plebiscites or international diplomacy have been emphasizing a return to grassroots organizing. Many activists—veteran and new—are engaged in the single-issue politics that characterize various movements for economic, environmental, and social justice in the United States. On the positive side this "new populism" promises to attract increasing numbers of ordinary people into political action. The downside is that populism, by itself, does not represent a systemic challenge to colonial or class domination.[32] Other activists concentrate on patriotic activities and educational campaigns to bolster national pride and challenge the colonial mentality. And then there is *Claridad*, the weekly newspaper that has consistently been a platform for the movement for close to forty years. In July 1996, the many streams of independence activism converged in a massive demonstration called *La Nación en Marcha* (Nation on the March), which was held to protest a meeting of the Conference of U.S. Governors being held in Fajardo, Puerto Rico. A turnout of some one hundred thousand persons assembled to make a powerful statement of national affirmation and independence. In the fall of 1997, many of these forces joined with the island's labor movement to mount a one-day work stoppage to protest the PNP's proposals for privatizing the public telephone company and other agencies. *El Paro Nacional* (the National Work Stoppage) became a resounding show of force and demonstration of labor solidarity.

And yet, despite signs of renewal and the deep commitment of thousands of individuals, Puerto Rico's movement for independence still lacks the broad support needed to transcend the politics of protest. The elections of 1996 returned the PNP to a second term, encouraging the annex-ationists to push ahead with their plans. As a new century approaches, it is clear that those making the case for an independent Puerto Rico have their work cut out for them. At a purely practical level, it would seem that the challenge of political unity is paramount, and the movement has yet to pass the test. Unless nationalists and socialists can find the basis for rallying around a strategic plan for national liberation, Puerto Ricans are at risk of indefinite subordination within the U.S. orbit. Without this stra-tegic unity, it is difficult to imagine how the island's various movements of cultural autonomy, social justice (including those seeking equality along lines of gender, race, and sexual orientation), and economic populism can be coalesced into a critical mass of anti-imperialism.

IN THE DIASPORA: The Future of Radical Politics

Meanwhile life in the diaspora proceeds apace. It is beyond the scope of this introductory chapter to rigorously outline future scenarios of the community in the United States. However, a few observations seem appro-priate. Socioeconomic data, one important clue to the future, paint a mixed picture. There is evidence of rising household income and a grow-ing middle-class, which is largely the product of two trends: among U.S.-raised Puerto Ricans, higher educational attainment and increasing access to public-sector employment, and a dramatic increase in migration of college-educated and professional persons from the island to the outer reaches of the diaspora, such as Texas, Florida, and California. New York and Chicago are no longer the dominant poles of attraction for the migra-tion stream. This has been taken as a sign of a modest incorporation into the U.S. mainstream.[33]

But there has been no diminution in the incidence of poverty and social dislocation. The HIV epidemic has struck hard, the prison population multiplies, and Puerto Rican youth face an intractable high-school drop-out problem. Reports from service providers indicate that the fiscal con-servatism of the last two decades has placed many of our families and youth in jeopardy. Most likely what we are seeing is a sharp bifurcation in the class structure of the community, with the traditional working-class strata being squeezed.

On the political front, there has been a significant expansion in the community's representation within governance structures, locally and na-tionally. This is exemplified in the presence of three Puerto Ricans in the U.S. House of Representatives and scores of state and city elected officials.[34] Unfortunately, these gains have come at a time when the public sphere has lost ground to the private sector. Nevertheless, few would deny that having a voice in municipal, county, and state government is a prerequisite for effective participation in the social and political struggles of the future. Concurrent with these political gains is the continuing existence of a broad network of groups involved in grassroots organizing, advocacy and policy analysis. There is a broad domain of activity involving social and economic justice issues.[35]

Culturally, there is a veritable renaissance in the arts, music, and literature within the Puerto Rican diaspora. It is fed partially by developments on the island, as well as by the swelling interest in the multicultural heritage of the United States itself. Also instrumental in this rebirth is the driving force of Puerto Rican and Latino youth. In their search for identity and cultural affirmation, they have broken new ground in these fields.[36]

Whether the two spheres of action—social/economic justice and cultural affirmation—will be translated into radical political power is another question. In the United States, Puerto Ricans with anti-imperialist, anti-capitalist sentiments face a double dilemma. First, the *independentista* agenda in the diaspora is heavily contingent on the state of movement politics in the homeland. Factionalism there curtails the effectiveness of political action within communities, as well as the enthusiasm of North Americans to engage in solidarity work. There is a second problem, namely, that the goal of a socialist transformation in the United States seems more distant than ever. If radicals are to remain an influence, they must recast their strategic goals so these are commensurate with reality.

Today this is a preeminent task facing Puerto Ricans who are moved by egalitarian and liberatory sensibilities. Whether informed by the politics of the sixties and seventies, or by other experiences, today's leadership of commitment is charged with the responsibility of creating a vision for the twenty-first century.

I.   THE CORE LEFT

Roberto P. Rodríguez-Morazzani

2   Political Cultures of the Puerto Rican Left
      in the United States

NOTHING IS SO hotly contested as the past. In discussing the
political experience of the Puerto Rican left in the United States during
the 1960s and the 1970s, we face a number of problems that we do not
encounter when discussing the North American, or for that matter, the
international Left. Primary among these problems is the dearth of written
accounts regarding experiences of the Puerto Rican Left in the United
States. Except for a few articles, mostly about the Young Lords, there is
no book-length treatment to be found. Such organizations as the Puerto
Rican Socialist Party, U.S. Branch, the Young Lords Party, El Comite–
MINP, and the Puerto Rican Student Union have not left a clear record of
what they accomplished or the impact that they had—either on the lives
of Puerto Rican people in the United Sates or even on those of their own
membership. The Puerto Rican left (defined as the social actors and the
organizations that they created) did, however, have a significant impact
not only amongst Puerto Ricans but also on other oppressed groups and
on the North American Left, and indeed, on the country as a whole. In the
absence of an adequate body of writing on the experience of Puerto Rican
radicalism, any attempt at analysis of that experience is necessarily tenta-
tive and provisional. However, this limitation notwithstanding, the undertaking is well worth the effort. The usefulness of any historical reconstruction is in the measure by which it acts as an open door through which
multiple reflections and debates are facilitated, thereby serving to further
our understanding of the past, present, and future.

At this time, there exists a hunger for the sharing of memories of Puerto
Ricans in the United States. This hunger is an effort to appropriate a past
that gives meaning to our community's existence and serves as a resource
in asserting a positive and an affirming identity. Hence, the search for oneself in history is closely connected to the question of the construction of
identity. While in the past this hunger has been most characteristic of
youth, today it cuts across the generational divide and even in a limited
way across certain sociological and ideological divisions. This hunger reveals the need to look at how the past is appropriated by oppressed groups
in everyday life. There also exists a hunger for the political-intellectual

resources required for understanding the present and for the construction of political identities through which to undertake change-oriented action on the part of activists and youth who are seeking to become involved in political struggle.

Any project of historical reconstruction must be critical if it is to be useful. Nostalgic and celebratory histories have no place in the intellectual project this essay proposes. As Perry Anderson points out: "The notion of history as an album of values to be bequeathed from individual to individual is nevertheless not a Marxist or even a specifically socialist one. Roll-calls of past lives, as moral exemplars for present struggles or aspirations, are a feature of very many political movements of the most opposing character—conservative or liberal as much as radical. Their original source is the romantic nationalism of the mid-nineteenth century, which very early patented resonant recollections of a ceremonial line of dead heroes."[1]

Self-serving liberal and neonationalist myth-making have come to dominate the way in which the histories of Puerto Rican radicalism are being presented in a number of political and academic settings. In reconstructing the past we should be careful not to fall into nostalgic romanticizing. Hero worship is a common phenomenon within nationalist historiography, as within politics, and has proven damaging to both.[2] Moreover, the hero, as representative of the aspirations of any group or as embodying an ideal, offers the opportunity to submit to an authority above and beyond the people who are the makers of history. The potential for creativity is lessened as submission to the hero tends to generate submission to a potentially repressive authority.[3]

This is not to say that the Puerto Rican women and men who were the actors in the movement and who took to the historical stage should not be recognized. In fact, it is their activity that is the focus of our investigations. Nevertheless, when considering the activities of these actors it would be useful to keep in mind Marx's view that "[m]en make their own history, but they do not make it under circumstances chosen by themselves, but under circumstances directly encountered, given and transmitted from the past."[4] It is within the context of those "circumstances directly encountered" that I wish to ground the activities of these social actors and their organizations.

The social movement that these individuals and collectivities created is best analyzed as a process in formation. All social life can be seen as a combination of action and construction, forms of practical activity that are informed by some underlying projects. Most often implicitly and even unconsciously, social action is conditioned by the actors' own "frames of reference" in constant interaction with the social environment or context. Action is neither predetermined nor completely self-willed; its meaning is derived from the context in which it is carried out, from the understanding that actors bring to such action, and from the emphasis on the creative role of consciousness in all human action, individual and collective. For these reasons, the focus of this essay is an attempt to transcend notions of linear progression in the constitution of political subjectivities and social movements.

The essay will also map out and explore the contexts and the interactions of a sector of the Puerto Rican community who emerged and engaged in the cultural, sociopolitical, and economic struggle from the 1960s until the early 1980s, historicizing and problematizing the political culture and identities of those who stood within a varied political spectrum on the Left. I argue that the shaping and constitution of the Puerto Rican Left in the United States was produced in a process of complex and contradictory historical conditions through which the so-called dichotomies between American–Puerto Rican, conservative-radical appear, disappear, and implode. Therefore, the historical experience of the Puerto Rican Left in the United States transcends dominant and traditional notions of history and radicalism. It is in the sixties that this political movement presents its most striking development, and it is this period that is my contextual reference.

In accounting for the historical development of the Puerto Rican radical generation of the 1960s–70s, I will look at selected factors that shaped the emergence of Left political culture: the transformations of the sociopolitical context of the Puerto Rican community in the postwar era and the impact of political repression; the decline of the Old Left, the university, Black Power, and Third World liberation movements; and the prison system.

Another way of viewing the object of this chapter is that it explores the process of political socialization its members underwent. Fred I. Greenstein offers a working definition of political socialization: "Narrowly conceived, political socialization is the deliberate inculcation of political information, values, and practices by instructional agents who have been formally charged with this responsibility. A broader conception would encompass all political learning, formal and informal, deliberate and unplanned, at every stage of the life cycle, including not only explicitly political learning but also nominally nonpolitical learning of politically relevant social attitudes and the acquisition of politically relevant personality characteristics." [5] This essay will operate under the broader definition by examining some of the formal and informal ways in which the political attitudes were learned, articulated, and transformed.

Political socialization took place for the generation of 1960s Puerto

Rican radicals in a variety of formal institutional settings (e.g., the family, school, playground, church, union, job, welfare programs, state agencies, etc.). Puerto Rican engagement in these institutional settings was conditioned by several factors; primary amongst these were the unequal relations of power that existed between Puerto Ricans and members of the dominant society, as well as amongst Puerto Ricans themselves (i.e., gender, race, class, sexuality). Within each of the institutional settings in which Puerto Ricans have found themselves, they have been confronted with a need to struggle against different forms of oppression. These struggles have taken the form of passive and active resistance and range from withdrawal from these institutional relations to the founding of alternative institutions and organizations.

The conflicts that took place within such arrangements made for a transformation of consciousness and behavior. Below I examine a number of these struggles within such institutions during the immediate postwar era. However, before proceeding it is important to situate the emergence of such struggles within the Puerto Rican community in the two decades following the Second World War.

THE POSTWAR TRANSFORMATION
OF THE PUERTO RICAN COMMUNITY

The Puerto Rican community of the fifties and sixties must be viewed as a diverse entity intersecting with the complex ways of the dominant society. If it is true that the American working class is stratified by skill, occupation, gender, race, and nationality, racialized groups or nationalities are far from homogeneous even within class boundaries. In looking at the sites of political socialization for the emergent generation of Puerto Rican radicals, a social world of greater complexity emerges and undermines any essentialized notion of what it meant to be a working-class Puerto Rican during the 1950s.

When looking back at the situation of Puerto Ricans in the United States during the 1950s, there is a tendency to imagine and describe the community as made up almost exclusively of poor or working-class families. Speaking little or no English, immigrants from Puerto Rico arrived in increasing numbers to the slums of New York, Chicago, and other U.S. cities are portrayed as unskilled and in possession of little or no "cultural capital." While it is certainly true, then and now, that Puerto Ricans have tended to be working-class and poor, it does not follow that *all* Puerto Ricans were either poor or working-class. Neither was it true that working-class Puerto Ricans were bereft of cultural capital. In fact, Puerto Ricans in the United States, while overwhelmingly working-class, were far from homogeneous. Class differences existed within the Puerto Rican community, and such classes were themselves stratified. For example, among workers there existed differences of skill, industry, education, etc. The same can be said of other social classes (e.g., professionals, merchants, the petty bourgeoisie, and so on). With the influx of tens of thousands of migrants from the island this internal stratification would increase.

While the postwar era marks the beginning of the mass migration, newly arrived Puerto Ricans did not construct a Puerto Rican community from scratch. In New York City, there already existed a significant Puerto Rican community dating back to the last quarter of the nineteenth century. The organizations of the Puerto Rican community, together with agencies of the state, provided the infrastructure for the incorporation of the newly arrived. Many who came did so with the assistance of family or extended family members. However, during this period the pressures exerted by the massive influx of immigrants, and the political social, and economic transformations then underway, would result in the dissolution of the earlier political culture of the Puerto Rican community.

The Puerto Rican community dating from the turn of the century up until the post–World War II era participated in the construction of working-class public spheres, both by joining and supporting the organizations of the labor and socialist movements and through the establishment of their own organizations and cultural spaces.[6] The development of this working-class cultural sphere wherein a socialist political culture can exist is not dependent only on explicitly political and economic factors but also on a wide range of cultural, social, and educational movements. Taken as a whole, these movements constitute communities that serve as a basis of resistance to capital and the State. These communities created forms of collective identity and collective subjectivity by offering their adherents a different view of themselves and their world—different, that is, from the characteristic worldviews and self-concepts of the social order that they were challenging.

Throughout this period, while continuously challenged by conservative elites, leadership of the Puerto Rican community was exercised from the bottom up by the labor movement and the Left. A similar situation existed in other communities in the United States prior to the Second World War. Paul Buhle, writing about the political culture of Italian-American immigrants, describes a situation similar to that which existed among Puerto Ricans and other working-class groups in New York City.

> Historians have failed to grasp the complex interactions of class and ethnicity within the ethnic community—divided against itself by class fissures but united at some points in a rough solidarity against the outside world. Immigrant radicals looked first to their communities, participating in industrial

union movements and class-conscious economic cooperatives foremost. Conservative ethnic forces, divided between the preservation of their own Old World prerogatives and their hopes for amicable relations with the American business community, were momentarily thrown on the defensive. The communities at large took a middle range position, supporting unions when they promised success, and defending ethnic victims of repression.[7]

As in the case of the Italian-American community that Buhle analyzes, the leadership of the early Puerto Rican community was effectively dominated by its most radical sectors. From the turn of the century this role was filled by members of progressive unions and organizations, such as the Socialist Labor Party and the Socialist Party of America. By the decade of the thirties Puerto Ricans would join the Communist Party U.S.A. (CPUSA) and participate in many of the organizations its Puerto Rican membership helped to establish. One example is the International Workers Order (IWO). Founded in 1930 by the Communist Party and left-wing members of the Workmen's Circle, the IWO was a multinational and multiracial order that was dedicated to providing affordable insurance and other services to its members and was dedicated also to the class struggle. The IWO organized campaigns in support of the unemployed, played an active role in the early years of the CIO, and provided aid to republican Spain. By 1947 the IWO had 187,226 members. The Spanish section of the IWO totaled more than ten thousand members, over half of whom were Puerto Rican.[8]

Within the Puerto Rican and other working-class immigrant communities, anarchist, trade unionist, socialist, and communist ideologies acted as counterhegemonic universals. While a national identity existed, it was not seen as central to the political identity of worker activists but as the modality through which a working-class identity was experienced. For Puerto Ricans and other Latinos, including Spaniards, the term *Hispano* inferred more than a common national history and language. It implied belonging to the working or popular classes as opposed to the rich immigrant class from Latin America.[9] The newspaper *Pueblos Hispanicos*, edited by Bernardo Vega, is an example of the meaning with which the term *Hispano* had been invested.

However, by the 1950s the combination of suburbanization, the internationalization of capital, Fordism, the pact between capital and American labor, the rise of the welfare state together with the emergence of mass culture and political repression was to signal an end to the old world of socialist working-class political culture. Moreover, in the postwar era there also occurred a rearticulation of race, which tended to displace class as the central component to the political identity of immigrant groups. In this period "ethnicity" increasingly replaced popular class identities as the primary social identity of immigrant groups. Thus, the type of multiracial working-class solidarity that had been possible in these working-class spheres also tended to be undermined.

Therefore, the world with which the newly arrived Puerto Rican worker came into contact resembled less and less the world of working-class political culture that the *Memoirs Of Bernardo Vega* described so vividly. By the mid-to-late 1950s the social landscape and the political context for Puerto Rican workers in the United States had dramatically changed, and community resistance was less based on a common identity rooted in class-specific ideologies.

A dramatic contrast between the political culture of the postwar era and the world of Bernardo Vega can be seen by viewing the effects of McCarthyism on Puerto Rican political culture. Named for the crusading anticommunist U.S. senator Joseph McCarthy, McCarthyism has been referred to as the American Inquisition.[10] This inquisition drove open left-wing opposition to monopoly, capitalism, and imperialism underground and made this part of American political culture invisible for more than a decade. Consequently, a repression of the political culture of the Puerto Rican took place.

THE FALL OF THE OLD LEFT AND THE PUERTO RICAN COMMUNITY OF THE FIFTIES

The mention of McCarthyism usually brings to mind images of the House Committee on Un-American Activities (HUAC) hearings and the blacklisting of writers, producers, and actors in Hollywood. While many individuals suffered persecution for supposedly holding "un-American" beliefs the overall effect of the witch hunts was not limited to those persecuted. For Puerto Ricans in the United States and in Puerto Rico, the impact on the political culture was significant. Before looking at the impact of McCarthyism on the Puerto Rican community in the U.S. it might be useful to describe the general effects of political repression.

Political repression can be described as a multifaceted phenomenon whose principal goals are to destroy the individual as a political being and to affect the individual as a person by severing links with family and other valued groups. To gain an understanding of the fear generated as a consequence of repression, it is necessary to analyze it in the context of the specific situation in which it occurs. Repression disrupts social practices and fragments social relations (job-related, familial, political) and alters any sense of continuity and achievement in people's lives. Individuals are at risk of interpreting these losses as irrevocable and surrendering to defeat. Fear is both an objective and subjective experience whose effects are initially on the individual but which, when occurring simultaneously in thousands of people, has serious repercussions for social and political behavior. Hence, fear can be described as an experience that is collective and observable as well as individual and denied, and one that acts on and shapes the forms of collective behavior.

Active radical engagement within most Puerto Rican homes, as is true for most groups in the 1950s, was to become extremely rare. The rise of the Cold War, McCarthyism, and the conducting of witch hunts in the United States was matched in Puerto Rico by *La Mordaza*, or the gag law. In 1948 the Puerto Rican version of the Smith Act, known as *la lea 53*, was passed by the Puerto Rican legislature and was not repealed until 1957. The main targets of *La Mordaza* were the Nationalist Party and the Communist Party of Puerto Rico.

The virtual outlawing of the Communist Party U.S.A., with the passage of the McCarran Act in 1950 and the decline of the American Labor Party, closed off two important avenues for radicalism amongst Puerto Ricans in the United States. Moreover, mainstream politics was not generally an avenue open to Puerto Ricans. Neither the Democratic nor Republican parties were very much interested in having Puerto Ricans participate in the political process. In fact, exclusion from the political process was the experience of Puerto Ricans.

The Nationalist uprising of October 1950 saw a wave of repression not only in Puerto Rico, but in the Puerto Rican communities of the United States. Puerto Rican Nationalists and socialists were placed under surveillance, and FBI agents made visits to a number of homes. The 1954 Nationalist attack on the Congress of the United States, led by Lolita Lebrón, resulted in the unleashing of another wave of political repression. As a result of the repression, views in favor of independence or socialism, if expressed at all by Puerto Ricans, were uttered in hushed tones. Visits from the FBI or the local "Red Squad" to the homes of Puerto Rican activists had a particularly chilling effect.

The combination of political repression and fear, both in the United States and in Puerto Rico, converged with the need for parents to protect themselves and their loved ones. To be involved in independence or left-wing politics was potentially dangerous. Visits from the FBI to one's home or place of work served to intimidate not only those who were active but also as a warning to those who were sympathetic or curious.

Visits by agents from repressive government organizations were only the tip of the iceberg. Repression directed against activists and sympathizers represented an elite strategy for suppressing dissent. Political repression through the culture of fear was effected on a societywide scale. In this the press and electronic media were very effective and colluded in maintaining the anticommunist political atmosphere.

During the fifties the wartime practice of civil defense drills was maintained. In schools, children were instructed on what to do in the case of nuclear attack by the Soviet Union. Many who went to school in the United States and Puerto Rico during the 1950s remember being told to line up and march to the nearest shelter or to crouch under their desks until the drill was over. In North American suburbs bunkers and bomb shelters were constructed; families stocked up on provisions and participated in civil defense drills. In many states participation in air drills by persons in public buildings was required by law.

Repression created a culture of fear that resulted in many cases in self-imposed inactivity and censorship. Silencing took place in the society at large at the level of the political. Alternative ways of thinking and counter-cultures would emerge throughout this period amongst subaltern groups, noticeably among artists and musicians. The jazz world of African Americans, the emergence of bebop, and the world inhabited by bohemians are vivid examples that would have an important influence in the next decade. However, at the level of formal politics, life had been frozen, and a thaw would not take place until the sixties. For Puerto Ricans the impact of the McCarthy era was also linked to coloniality and race. Anticommunism in the United States has historically been linked to antiimmigrant sentiments rooted in a racist and xenophobic nativism. Thus, the foreign-born and Jews were especially susceptible to being scapegoated by the conservative media. Despite being citizens since 1917, Puerto Ricans were considered a foreign presence. Therefore, distancing oneself from radicalism, especially nationalism and communism, was a way of being less foreign in the eyes of the dominant society. Hence, assimilation, as a dominant strategy in the 1950s and 1960s, for Puerto Ricans involved a political as well as a sociocultural dimension.

It is little wonder that many Puerto Ricans growing up during this time experienced a rupture with the oppositional political culture of the Old Left, and the various strains of Puerto Rican nationalism since they had been silenced. This silencing not only engendered a political rupture but caused a fragmenting of memory. Puerto Rican radicals in the sixties would seek to recapture and create a collective memory of Puerto Rican activism that could serve in the formation of a political identity and radical project.

THE UNIVERSITY, BLACK POWER, AND NATIONALISM

The student movement in the United States, as in Western Europe, became the archetypal movement of opposition of the late sixties. It came to represent and symbolize new forms of rebellion and discontent as it was not a residue of older historical antagonisms and arose in a period of relative growth and prosperity. Education was widely heralded by the society at large, and by liberal theorists and policymakers in particular, as the means of leveling social inequalities, broadening the basis of citizenship, and guaranteeing future prosperity. However, it produced the bitter fruit of conflict. Youth—the generation destined to create the future utopia— became a social problem and the angry conscience of a divided society.

The impact of the student movement owed much to the fact that it was an aspect of an organic crisis. Students were the second group to mobilize en masse. It was the first time that students emerged as a social group in their own right. Previously, as in the 1930s and 1940s, they had acted in support of other groups in a subordinate capacity. They had taken up general political questions. By the sixties, with the extension of schooling at the postsecondary level, students became more important numerically. The student movement's novelty and its significance gave it a historical role out of all proportion to the students' relatively marginal position in society. As the student movement was gathering momentum, the Civil Rights Movement was entering a new phase known as the Black Power Movement. The student movement in the United States, while a reflection of a number of sociopolitical transformations, was initially inspired by the continuation of a struggle that had defined (and continues to define) the country since its founding—the African American struggle for freedom.

From the early stages of the modern Civil Rights Movement, young African American students and their White counterparts from northern U.S. cities participated in the numerous campaigns to end Jim Crow segregation in the South. By the mid-sixties the Civil Rights Movement had reached an impasse. The passage of the Voting Rights Act of 1965 was increasingly viewed as inadequate to meeting the freedom struggle. Among younger Black Civil Rights activists, disillusionment with the political process stemmed from a belief that the federal government was not doing all that could be done to ensure compliance with civil rights and with the War on Poverty legislation. Together with new and increasingly sophisticated legal evasions, meaningless tokenism, half-hearted searches for "qualified" minorities, and the ongoing problem of de facto segregation guaranteed further frustration with the pace of the freedom struggle. In addition, the Johnson administration's growing commitment to the Southeast Asian war and the uneasiness evidenced within the White liberal camp after the Watts Riot (rebellion) seemed to bode ill for increased funding of civil rights enforcement. These developments resulted in a loss of faith in both the leadership of the movement and the tactics that had been employed and finally with the dominant interpretation of Black freedom as achievable through integration.

As the movement reached a crossroads, Black youth confronted the old

Civil Rights Movement with the limitations of the strategy and tactics being pursued and in the process supplanted the old leadership. In doing so they articulated a different paradigm for achieving freedom. Black Power was at once a slogan and a variously defined political, socioeconomic, and cultural philosophy. This reorientation included a geopolitical shift from rural areas in the South to urban centers in the North and in western parts of the country.

The Black Power Movement reflected both an impasse in the Black freedom movement and the appropriation and rearticulation of a number of ideological and political trends within African American political culture dating back to at least the 1920s on the part of Black youth. From the "Back to Africa" movement led by Marcus Garvey to the Nation of Islam and the Deacons for Defense, there had been a tradition of political struggle that was inspired less by the teachings of M. Gandhi than by the example of Nat Turner. These political traditions that included socialists as well as nationalists had, with the rise of a Black bourgeoisie and middle-class leadership together with White liberals dominating the movement, been temporarily eclipsed. As Robert L. Allen points out: "The civil rights movement began as an independent black struggle, but it started declining partly because its middle-class leadership merged with white liberals and allowed them to define goals and tactics. The concept of 'Black Power' as articulated in the sixties represented a reassertion of black independence." [11]

For many African American youth activists Martin Luther King Jr. no longer inspired their activism — instead he was increasingly viewed as a representative of a leadership given to compromise and dependent on paternalistic support of White liberals. Instead of looking for leadership and direction from the Southern Christian Leadership Conference (SCLC) or the National Association for the Advancement of Colored People (NAACP), Black youth, such as those in the leadership of the Student Nonviolent Coordinating Committee (SNCC) and Stokley Carmichael, looked increasingly toward the former minister of the Nation of Islam, Malcolm X. In 1966, a year after the assassination of Malcolm X, the leadership of SNCC introduced the slogan of Black Power, the achievement of which was the precondition for freedom. Within the movement Black Power represented a shift from a liberal ethnic paradigm to paradigms operating within a framework that posited race, class, or nation as the central analytical category for understanding oppression.

As the movement entered its Black Power phase, African American students who in past summers traveled to the South to struggle against segregation, now focused their attention on institutional racism within the university. Young African American students also began to distance themselves from many of the White students who had been active in the Civil Rights Movement. The major reason for this distancing was the paternalism that Black students perceived on the part of White students. This paternalism was seen as being rooted in a complex of guilt and a search for meaning within the Civil Rights Movement: White college students could, via participation in the Civil Rights Movement, alleviate their guilt and give meaning to their sterile, White middle-class existence; White liberals who were active in the movement would continue to see African Americans as victims or problems but never as true equals.

The assertion of Black pride and self-sufficiency together with a rejection of nonviolence as the sole tactic to be employed to achieve freedom by Black youth led to the alienation of young Whites from the Black freedom movement. White students would increasingly turn to the growing antiwar movement and to participation in different aspects of the sixties counterculture. Black students would also protest against the war, however from a different standpoint. As they struggled against institutionalized racism within the university they also fought to maintain links with the Black community.

During this period of transition, Puerto Rican youth began to enter the university in small numbers. Many of them were the first members of their families to pursue higher education. Their admission was the result of two different strategies. First, the leadership of the Puerto Rican community was pursuing a strategy of community advancement through educational achievement. Identical to the perspective of their African American counterparts, their strategy was premised on a conception of a pluralist society, composed of various ethnic and interest groups, all of whom were competing with one another for goods and services. This being the case, equal opportunities, privileges, and respect must be accorded to all groups. The amicable coexistence allows each subculture to remain relatively intact. If granted equal access to power and allowed to strengthen and renew their unique cultural roots, the groups would form a multicultural society in which each component supported and enriched all others.

A second strategy was that pursued by certain factions of capital- and liberal-minded state elites. It was believed by policymakers that the recruitment of "nontraditional" students, that is, African Americans and Puerto Ricans, would be the best way of creating acceptance of the prevailing social system. An expanded minority bourgeoisie and middle class would have an active, vested interest in its benefits and thus would serve as a stabilizing force among the urban masses. Of course, the numbers who would be allowed in the university would be restricted to a few. Hence, interestingly there existed a convergence between the strategy of ethnic group advancement and the maintenance of the status quo.

Following in the footsteps of the previous generation of political actors within the Puerto Rican community, many young Puerto Ricans who entered the university were determined to undertake studies in professional fields. As professionals (i.e., social workers, educators, doctors, and lawyers), they could improve their socioeconomic status while providing some types of community service.

As they entered the university they found that there were many barriers to the educational and professional goals they had set for themselves. It is within the context of struggling against the institutional and individual racism in higher education that many came into contact with the existing student movement and alternative ideas that would change the way many would think about the world and about themselves. Primary of the different movements that they came in contact with was that of African Americans.

While Puerto Rican youth had been exposed to the political culture of the Black community in their own neighborhoods and witnessed the Civil Rights Movement through the mass media, for many Puerto Rican youth the organizing of student organizations was the first type of overt political activity in which they had engaged. And for those who had experience in the youth groups, such as Aspira, this was an opportunity to engage in activity independent of the agency staff who ran the youth programs. In the course of the late sixties dozens of Puerto Rican student organizations were founded. The largest and perhaps the best known of these was the Puerto Rican Student Union.

For Puerto Rican youth, like their African American counterparts, the struggle was not only focused on questions of racism, social justice, and exploitation, but it also involved a struggle of definition, of identity. The psychological battle against the crippling effects of racism was seen to be as important as the struggle against its institutional forms. In their search for an affirming identity, many would first encounter not only the active movement of African Americans but also the corpus of African American writings. It is important to note that in the midsixties there existed very little written or translated into English about Puerto Rico, and even less about Puerto Ricans in the United States that was not derogatory or a distortion of the Puerto Rican experience.

Exposure to the African American political and literary culture led many Puerto Rican youth to seek out resources for the exploration of their own identity. The impact of two events that registered in the Puerto Rican community were to be explored in earnest by Puerto Rican students. On February 21, 1965, Malcolm X was assassinated while addressing an audience at the Audubon Ballroom in New York City. Across the country African Americans, many who had disagreed with the philosophy of

Revolutionary Black Nationalism Malcolm X espoused while he was alive, mourned his death. The influence of Malcolm X has been the subject of a large number of studies on the politics of the Black community in the United States. However, his impact on the lives of Puerto Ricans has not been explored.

For many young Puerto Ricans in New York City, Malcolm X was a familiar figure. Oftentimes when Malcolm X was the main spokesperson for the Nation of Islam and addressed rallies in Harlem, Puerto Ricans who lived in East and West Harlem would hear him speak. The newspaper *Mohammed Speaks* was peddled on the streets of neighborhoods where the residents were both Black and Puerto Rican.

While for an older generation of Puerto Ricans, the philosophy of the Nation of Islam (or for that matter Malcolm X's post–Nation of Islam perspective) was anathema, at least officially, his denunciation of White racism and call for Black pride resonated among young Puerto Ricans. Puerto Rican youth read his autobiography, which related his struggle against racism and called for a reaffirmation of Blackness, and likened it to their own experience as a racialized group in the United States. In fact many Puerto Rican activists cite Malcolm X and the reading of his autobiography and speeches as a major turning point in their lives. Malcolm inspired in young people a search for their own roots and historically relevant political figures.

On April 21, 1965, Pedro Albizu Campos, the leader of the Puerto Rican Nationalist Party, passed away. For Puerto Rican youth in the United States, Albizu Campos was a relatively unknown figure. Most of the sixties activists had been infants when the Nationalist Party had staged an uprising in 1950 and were not much older when Puerto Rican Nationalists made an armed attack on the U.S. Congress. These events were not yet a part of the historical memory of this youthful generation, having been suppressed by the silence imposed by the Cold War. The memories of those who had lived the experience had been fractured, made ephemeral, and almost forgotten. The death of the Nationalist leader together with the social upheavals then taking place jarred the social memory of the Puerto Rican community.

For the emergent generation of Puerto Rican radicals the legacy of Pedro Albizu Campos was to be appropriated and invested with a number of meanings. As a symbol of unwavering militant opposition to U.S. colonialism, Albizu Campos could be viewed as Puerto Ricans' Malcolm X. In Puerto Rico, Albizu Campos was rediscovered by student activists, and like their U.S. counterparts, they demanded to know who he was and why knowledge about him had been suppressed.

As Puerto Rican college students and youth began to form organizations, many of the groups were named after the late leader. Among these was the Sociedad de Albizu Campos, the precursor of the Young Lords Party in New York City. Puerto Rican Nationalism as represented by Albizu Campos and the Nationalist Party was to be rearticulated and incorporated as a part of the ideology of the Puerto Rican Left, as were a number of other ideological currents. The strident nationalism of Albizu Campos was appropriated as the more conservative class and cultural dimensions of *Albizuismo* were ignored. Also, the definition of what constituted a Puerto Rican for Albizu Campos would have excluded many of the young U.S.-born Puerto Ricans.

THIRD WORLDISM, CUBA, AND CHINA

Another influence on the emergent Puerto Rican Left, and on the Left internationally, was the Cuban Revolution and the example of its leaders, Fidel Castro and Ernesto "Che" Guevara. The July 26 movement underwent a rapid radicalization, in no small part as a result of the pressures of the U.S. government, but also as part of an internal political process. The impact on the American Left has been generally acknowledged, with at least one view that the Cuban Revolution was instrumental in sparking the rebirth of left-wing politics in the U.S.[12]

In Puerto Rico the fall of U.S.-backed Cuban dictator Fulgencio Batista was met by Nationalists and socialists alike with great optimism. That same year the Movimiento Pro Independencia (MPI) was founded. In New York a section of the MPI was organized by a group of proindependence intellectuals. By the late sixties the MPI in New York, fed by student and other sectors, increased in size. A new wave of political literature became influential among radicalized youth. Collected writings and speeches by Fidel Castro together with *Reminiscences of the Cuban Revolutionary War, Guerrilla Warfare,* the *Bolivian Diaries,* and the pamphlet "Socialism and Man in Cuba" by Che Guevara were widely read. Also, a large volume of books written by supporters of the revolution were published. Influential on the Left in the U.S. were *Listen Yankee* by C. Wright Mills and *Cuba: Anatomy of a Revolution* and *Socialism in Cuba* by Leo Huberman and Paul Sweezy. One of the most influential books to appear that presented the Cuban Revolution as a paradigm for revolution for Latin America was Regis Debray's *Revolution in the Revolution.*

The impact of the Cuban and other Latin American revolutions on the Puerto Rican Left was significant for a number of reasons. The romantic image of the young *guerrillero* leadership marching into Havana at the head of the rebel army, the heroic and defiant stance taken toward the United States in defense of Cuba's sovereignty, and the commitment to eradicate poverty and ignorance captured the imagination of radicalized youth internationally. That the leadership of the Cuban Revolution supported revolutionary movements abroad, and in particular supported the independence of Puerto Rico, was for Puerto Ricans on the island and in the United States of particular importance. In fact, establishing the historical links between the Cuban Revolution and Cuba's anticolonial struggle with that of Puerto Rico was of particular importance for most sectors of the movement. That the contemporary struggles being waged for independence could be linked to the Cuban Revolution, the struggles waged in the nineteenth century against Spanish colonialism, and the movements against imperialism in the twentieth century, gave these a certain continuity and legitimacy.

The establishment of links between the past and present is important to any counterhegemonic movement. As Walter Benjamin understood "[i]nsofar as the past has been transmitted as tradition, it possesses authority; insofar as authority presents itself historically, it becomes tradition." The past is legitimate because it is authentic. The political movements of the sixties, like all movements, sought to establish links with the past and to establish itself as the continuation of those traditions, even in dramatically changed circumstances. In this way, figures from the nineteenth-century independence struggle were brought back to life and walked side by side with martyrs from this century together with contemporary leaders. This aspect of the movement was to prove problematic at a number of levels, which will be discussed later. However, during initial stages of the movement it proved useful insofar as all movements require myths, as a means of both legitimation and as a way of marking off the boundaries between itself and those outside the tradition that is being claimed.

ON THE INTERNATIONAL scene there was another development that was particularly significant for the development of the Left in the United States, and in particular for Chinese, African Americans, and Latinos— the Chinese Cultural Revolution.

The appeal for most groups in the United States had mostly to do with the emergence of a model of socialism that appeared to be carrying out a thorough social transformation placing "politics in command," as opposed to the Soviet example that held little appeal for an emergent Left. Because the sixties movements were largly moved by a voluntaristic spirit, the Chinese model held a special appeal. Also, the existence of a leadership, especially Mao Tse Tung, whose legitimacy was at the time unquestionable, should be noted. Neither Nikita S. Khrushchev nor Leonid I. Brezhnev could claim to have led a revolution. To be a leader of a revolution in the most populous nation on earth was an asset possessed by no other party. In addition, the image of the Cultural Revolution being carried out by the Red Guards (Chinese youth) was especially appealing for a movement that was from its inception a movement of young people. For African Americans and Puerto Ricans, the Chinese Cultural Revolution was, in addition to the above, appealing for a variety of other reasons. That the center of world revolution was seen as being located in the Third World, and a nuclear power at that, as opposed to the Soviet Union (which was, whether socialist or not, still a European power) was an important factor.

While a number of splinter groups from the Old Left had since the Sino-Soviet split been supporters of the Chinese line in the international communist movement, their influence amongst Puerto Rican and African American militants was negligible.[13] The best known of these organizations, the Progressive Labor Party, while successful in attracting a few Puerto Ricans to its periphery in the early sixties, was never able to attract more than a few members.[14]

In the late sixties a number of African American radicals were attracted to Marxism via Mao Tse Tung's thought. In early 1967 on the campus of the University of California at Berkeley, leaders of the Black Panther Party, Huey P. Newton, Bobby Seale, and Bobby Hutton, had set up a table and began selling Chairman Mao's *Little Red Book*. The Black Panthers' promotion of Chairman Mao's writings was an important influence on Puerto Ricans who identified with the Black Power Movement. The Young Lords Party was more so than any other Puerto Rican group in tune with developments in the Black community.

The turn to Maoism on the part of a section of the Puerto Rican Left became an integral part of a Third Worldist perspective. Third Worldism can be seen as a response to the racism of the traditional U.S. Left. The New Communist Movement's support for Third World liberation struggles and its resurrection of the 1928 and 1930 Comintern thesis, which called for national self-determination of the Black nation in the U.S. South, were key factors in the movement's appeal to oppressed racial groups in the United States.

Another reason that U.S. Maoism was seen as an alternative was the experience many Puerto Rican radicals had with the leadership of the Movimiento Pro Independencia and later with the Partido Socialista Puertorriqueña (PSP) and the organization's ambivalence toward the struggles of Puerto Ricans in the United States.

Many of those who gravitated toward the section of the Puerto Rican Left that entered the New Communist Movement identified the leadership of the PSP as being composed of upper-class Whites from Puerto Rico who looked down their noses at poor and working-class darker-skinned Puerto Ricans born in the United States.

The class and racial differences between the PSP leadership from Puerto Rico and Puerto Ricans in the United States was a disappointment for many young Puerto Ricans who were born and/or raised in the United States. In this respect, language took on an added dimension as many Puerto Ricans raised in the United States were English-dominant. The PSP adhered to a linguistic chauvinism that privileged Spanish over English and saw language, and other cultural markers, as defining nationality. Added to this was the PSP's failure to adequately address the relation between the independence aims of the party and the urgent economic and social problems of Puerto Ricans in the diaspora.

The PSP's failure to address the question of the two million Puerto Ricans who lived in the United States alienated many young Puerto Ricans and created tensions within the ranks of the membership of the U.S. section of the PSP. For such groups as the Young Lords Party (which later became the Puerto Rican Revolutionary Workers Organization), in addition to being a revisionist organization like the CPUSA, the PSP maintained a relationship with Puerto Ricans in the United States as a type of "subimperialism." Puerto Ricans in the United States were to submit to a leadership that was not concerned with the particular struggles of poor and working-class Puerto Ricans here and whose primary task was to support the struggle for independence that would be led by the PSP.

However, while the leadership of the PSP may have seen the task of decolonization as primary for Puerto Ricans in the United States, the membership of the U.S. branch was involved in many organizing efforts at the local community level. PSP organizing around housing issues in parts of New York, such as Williamsburg, and in Chicago were significant, as were organizing efforts in the labor movement. It is important to note the divergence between what the political line of the party established by the leadership was and how the membership may have interpreted it. In recent scholarship on the Communist Party, the study of this divergence has been instrumental in providing a more nuanced analysis of the CPUSA's history.[15]

The breach between the two major tendencies of the Puerto Rican Left was rooted in the ideological and political split in the international communist and liberation movements but was also tied to internal class and racial differences linked to the politics of identity. Puerto Rican radicals in the United States were not only involved in struggles at the economic and political level but also were involved in constructing a political identity framed by class, race, and coloniality. The assumption of a subordinate role by Puerto Ricans in the United States to an upper-class leadership from Puerto Rico was viewed by some participants as a relationship of domination and subordination.

INSIDE PRISON

As the war in Vietnam raged overseas, the political ferment generated at home slipped through penitentiary bars, providing African American and Puerto Rican inmates with alternative perspectives on society and their role in that society. Throughout the late sixties and early seventies American prisons were increasingly the site for unrest. While U.S. prisons have always held political prisoners, this period marked the first time that prisoners en masse were becoming politicized.

During this period, movement activists provided a detailed critique of crime and punishment in the United States. Many had first-hand knowledge of the institutions and practices that were described and, therefore, they could provide vivid accounts of the system. *The Autobiography of Malcolm X* offered a trenchant critique of the American criminal justice system and the impact of racism on African Americans who were unfortunate enough to be subject to that system.

Criticism of the criminal justice system included inferior treatment for non-White and poor defendants provided by uncaring or insensitive public defenders, jurors who were seldom the prisoners' socioeconomic peers, and judges who were racist and ardent defenders of the system. In the case that the judge was liberal, he or she was usually so overburdened with the task of diminishing a backlog of cases that this task had become much more important than dispensing justice. For these reasons, it was argued that many African Americans and Latinos were being sent to prison for crimes for which Whites were seldom tried much less convicted.

The critique of racism within the criminal justice system was joined to a critique of capitalism and racism in America. If Black and in prison for an economic crime, one was in effect a political prisoner. The category of political prisoner was recast to encompass a larger segment of the inmate population. Also, the activities of the ruling class were seen as constituting criminal activity. The process of capital accumulation and the running of the repressive apparatus of the state were viewed as criminal, if legally sanctioned, activity.[16]

After Malcolm X, whose autobiography was passed from inmate to inmate, the most influential African American writing from the position of an inmate was that of Eldridge Cleaver. Cleaver's *Soul on Ice,* a collection of essays that had appeared in the radical magazine *Ramparts,* was widely read. While described by Cornel West, among others, as a sociopath because of his misogynistic advocacy of rape, Cleaver's essays in many ways crystallized the frustrations of many African American youth, especially those on the margins of society.

As the Black movement progressed, African American inmates began to form groups within the prisons. While the Nation of Islam had a presence within the prison system, it was never able to influence more than a handful of prisoners. Moreover, the Nation's demonology and lack of a coherent strategy prevented it from achieving the broad appeal that other brands of Black Nationalism held.

Following the example of Malcolm X, some inmates used the serving of "hard time" to cultivate self-awareness, spur intellectual growth, and develop ideological coherence. However, for most inmates, the prison experience served only as formal recognition that they had been consigned to the very bottom of the U.S. social structure. And while they did not join the different Black Nationalist groups, they remained receptive to appeals from politicized inmates and political prisoners who came into the system.

That prison conditions in the United States are brutal has long been acknowledged. However, during the sixties conditions were to become increasingly abysmal. For the non-White inmate, once sentenced to a correctional facility, the experience would prove to be worse than that for his White counterpart. Along with ineffective rehabilitation programs and increasingly intolerable living conditions, advocates of prison reform critiqued both correctional officers and administrators. The guards harassed and brutalized non-White inmates. They also enlisted White prisoners to help enforce their system of internal racial control. In many instances White prisoners were provided with knives and zip guns and directed to ensure that facilities remained segregated. If an interracial altercation broke out, levying harsher punishment on the darker of the two combatants was the rule. In a number of prisons, guards and White inmates were organized into chapters of the Ku Klux Klan and other White supremacist groups.

Prison system administrators were criticized for far more than simply allowing such conditions to exist. They were accused of developing and implementing policies that defined many, if not most, militant African Americans or Latinos as "political" prisoners. Once prisoners were labeled in this fashion, they found their reading material censored, their privileges limited, and their chances for parole greatly diminished. No longer mere criminals, they had become enemies of the social order—to be kept under long-term surveillance by the predominantly White occupiers of the largely non-White penal colony. When such prisoners appeared before a parole board, their views on contemporary social issues immediately became the primary issue of interest. If an inmate was honest and told the truth, he would be termed unrepentant and denied parole.

The death of a politicized inmate under suspicious circumstances was to channel the anger of the inmate population across the country and spark a series of prison rebellions. On August 21, 1971, George L. Jackson was killed inside San Quentin Prison. The author of *Soledad Brother* (1970) and *Blood In My Eye* (1972) was to become a symbol, both within and outside of the prison system, of what was in store for inmates who developed politically and stood up against oppression. As news traveled from prison to prison, politicized inmates, and those who were receptive to oppositional politics, held moments of silence in honor of the slain inmate. At Attica Correctional Facility in New York, seven-eights of the inmate population participated in a George Jackson memorial. The day was observed by a boycott of food served in the mess hall, silence in the mess hall and the corridors, and the wearing of black armbands as a sign of mourning.

On September 9, 1971, 1,281 men imprisoned in New York's Attica Correctional Facility forced their way into the consciousness of the country by rising up against intolerable conditions and taking hostages. Prisoners issued a list of thirty-three demands, which included: administrative and legal amnesty for all who participated in the rebellion, freedom of religion, application of minimum-wage laws to work done by inmates, the allowance of prisoners to be politically active without fear of intimidation or reprisal, the end of censorship of letters and all publications and books, the provision of a Spanish-language library, provision of adequate health care and nutrition, the modernization of the educational system, and provision of bilingual services for Spanish-speaking inmates. Demands for bilingual services and a Spanish library were made by Puerto Rican inmates, such as Mariano Gonzalez.

The uprising was squelched on the morning of September 13, when an assault, approved by Gov. Nelson Rockefeller, was carried out by state police. After shooting ended, forty-three men were dead, and eighty-nine had serious gunshot wounds. Retribution against the leaders would go on throughout the night as guards went from cell to cell identifying inmates who were involved in the uprising, and those individuals were punished accordingly.

The Attica uprising had not been the first to take place during this period. On August 10, 1970, the "Tombs" (the Manhattan House of Detention) experienced a one-day rebellion of Black and Puerto Rican prisoners.

On October 2, 1970, several New York City jails experienced similar uprisings. In all these, Puerto Rican inmates were at the center of the rebellions and made demands particular to their needs. However, it was the death of George Jackson and the Attica uprising that brought attention to the different social movements and the situation of prisoners, especially non-White inmates, in U.S. prisons.

Throughout the early seventies Puerto Rican prisoners were to establish contact with Puerto Rican organizations and establish their own organizations inside the prisons. At Attica, prison inmates established a chapter of the Young Lords Party. Puerto Rican inmates, once politicized and involved in organizing groups, would be identified by prison administrators and sent to different prisons in an effort to break up these organizations. However, inmates who were sent to other prisons would start their organizing efforts anew, increasing the networks among Puerto Rican inmates. These networks were also connected to political prisoner defense committees, prisoners' rights groups, and attorneys. Upon release from prison, former prisoners joined several Puerto Rican Left groups and devoted themselves to working on prison reform issues in addition to working for the release of the Puerto Rican Nationalists and other political prisoners.

The significance of the prison rebellions of the early 1970s for the Puerto Rican movement was that it served to challenge a rather traditional conception within the community and sections of the Left that tended to view prisoners strictly as criminal or *lumpen* elements who were lost to society. A sector of the Puerto Rican community (prisoners) that was marginalized was resisting oppression and seeking to move toward an identity, which young radicals were creating. Race and class assumed a centrality in this process because the perspective of the movement was that those who were non-White and poor were more likely to end up in prison. Simultaneously, some sectors of the movement tended to romanticize the rebellions within the prisons and moved from working with privileged students or the working class to the *lumpen proletariat*. The Young Lords Party early in its development called for the organizing of the *lumpen proletariat*. A certain romanticizing about prisoners and their revolutionary potential was common during the sixties. This was, in part, a response to the racial and social devaluation of the *lumpen proletariat* by the traditional Left in the United States and in Puerto Rico. Moreover, because the U.S. working class had not realized its "historic mission" (either because of racism, and/or because workers were bourgeoisie) the issue of finding a social agent capable of transforming society led some to pose the *lumpen* as the agent capable of undertaking this task.

Conclusion

This essay examines some of the main constitutive processes affecting the new generation of Puerto Rican radicals that entered the political stage starting in the late 1960s. Other aspects of their formation not addressed here include: mass culture of the "baby boomer" generation, exposure to the ideas of existentialism and the mass culture in general, the military, and the antiwar movement. Taken together, these forces were fundamental influences in the political formation of this generation.

JOSÉ E. VELÁZQUEZ

3   Coming Full Circle

The Puerto Rican Socialist Party, U.S. Branch

IN APRIL of 1973 three thousand people gathered in New York City to witness the inaugural congress of the U.S. branch of the Puerto Rican Socialist Party, or PSP (Partido Socialista Puertorriqueño).[1] From 1959 to 1971 the organization was known as the MPI, or the Movement for Independence (Movimiento Pro Independencia); in 1971 the group changed its name to PSP. The 1973 assembly was an historic event, in which the group announced its new political direction. The PSP would try to do what the island's independence movement had never seriously attempted: organize a massive revolutionary organization that simultaneously dealt with the crusade for Puerto Rican independence and the social and political struggles of Puerto Ricans in the United States.

This milestone event signaled new opportunities, as well as challenges, for the independence movement in Puerto Rico and for the mainland Puerto Rican radical movements of the late 1960s. Both these forces were to coalesce and develop a cohesive Puerto Rican revolutionary movement in the United States well into the 1980s. Along with the Young Lords Party and El Comité, the PSP represented one of the leading forces within the Puerto Rican movement.

In the early 1970s, the PSP, armed with a new party program for the United States, created chapters in several major cities; nourished itself with experienced cadre from other Puerto Rican radical organizations; and recruited hundreds of young and old, first- and second-generation Puerto Ricans. It also gained credibility and influence among major sectors of the North American Left. By the mid-1970s, the PSP became the dominant organization within the Puerto Rican Left in the United States, overshadowing the Young Lords Party, which remained entrapped in factional and ideological conflicts.

However, by the late 1970s, the PSP experienced a period of rapid decline stemming from its failure to develop a clear and consistent political theory and practice for organizing the Puerto Rican community in the United States. At the heart of this decline was the party's inability to programmatically link the struggle for the independence of Puerto Rico to the political, social, and cultural struggle of Puerto Ricans in the United

48

States, a task that the PSP defined as the "struggle for democratic rights." Despite making deep inroads within the Puerto Rican community in the United States, the PSP would never transcend its traditional role of primarily building solidarity for the independence struggle in Puerto Rico.

An analysis of the PSP's demise in the United States reveals the complexities involved, despite claims of autonomy, in building a revolutionary organization that received direct leadership from Puerto Rico. The organization's decline was accompanied, and to some extent caused, by continual ideological differences among the PSP leadership in Puerto Rico. The intensive involvement of the U.S. branch in these debates effectively hindered the group's organizing efforts and left little room for much-needed theoretical discussions about its role in organizing Puerto Ricans in the United States. By the early 1980s, many of the mainland Puerto Ricans who had joined the PSP during the previous decade came full circle, giving up any hope that the organization would play a leading role in the Puerto Rican struggle in the United States. This essay attempts to convey the experiences of some of the mainland Puerto Ricans who participated in the development of the PSP, U.S. Branch. It also attempts to give a chronological survey of the major events and debates that shaped the development of the PSP from the early 1970s until the early 1980s.[2]

Despite failure to attain its goals, the PSP demonstrated the potential for the development of a mass-based, revolutionary movement that would link the struggle for the independence of Puerto Rico with the struggle of Puerto Ricans within the United States. The PSP successfully recruited among several generations of Puerto Ricans on the mainland, organized hundreds of activists, and influenced tens of thousands of people, Puerto Rican and non–Puerto Rican. Though its leadership was essentially comprised of former student and youth activists, the party developed an extensive working-class membership. The Puerto Rican revolutionary movement of the 1960s and 1970s left an enduring legacy that continues to influence present-day Puerto Rican political, social, and cultural manifestations. The decline of the PSP, as well as other Puerto Rican revolutionary organizations, however, left a vacuum in the level of organization and the ideological content of present-day activism in the Puerto Rican community. In this regard, the PSP's experience can provide valuable lessons for the Puerto Rican revolutionary movement of today and tomorrow.

THE FORMATIVE YEARS

The Puerto Rican Socialist Party had its roots in the MPI, a group established in Puerto Rico in 1959 and that subsequently organized the Vito Marcantonio Mission in New York City in 1964. Based in East Harlem and the Lower East Side during the 1960s, the MPI was involved in traditional patriotic mobilizations, Puerto Rican parades, and local community struggles. Comprised essentially of first-generation Puerto Ricans, many of whom had ties to the Nationalist movement of the 1950s, the MPI saw its main role as being a financial and propagandistic support group for the independence movement in Puerto Rico. By the mid-1960s, several major events had a radicalizing effect on island politics, especially among the youth: the Cuban Revolution, the Vietnamese national liberation struggle, the North American antiwar movement, and the Black liberation struggle—all had a radicalizing effect on the struggle in Puerto Rico. It was a struggle increasingly characterized by labor strife, militant student protests, antiwar mobilizations, and proindependence activity, and this struggle was led by the MPI and the Puerto Rican Independence Party (PIP).

By the late 1960s, radical organizations were developing in the Puerto Rican community in the United States. Many, such as the Sociedad Don Pedro Albizu Campos, predecessor of the Young Lords Party (YLP), were strongly influenced by the Black liberation movement, as well as by the struggle for the independence of Puerto Rico. Operating simultaneously with the YLP were a host of Puerto Rican radical groups primarily based in New York City; these groups included the Puerto Rican Student Union; the Third World Revelationists, the Eduardo "Pancho" Cruz Defense Committee; the Carlos Feliciano Defense Committee; La Unión Latina; El Comité; Resistencia Puertorriqueña; and Puerto Ricans for Self-Determination (PRSD). Outside New York, other collectives and organizations proliferated.

The MPI would not be immune to the changes occurring in the Puerto Rican community. By the late 1960s, having made a decision to transform itself into a Marxist-Leninist party, it increasingly supported such struggles as the student takeover of City College in New York City during 1969; the YLP takeover of the 110th Street church in East Harlem; and the march to the United Nations in 1970 in support of the independence of Puerto Rico. The MPI leadership was uneasy about opening up the organization to second-generation youth from the mainland. Nevertheless they began a conscious effort to establish roots among Puerto Ricans raised on the mainland who were now spearheading new radical movements. Learning from the Vietnamese experience, the MPI recognized furthermore that a successful struggle for independence would require a strong solidarity movement within the United States.

In the late 1960s, the MPI expanded from its home base in New York City to New Jersey, Pennsylvania, Connecticut, Massachusetts, and the Midwest, especially Chicago; it developed a broad-based organization of political activists involved in local issues, while it also raised demands for the independence of Puerto Rico. The transition from MPI to PSP in 1971 attracted new recruits, many of whom were in their early twenties, were born and raised in the United States, were mostly bilingual or English-dominant speakers, and were from working-class backgrounds. New members were also drawn from other Puerto Rican radical organizations, including many individuals with deep roots in their respective communities. In March 1972, the publication of a bilingual supplement to the party newspaper, *Claridad,* provided an important vehicle of communication and outreach to Puerto Ricans raised in the United States.

These mainland based forces, along with MPI veterans, fashioned a new leadership and political perspective for the emerging Puerto Rican Socialist Party. Many of these activists joined the PSP because they viewed it as a serious Marxist organization committed to building a working-class movement, as opposed to the YLP, who many mistakenly perceived as having based its organizational strategy on street youth, who were referred to as the *lumpen proletariat*.[3] The PSP also provided its members an organic link to the rich tradition of struggle in Puerto Rico and had the benefit of international recognition. Furthermore, the PSP seemingly bridged differences between Puerto Ricans residing in the United States and those living in Puerto Rico;—in a sense, providing a reaffirmation of Puerto Rican national identity.

THE FIRST CONGRESS OF 1973 AND *DESDE LAS ENTRAÑAS*

An intensive organizing effort led to the celebration of the First Congress of the U.S. branch of the PSP, held on April 8, 1973, at New York City's Manhattan Center. With the concluding session attended by more than three thousand people, the PSP announced itself, in a style typical of the time, as the "vanguard" of the revolutionary movement. The congress adopted a political declaration published in pamphlet form and entitled *Desde Las Entrañas (From the Belly of the Beast)*, the key premise of which was that Puerto Ricans in the United States were not simply another "national minority" but rather an integral part of the Puerto Rican nation. Since the U.S. community maintains extensive economic, cultural, and psychological ties with Puerto Rico, it was argued that the implications for strategy were clear:

> The Puerto Rican Socialist Party is organized to direct the national liberation struggle of our people and to take state power, to transform the present structure completely and direct the working class in the construction of a new society in Puerto Rico, a socialist and revolutionary society.

> Its primary role in the United States is to unleash that national liberation struggle, in all its fury, in the very hearts of North American cities to which a significant portion of our colonized population was forced, and to link that struggle to the struggle for revolutionary transformation of North American society.[4]

To give weight to the importance of this "link," the political program further stated, "The construction of socialism here is *also a priority* [author's emphasis] for Puerto Ricans living in the United States. This is the only way to end the superexploitation that we suffer in the United States. The effective participation of Puerto Rican workers in the radical struggles of North American society will be an important contribution in raising the level of class struggle in this country, besides contributing in a decisive way to the securing of independence and socialism in Puerto Rico."[5]

In effect, a compromise was struck within the organization. This formulation allowed the PSP, U.S. Branch, to say that its strategic conception embodied a "dual priority"—independence for Puerto Rico and the struggle for socialism in the United States. This terminology recognized that, though Puerto Ricans on the mainland were a part of the Puerto Rican nation, they also formed part of the U.S. working class and therefore also needed to bring about revolutionary change in the United States. Whether the old-line leadership in both Puerto Rico and the United States really bought into this concept is another question.

There was quite a bit of ambiguity in the notion of dual priority, for in reality, the dominant perspective was that the independence of Puerto Rico would serve as a spark for revolutionary change in the United States. The *primary* objective of the PSP was to organize Puerto Ricans on the mainland who were viewed as having a potentially decisive role in achieving the independence of Puerto Rico. Since independence was viewed as imminent, this objective, in practice, received top priority. This viewpoint also led to the party's thesis that Puerto Ricans in the United States would emerge as a distinct ethnicity (a "national minority") *only* upon the advent of independence.

The PSP's *Desde Las Entrañas* was a huge step forward when compared to the programmatic ideas of the MPI of the 1960s. The emerging PSP reflected the entire range of the Puerto Rican community: young and old; Nationalists; post-1959 *independentistas;* young, mainland Puerto Rican radicals; and New York and non–New York Puerto Ricans—all of whom brought their experiences and unique perspectives into a flourishing organization. By 1973, a consensus was reached to promote both aspects of the dual priority, which represented a giant step forward for the traditional Nationalist elements within the PSP. This is not to deny that there were real fears among the leadership in Puerto Rico that the struggle on the mainland would divorce itself from the issue of independence or that it might possibly fall into a reformist or assimilationist mode. The dual priority formulation reflected the correlation of forces within the PSP at the time: those members who saw the independence of Puerto Rico as the sole priority, and the new recruits who joined the PSP and saw both the necessity of developing the democratic-rights struggle of Puerto Ricans in the United States and the importance of the struggle for independence in Puerto Rico. This dichotomy would be a source of tension in the daily practice of the PSP throughout its existence, as well as among the entire Puerto Rican Left in the United States.

"*TODOS PA'L GARDEN*": The "National Day of Solidarity with the Independence of Puerto Rico"

Having successfully completed its first congress, the newly formed Central Committee of the PSP met on April 22, 1973, to chart out the course for the "Year of Consolidation of the Party." The party's leadership in Puerto Rico had characterized this period as the beginning of a prerevolutionary stage of the struggle in Puerto Rico. During 1973 and early 1974, the mainland leadership viewed the key to party growth as increasing its activity in democratic-rights issues that affected Puerto Ricans in the United States and not solely limiting itself to the solidarity campaign for the independence of Puerto Rico. During these years, the PSP dealt with such issues as organizing migrant workers, denouncing police brutality, housing struggles, arson (the wholesale burning by landlords of older tenements in urban ghettos) and displacement of communities, welfare rights, student struggles, the effects of the energy crisis, and establishing trade union democracy. The party paid special attention to increasing its organizational efforts among workers and to the development of a progressive Puerto Rican trade union leadership.

A first turning point for the organization began with what became the de facto priority for 1974: the "National Day of Solidarity with the Independence of Puerto Rico," which was held on October 27, 1974, at Madison Square Garden. This political and media event was designed to have an international impact, and the decision to organize the activity was made at the highest levels of the party in Puerto Rico in early 1974. With minimal opposition, the U.S. leadership made a sharp detour from its previous emphasis on democratic-rights struggles, reflecting the top-down decision-making process that would continually plague the PSP. Those individuals who joined the PSP in the early 1970s had the greatest admiration and respect for the party leadership in Puerto Rico—a fact that served to minimize their opposition. Moreover, the development of a

North American solidarity movement for the independence of Puerto Rico was viewed as having strategic importance for the party, especially during a period characterized by the leadership as "prerevolutionary." Furthermore, it was assumed that the National Day of Solidarity would become a priority for the North American Left, who would shoulder most of the financial and political responsibility for the activity, leaving the PSP free to concentrate on its activities within the U.S. Puerto Rican community. This assumption proved to be wrong.

The "National Day of Solidarity" was a huge success from the standpoint of public impact. Twenty thousand people were mobilized, filling up Madison Square Garden in solidarity for the independence of Puerto Rico. However, there were visible signs of the negative impact on the PSP's infrastructure and objectives in other areas caused by the strain of organizing the event. The financial burden that the party assumed in the spring of 1974 was overwhelming. The harsh reality of meeting the goals for this activity completely absorbed party attention and resources to the detriment of the objectives, spelled out in early 1974, concerning democratic-rights issues. A clear example was the decision to reassign the party's secretary for community affairs, the individual (along with his department) responsible for community-based organizing, to the position of national coordinator for the "National Day of Solidarity." Organizing the event also led to the development of a large party bureaucracy, as the number of full-time cadre assigned to central headquarters in New York City rose dramatically, and intermediate leadership groups in different cities were expanded at the expense of local chapters.

GROWING PAINS, GROWING CONTRADICTIONS

In early 1975, the Central Committee in the United States acknowledged that the party, in detriment to other strategic objectives, had focused its greatest efforts on achieving support from North Americans for Puerto Rican independence.[6] The formation of the Committee for Puerto Rican Decolonization (CPRD), the "National Day of Solidarity," and a proposed bicentennial campaign for 1976 were seen as qualitative leaps in garnering solidarity from within the colonizing nation. In a self-critical tone, the U.S. leadership noted that it had paid little attention to the struggle of the Puerto Rican people in the United States for their basic democratic rights within the United States. Aside from the establishment of the Federation of Puerto Rican Socialist University Students (FUSP) on several college campuses, the PSP lagged behind in accomplishing its other key organizational goals. The leadership recognized the need to balance the party's work in 1975, described as the "Year of the Decisive Advance"

(Año Del Avance Decisivo). This balance would be achieved through reaping the benefits of the "National Day of Solidarity" and by emphasizing organizational objectives aside from solidarity work. To make the proper adjustments, the organization would have to return to basics: focusing on workplace and union organizing, the struggle for democratic rights, expanding the party's influence among high-school youth, and recruitment of new members.

During 1975, the PSP developed significant campaigns relating to the democratic-rights struggles of Puerto Ricans in the United States. It played a pivotal role in the campaign to save Hostos Community College in New York City and in the development of Accion Boricua (Puerto Rican Action), a coalition organized to work for democratic rights. In New York's Lower East Side, the party ran candidates for the district community school board. During the Puerto Rican Day Parade in New York, the PSP went beyond the traditional independence contingent and led a "people's contingent" under the slogan "Parade One Day, Poverty Every Day!" ("¡Desfile Un Dia, Pobreza Todos Los Dias!"). Similar coalitions were formed to lead protest contingents in Chicago and in Newark, New Jersey. In New Jersey, the PSP helped expand the statewide Puerto Rican Congress (Congreso Boricua) and was in the forefront of protests in Trenton against education budget cutbacks. In Paterson, New Jersey, the group led a community task force against cutbacks in senior citizen services and bilingual education. In Hartford, Connecticut, the party confronted the powerful insurance companies that spearheaded plans to fence in the Puerto Rican community under the guise of an urban renewal project. The PSP also increased its participation throughout the country in support of labor actions and in the development of Hispanic labor committees in various cities. Serious groundwork was being laid for the formation of the Brotherhood of Latin Workers (Hermandad de Trabajadores Latinos), a strategic goal outlined by the 1973 congress. By the end of the year, as a result of the success of its many campaigns, the PSP leadership was planning to spur the formation of a national Puerto Rican organization focusing on the democratic-rights struggle.

THE 1976 BICENTENNIAL CAMPAIGN

Nineteen seventy-six brought another reversal of direction for the PSP. The party would again de-emphasize its focus on democratic rights in favor of traditional solidarity mobilizations, thus setting the stage for the beginning of an irreversible internal crisis. Although there had been agreement to preserve the dual priority strategy, by April 1976 the real emphasis became the "Bicentennial without Colonies" (Bicentenario Sin

Colonias) campaign. This initiative originated in a speech given by PSP Sec. Gen. Juan Mari Brás at the October 1974 Madison Square Garden rally, where he pointed out the irony of celebrating the bicentennial of America's independence when this country was still holding onto one of the world's last colonies. He called for an anticolonial demonstration that would serve to unite all anti-imperialist and progressive forces in the United States. Mari Brás repeated this proposal at the First Extraordinary Congress of the PSP held in Puerto Rico in November of 1975, stating that the bicentennial campaign would be a major goal of the PSP in the United States for 1976. For reasons discussed earlier, though the PSP in the United States had organizational autonomy, it usually went along with directives emanating from the leadership in Puerto Rico, often despite doubts as to the impact on the U.S. branch's activities on the mainland.

Primarily conceived as a demonstration in solidarity for the independence of Puerto Rico, the bicentennial campaign evolved into an event aimed at uniting the entire progressive and anti-imperialist movement in the United States on multiple issues. By April 1976, key PSP cadre from the Central Committee, the newspaper *Claridad,* and intermediate leadership levels were shifted from their party assignments to work within the July Fourth Coalition, a group created to lead the bicentennial campaign. Reassignment of many cadre, with negative consequences for party stability, had already occurred in 1974 during the "National Day of Solidarity" campaign. Those in the leadership who raised concerns about the other "priorities" were told that the struggle for democratic rights and the consolidation of the party could be achieved within the goals of the bicentennial campaign. To make matters worse, the highly anticipated second congress of the U.S. branch, at which many members hoped to reexamine organizational theory and practice, was indefinitely postponed.

The bicentennial rallies, held on July Fourth in Philadelphia and San Francisco, made their mark and received extensive coverage by the media. Estimates were that more than fifty thousand people attended the two, all-day affairs. The rest of the country was swallowed up in an unabashed commercialism and a one-sided view of the origins of the "American dream." The Left, however, proved capable of mounting a political and educational campaign calling attention to the idea that democracy is not real democracy if it tolerates imperialism abroad, racism, and gross social and economic inequality at home. The demonstrations brought together much of the radical Left that had remained active since its heyday in the late 1960s. In the middle of it all was the PSP, by now one of the largest of the remaining leftist organizations in the United States. Since early 1973, when it transformed itself from the MPI, the PSP, U.S. Branch, could point to a continuous progression of larger and larger actions. The PSP was seen as a radical group with deep and varied roots and a real capacity to mobilize many people—not just Puerto Ricans. Increasingly, independent leftists and progressives within other sectors and movements—tired of sectarianism and dogmatism—looked to the PSP to lead collaborative efforts on rebuilding the U.S. Left. On the surface, it appeared that the organization was poised to make another strategic leap.

In August 1976, the Central Committee highlighted the inability of the organization to make progress on most of its strategic objectives, with the exception of the solidarity movement fostered by the bicentennial campaign. The overwhelming consensus was that the organization had overextended itself and on the whole was weakened internally by the bicentennial campaign. The PSP leadership now turned its attention to the previously postponed second congress, now planned for the spring of 1977. The planning for this congress served at least to diminish increasing manifestations of internal unrest within the organization at all levels. No one could predict that events would delay this second congress yet again until late 1978.

PROBE AND PARRY: Indirect Repression

In the interim, the bicentennial campaign led the PSP leadership to pay closer attention to attempts at political repression of the party by government agencies. Since the late 1960s, members of the MPI, and later the PSP, had been the target of surveillance and harassment. The party did its best to control the infiltration of the organization by informers and provocateurs through a fairly clear set of rules for becoming a participant; but basically, the PSP believed that the best protection was to have an open organization with a large membership. Another method used by government agencies to repress the PSP was to try to draw the group into conflicts with other organizations of the Left and with Cuban exile groups.

In July 1975, the Senate Committee on the Judiciary began its hearings on the so-called "Cuban Connection," which centered on the PSP as a tool of "Cuban-inspired terrorism." The hearings involved testimony from informants and FBI officials who attempted to connect the PSP to the FALN.[7] During the same year PSP members in several chapters were investigated for involvement in illegal activities, including the late Lureida Torres who was imprisoned for allegedly assisting the FALN.[8] Insinuating that the PSP and the July Fourth Coalition could be planning to disrupt the official government bicentennial activities, the FBI called for greater controls over the activities of these organizations. On May 28, 1976, the FBI announced that it would investigate the July Fourth Coalition. On May 30, Mayor Frank L. Rizzo of Philadelphia requested fifteen thousand troops to handle the bicentennial demonstration. However, by late June, the federal government, still reeling from public exposure of other more obvious illegal and antidemocratic practices of the FBI and CIA, expressed its opposition to the mobilization of troops in Philadelphia and backed off bringing any conspiracy charges against the coalition.

After the bicentennial, the PSP leadership was acutely aware of the status it had achieved in the eyes of the FBI and other repressive agencies. The lessons of the assassinations of Malcolm X and Martin Luther King Jr. and the destruction of the Black Panther Party, precisely as they led efforts to build multinational unity, were not lost on the PSP. Further levels of repression were expected, and the leadership prepared for this eventuality through various means, including a possible class-action lawsuit by Third World groups against the FBI. The organization also tightened its internal security by tracking the activities of suspected informants and prepared itself for the potential necessity of going underground.

However serious the government efforts against the PSP, they were not the main reason for the group's decline. In addition to its still significant support network within the community at large, the PSP had fairly rigorous requirements for membership; leadership appointments and promotions were even more carefully monitored. The organization took pains to implement counterintelligence measures. Furthermore, the ideological debates of the following years, although heated and personal, did not degenerate into violent confrontations, as happened with a number of revolutionary and militant groups of the time. The stagnation of the PSP had its roots in unresolved ideological and organizational problems, which erupted in an internal crisis in 1977. In the following years, these conflicts would cause many members, both leadership and rank and file, to come full circle and question the ability of the party to lead the struggle in the United States.

CRISIS AND STAGNATION: 1977–1978

In the aftermath of the November 1976 elections in Puerto Rico, the PSP entered into a crisis period characterized by extensive internal evaluations and ideological struggles that continued well into the 1980s. In deciding to participate in the 1976 elections the PSP acknowledged that, despite previous claims, Puerto Rico was not nearing a "prerevolutionary situation." This was how the party leadership had frequently described the situation, implying that the independence movement would soon be ready to take state power (in Puerto Rico) through a combination of mass mobilization and military assault. The average PSP member imagined something like the Cuban Revolution of 1959. But when the PSP announced in 1975 that it would actually run an electoral campaign, this seemed to take the wind out of the sails of revolutionary impulse. When the election results showed that the PSP received less than 1 percent of the total vote, it was time for a serious "reality check."

Though the PSP's participation in the elections meant an increased national presence, its showing at the ballot box fell far short of its expectations and exposed its weak support among the masses. Under the slogan "To Rectify Is to Advance" ("*Rectificar Es Avanzar*") the party leadership unleashed a period of profound introspection that would culminate in a Second Extraordinary Congress in Puerto Rico during September 1978.

Similarly, the PSP in the United States embarked on an intense self-assessment. The Central Committee began this process in January 1977 by taking note of "a new political situation," referring to the electoral victory of the proannexation forces in Puerto Rico and subsequent pros-tatehood pronouncements by Pres. Gerald Ford. The leadership also analyzed the declining social and economic situation of the Puerto Rican community on the mainland, highlighting the skyrocketing unemployment rate, drastic reductions in social services, and the impact of urban housing policies that caused displacement of many Puerto Rican neighborhoods. A key part of this analysis centered on the ineffective political response of the community, the vacuum in mainstream political leadership, and the declining influence of Puerto Rican leaders associated with the Democratic Party. Although the PSP was acutely aware of this critical situation, the emphasis on solidarity mobilizations prohibited it from mustering resources to lead the struggle in these arenas.

The leadership stated that the party's main problem was its organizational instability and ideological weakness. Organizational reports reflect that the membership had remained stagnant since 1975. The leadership faulted itself for a lack of focus on the struggle of Puerto Ricans in the United States and for neglecting the development of the party itself. Admitting the negative consequences of the bicentennial campaign on the consolidation and growth of the party, the leadership, nonetheless, called on the membership to look favorably upon the campaign because it served to expand the solidarity of the North American people for the independence of Puerto Rico. On the other hand, though the July Fourth Coalition had managed to unite most of the anti-imperialist forces for this event, the possibilities of long-term unity were slim. This was quickly borne out, as the July Fourth Coalition soon ceased to exist, and the PSP would be severely shaken up by its own rectification process.

Guiding the rectification campaign was a consensus resolution adopted by the Central Committee on April 24, 1977, stating that once the PSP finished the period of rectification, the areas of concentration would be the consolidation of the party and the staging of the previously post-poned second congress of the PSP. In reality, the party would spend the following two years in the rectification process and in reacting to the ideo-logical conflicts that developed among the leadership in Puerto Rico. The second congress would again be postponed to late 1978, and the PSP, U.S. Branch, had the added impediment of simultaneously preparing for the party congress in Puerto Rico, which was to be held in September of the same year.

In the United States, the rectification process sought to correct un-healthy organizational practices ("gigantism," preoccupation with inter-nal processes and meetings, and voluntarism) rather than the party's po-litical theory. Especially targeted was a reduction in the superstructure created during the previous years. Generally, the leadership underesti-mated how the rectification process would lead to a reduction in mass activity and in a long period of internalized discussion, which lasted until late 1978. In November 1977, the FUSP (the student arm of the party) decided to dissolve itself after a period of intensive evaluation. By late 1977, the party had experienced zero growth and a 25 percent drop in the circulation of the party newspaper, *Claridad*. On a positive note, the central leadership group of the organization had remained fairly intact. Furthermore, owing to the number of previously full-time party cadre who had recently entered the workforce, the PSP had also greatly ex-panded its trade union activity.

For many years, the leadership had stressed the necessity of a second congress to update its theory and practice concerning the reality of Puerto Ricans in the United States since the adoption of *Desde Las Entrañas* in 1973. However, the second congress, now set for November 1978, would essentially serve as the culmination of the rectification process, now two years in the making. A hastily composed *Ante Proyecto de Tesis* (*Draft Thesis*), which responded to the internal debates prevalent at the time, was overshadowed by the discussion documents pertaining to the congress of the entire party being held in Puerto Rico; the thesis never became the focus of discussion at the second congress of the PSP in the United States.[9] *Ante Proyecto de Tesis* analyzed the factors that reinforced how Puerto Ricans in the United States continued to form part of the Puerto Rican nation, while at the same time forming an "oppressed nationality" *within* the United States (as opposed to a "national minority") and a super-exploited segment of the North American working class. These factors were the two-way migration process, a "ghettoization" similar to that of African Americans, geographic isolation, stratification within the work-force, cultural isolation, racism and discrimination by the dominant society—all of which were viewed as reinforcing national consciousness and the potential for collective action. *Ante Proyecto de Tesis* emphasized that though the PSP had a two-dimensional goal of achieving socialism both in Puerto Rico and in the United States, its main contribution to the revolution in the United States would be to weaken imperialism by attaining the independence of Puerto Rico.

In an effort to make up for the lack of systematic work in defense of the democratic rights of Puerto Ricans in the United States, *Ante Proyecto de Tesis* attempted to outline a program of action in this arena. Nevertheless, the document contributed little to answering the concerns regarding the relationship between the struggle for the independence of Puerto Rico and the democratic-rights struggle of Puerto Ricans in the United States. For the most part, the document's arguments were aimed at dogmatic formulations by sectors of the North American Left who viewed Puerto Ricans solely as a "national minority" as opposed to being part of the Puerto Rican nation and chided the PSP for affirming its right to organize separately from other Marxist organizations. However, *Ante Proyecto de Tesis* did little to resolve the ideological conflicts within the PSP because internally no one was arguing that Puerto Ricans in the United States *were not* part of the Puerto Rican nation, but rather they were arguing over how the party was mishandling the dual priorities established for the U.S. branch. Furthermore, the document posed two contradictory views: that the independence of Puerto Rico was imminent on the one hand, and on the other hand, that the very survival of the Puerto Rican nation was at stake. In practice, both views meant that all other objectives of the PSP in the United States were secondary and had to revolve around the issue of the independence of Puerto Rico.

DECLINE AND FINAL RUPTURE: 1979–1983

In 1979, attempting to recover from the rectification process and the lackluster second congress, the PSP, under the slogan "For National Survival, Independence, and Socialism" (*"Por La Sobrevivencia Nacional, Independencia, y El Socialismo"*), established two major goals for the next few years: the restructuring and consolidation of the party and combating the annexationist offensive. An inventory of the party's campaigns during these years confirms that the organization once again reverted to concentrating its efforts on solidarity for the independence of Puerto Rico. These campaigns included an antiannexationist offensive; the freedom of five Nationalist prisoners;[10] solidarity with the movement to protect Vieques from U.S. Navy bombardment exercises; mobilizations for the United Nations Decolonization Committee hearings; planned protests at the 1980 Democratic Convention; and support for the PSP's participation in the

1980 elections in Puerto Rico. Providing few practical guidelines or assistance to local chapters on democratic rights-struggles, instructions were given to attend to these issues *only after* these priority campaigns were accomplished.

Juggling Mass Work, Solidarity Campaigns, and Ideological Debate

By the turn of the decade, considerable turnover in the core membership and leadership of the party was evident. Some members relocated to Puerto Rico; some left to attend to pressing family and economic obligations; and others resigned because of political differences or disenchantment with the movement. The constant mobilization and solidarity campaigns, which virtually turned the members into peddlers of newspapers, buttons, raffles, tickets, and other fund-raisers, led to burnout among the ranks. The vacuum was partially filled by new cadre recruited during the mid- to late 1970s, who now had to assume greater leadership.

Serious divisions in the ranks of the party crystallized during the early 1980s based on the lack of participation in the struggle for the democratic rights of Puerto Ricans in the United States. In November 1980, the general consensus of the Central Committee was that recent fund-raising tasks and patriotic mobilizations, coupled with the lack of resources, had again stifled local campaigns concerning democratic-rights issues. The political commission of the Central Committee, however, emphasized that these mobilizations had strengthened the patriotic unity of the Puerto Rican independence forces in the United States and had been successful in projecting the colonial case of Puerto Rico on a national level. A significant minority of the Central Committee voiced disagreement with this evaluation and argued that the party would have no basis to unite with the North American working class or the Left if it did not develop roots in the community and trade unions based on fundamental issues affecting Puerto Ricans in the United States. It pointed out that, once again, the organization had reverted to what it had traditionally done—led patriotic mobilizations. This debate was the beginning of a series of conflicts between the political commission and other members of the Central Committee that characterized the leadership body in the early 1980s.

Meanwhile, the Central Committee discussed the upcoming founding of the National Congress for Puerto Rican Rights to be held in April 1981. The PSP leadership expressed concerns about the reluctance of some of the organizers to discuss the colonial status of Puerto Rico, as well as concerns about the absence at the conference of many important leaders in the Puerto Rican community. Concerns were raised about ex-members of the Young Lords Party, who were in the leadership of this conference and with whom the PSP had ongoing ideological differences. Nevertheless, the PSP leadership felt it important to participate and to ensure that issues concerning the colonial situation of Puerto Rico would also be on the agenda. Thus was born the PSP's passive participation in what aspired to be a national organization to lead the struggle for democratic rights; a goal that the party itself had hoped to realize in previous years. There were key members who became actively involved in the organizing of the congress, but these individuals were acting largely out of personal initiative and did not receive the full-scale backing of the party. The PSP's lack of influence within the National Congress during the following years was a reflection of its own internal weakness and sectarian attitudes, as well as its ideological ambivalence toward the democratic-rights struggle.

In June of 1981, the Central Committee met to discuss a proposal that would significantly shift the party's focus of activity in New York City to the electoral arena and eventually would become a point of controversy within the entire organization. This proposal called for the endorsement of Gerena Valentín and José Rivera in upcoming elections and Frank Barbaro for New York City mayor. Valentín and Rivera, who were both well respected by progressive Puerto Ricans because of their strong support of independence and democratic rights, launched their candidacies within the Democratic and Liberal Parties. They were also part of a new entity, the Unity Party, which was a citywide coalition of labor, minorities, and progressive forces within which the PSP had been active too. The Unity Party served as the vehicle for the mayoral campaign of long-time Democratic State Assemblyman from Brooklyn, Frank Barbaro. As long as the two veteran Puerto Rican activists confined their campaigns to the Unity Party, PSP members did not have a problem with the candidates' efforts. However, this was not the case as the two were also competing for Democratic and Liberal Parties support, and the PSP had always denounced the capitalist two-party system.[11] Straining its Marxist-Leninist principles to the limit, the PSP's Central Committee decided to back Valentín and Rivera in the primaries and general election, with the stipulation that support for the candidates should not be interpreted as an endorsement of the Democratic Party. Accepting the argument that Valentín and Rivera represented a special case, the PSP leadership decided to support the candidates, promising to help in the petition drive and organizing support activities.

The discussions ended in a consensus, but they also stirred up concern among a section of the membership that electoral activity might become the PSP's main form of organizing around democratic rights and would hamper the party's own growth and consolidation. These concerns were partially offset when Gerena Valentín achieved victory in his bid to represent a district in the South Bronx, thus becoming the first Puerto Rican *independentista* and socialist to sit on the New York City Council. In the mayoral race, despite his loss to Ed Koch, Frank Barbaro won an impressive 36 percent of the primary vote, including the majority of the Puerto Rican vote. This Puerto Rican support for the Barbaro candidacy was viewed by the PSP as an opportunity to develop an electoral alliance in New York City with African American and progressive forces on the Left. However, the enthusiasm surrounding these electoral campaigns would soon be overshadowed by events in Puerto Rico at the close of 1981.

FINAL CRISIS

Nineteen eighty-two was a key period in the final crisis of the PSP. At the annual rally commemorating the birthday of Puerto Rican patriot Eugenio María de Hostos, on January 11, 1982, the secretary general of the PSP, Juan Mari Brás, announced the PSP's intention to foster a "socialist re-grouping," including Christian and nonaffiliated socialists. There was an immediate recognition that fundamental changes were being proposed that brought into question the very existence of an organization based on Marxism-Leninism. It soon became evident that the Central Committee in Puerto Rico was divided into two antagonistic tendencies. One tendency called for a broad regrouping of socialist forces into a new political entity, the rejection of Marxism-Leninism as a point of unity, and an emphasis on the urgent and immediate task of independence for Puerto Rico. The other tendency, while agreeing with the urgent task of achieving the independence of Puerto Rico, stressed the need for an independent, anti-dogmatic Marxist-Leninist party; this tendency identified the problems of the PSP as being centered in the leadership's inability to apply the political and organizational objectives adopted by the party congress of 1978 in Puerto Rico.

A major falling-out occurred within the leadership of the PSP in Puerto Rico and sent shock waves throughout the party in the United States, whereupon the membership was divided in accepting or rejecting the proposals of the Central Committee in Puerto Rico. The debates carried over to how the party leadership in the United States viewed the organizational state of the U.S. branch and its tasks set for 1982. During the previous four years, more than one-third of the U.S. membership had moved to other areas, primarily Puerto Rico, adding to the instability of the organization. The circulation of the party newspaper, *Claridad,* had dropped by a third in New York and by more than half in other states. Several important chapters throughout New England and the Mid-Atlantic and Midwest regions, as well as in New York City, had basically stopped functioning. The Central Committee, in a resolution addressed to the entire membership in April 1982, called for the convening of a third party congress in the United States to be held the following year, with the purpose of resolving ideological and organizational problems. However, with the very existence of the party in question, discussions leading toward the November 1982 main party congress in Puerto Rico would take center stage over these concerns.

In the interim, the party's continued involvement in the New York City Council elections caused a deep rift among key members of the Central Committee and throughout the organization in New York City. Though the PSP had made clear its opposition to getting involved with the Democratic Party, throughout early 1982 the political commission had assigned party members and resources to work in a number of Democratic primary battles—without authorization from the Central Committee. This behavior on the part of the political commission led to severe criticisms and resignations by several veteran members of the Central Committee foreshadowing the disintegration of the leadership body, which would occur after the November 1982 party congress in Puerto Rico.

The ideological crisis in the party in Puerto Rico had heightened personal and ideological differences among the membership in the United States. Many leaders who were critical of the organization's emphasis on solidarity work now found themselves generally supporting the opposition that rallied around a platform of socialist affirmation. Others rallied around the majority positions of the Central Committee, particularly those expressed by Sec. Gen. Juan Mari Brás. Adding fuel to the fire was the severely limited discussion within the party in the United States as a result of not receiving precongress discussion documents in a timely fashion.

The party sent a large—but divided—delegation to the November 1982 congress in Puerto Rico. Though the major issues of the congress revolved around the very existence of the PSP, the delegates from the United States were astounded by the lack of any meaningful discussion about the situation of Puerto Ricans in the United States. Many delegates returned with painful reminders of how foreign the party's work in the United States was for most of the membership in Puerto Rico, and how this work was generally viewed only from a perspective of solidarity for the independence of Puerto Rico. The turn toward a Nationalist stance (within the party in general) had the side effect of devaluing the U.S. branch's role in organizing around democratic rights in U.S. communities.

Immediately after the congress, the organization experienced a host of resignations from Central Committee and rank-and-file members throughout the United States. These resignations, though sparked by the results of the congress in Puerto Rico, were in reality the culmination of years of ideological conflicts within the U.S. branch. They reflected a realization by many members that the PSP could no longer fulfill a dual role of leading the struggle for independence of Puerto Rico and the democratic-rights struggle of Puerto Ricans in the United States. Many who resigned faded away without public comment, while others bid farewell in open letters to the party membership. By year's end, former members were meeting to discuss their future political work and the possibilities of a reorganization of the Puerto Rican Left in the United States. This group included many of the members who in the 1970s promoted changes from the old MPI to the new PSP, and who now came full circle with their resignations from the party. Their efforts extended over a two-year period, but the former PSPers were not successful in reinvigorating the Puerto Rican Left. In retrospect, these individuals were too exhausted politically and physically to reverse the decline that affected the movement throughout the 1980s.

By early 1983, the PSP had lost its political momentum on the mainland, and for the next few years it would be limited to the commemoration of patriotic events with an occassional foray into specific electoral and democratic-rights issues. Under the slogan "For Puerto Rican Unity, Social Justice, and National Independence" ("*Por La Unidad Boricua, la Justicia Social, y la Independencia Nacional*"), the organization held a third congress in May 1983. This congress essentially rehashed the 1978 *Ante Proyecto de Tesis,* endorsed the concept of the formation of a National Liberation Front in Puerto Rico, and discussed the ways in which the party in the United States fit into this new strategy. In succeeding years, many members returned to Puerto Rico where they continued their involvement in the independence movement. Eventually in 1995, the PSP in Puerto Rico dissolved itself and initiated the formation of the NMI—the New Independence Movement (*Nuevo Movimiento Independentista*). It is one of many forces trying to forge a new national liberation movement on the island. The remaining members of the PSP in the United States followed suit and continue to work with this new movement.

CONCLUSION

The demise of the Puerto Rican Socialist Party was a serious setback for the Puerto Rican Left in the United States. At its best, the PSP demonstrated the revolutionary potential in linking the struggle for the independence of Puerto Rico with the struggle for the democratic rights of Puerto Ricans in the United States. The PSP left an enduring legacy. It was an *escuela de cuadros* (school for cadre) directly training hundreds of activists throughout scores of communities in the United States. Its influence continues to have an impact on the political and cultural fabric of the Puerto Rican community today. Unfortunately, the PSP missed the opportunity to unleash the revolutionary dynamics of the Puerto Rican struggle on the mainland, by generally viewing the struggle in the United States solely through the prism of island politics and solidarity with the independence movement of Puerto Rico.

Generally, the PSP's policies were divorced from the day-to-day reality of Puerto Ricans on the mainland. Notwithstanding continued ties to the island, the Puerto Rican situation in the United States presents a distinctly different reality from that in Puerto Rico and demands its own political strategy. Of the some 2.8 million Puerto Ricans on the mainland, the vast majority are here to stay—even with an independent Puerto Rico. They will continue to forge their destiny as an oppressed nationality within the United States. The PSP did not fully accept the implications of the fact that U.S. Puerto Ricans constitute an oppressed nationality that faces class exploitation and racial oppression *irrespective* of Puerto Rico's political status. The PSP remained caught up in the old debates about the "national question," constantly insisting that the mainland community is part of the Puerto Rican nation and not a "national minority." But this dichotomy— which pitted the two concepts as mutually exclusive ideas—lost political significance by the early 1980s and prevented the organization from adapting to the rise of conservative ideology throughout the United States.

Furthermore, the PSP leadership completely misread the reality of the situation in Puerto Rico. By continually stressing an impending crisis of colonialism and an imminent revolutionary upheaval, the party dismissed as secondary the day-to-day, grassroots organizing around democratic-rights issues in the United States. Though periodic evaluations consistently noted this misjudgement, the leadership continually reverted to traditional solidarity mobilizations. Particularly in its later years, though having deep roots among mainland Puerto Ricans, the PSP came to be viewed by many Puerto Rican activists as an organization whose only role was to foster solidarity for the independence of Puerto Rico.

The forces of renewal who joined the organization starting in the late 1960s, during the organization's transition from MPI to PSP, displayed loyalty to an organization that was not always comfortable with the incursion of Puerto Ricans from the diaspora. Their committment to a system of democratic centralism often minimized debate, as the minority was to adhere to the rule of the majority without dissent. Political dissidence was generally inarticulate, fragmented, and disorganized. In addition, their respect and admiration for the party leadership in Puerto Rico served to soften their opposition when, in fact, open criticism was needed. The absence of meaningful ideological development, especially after 1976, led to the party's failure to develop a clear and consistent theory and program for its work in the United States.

The decline of the PSP, as well as that of other Puerto Rican leftist organizations, raises serious concerns as to whether the Puerto Rican Left can rebound from the experience of the 1980s and articulate a new revolutionary program of action within the United States. What is evident from the experience of the PSP is that a mass Puerto Rican radical movement cannot be successfully directed from Puerto Rico. This movement will have to be independently led and based on the reality of life in the United States, while developing ties and coordination with revolutionary forces on the island.

Notwithstanding the demise of the PSP, the Young Lords Party (which later became the PRRWO), El Comité (later known as the MINP), and other revolutionary organizations, many Puerto Rican activists continue to play leading roles in the struggles of the Puerto Rican community. However, generally these struggles lack a national focus and are mostly limited to local levels and minor reforms. The limited success of the PSP, the Young Lords Party (PRRWO), El Comité–MINP, and other organizations during the 1970s verified the need for a vanguard organization of the Left that can give the democratic-rights struggle a revolutionary impetus. History waits to see whether the Puerto Rican Left can meet the challenges ahead.

JOSÉ E. CRUZ

4 Pushing Left to Get to the Center

Puerto Rican Radicalism in Hartford, Connecticut

Each time in the continuing struggle for coherent practice and revolutionary theory, there is a spinning out, a drawing of conclusions, an expansion of hope and of conviction, and then a disappointment, a painful drawing up at the limits of a theoretical orientation, which in turn forces a new beginning.

—Andrea Nye, *Feminist Theory and the Philosophies of Man*

Sisyphus watches the stone rush down in a few moments toward that lower world whence he will have to push it up again toward the summit. He goes back down to the plain. It is during that return, that pause, that Sisyphus interests me. . . . That hour like a breathing-space which returns as surely as his suffering, that is the hour of consciousness.

—Albert Camus, *The Myth of Sisyphus*

THIS CHAPTER focuses on the emergence, development, and significance of the Puerto Rican Socialist Party (PSP) in Hartford, Connecticut, during the period from 1970 to 1983.[1] The PSP is singled out from radical political movements in the city for reasons of space but also because of its importance relative to other organizations. In contrast to the record of the People's Liberation Party (PLP), formed in 1969 and the first Puerto Rican radical group in the city, PSP activities extended for more than a decade. The party had a clearly articulated platform and a national presence. In Hartford, it challenged the legitimacy of the mainstream community leadership, and its issues became a rallying point for the White and ethnic Left. Its presence in the record is prominent as it also was in various local struggles. PSP initiatives often provided the impetus for ancillary action through ad hoc groups, including ventures in labor organizing.

The chapter addresses two types of questions, each in turn. Descriptive questions include the following: What was the context in which the PSP emerged? What were its goals, and how did it pursue them? How did the party relate to other radical groups in the city? The analytical questions are: What was the relationship between mainstream leaders and radicals? How effective was the Puerto Rican Left? What was the contribution of

Puerto Rican radicals? What explains the PSP's decline? Are there any lessons in this experience relevant to the current status of Puerto Ricans in the United States?

This is a story full of disappointments, most of which can only be hinted at here. But it is precisely because nothing really worked out the way it was originally expected by radicals that it is necessary, as Andrea Nye suggests, to turn back, retrace steps, and think through what happened, hopefully to force a new beginning. The experience of Puerto Rican radicals is not unlike that of Sisyphus, who after pushing the rock uphill had to painfully watch it roll back down. Looking into the past is like watching the rock descend. As we climb down from the summit we prepare ourselves to start anew, and in that extended moment we imagine new possibilities; as Camus suggests in the quote above, such is the moment of consciousness. For him that moment is when the present becomes clear; to me it is the moment in which we make sense of the past.

THE CONTEXT: Puerto Ricans in Hartford

The presence of Puerto Ricans in Hartford can be dated to 1941 with the arrival of Olga Mele shortly after her marriage to a U.S. serviceman in Puerto Rico. By 1954 an estimated five hundred Puerto Ricans had settled in the city, and by 1959 their presence was twelve times that number. They were brought to Hartford by a mixture of ambition and circumstances; once there the migrants sought better education, better jobs, and home ownership, while area restaurants, stores, factories, and farms were coping with a tight labor market.[2]

In 1952, the government of Puerto Rico expanded the migration division of its Department of Labor to cover Hartford and other cities in Massachusetts and Rhode Island. Four years later, the San Juan Catholic Center opened its doors under the sponsorship of the Greater Hartford Council of Churches to offer family counseling, translation, and referral services. These two initiatives were clear signs of a growing community.

In 1957 the local press reported, with surprise, that two hundred Puerto Ricans had registered to vote the year before.[3] Their availability to vote in the 1957 election was important, especially to aspiring mayor James Kinsella. Believing that no group of voters was insignificant enough to be ignored, Kinsella approached the director of the San Juan Catholic Center for help with the Puerto Ricans.[4] The response was enthusiastic. Community leaders were asked to register and mobilize voters. They did, thus making 1957 the year that Puerto Ricans first entered the local political process.

During the 1960s, social unrest coincided with political change in the city. Partisan elections were restored in 1967, and by 1971 the Democrats had managed to take full advantage of this change. In that year the party achieved control of the mayoralty and the city council. Nearly two-thirds of the voters had been registering as Democrats since 1966 making Hartford a de facto one-party city even before the party managed to wrest total control from Republicans and Independents. Interparty competition waned. Intraparty divisions waxed. Electoral contests began to be fueled by the politics of race, ethnicity, and turf.

Economically, Hartford was rapidly becoming a postindustrial city. Between 1965 and 1975, manufacturing jobs fell from 20 to 9 percent of the total nonagricultural employment in the city, while service jobs climbed from 19 to 23 percent. Changes in the proportion of jobs in the financial, insurance, and real-estate sectors were also significant during this period. These climbed from 24 percent of the total in 1965 to 31 percent in 1975. The consequences of this shift were manifold but among the most significant was the decreasing capacity of city residents to get a city job. Between 1960 and 1970 city jobs increased by 16 percent while the number held by Hartford residents decreased by a whopping 24 percent.[5]

During this period the city's business elite kept itself politically busy. In fact, the local chamber of commerce was the prime mover in the effort to reinstate partisan elections. Inspired by the example of Richard Lee in New Haven, business leaders also wanted to establish a strong mayoralty that would spur downtown development. In this the business establishment was not successful, but it nonetheless found in Nicholas Carbone—Hartford's most powerful politician during the 1970s—a more than adequate surrogate for the kind of strong executive that it had in mind.

Carbone first made his way into the city council in 1969. The focus of his strategy for tackling Hartford's social and economic ills was an alliance between public and private power represented respectively by the city council and the chamber of commerce. The terms of this alliance were deceptively simple: Redistributive measures had to be linked to downtown development. According to Carbone, in order to have redistributive impact, public policy had to go with the flow of current corporate preferences and interests. Thus, development strategies favored office construction, gentrification, and real-estate speculation, as well as upscale retail centers rather than neighborhood revitalization, housing construction, or neighborhood retail outlets.

This strategy was not good for Puerto Rican interests, but in 1970 this was not absolutely clear. In fact, even Puerto Rican numbers were in question. According to the Census Bureau, the Puerto Rican count was 8,543 that year, a mere 5 percent of Hartford's 158,000 inhabitants. Local estimates, however, placed the number at more than 20,000.[6] By the end of the decade the official figure was 24,615, or 18 percent of the total, but in public forums community leaders spoke on behalf of the "30,000 Hispanics that live in this city."[7] By then it was clear that Carbone's strategy had left out Puerto Ricans as they suffered the triple whammy of displacement, unemployment, and relative political invisibility.[8]

The Puerto Rican Socialist Party: Means and Ends

The Puerto Rico–based Movimiento Pro Independencia (MPI) began its activities in Hartford in December 1971. In November of that year the MPI changed its name to Partido Socialista Puertorriqueño-Movimiento Pro Independencia (PSP-MPI), but it was not until 1972 that the Hartford chapter followed suit, after the MPI in the United States became the "United States branch of the Puerto Rican Socialist Party."

In March 1972, the U.S. branch published the first issue of the mainland edition of *Claridad*, as a supplement to the island-based newspaper. The first editorial of the supplement declared: "[W]ithin the fight for our rights here, the fight for independence and socialism in Puerto Rico constitutes our priority."[9] A year later, on April 1, 1973, U.S. members adopted a platform that stated: "[O]ur fundamental objective is the transformation of the existing colonial-capitalist structure in Puerto Rico into a Socialist and Democratic Republic of the Puerto Rican Workers."[10]

Between 1972 and 1983 only twelve PSP-related stories were written in Hartford's daily press. In the community press the party was virtually invisible, with only six stories reporting on its activities between August 1974 and November 1983. In 1974, several editions of one community paper carried an advertisement for a national rally. Between 1972 and 1983 *Claridad* carried 35 stories about Hartford for an average of 2.7 stories per year. Two letters from a Hartford resident were published in 1980 and 1982. Hartford was mentioned in two columns during this eleven-year period. At least one newsletter of a sister organization, the Connecticut Defense Coalition (CDC), a local affiliate of the National Alliance Against Racist and Political Repression, discussed regularly issues in which it had a common interest with the PSP. The PSP had its own newsletter and members sold *Claridad* in local stores and in Puerto Rican neighborhoods.

In New York City, this would amount to invisibility. But in Hartford it translated into an uneven presence. The PSP was: 1. fairly well-known within the community 2. a familiar presence within elite circles 3. but relatively invisible among the middle- and upper-income segments of the population at large. There was a systematic pattern of partisan activities, more or less as follows: weekly meetings, regular distribution of *Claridad*, occasional distribution of newsletters and leaflets, and mobilization to national rallies. Local demonstrations and meetings with elected officials, such as the mayor, took place irregularly as circumstances required. The party also offered weekly political education and culture classes. On special occasions forums were held, sometimes in collaboration with other groups. *Claridad* was used to publicize problems, such as high rents in dilapidated buildings, and to document cases of abuse or discrimination against Puerto Ricans. The weekly was also a vehicle for attacks on city hall.[11]

The PSP targeted its organizing efforts to migrant workers. "The struggle has begun in Hartford," reads the first issue of *Mete Mano*, the group's newsletter, "and the exploiters of our people are trembling." A section titled *"El Trabajador Migrante en Los Campamentos Agrícolas"* ("The Migrant Farmworker"), described the housing provided to farmworkers as concentration camps and referred to Puerto Ricans as "slaves of the tyrants ruling our homeland."[12]

The task of organizing farmworkers fell on José La Luz, a native of the town of Ciales, located in Puerto Rico's central region, whose parents moved to Bridgeport in 1964. According to La Luz, the MPI, and subsequently the PSP, was behind the creation of such groups as CAMP, the Comité de Apoyo al Migrante Puertorriqueño (Puerto Rican Migrant Support Committee), ATA, the Asociación de Trabajadores Agrícolas (Agricultural Workers Association), and even META, the Ministerio Ecuménico de Trabajadores Agrícolas (Ecumenical Ministry of Agricultural Workers), run by Rev. William Loperena.[13]

La Luz recalled that organizing proceeded at a feverish pace. But the focus of partisan activities was not just the working class. A forum organized on March 21, 1972, to commemorate the Ponce Massacre focused on the national question. Two days later, a seminar led by Angel Agosto, the party's national secretary of labor affairs, discussed the situation of migrant workers. This juxtaposition defined the party from the outset and dominated its actions throughout its short life.[14]

Impressed by what he saw in Hartford, Agosto declared in a *Claridad* column that PSP work among Puerto Rican workers in the United States was on the rise. He referred to the city as an example, saying that party members "have organized several workplaces and they are in the process of organizing the farmworkers in the area."[15]

This was in contrast with complaints by La Luz that party members were not always on top of local issues and that sometimes they were indifferent to the situation within the community. The solution to this, he declared, was to organize campaigns "around the problems which affect the respective communities." Then, a few months later, the party organized a demonstration to protest Puerto Rico's colonial status. During the protest La Luz announced the beginning of a campaign to pressure the local dailies, the *Hartford Courant* and the *Hartford Times*, to hire Puerto Ricans and to cover the news of the community.[16]

Within the community the PSP was not particularly good at developing alliances that cut across class, ideology, or generation. The party paid little, if any, respect to the leadership that preceded it in Hartford. It also treated the more affluent members of the community with disdain, an attitude that many of these individuals reciprocated.[17]

Yet, according to Juan Fuentes, a journalist, photographer, and community activist living in Hartford since 1963: "The Partido Socialista was a force behind the development of positive activities in the Puerto Rican community. Because in many instances they forced the issue. They were people with a clear vision of the troubles. They were instrumental in opening the eyes of many individuals."[18]

This is all true even if the quality of the "vision" that was offered is open to question. What is also a fact is that there was much dissonance between the party and the community. Migrant workers wanted better working conditions, and the PSP offered them Marxism-Leninism. The community sought political representation in Hartford, and the party organized rallies in support of labor strikes in Puerto Rico. While PSP members booed and heckled Geraldo Rivera at a rally in 1974, Hartford businessmen gave him a humanitarian award.[19]

On occasion, the PSP was able to make its positions resonate among Puerto Ricans. People responded to the message even if the messenger was doubtful. Yet even when the party's critique was on target, its terms were crude and formulaic. In 1974, for example, the party agitated intensely around an anticrime proposal put forth by the Hartford Institute of Social and Criminal Justice, which included such measures as fencing off certain neighborhoods, increasing police manpower, and the acquisition of more powerful weapons. The PSP was convinced that this proposal would have a negative impact, disproportionately affecting Puerto Ricans. In this they were on the mark. Criminal justice statistics indicated that the person most likely to be arrested in the city was young, unemployed, male, and Puerto Rican. Moreover, although the evidence was not conclusive, an analysis of the disposition of cases strongly suggested a law enforcement system "biased in favor of light-skinned defendants, especially those for whom English is a native language." Thus, on this issue the party obtained a positive response from the community. But instead of providing these facts, they simply claimed that the fencing proposal was a conspiracy, "part of a national plan developed by the ruling class."[20]

Similarly, when in 1975 Puerto Ricans mobilized against the Greater

Hartford Process (GHP)—a corporation that proposed limiting Puerto Rican migration to the city, segregating Puerto Rican and Black neighborhoods, and an upward redistribution of public investment and services—the PSP was in synchrony with the community even if its accusation was ludicrous. This time party leaders charged GHP with trying to destroy Puerto Ricans because they refused to assimilate. In this case the ring of conspirators included the corporate sector, its branches in Puerto Rico, and the government of the island.[21]

For nearly five years the party sustained an intense schedule of demand-protest activities. Then, in 1976, events in Puerto Rico turned the world of the party upside down. After the 1976 general election, a crisis developed, triggered by the party's poor electoral performance on the island. Of 1.7 million voters, 86 percent turned out. Of these, only 9,761, or 0.6 percent, voted socialist. These results prompted a debate between those who emphasized the national question and those who emphasized socialism. The party's organizing strategy and its operational style were two other important issues. The debate quickly became a "holy war," and in two years the party tore itself apart, on the island and the mainland, piece by piece, gradually but bitterly.[22]

In Hartford, a sense of disappointment enveloped party members. Many began to realize that their work was not as effective as they had thought. According to Aida Claudio:

> There came a lot of fighting amongst some of the leaders and everyone seemed to be pulling in different directions because of the chaos that was going on in New York and that's where we got our leadership and direction from. . . . There was loss of membership, people started to go in different directions, philosophies started to change, strategies started to change and after that the party wasn't around a lot longer . . . some of us became more involved directly with the electoral process in Hartford, we [the PSP] got new membership from the island . . . and they believed that we should only think about independence. . . . So a lot of us just got out, resented the difference in philosophy, the direction that some of the new leaders were taking the movement and I think that changed to the point where it just disbanded.[23]

PUERTO RICANS, BLACKS, AND THE WHITE/ETHNIC LEFT

The relationship between African American and Puerto Rican radical groups was virtually nonexistent. Some Puerto Ricans used the Black Panther Party as a model but no joint actions or campaigns ever took place. The model lost its appeal quickly. The 1969 trial of Bobby Seale in New Haven signaled the demise of the party in Connecticut, reducing further the opportunities for joint work. In Hartford, most Puerto Rican activists had never even heard of the radical Black Caucus, a group that used obscene language to urge Blacks to resort to violence. According to Aida Claudio, Puerto Rican radicals "received a lot of support from the leftist movement within the white community. . . . [But] it was different with the African-American community. . . . Although we might be fighting for the same goals we didn't want to do it together mainly because the black community did not want to get involved with us."[24] Puerto Ricans did work, however, with individual Black radicals within the umbrella of the White/ethnic Left.

Such groups as the CDC readily mobilized in support of Puerto Rican issues in Hartford, New Britain, and elsewhere. The CDC in particular publicized the organizing activities of ATA, and some of its members participated in the activities of an ad hoc group that supported ATA's work. They worked for the release of Puerto Rican political prisoners and joined others in the repudiation of the Greater Hartford Process.

In such circles, Puerto Ricans collaborated with African American, Jewish, Native American, and White radicals who helped mobilize non–Puerto Ricans to such events as National Solidarity Day in 1974 and the Bicentennial without Colonies rally in Philadelphia in 1976. Puerto Ricans in turn agitated and mobilized against political repression, helping organize conferences and marches in support of its victims.

Intergroup conflict was not absent. Electoral participation was shunned and therefore there was no representation, which is the harbinger of conflict over distributive shares. On the rare occasion in which there was a brush with electoral politics the objective was not to win but to raise issues. Thus, conflict was about "the party line," about violations to the code of revolutionary ethics, about setting priorities, about personal rivalries, and about how to do what.[25]

In short, the White/ethnic Left was to Puerto Rican radicals what the political machine was to their mainstream counterparts. There was only one important difference: The Left accepted Puerto Ricans readily, but it failed to give them a model for success. To be effective Puerto Rican radicals had to take a second look at a model of political mobilization they rejected from the outset of their activities in Hartford.

PUSHING LEFT TO GET TO THE CENTER

Before 1977 two approaches to politics prevailed in the Puerto Rican community in Hartford. One strategy was to join the Democratic Party and work from within to exact programs and services. A second alternative was to work outside the party, challenging the city council and mobilizing the community to demand services. Mainstream leaders and radicals embodied these respective strategies, sometimes working in collaboration but mostly acting at some distance from each other. Aside from the common bond of ethnicity, there were few reasons why the twain should meet. But in 1977 a strategic convergence between mainstream and radical approaches took place. This is the phenomenon I refer to as "pushing left to get to the center."

Two PSP members embody and best exemplify the convergence of the two alternatives: José La Luz and Edwin Vargas. La Luz and Vargas articulated and put in practice a strategy that combined bargaining and compromise with demand-protest actions, using open challenges to the Democratic Party as a point of entry and platform. The most visible and significant instance of convergence took place after the 1976 debacle in the PSP, when Vargas declared his candidacy for city council. On August 2, 1977, accompanied by community leaders Eugenio Caro, Mildred Torres, Cesar Carmona, Angel Ocasio, and by José La Luz, Vargas announced the formation of the Puerto Rican Political Action Committee, a nonpartisan organization designed to increase voter education and elect Puerto Ricans to office. The group was formed after Vargas failed to win the endorsement of the Democratic Party to be on the slate for city council. La Luz, who at this point was an employment specialist at La Casa de Puerto Rico, an antipoverty agency, declared, "We should pressure the political parties to become more responsive to the needs of this community." [26] A public challenge to the Democratic Party by Puerto Ricans was unprecedented. As such it became the link between radical and mainstream politics.

Within the PSP this was the end for La Luz. Vargas was also suspended from its ranks. During one of its regular meetings, held on August 27, 1977, the Central Committee of the party rescinded Vargas's membership because of the "violation of democratic-centralism and party rules in your decision to run for office without consulting first with the party." [27]

Vargas lost his bid, but the race became the starting point for convergence, even if anticolonialism was no longer the rationale, and the goal of Puerto Rican independence was absent. The socialist rhetoric was muted, but the democratic impulse behind the socialist program was not abandoned. The project was now to develop an autonomous power base to pressure the Democratic Party into adopting a more responsive stance. This would lead to representation and the ability to influence public policy.

The 1977 convergence was not equivalent to selling out, although some defined the transition as such. [28] Instead, like the dialectic that first brought Puerto Ricans to Hartford, a combination of circumstances and ambition drove radicals to look toward the electoral process and the Democratic

Party. No matter how strong their nationalist feelings, their place was no longer Puerto Rico but Hartford. The political behavior of the community had consistently shown that its support of independence for Puerto Rico was not in the cards. To be a cultural nationalist was one thing but to support independence and socialism was quite another. The PSP, on the other hand, was not willing to entertain amendments to its strategy and did not welcome those who refused to toe the line. For radicals, to move beyond "raising issues" and to score actual victories, convergence was necessary. By 1977, Vargas and La Luz, among others, realized that to win something for the community (better education, better housing), it was necessary to stop subordinating the struggle for democratic rights to the struggle for national liberation. Putting the national question aside, they continued to push left from outside the party but now with the objective of penetrating the establishment.

By 1978 Vargas and La Luz were joining forces with the new leadership at the office of the Commonwealth of Puerto Rico in Hartford to organize a coalition to lobby the state legislature.[29] In the eyes of the PSP, they were traitors. La Luz in particular had scorned the commonwealth's office as an agent of colonial exploitation. Now the office was an ally. In retrospect, one can either view their actions as inconsistent or cynical, or as a sign of political maturity, as an admission that they had been wrong in the past.

PUERTO RICAN RADICALISM AND PUERTO RICAN POLITICAL DEVELOPMENT

How Effective was the Puerto Rican Left?

Because of its heavy emphasis on the national question, the PSP deviated the attention of many within the Hartford community from day-to-day issues. Mainstream leaders wanted Puerto Ricans to register to vote in Hartford. The PSP registered voters to cast absentee ballots in elections in Puerto Rico. It even recruited poll-watchers to volunteer their services on the island. Everywhere the PSP went it tried to route the community's attention away from mainland issues. At the 1982 Connecticut State-wide Puerto Rican Convention, a Hartford-based initiative, PSP members pushed so hard for the adoption of their program that many participants were alienated.[30] This impaired the party's effectiveness.

The organizational impetus of the Hartford community was not terribly diminished by the PSP; the most that can be said about the party's impact in this regard is that it generated dissension and conflict and that it was distracting. What seems clear, however, is that the emphasis on the national question prevented the PSP from developing a solid base of support among the masses, thereby undercutting its potential. This is ironic because in Hartford mainstream Puerto Rican politics was driven by culture and language. But the cultural nationalism of community leaders was a platform for incorporation, and this was something the PSP did not want to promote; its radical nationalism invited separation instead. Most Puerto Ricans wanted to incorporate more than they wanted to return to a sovereign homeland; they wanted economic progress, and they understood that to achieve upward mobility they needed political representation, not the destruction of the establishment.[31]

The actions of the office of the Commonwealth of Puerto Rico in Hartford blunted the edge of radical critiques of the Puerto Rican condition and reduced the incentives for joining such organizations as the PSP. It is not strange that the initial focus of the party was on Puerto Rican farmworkers. They were the natural constituency of a group that emphasized economic disadvantage, political disfranchisement, and colonial exploitation as inducements for political mobilization. But the revolutionary potential of farmworkers never developed in full, in part because PSP activities strengthened the resolve of the commonwealth's office to serve the community—and particularly migrant workers. The PSP also had to compete with other groups, such as the New England Farmworkers Council, which were better prepared, had more resources, and more access to the workers themselves.

Ironically, the PSP's strategy of organizing through fronts—such as META and CAMP—and of promoting autonomous organizing among workers was counterproductive. The impulse behind the strategy was commendable, at least in part. The idea was to assist the working class in the development of its own institutions, provided, of course, that they subject themselves to the guidance of the "more advanced sectors" of the class, namely the PSP. Farmworkers understood that the party was their ally but their bond was pragmatic rather than ideological. Despite the insistence of the PSP that the government of Puerto Rico, acting in league with the tobacco growers, was responsible for their miserable situation, many workers saw commonwealth officials as their representatives. In 1973, for example, in a letter to the governor of Puerto Rico, a group of farmworkers complained about a breach of contract by the tobacco growers' association. They wanted the governor to intervene on their behalf to negotiate a new contract, including worker representation in the process.[32]

The Contribution of Puerto Rican Radicalism

The contribution of the radical movement as such to Puerto Rican political development was limited. More substantial was the contribution of individual radicals. But there is a link between the two simply because their lack of party affiliation after 1976 did not prevent such individuals as Vargas and La Luz from carrying the movement in their heads. They were removed from the PSP, but the PSP was not entirely removed from them. Thus, there was a positive association between their tempered extrapartisan radicalism—measured by their methods, strategy, and populist attitude—and their effectiveness.

In 1976 the PSP decried what it called a "traditional view of Puerto Rican politicians in this country." According to the party, those politicians did the community a disservice by promoting the idea that "elections on the island have nothing to do with *Boricuas* who reside in the U.S." This is interesting in view of the claim, made by James Jennings, that during the 1970s the Puerto Rican community in the United States experienced a shift in attitude, from a concern with island-based issues to an interest in mainland-based agendas. According to this claim, the activities of radical groups gave the coup d'grace to the old attitude.[33] In reality, there was no *community* shift since *interest in mainland politics was the traditional attitude*. To be sure, there were mainstream leaders who were interested in the national question as well as radicals who had their feet planted in mainland realities. But, in a sociological sense, the shift took place *amongst radicals*. The irony of this development is that it enhanced the arsenal of strategies available to those interested in electoral politics. This is what the Hartford case demonstrates. There, the traditional attitude was focused on electoral politics, and during the 1970s the PSP was not happy about it. If Puerto Ricans on the mainland ignored island politics, the party reasoned, they would never understand the real issues of colonial exploitation and forced migration. But most did ignore island politics, and by joining them radicals boosted their local political capacity.

Puerto Rican radicals in Hartford created openings for more mainstream groups, such as the Puerto Rican Businessmen Association (PRBA). In 1973 PRBA took advantage of the PSP's lead in a fight against the mayor of West Hartford in order to seek business opportunities for minorities.[34] In cases such as this, radicals acted as shock troops, forcing institutional responses and keeping regular community leaders honest.

Radicals raised issues, promoted a positive identity for Puerto Ricans, and were highly critical of what they thought to be intolerable inequities in the distribution of wealth and power. Their membership in community organizations was irritating when they tried to push their political agenda, but when they didn't, it was invigorating because they worked hard.

Their devotion to conspiracy theories and their apocalyptic tone was quite off the mark, but their critique was part of the necessary mixture of moderation and excess that helps the polity survive.[35] This, of course, must be appreciated as an unintended consequence. But one can nonetheless say that their discourse and actions give credence to William Blake's dictum that "the road of excess leads to the palace of wisdom." By pushing to the left Puerto Rican radicals helped the community get to the center; not all radicals got there, but those who did made significant contributions to the community's enfranchisement. They helped open the sphere of representation and gave political discourse in the city a more critical and pluralistic edge.

Reasons for Decline

Studies of the immigrant Left cite nativism, repression, Bolshevization, emigration, consumerism, the erosion of the demographic base of the community, and social mobility as factors that account for the decline of radicalism among ethnic groups.[36] Some of these factors contributed to the failure of Puerto Rican radicals, but their experience is different in many ways. The demise of the PSP is complex and the explanation is multivariate.

One debilitating factor was the promotion and eventual loss of able leaders. José La Luz was, without question, the top socialist leader and organizer in Hartford. By June 1973 he was promoted to regional secretary for New England. Then on December 1974 the party decided to appoint him to the U.S. branch secretariat, leaving the New England region in the hands of Ramón Lugo, an organizer from New Britain. These transitions created a leadership vacuum in the city.

The behavior of some leaders in New York, characterized as "cold," "elitist," "cliquish," and "arrogant" did not help strengthen the party.[37] New York leaders demanded much and provided little. This was also the case in Hartford. Local leaders were pretentious and detached. The party's hierarchy and its organizational strategy drove away supporters and kept sympathizers at arm's length. "Why is it that the party is not open to the people?" This incredible question was publicly asked in Hartford by a local resident in 1982 who concluded that it was "easier to hit a pitch from Rich Gossage blindfolded than to become a member of the Socialist Party."[38]

Burn-out was another factor. La Luz, for example, divided his time between local, regional, and national meetings. He wrote occasional news articles and columns for *Claridad*. For at least two years he organized and was spokesperson for every single march and rally the PSP conducted in Hartford. He was also behind the PSP's organizing efforts among migrant workers. No leader could sustain such a demanding workload indefinitely. Similarly, the pressure on rank-and-file members was phenomenal. Not a year had passed since National Solidarity Day—a mobilization effort that brought nearly twenty thousand activists to Madison Square Garden in 1974—and the party was already committed 1. to a national mobilization to Philadelphia on the bicentennial 2. to mobilizing thousands to a demonstration during the discussion of Puerto Rico's case at the United Nations, and 3. to register voters, raise money, and recruit poll-watchers for the 1976 election in Puerto Rico. This was not an extraordinary situation but the typical pattern of PSP demands on its members. According to the leadership, the only alternative was to "increase our ability to work at many levels at the same time." As if this was not daunting enough, members had to improve their efficiency while simultaneously resolving "serious problems of political education, development of affiliates and cadre, in addition to recruitment."[39]

In fairness to the PSP it must be recognized that, while the White/ethnic Left provided socialization guidance, it did not provide a model for success. The Hartford Left was not exempt from the deficiencies that have afflicted the U.S. Left, including the feebleness that inevitably accompanies a movement of "followerless cadres," sectarianism, pigheadedness, petty infighting, and the dissolving effects of political faddism.[40] Thus, the failure of Puerto Rican radicals was also determined, in part, by the company they kept.

As noted above, the party's critique was overweening. I have provided examples of their bent for conspiracy theories and ready-made formulas that substituted ideology for analysis. In retrospect, the party's self-righteous stand, its dogmatic tone, and its disregard for standards of evidence feels jarring and offensive to many former PSP members.[41] That was not the case when they were in the heat of activism, and, in fact, the air of certainty that enveloped the party and its crusading approach were appealing rather than repellent. Yet these features must have also prevented more sensible people from joining and therefore ought to be counted among the reasons for the party's decline.

During ten years of activity in the city, the PSP was subject to surveillance, intimidation, and harassment. A few of its members were punished with the loss of jobs, trumped-up charges, and jail. The group was successful in its campaign on behalf of José "Pepe" Torres and Rubén Vega, two members accused of firebombing a police car in 1970, but it had to pay a substantial price in terms of time, energy, and resources. Repression did not wipe out the party, but it certainly undermined its capacity.[42]

One is really hard-pressed to find ideological co-optation as a reason for decline, but upward mobility sometimes made activism more difficult, if only because being an activist in the city while living or working in the suburbs was logistically complex. To survive, radicals often found themselves working for community agencies they despised. Some worked for mainstream organizations, such as Hartford Hospital, or for public institutions, such as the school system, during and after the heyday of radical activities in the city. In time, the lifestyle and appearance of most became decidedly middle class. In some cases there was a middle-class background from the start. In these cases the tendency was for individual radicals to make more money, dress better, and drive bigger and more expensive cars as the years went by. Yet, for the most part, these changes affected their tone or their image but not the substance of their discourse. For example, in 1993, La Luz declared, "People should be involved in formulating policies and programs that affect their daily lives. . . . And that calls for, in fact, as you characterize it, a radical approach to democracy." In 1994, Vargas arrived at a Hartford forum in his Lincoln Town Car, wearing a very elegant suit and tie. The first thing he did was to define himself as a democratic socialist, a label that is consonant with his political record.[43]

A crucial factor was the party's focus on the national question. Interestingly, the dissonance between the struggle for national liberation in Puerto Rico and the struggle for democracy and economic progress in the United States fueled the convergence of demand-protest and electoral politics, which in turn contributed further to the decline. The party's schizophrenic approach persisted beyond the 1976 crisis. In January 1982 Hartford leaders declared, for the nth time, their intention to immerse the party in the everyday struggles of the community. At the same time, they made support for independence and support for the withdrawal of the U.S. Navy from Vieques the litmus test of coalition-building efforts. At a forum in June, Antonio Gaztambide, from Puerto Rico, and Carmelo Ruiz, from Hartford, declared that independence continued to be the party's first priority. In December, at a meeting to discuss the relationship between the electoral process and the struggle for democratic rights, José Alberto Alvarez, from New York, made it clear that to be acceptable, the party's electoral participation had to contribute to the goals of independence and socialism for Puerto Rico.[44]

WHAT IS TO BE LEARNED?

Are there any lessons in this experience that might help the Puerto Rican community in the United States understand and overcome its plight? Several discoveries and insights emerge from the foregoing narrative and analysis.

First, while ethnic identity was politically important to Puerto Ricans, theirs was a cultural nationalism that promoted incorporation and was therefore at odds with a radical nationalism that advocated separation and the destruction of the establishment. This dissonance explains why the national question did not turn out to be as effective a mobilization strategy as radicals thought it would be. It is clear that Puerto Ricans in the United States, radical or otherwise, need to be careful about how much attention they devote to issues on the island. This is, perhaps, the most important lesson of this history if only because the national question is the Dracula of Puerto Rican politics in the United States; no matter how many times we drive a stake through its heart it comes back to haunt us. In 1996 Republican congressman Don Young introduced a bill to the House of Representatives to redefine the political relationship between the United States and Puerto Rico, enticing Puerto Ricans on the mainland, albeit briefly, to divide the focus of their attention. The bill was withdrawn because of Young's refusal to include an amendment requiring English as the official language of Puerto Rico under statehood. The following year, the congressman introduced a new bill, this time with fifty-two additional cosponsors.[45] Meanwhile, a lively debate took place among Puerto Rican intellectuals and activists on what the stateside community should do on the one hundredth anniversary of American colonial intervention in Puerto Rico.

Second, the shift in attitude concerning the relationship between island and mainland issues attributed to the community was actually experienced by Puerto Rican radicals. They pushed left, ended up in the center, and consequently enriched the arsenal of mobilization strategies available to Puerto Ricans in general. It is clear that incorporation was not hurt but was rather helped by a mixture of moderation and excess. In this there is a similarity with the Black Power experience described by Kwame Ture and Charles Hamilton, except that in the Puerto Rican case the outcome was, in part, unintended and, therefore, it brings into question the teleological and functionalist assumptions they incorporate into their analysis. Ture and Hamilton dismiss outsiders who tone down their discourse in order to become insiders by arguing that by doing so they achieve only "meaningless, token rewards that an affluent society is perfectly willing to give."[46] Political representation, however, was not meaningless to Puerto Ricans, and it was not willingly given to them.

Third, this story suggests that to be effective leaders, radicals must be superior followers. This is problematic because even though radicals toned down their discourse to make it meet the requirements of electoral politics, they did not necessarily become more credible. They helped the community but at great political cost. No radical was ever able to gain elected office, and there was no radical group succession. It seems that in order for radicalism to develop a popular following it must emphasize construction rather than destruction, espousing a variety of progress that enhances positive institutions, meaningful relationships, and cherished values. The irony here is that, in order to win popular support, even such an approach would probably require dissociation from the label of "radical." A politics of protest, although not automatically legitimate, appears to be more acceptable than a politics of radical transformation, if the latter is understood to be at odds with the prevailing framework of ideals and values.

The issue of leadership raises a related question: Must radicals dilute the terms of their critique in order to succeed? There is no clear or easy answer to this question. The Puerto Rican experience in Hartford is fraught with ambiguity. Vargas's shift to the center was not followed by immediate electoral success, yet radical methods were productive in some electoral battles. During the 1977 campaign Vargas was red-baited, but he was also supported by María Sánchez, a dedicated and respected but quite conservative community leader.[47] What occurred in 1977 was not a turnaround, but rather a troublesome transition. No radical group of consequence stepped in to fill the vacuum left by the demise of the PSP. After 1977, the systemic critique, however crude it was, that distinguished the discourse of Puerto Rican radicals receded into the background.

Was convergence a recognition that, as Marx noted in the *Communist Manifesto*, "the first step in the revolution by the working class . . . is to win the battle of democracy?" According to Marx and Engels, communists ought to fight for the "immediate aims" and "momentary interests" of the working class, without losing track of the long-term goals and interests of the revolutionary movement.[48] Was the focus on mainland issues and electoral politics on the part of Vargas and La Luz a local application of this world-historical dictum? I have suggested that this was the case. Two decades later it is also apparent that the "momentary" battle for democracy continues and that the signs of a systemic transformation are weaker than ever. What is not entirely clear is whether this is because of the dilution of systemic critiques or because of the absence of a revolutionary critique that is realistic and persuasive.

Finally, there is the larger question of how to apply what we learn— a question that those who suggest that experience can help formulate current strategies rarely examine.[49] How do we use political historiography to make the past work for the present? I suggest that we do it the way porcupines make love: very carefully.

After looking back at the Puerto Rican Left in Hartford, it is clear that one can make sense of the past through opportunities that only come up in the present. We understand what went on then in light of what we know now. Thus, retrospective knowledge allows us to understand that the emphasis of the PSP on the national question was a recipe for failure because it was at odds with the cultural nationalism used by the community to promote enfranchisement and representation. This understanding is the result of interpretation but, also, a matter of access to the facts. Thus the truth about the past can only be ascertained in the present because it is at that moment that one usually has access to all the facts one can possibly recover and assemble about that past; this is rarely possible when the past is happening, when it is the present. Because the truth about now can only be found later, the present is an intermediate stage, a point of transition, *an imaginary moment* that happens but that is somewhat *unreal*. The present illuminates a previous moment, and it is clarified by a succeeding one.

This relationship between past-present-future raises an important question about the notion of wisdom, understood as insights based on retrospective learning. Namely, how do we transform wisdom into action, how do we make it *practical* wisdom? Simply put, political practice is most unintelligible when it matters the most to know what is going on—in the present, when things are happening. By looking back, we learn what went wrong; this makes us wise. But the knowledge gained does not necessarily tells us what will work now. Thus the usefulness of the past for present action is questionable.

This research might enhance our understanding of the Puerto Rican radical experience, but it might not necessarily offer a sound course of action under current circumstances. As the present rapidly becomes past we face a dissonance between what we know happened and what is happening now. This creates a situation in which we might try to solve a new problem with an old solution, that is, *with a solution that might have worked yesterday but that will not work today*. For example, the PSP was unable to set priorities. In retrospect it is evident that this was a debilitating factor. Thus to avoid inefficiency in the present one would be well advised to find a match between capability and action. This still might not work because one might settle on the wrong issue, thus missing out on a better opportunity; or one's energies might be focused on the right issue, while blundering on strategy.

A second problem has to do with the *accuracy of representation*. Given the fragmentary and incomplete nature of the materials we use to reconstruct the past, how do we know we got the story right? This increases the possibility of dissonance between past and present because what we think we know might not be what it was. Is it really appropriate to talk about the decline of the Puerto Rican Left in Hartford? How do we know that all the references in *Claridad* to "significant growth," "workplace organizing," "glorious campaigns," "successful assemblies," and "leaps in organizational development" are true? Conlin has noted that the radical press in the United States was often nothing more than "a desk, a typewriter, a printing press, and a busy mind." Although *Claridad* was more than that, it is not beyond the pale to think that, like in the U.S. radical press, many of the "successful rallies" and "intense organizing campaigns" reported in the weekly were nothing more than, as Conlin puts it, "reveries or the ill-advised propaganda devices of a revolutionary journalist."[50]

Even if these two difficulties are overcome we still have to contend with the rather indeterminate relationship between past and present. The problem is, essentially, that as insights derived from the past decrease in generality so does their applicability in the present. For example, the story of Puerto Rican radicals in Hartford suggests that effective leaders must have their ear close to the ground, that in order to lead the masses they must learn how to listen to them and must respect their wishes and aspirations. This is fine, but what exactly do we do when a community is motivated by ignorance or prejudice? How do we decide what to listen for? How do we know who in the community is right?

These are difficult, not unanswerable, questions. The point is that while sometimes we can be certain, most of the time all we have is a dimly perceived approximation to an answer. In 1987 Alfredo Lopez wrote, "Puerto Rico's past makes clear that periods of organizational disarray in the independence movement are only moments, short pauses really, in the history of what has proven to be a powerful and resilient movement."[51] In Puerto Rico the Nationalist Party was wiped out in 1950. The MPI came about nine years later; the PSP emerged a decade after that. Thus it took twenty years for the independence movement to overcome the disarray that followed the demise of the Nationalist Party. If we date the collapse of the PSP in the United States to around the mid-1980s, assuming that the cycle of decline and renewal takes a full generation, a new movement should begin to show its signs by 2005 or thereabouts. This is, of course, pure speculation. But at least one can say that while it might be too late to be certain about the promise of renewal, it is still too early to declare that it is an empty promise. Renewal is possible; we can use the "lessons" that political historiography reveals, but we must do this with sobriety by recognizing that what we learn from experience is rarely, if ever, tried and true knowledge.

JOSÉ E. VELÁZQUEZ

5   Another West Side Story
An Interview with Members of El Comité–MINP

DURING THE 1950s, on the West Side of Manhattan an enormous working-class community stretched from the edges of Chelsea to the Upper West Side and Harlem. This community was predominantly Puerto Rican but also included a large number of Dominicans, Cubans, African Americans, and Whites. During the 1960s, this area was targeted by the Urban Renewal/Model Cities Program to be part of a master plan to gentrify the area through the building of middle-income and luxury housing. Having already removed thousands of poor and working people for the Lincoln Center development, the city embarked on a plan to remove thousands more while promising that they would eventually return to new housing developments in the area. As this displacement got under way, the city government acquired empty tenement buildings that were to be demolished in order to make room for new high-rise developments. This gave rise to an often spontaneous, but significantly large, movement of squatters who invaded these tenements, openly challenging the city government to remove them.

As part of that squatters' movement, in early 1970 a group of residents—made up of Vietnam veterans, factory and construction workers, the unemployed, and former gang members—took over a storefront on 88th Street and Columbus Avenue and began to craft a political response to the city's plan for what these residents termed "urban removal." Led by Federíco Lora, a Vietnam Veteran of Dominican heritage with strong ties to the Puerto Rican community, this group of mostly Puerto Ricans and other Latinos called itself "El Comité" and began to make its presence felt in the housing struggle on the West Side. Furthermore, it began to rally support for bilingual education and community control of the school district.

Increasingly radicalized by national and international events, El Comité emerged as one of the organizations of the Puerto Rican Left, although differing in many aspects from the already established Young Lords Party and the Puerto Rican Socialist Party (PSP). While primarily involved in local community issues, El Comité would later adopt a Marxist-Leninist philosophy and proclaim the building of socialism in the United States as its long-term goal. In January 1975 in New York City, the organization held a constituent assembly that officially gave birth to El Comité–Movimiento de Izquierda Nacional Puertorriqueño (or MINP; Puerto Rican National Left Movement). This assembly concluded a period of formation of chapters in New York City's West Side, Lower East Side, East Harlem, the Bronx, and Brooklyn. The organization also had supporters in Long Island, New York; Camden, New Jersey; Boston, Massachusetts; Washington, D.C.; and California.

Rejecting earlier theoretical formulations of the Puerto Rican Left that viewed Puerto Ricans in the United States as "part of the Puerto Rican nation" or a "divided nation," El Comité–MINP defined *Boricuas* in the United States as a "national minority" within the U.S. working class. While supporting the need for Puerto Ricans to organize independently and to play a special role in solidarity with the independence of Puerto Rico, El Comité–MINP called for the formation of a new multinational Communist Party to lead the struggle for socialism in the United States.

In the late 1970s, several key members of the organization who felt that the struggle for the independence of Puerto Rico was primary in their lives relocated to Puerto Rico, including Federico Lora, the organization's founder and First Secretary. Subsequently, after its first assembly, held in November 1978, El Comité–MINP would give greater attention to the building of a new communist movement in the United States. Joining the "antirevisionist, antidogmatic" wing of this movement, El Comité–MINP criticized the class composition, dogmatism, and sectarianism of those groups in the North American Left who had proclaimed themselves to be the "New Communist Party," while having little political influence or support among working people. It also differed with those in its own wing who attempted to prematurely create "ideological centers," arguing instead that theoretical formulations had to be preceded by building roots among the working class.

As El Comité–MINP continued its activity, by January 1981 a factional conflict based on ideological and personal differences had developed within the organization. The leadership took measures to expel those members involved in factional activity, creating even further instability within the organization. Taking a personal and political toll on the organization, this split would lead to the eventual dissolution of El Comité–MINP in 1982.

The following interviews explore the origins and development of El Comité–MINP through the eyes of some individuals who played key roles in the organization from its beginning to its eventual demise. Participating in this interview, conducted during the summer of 1996, were Carmen Martell and Elizabeth Figueroa, both early members of El Comité–MINP and individuals who continue to be activists on health and labor issues; Julio Pabón, also an early member, who presently presides over a multi-faceted sports-marketing company; and Sandra Trujillo, who joined the organization in the mid-1970s and who continues to be an activist on issues affecting children and families. In a postscript, I also interview Federíco Lora, founder of El Comité–MINP and presently a practicing labor attorney and proindependence activist in Puerto Rico. Lora, who relocated to Puerto Rico in 1978, discusses his experiences upon his return to and incorporation into the struggle on the island.

Origins and Development

JOSÉ VELÁZQUEZ: Can you describe some of the experiences that led you to become involved with an organization that was talking about revolutionary change?

CARMEN MARTELL: El Comité was an organization that very few people know the history of, beginning with its origins on the upper West Side and its connection with the squatters' movement. We were instrumental when it came to demonstrating against urban renewal—what we called at that time "urban removal,"—as thousands of housing units on the West Side were destroyed by the city administration who broke its promise to replace them with low-income housing. So, to organize against it [renewal] was a great achievement because we were not political; we were just people that wanted to get involved with issues affecting our community. At the time, we were aware of the activities of the Young Lords Party and MPI [which later became PSP]. We supported the Young Lords' takeover of the 110th Street Methodist Church by collecting any type of donations that could contribute to its success. We would go to MPI activities on Fridays and to political-education classes at the Young Lords' storefront in East Harlem, learning from both organizations. Of course we had our leader, Federíco Lora, and later added Américo Badillo, who became a political mentor. Américo was from Puerto Rico and had a knowledge of the history of Puerto Rico that we desperately sought. Federíco became our spokesperson from the beginning, representing us at school board meetings and in meetings with different housing officials. In 1970, we decided to participate in a rally on 138th Street in the South Bronx, and that was the first time Federíco addressed a mass rally organized by the Puerto Rican Left.

JULIO PABÓN: I had not heard of El Comité prior to that rally in the South Bronx. A lot of us didn't know that there was a humongous Puerto

Rican community on the West Side that was being forcibly removed to gentrify the area. At the rally, most of the other organizations were concerned with the issue of Puerto Rican independence, the war in Vietnam, and police brutality. However, El Comité was one of the few organizations that seemed to touch upon a major issue in the community when they described the squatters' movement. As a South Bronx resident who had never been to the West Side, after hearing Federíco speak I went to meet him at [El Comité's] headquarters, and that's how I became a member of the organization. In 1970–71, Victor Quintana, myself, and other students organized El Frente Unido (United Front), a Puerto Rican student club at Lehman College. Later Victor became a member of El Comité, and we began to go to the classes on Puerto Rican history. I was the first one from Caldwell Street to go to the West Side, and that's the link from the South Bronx to the West Side.

ELIZABETH FIGUEROA: When I was in high school, I lived in *El Barrio* (East Harlem) on 115th Street and Madison Avenue. So, I had already been introduced to the Young Lords, but it was not until I attended Lehman College that I met members of El Comité and became attracted to their politics. Everybody in El Comité followed rule number one—you had to be in some kind of mass organization. It was embarrassing to go to a meeting of El Comité and not report on what your organization was doing. We didn't care what it was—a baseball team, a domino club, a student group, a factory unit, or a group of women who got together to go dancing at clubs.

PABÓN: Having grown up on Caldwell Avenue in the Bronx, I was streetwise, and what attracted me to the movement was seeing how cops in the South Bronx would stop and search Latinos who were just driving cars or hanging out. It was like an occupied territory, and the police were the occupying force. Although I saw the Black Panthers on television pulling out guns against cops, I did not see this on my block. All of a sudden, you began to see a group of young people, called the Young Lords, confronting the police and saying that we were somebody. I became a member of the Young Lords for about six or seven months; but what attracted me to El Comité was the passion and seriousness of Federíco Lora's speech at that rally in the South Bronx. My experience was that people in the [Young Lords] movement during the day did very serious work; such as TB and lead-poisoning testing and distributing newspapers. However, at night, people were smoking joints and stuff like that. Meanwhile, I'm saying, "Wait, we're talking about cops and guns, and you know, we could get killed." I took this seriously because I saw it happen on my block. The first group that I saw that was also very serious about this situation was El Comité, and that is why I became a member.

MARTELL: Some of the founders of El Comité had served in the U.S. Marines and completed tours in Vietnam. Having returned home, they saw people being dislocated, and the squatters resisting these policies by taking over buildings. There was a sense of "Hey, the government is destroying our community. We are not going to let them do it." Personally, I went a different route. I was at MPI activities most of the time, and Federíco Lora (my former husband) would ask why I had not joined El Comité. However, I shied away from the male dominance prevalent within the group. In the beginning, there were very few women; Esperanza Martell was one of the few women in the organization. She would take on all of the men at that time. Later, Americo Badillo had been drawn to El Comité and began to teach us Puerto Rican history. From then on we began to develop an identity—a Puerto Rican identity.

FIGUEROA: For me, it was the Vietnam War and the antiwar protests that led to my early political involvement. Though I did not understand the international political connections, I knew that we were in a war that we did not belong in, and that the Vietnamese were people of color. It was the antiwar experience that drew me to want to know about my roots in Puerto Rico because there was always a link. We were talking about Vietnam. and all of a sudden someone would shout, "U.S.A. out of Puerto Rico." This was also a time when social norms were being questioned, and various social issues were linked together because of the war. When I went to college, all of this experience now fed into the struggle for the independence of Puerto Rico. My father was a real Nationalist who talked all the time about Puerto Rico. On the college campus, the struggle for Puerto Rican studies became a major issue. Initially, that's how I got involved with El Comité because they were active in the student club and leading the fight for Puerto Rican studies.

SANDRA TRUJILLO: I'm originally from San Francisco where I was active around youth and community empowerment issues, which instilled in me a sense of ethnic pride and commitment to social change. I became radicalized by those issues and by the influences of the Black Panther, Brown Beret, and anti–Vietnam War movements, as well as the struggles taking place in Latin America. In 1970, I was recruited to attend Barnard College where I immediately became active in the Latin American Student Organization (LASO), organizing around issues affecting Latino students on campus, as well as supporting the nearby squatters' movement on the West Side. I subsequently spent two years in Puerto Rico, where I participated in a student occupation at the University of Puerto Rico and attended other proindependence activities. As much as I came to love Puerto Rico, I also longed to return to the United States to resume my involvement in the struggle for social justice. Returning to the United States in 1974, I met some members of El Comité, including Carmen Lora [Martell, who is also a part of this interview], who along with other women were preparing a presentation on the reality of Latin women in the United States for a Vietnamese Women's Solidarity Conference in Canada. That effort later became the impetus for the creation of the Latin Women's Collective. Being impressed by the seriousness of Carmen and other members of El Comité, I eagerly accepted Carmen's invitation to join a study group, which was the first step toward becoming a member of the organization.

VELÁZQUEZ: How did El Comité develop from a local community group into a political organization with its own identity, and how did it differ from the other established organizations of the Puerto Rican Left?

FIGUEROA: The first phase was the local community struggles concerning housing, education, and jobs. At some point, the influence of existing political groups made us more international in our perspective. Then, we embarked upon a conscious effort to learn about our own history through Puerto Rican history classes. So, we went from local community activists to being Nationalists, including some members who became die-hard Nationalists.

PABÓN: These classes were no joking matter. First of all, you had to study for a test once a week. We had books to read. So, no matter if you were in college and had ten term papers to write, or whether you were a factory worker who worked ten hour days, or a housewife who had to cook for her husband—if you came to the classes unprepared, it was the worst disgrace that you could possibly imagine. The part that you dreaded most was the criticism sessions.

MARTELL: When El Comité put a Puerto Rican and a Lares flag on its West Side storefront, we finally had some basis to argue that we were a political group doing community organizing on the West Side. Now remember, we were from the West Side and had a high level of pride and arrogance. We had Puerto Ricans who were recent migrants but also Puerto Ricans that had been here for a long time and felt very much a part of this country. We would go and ask for advice and help from the Young

Lords and MPI, and what we got back was sort of, "Well, if you will be our chapter, maybe we can help you."

PABÓN: El Comité's political work started out as a reaction to social conditions in our community. Then, from there it started growing because of national and international events that were taking place in Vietnam, Latin America, and Africa. At the time, the Left movement as a whole was growing and developing; El Comité was changing just like the MPI became the Puerto Rican Socialist Party (PSP), and the Young Lords became the Puerto Rican Revolutionary Workers' Organization (PRRWO). El Comité went through a similar transition from a community organization to what became known as the Movimiento de Izquierda Nacional Puertorriqueño (MINP). It is interesting to note that throughout this period the organization was still very Nationalist, even though we had people that were not Puerto Rican.

TRUJILLO: As El Comité developed, we came in contact with members of both the Puerto Rican and North American Left. Irwin Kaplan (Kappy), an elderly man who had a rich and lengthy experience in the U.S. labor and Communist movements, lived in the West Side and took an interest in the young people gathering at 88th Street. He became an early mentor and supporter and helped guide our early political formation. In general, most Left organizations, in chauvinist fashion, sought to incorporate us into their formations, rather than offer to help us in our own development. As time passed, we began to study Marxism-Leninism and other writings in an organized and deliberate fashion. Eventually, we proclaimed ourselves to be an integral part of the Puerto Rican Left, as well as part of the U.S. Left working toward the development of a new Communist Party.

THE NATIONAL QUESTION

VELÁZQUEZ: One issue that was a constant source of controversy among the Left was the Puerto Rican national question. Some viewed Puerto Ricans on the mainland as an oppressed national minority within the United States, while others affirmed that they were part of the Puerto Rican nation. How did you view the national question?

PABÓN: When the question came up, we were clear that we were Puerto Ricans who happened to be living here, and, although I love Puerto Rico, we were a national minority. The issues here were about better services at Lincoln Hospital or about the quality of the schools that our people attended. Some of us experienced that directly because we had children and had to deal with the reality that when your kid got sick, you had to go to Lincoln Hospital and wait six or seven hours to see a doctor. So, then you leave there to go to a meeting to talk about issues in Puerto Rico or Angola?

TRUJILLO: What attracted me to El Comité–MINP was precisely the debate on the national question. Although truthfully, I probably didn't comprehend the significance of the different positions, I viewed it in a very concrete way. My perception of the Young Lords and the PSP was that, in practice, they seemed to only be involved in issues related to Puerto Rico's independence, while hardly addressing the pressing issues affecting Puerto Ricans in the United States. El Comité, on the other hand, did support work for Puerto Rican independence but not as its primary activity. Most of its day-to-day work was in community, student, or work-related struggles. As a Chicana, I identified myself as a "national minority" whose primary struggle was in this country.

FIGUEROA: We were not at all critical of the PSP in Puerto Rico. What they did on the island was quite appropriate: fight for Puerto Rican independence. However, it should not have been the only and ultimate focus for the PSP in the United States, as there were other issues to address that were not directly connected with the status of Puerto Rico.

PABÓN: We realized that once you organized around deteriorating conditions here, then you could get into discussions about Puerto Rican independence. While we went into the community to organize around local issues, other organizations seemed to want to focus on the independence of Puerto Rico. When building our local base, we were not about to get caught up arguing that everything had to be about Puerto Rican independence. That distinguished us from other Puerto Rican Left organizations, and, to some degree, I think that's what kept El Comité alive for so long.

TRUJILLO: That doesn't mean we didn't do solidarity work in support of Puerto Rico's independence; we did both. We worked on local community issues while also conducting Puerto Rico solidarity work in coalition with other individuals and organizations. We were active in such efforts as the Puerto Rico Solidarity Committee (PRSC) and later in the New York Committee in Support of Vieques. So, for us the independence of Puerto Rico was fundamental. However, we believed that all Americans should support Puerto Rico's right to self-determination and independence because it is the major colony of the United States.

THE HIGH POINTS

VELÁZQUEZ: What were some of the main accomplishments of El Comité–MINP?

PABÓN: One good thing about El Comité is that eventually it had so many women in leadership, which allowed male chauvinist Latinos, like myself, to theoretically and practically address the issue of women in leadership. Another highlight for me was how we dealt with the issue of Angola, where rival organizations, the MPLA and UNITA, clashed in their battle against Portuguese colonialism. The Soviet Union supported the MPLA, and the United States and China lent their support to UNITA. Most Left organizations followed either a Soviet or Chinese political line. We had no links to China, Havana, or the Soviet Union, so we were forced to research the situation and arrive at our own conclusion to support the MPLA, as opposed to blindly following some international line.

FIGUEROA: Support of Cuba through demonstrations, cultural activities, and rallies at the United Nations was also a highlight of El Comité. We were always sponsoring activities aimed at showing that what was happening to working people in the United States was directly linked to the struggles in Puerto Rico, Chile, Nicaragua, Angola, etc. There was a period of three or four years when we had a high level of participation in all activities and issues addressed by the movement. I know the impression was that El Comité "fit in a Volkswagen," but I think that speaks to our being very security-conscious. We learned from the experiences of other organizations, and while not being paranoid about police infiltration, we structured the organization to limit its effects. El Comité was prepared and ready to be supportive of the Puerto Rican people if they decided they wanted independence.

MARTELL: We were instrumental in organizing a national conference in 1971 around the campaign to free the five Puerto Rican Nationalist prisoners. Our main emphasis was to have a successful conference, not to get the credit. The press reported that the MPI-PSP and the Young Lords spearheaded the conference. Often the mass media attributed many of our actions on the West Side to the Young Lords Party.

Nevertheless, our main emphasis was not who was responsible, but whether we got our message across. Though we had our differences, we tried to work in coalition with the Young Lords Party, PRRWO, and the PSP on a principled basis. However, our efforts were not always successful.

PABÓN: We were very much a part of the successful campaign to free the five Puerto Rican Nationalist prisoners. For one of the first and few times, we had to work closely with politicians, such as former congressman Robert García and others, who were urging President Carter to commute the sentences for the Nationalists. However, a strong community-based campaign to support this effort was the key, and this was accomplished as a result of the unity of the Puerto Rican Left. Seeing these people freed as a result of some of the work that we did was definitely a high point for El Comité and the entire movement.

TRUJILLO: One of the best characteristics of El Comité was its emphasis on development, leadership, morality, and commitment. I believe most of our members were extremely responsible and hardworking. We were not into just getting sound bites, focusing instead on grassroots, day-to-day organizing and helping to build effective mass organizations. The other significant accomplishment was our role in helping to build the Latin Women's Collective (LWC), the first and only, in my opinion, Latina progressive organization in New York that really organized women in a way that was different from the feminist movement. We were critical of the feminist movement because we perceived it as being primarily an antimale movement that did not address the issues affecting working women, particularly women of color. The LWC focused on the issues facing working-class Latina women in the areas of education, day care, health, and labor. At our peak period, there were fifty or sixty active women attending weekly meetings and working on a variety of projects.

MARTELL: Esperanza Martell, a member of El Comité, spearheaded the efforts at building some type of women's organization. We decided that it was important to get together with other women who were not members of El Comité. Many women from different organizations wanted to be part of this effort, as long as no one organization controlled it. The Latin Women's Collective became a truly independent mass organization capable of recruiting women at all levels.

VELÁZQUEZ: Can you talk about the "Gypsy Cab" movement and the role El Comité played in this struggle?

PABÓN: That was also a high point for the organization. Basically, it began when a handful of unemployed Puerto Ricans in New York City discovered that putting a flashlight on the hood of a four-door car at night makes it look like a Yellow Cab. You could actually make a living by picking up passengers, as Yellow Cabs usually bypassed nonwhite passengers or refused to service areas like the South Bronx. People like Tati Rivera, a former member of the Young Lords, José Rivera, a community activist (now a New York City councilman), and Freddy Pérez, an organizer in the South Bronx, were basically the founders of the "Gypsy Cab" movement. They reached out to college students for support, and we held dances to raise money for this coalition of livery car owners. As a result of government opposition and police harassment, there were major confrontations—the largest occurring on the Willis Avenue Bridge when numerous cab drivers blockaded traffic. The cops came, and heads were busted, sparking major riots in the South Bronx. The Puerto Rican Left provided much of the support and leadership for what today is a large industry [owning livery cars], now run by a Dominican majority.

DECLINE

VELÁZQUEZ: Can you pinpoint a particular moment or turning point leading to the demise of El Comité?

MARTELL: As we developed new chapters and recruited members throughout the country, we allowed many Marxist-Leninists, who at one time were former leaders or members of other organizations, to become part of El Comité. One of the things that had kept us viable over the years was our consistent efforts at building mass organizations. However, with more theoretically oriented members, political debates about "party building" became the main preoccupation within the leadership. People began to separate themselves from mass organizations. Our discussions began to focus on which national effort should we become part of to build a new Communist Party. In the last few years, we began to see the negative influence of those members who joined the organization in the later period, and who began to take to take control of its ideological agenda.

FIGUEROA: What Carmen said is significant and would not have occurred during El Comité's earlier period. There was a dismissal of our work in mass organizations as a "petty bourgeois" waste of time and arguments that it was more important for us to teach people about Marxism-Leninism. The members from the old guard sat there and said, "Wait a minute, you don't educate people by solely preaching Marxism-Leninism; they won't know what the hell you are talking about." Those kinds of debates never took place in El Comité–MINP until after the 1978 assembly. I don't know how to say this gently, so I'm just going to say it; and again, hindsight is twenty/twenty. Generally, the White members had a completely different outlook from us. When we talked about Puerto

Rico, Chile, Nicaragua, etc., it came from an intimate understanding of their realities because of the cultural similarities. So, if a woman could not come to a meeting because of problems with her husband, we all understood. We said, "That's her husband, we've got to work with him," whereas White members sat there and said, "You know, he's this, he's that." We were not accustomed to that kind of reaction either. Looking back, if I had to do it all over again, I would not allow any White members in the organization.

MARTELL: It was not the Whites who had been long-standing members of the organization, but rather those from other Left tendencies that came in during the later period. Let's also remember that during this time a number of former leaders and members of El Comité–MINP relocated to Puerto Rico. That exodus of a significant part of the leadership left a large vacuum in the organization.

PABÓN: Although some of the leadership had left to Puerto Rico, it wasn't because they were in disagreement with El Comité's stance on the national question. They agreed that Puerto Ricans were here to stay, and although some said "This ain't mine," nevertheless they worked on issues affecting people here. Later, they reached a point in their lives where they wanted to directly commit themselves to the struggle in Puerto Rico. There was no anger whatsoever. What happened later, leading to a split in the organization, was a direct challenge to the core principles of El Comité–MINP. I also think its important to look at the historical context. This took place after Ronald Reagan's election, when the police apparatus sought to destroy the remnants of the earlier Left movements.

TRUJILLO: After the split, some of us, through the Freedom of Information Act, retrieved our FBI files, which reveal attempts by the FBI to infiltrate the organization almost from its inception. Shortly before the split, some people began to promote the position that ideological formation was primary over organizing efforts. They advocated that we should play a leading role in the national party-building efforts taking place at that time. They also disparaged some of our grassroots organizing, calling it "reformist" and labeled other members as "Nationalists," concerned only with Puerto Rico. At that time, we were functioning under "democratic centralism," where once decisions were arrived at, everyone was expected to adhere to the collective will. Not being able to secure a majority for their viewpoints, some of these individuals began to secretly hold meetings outside of the organization's structure and lobbied individuals in different chapters to support their views. This factional activity unleashed a series of events that promoted internal divisions within the organization—divisions that would lead to our eventual dissolution.

MARTELL: We did not know how to react in this situation. We were given a letter, which was more like an ultimatum, by this faction who demanded a meeting of cadres. It included signatures of cadres from different chapters, proof that this faction was actively organizing outside the realm of the Central Committee and our organizational structures. It was a sort of betrayal because El Comité had gone so far and done so much; and we always felt there was room for debates within the organization. We felt that some of the people that joined this faction were destroying something we had built. So we purged those people whose signatures appeared in the letter. There were people at many different levels who were hurt by all of this because they did not know how to take sides. There were many folks that even to this day don't understand what happened.

TRUJILLO: This period of internal factionalism led to our ultimate demise. I think from that point, we started a process of dealing both with our rage and also our hurt; dealing with feeling like half of our family was cut off because it drove the organization apart. We were all committed to continuing our work and actually used that opportunity to examine and try to redouble our grassroots organizing efforts. However, the internal situation drained us, and with less people holding the organization together, our efforts proved exhausting.

MARTELL: In late 1981, we decided to dissolve the organization. Some people continued doing some type of mass work with other organizations, but El Comité as a political entity had come to an end.

VELÁZQUEZ: In the late 1970s, the organization endorsed participating in the strategy to build a new Communist Party. What were some of the consequences of this decision?

PABÓN: The issue of party building and its relationship to a mass movement across America was part of a historical period that developed independently of the people who joined El Comité in its later period. However, the undemocratic and destructive ways these individuals promoted the issues within the organization was unprincipled. By the time the leadership purged these individuals, there was no other alternative because they had broken every rule of the organization, and if they remained it could have developed into a nasty situation. Thank God that the leadership stopped it cold, avoiding the vengeful actions that erupted in other organizations of the Left during similar conflicts.

TRUJILLO: If we look at this faction's criticism of El Comité as reformists and as not being up to the challenge of party building, it is interesting to note that after being expelled from the organization, eventually their focus became solidarity activities with the independence of Puerto Rico. It's interesting how they came full circle after criticizing us for being Nationalists or reformists. The bottom line is, their activities within El Comité led to the destruction of an organization that had a lot of promise.

FIGUEROA: If you want to build a movement, you have to start with what you know—the Latino community. Though I believe in coalition building, you have to work with your group first, and then come together on common grounds with other groups. I think it was a grave mistake to merge, as quickly as we did, with sectors of the North American Left when we had not consolidated our own level of development and organization.

THE MOVEMENT'S LEGACY

VELÁZQUEZ: How would you sum up the experience of the Puerto Rican Left during this period?

TRUJILLO: I think that El Comité emerged in response to the racism and national oppression that our people faced, as well as to fill the vacuum left by the failure or inability of the North American Left to address our needs. We were an organization comprised of people who were genuinely dedicated and committed to our cause, participating in many key reform struggles in the areas of housing, education, health, and labor. In retrospect, we really had no clue of the "bigger picture," of political empowerment, and how to make long-lasting changes to benefit our communities. We shunned electoral politics as "reformist" and ultimately failed to develop the necessary leadership and community structures to safeguard our achievements. Unfortunately, many of our present elected leadership lack that history of struggle and commitment.

PABÓN: Coming from a broken home, one of the things that I'm grateful for is that the movement gave me structure and opportunity for personal development. One of the negative aspects was that we totally disassociated ourselves from making money or investing it. Furthermore, we left a serious leadership void in our community, allowing many opportunists to fill this vacuum. To a great degree we have to take responsibility for that because of our opposition to electoral politics. In 1984, when I was running Congressman José Serrano's campaign, I was criticized by a lot of people for being a reformist or getting involved with the system. Now, I think everyone on the Left has been involved, to some degree, in electoral politics. On the other hand, one of the things that we must do is develop economic power. It took me about six years of personal development and growth to not fear wanting to be a businessperson. I was totally convinced that capitalism was evil and that making money was bad, thereby failing to recognize that there are a lot of progressive businesspeople. I've been able to take things that I learned in the movement and apply them to make money and put back into the community. Nonetheless, the movement gave us a lot to be proud of. If you were to omit the 1960s and 1970s and look at our community today, I think we would be ten years behind. Even though our conditions continue to be deficient, relatively speaking, I think that the movement did a lot to improve those conditions.

TRUJILLO: In the late 1980s, some former members of El Comité helped to create, along with others, the necessary coalitions leading to the election of David Dinkins as mayor of New York City. We helped spearhead "Latinos for Dinkins," which brought together progressive Latinos, many of whom were former members of Puerto Rican and Dominican organizations on the Left, and other Latino leadership from community and labor struggles. This group played an important role in mobilizing the Latino vote for Dinkins's candidacy. We were able to bring the commitment, experience, and expertise of the progressive movement to support Dinkins's candidacy. Many of us have continued to stay active in the realm of electoral politics.

VELÁZQUEZ: You committed your lives for a number of decades to two main goals: the independence of Puerto Rico and the democratic-rights struggle of Puerto Ricans in the United States. What is your sense of the prospects for the independence of Puerto Rico?

FIGUEROA: I've always used my parents as a barometer to measure what's going on. I think that the tremendous fear about Puerto Rican independence is partly a result of right-wing Cuban influence in Puerto Rico. I also think that we have been a colony for so long that now we don't know how to make that transition to independence. There is just this tremendous dependency on the United States. I think that the movement in Puerto Rico must develop a public awareness of the viability of independence and a greater level of activism.

PABÓN: I am still a firm believer in Puerto Rico's right to self-determination and independence—now, more than ever. The business sector in Puerto Rico is beginning to recognize that opportunities exist for us to survive without the United States. I think there are people who believe that Puerto Rico can become a bridge between the United States and developing nations in Latin America that need advanced technology. Puerto Rico is one of the most technologically developed countries, not just in the Caribbean, but in the world. There is a sector in Puerto Rico that believes the mood within the United States is shifting in favor of Puerto Rico becoming an independent country. The United States is doing everything possible to move away from Puerto Rico becoming a tax burden. Section 936 was recently eliminated, and to our surprise, it was a sector of our own leadership in Puerto Rico that pushed for that Republican dream. I think there are other indicators that something is in the works, such as the State Department allowing people to relinquish their American citizenship, return to Puerto Rico, and travel without any problem. I will continue to support independence, but I don't think it is going to be achieved through armed struggle or any other struggle that we talked about earlier.

MARTELL: I think the majority of the people that were in our organization still believe in the independence of Puerto Rico and are willing to do anything to help achieve this goal. There is a lot of consciousness-raising about the status of Puerto Rico that must take place. We can only hope that independence will be achieved in our lifetime or in our children's lifetime. I strongly believe that Puerto Rico can and should be free.

VELÁZQUEZ: Julio, you were very active recently in promoting a visit by Fidel Castro to the Bronx. Can you tell us about this experience?

PABÓN: That's right. We are aligning ourselves with a lot of upstart companies that are very young and progressive minded. I was able to take a proposal for Castro's visit to members of the Puerto Rican Business Council, who are majority Republican and conservative. However, they recognized that in terms of future business development in Cuba, it was in their best interest to open channels for dialogue. To be honest with you, we did not think Fidel would accept the invitation. We just thought that it would be symbolic for Puerto Ricans from the South Bronx to invite Fidel for dinner after Mayor Guiliani's rejection, and Castro's subsequent visit to Harlem. I had to convince some people to undertake this risk, and I also had to be prepared to take the heat. I lost contracts immediately afterward, my radio program was cut, and some of my sponsors pulled out. So I took the heat, but I know the rewards will come back to us in many other ways because I think we are the future.

VELÁZQUEZ: What concerns do you have about the future directions of the Puerto Rican struggle in the United States?

TRUJILLO: I'm really concerned about the next five to ten years because we lack leadership and organization. We are in the midst of a reactionary swing toward the Right, a swing that is anti-immigrant, anti–people of color, anti-urban centers; and we are not prepared for it. We are also going to be faced with unprecedented cuts in social services and public assistance. Being that the Puerto Rican community is a poor community, there is a greater dependency on the social support they receive. I believe that major lobbying and organizing efforts must take place concerning these issues, especially as they affect children and families. Unfortunately, I find very few Latinos that are out there advocating around these issues.

PABÓN: One of my concerns is that almost half of the total population of Puerto Rico now resides in the United States. I think there is only one or two other countries that could say that half of their population resides outside their national territory. What I think is also significant is that there is a renaissance taking place among young Puerto Ricans and Latinos as a whole, in wanting to identify with their roots. In every state of the union, due to this rising nationalism, we are beginning to unite around being Puerto Rican and Latino. New York should have been the mecca, but it is not becoming the mecca of leadership. We are still looking to see from where the future leadership and political direction will arise in the Puerto Rican community.

Postcript: Speaking with Federíco Lora from Puerto Rico

VELÁZQUEZ: At one point, you and other members of El Comité made a decision to return to Puerto Rico. Can you tell me the reasons for this decision and its effect on the organization?

LORA: I think that the organization was prepared and dealt with the problem quite well. At our constituent assembly in 1975, we felt that it would have been irresponsible not to inform the membership that a number of us understood that our role in the revolutionary process was in Puerto Rico and not in the United States. Since it was a significant number of people, we decided not to leave all at once. As a matter of fact, I was the last one to leave. We felt that it was necessary to do a PSP in reverse, that is, to educate the Left in Puerto Rico about Puerto Ricans in the United States. It was like a reverse migration of leftists. Over the years, El Comité had organized activities in the United States with labor leaders from Puerto Rico and had developed close relationships with sectors of the labor movement that were independent of the PSP. So, our assumption was that we would return to Puerto Rico and join the labor movement, while spreading greater knowledge about the reality of Puerto Ricans in the United States among the Left on the island.

VELÁZQUEZ: You have been in Puerto Rico for more than twenty years. How would you assess the strengths and weaknesses of the independence movement?

LORA: I think we are at the weakest moment since the formation of the Movement for Puerto Rican Independence (MPI) in 1959. Electorally there is stagnation, many independence supporters not even voting for the Puerto Rican Independence Party (PIP). The organizations to the Left of the PSP drew very little support among the masses during the last two decades. The PSP, which transformed itself into the Nuevo Movimiento Independentista (New Movement for Independence), has not been able to develop a viable alternative for the Left. The clandestine Left suffered devastating blows as a result of a series of arrests and subsequent repressions. The inability to gain support among the masses has put the movement in a difficult position, at a time when the prostatehood movement, as evident by recent elections, continues to develop a fast rate of support. There is a possibility that we may face a situation where the majority of people support statehood for Puerto Rico, and we'll have to be prepared for that not very encouraging situation.

   On the other hand, the Left has continued to provide leadership for the labor movement, which has remained solidly organized among certain sectors, though not as a percentage of the working force. Though the labor movement lacks a clear political direction, it continues to serve as a bedrock for the working class. Undoubtedly, the dissolution of the PSP weakened the political direction of the labor movement.

   I think that we on the Left were sympathizers of Marxism but were not Marxists; we were sympathizers of socialism but were not socialists. Once the Berlin Wall came down, so did much of the Left because we were dependent, not so much upon our work among the masses but upon world socialism, which provided much of our posture and political discourse. In the process, we became so sectarian and committed major errors, making it difficult to promote unity among the Left today because of past events. For example, there is still animosity between the PIP and other sectors of the Left over issues that occurred fifteen to twenty years ago and that have no relevance to issues that demand our attention today. There are many of us whose existence was to criticize what the PSP was doing or not doing, rather than doing what needed to be done. In the process, we caused a lot of distrust among those forces committed to independence and socialism. Partly because we didn't have a clear political direction, we served to cancel each other's efforts rather than work toward a common cause.

VELÁZQUEZ: You made reference to the decline of world socialism and its effects on the independence movement in Puerto Rico. Does the independence movement have a realistic program for changing the complex reality of today's Puerto Rico?

LORA: The Marxist Left, as well as the non-Marxist Left, has never really developed this program. It's not sufficient to preach independence during the elections without providing a viable alternative that can convince the people of the benefits of independence. My concern during the recent elections was that we are losing our support among the youth and not speaking to how independence is viable to them and to their interests. The opposing statehood forces have taken our emblems, our culture, even our anticolonial discourse, and used them to garner support among young people. Furthermore, there are sectors of the independence movement that are placing a big gamble on the hopes that the U.S. Congress will reject statehood. Undoubtedly, the best way to get Congress to reject statehood is to let them know that there is a strong independence movement that will make statehood an untenable proposition.

CARMEN TERESA WHALEN

6   Bridging Homeland and Barrio Politics
The Young Lords in Philadelphia

ON AUGUST 10, 1970, the *Philadelphia Inquirer* announced
their arrival: "Young Lords Come to the City; Ask Food, Shun Strife,
Dope." The reporter described the event: "A Cuban flag waved lazily from
a street sign in a hot gentle breeze as various Lords barked messages of
socialism over a loud speaker and young brown faces smiled as they tasted
the pasteles." For some Philadelphians, these were ominous images—the
Cuban flag, the socialist message, and this: "Some compare the Young
Lords with the Black Panthers and place them in the danger area of the
new left." Yet, these images were tempered with that of smiling children
eating ethnic food and with the assurance that "the Lords denounce violence as a means of securing their objective—promoting socialism and
Puerto Rican consciousness." The Young Lords planned "to 'politicize'
any who will accept their gifts of food or clothing." The reporter captured
the Young Lords' emerging program that bridged independence for Puerto
Rico with local community issues. He also revealed the Lords' ambivalent
reception in Philadelphia. The festival took place "under the wary eye of
the police department" and only after "the determined young organizers
overcame obstacles in obtaining a permit." The permit "was finally issued
to a Catholic nun." [1]

In the early 1970s, Puerto Rican youth defined a politics that bridged
the homeland politics of Puerto Rico with the reality of their lives in *El
Barrio*. These youth, born or raised in Philadelphia, confronted the poverty and discrimination that affected their working-class neighborhoods.
In looking to Puerto Rico, they asserted an identity that was proudly
Puerto Rican and that both connected these youth to their island ancestry
and allied them with the struggles of people of color in the United States.
They linked the colonization of Puerto Rico to the poverty of Puerto Ricans in the United States and defined the issues as imperialism, capitalism,
and racism. They defined the solutions as independence for Puerto Rico
and socialism. This coupling of homeland and barrio politics were important in several regards. First, it strengthened their sense of Puerto Rican
identity and their political analysis of the larger forces affecting their lives.
Second, it created strategic challenges. Although activists saw the two as

intricately connected, they found it difficult to balance homeland and local concerns. Third, this bridging shaped the Young Lords' allies and adversaries. The Young Lords were supported by several clergy, who focused on their community work while dismissing their political ideology. The city administration and the police, however, perceived the Young Lords as "radicals" and responded harshly. Finally, the Lords' ideology and confrontational style challenged the established Puerto Rican leadership and forged a realignment of Puerto Rican politics in the city.[2]

Although their tenure as an organization was short-lived, the Young Lords had a lasting impact on Puerto Rican politics in Philadelphia, and their bridging of homeland and barrio politics is key to understanding that impact. This essay examines the emergence of the Young Lords in Philadelphia, their politics and ideology, and their impact on Puerto Rican politics in the city.

THE ORIGINS OF PUERTO RICAN ACTIVISM

Juan Ramos reminisces about the beginnings of the Young Lords in Philadelphia: "It came about in a period where we were looking for our identity in high school. . . . I'd say in the spring of 1970, there was a big transformation and almost a clear identity came into shape—who we are. And then good things started to happen that eventually helped the community."

In recalling the factors that sparked their political activism, Juan Ramos, Wilfredo Rojas, and Rafaela Colón emphasized their emerging sense of Puerto Rican identity and the poverty and racial discrimination that affected themselves, their families, and the entire Puerto Rican community.[3] They perceived the economic conditions and discrimination as unfair and intertwined these factors in their interviews. They also pointed to a sense of collective responsibility that was rooted in their families and their religion. Their politics began as personal experiences and broadened as they began to question the institutions that affected their daily lives and as they became aware of other social movements both within and beyond the city's limits. Their organizing efforts broadened as well. Ramos and Rojas organized high school clubs, then the Young Revolutionaries for Independence, and finally the Philadelphia branch of the Young Lords.

These future activists were struck by the fact that their parents worked hard and remained poor. Rojas recalls, "I became very political . . . because I saw that something was not right. . . . My father cut sugarcane, came from Yabucoa, Puerto Rico. Here he went through years of discrimination." The contrasts were stark and the place of Puerto Rican men in the community was clear: "The Embassador Hotel was the best, classiest Jewish restaurant in the city, right across the street from my house, and all the cooks were Puerto Ricans, in the back." Ramos' father worked at the hotel for years. Colón's father migrated as a seasonal agricultural laborer, and her mother cooked and washed for the farmworkers. When her family moved to the city, her father worked in a factory, and her mother stayed home to care for their nine children. Colón says, "I think [about] being in the middle and having to use hand-me-downs . . . the little ones got the milk, and I was one of the older ones so I didn't get any milk, because we were poor—dirt poor." She explains the impact: "One of the things that I always looked at, since I was little, [was that] we were poor. . . . I knew I wanted it to be different . . . I knew something was wrong with the picture because my father worked, we were church-going, God-loving people."

The three Puerto Rican youths' interactions with the larger society reinforced their sense that "something was wrong with the picture." Rojas felt that his neighborhood was deteriorating: "I saw my neighborhood go from being a Ukrainian, German, Irish, stable neighborhood to being a ghetto. Those things begin to weigh on you. Why is it that when we get here it becomes a ghetto, and all the other Europeans move away?" At school, Rojas and Ramos confronted racism when they were in seventh grade. Rojas explains, "A nun would call us spics [and say] 'you're ruining the neighborhood,' she would smack us around. . . . and this lady would say it, and we would have to take this from this nun." They led a student "walk-out" to the principal's office. For Rojas, confronting this racism was an affirmation of his Catholicism: "That was a stand that we took. So we were very Catholic." By the age of fourteen, Colón had to work: "Every weekend I was either baby sitting . . . for rich people's kids or cleaning some lady's house. . . . I ironed and washed for her every weekend, and she paid me five dollars. . . . I was exploited." In spite, or perhaps because, of this experience, Colón says she knew that she wanted to work and go to school. Describing her mother as "a wonderful human being," Colón says: "I knew that I loved my mom, and I knew that I wasn't going to be like that . . . the fact that, OK, [my father] worked and busted his chops. So did she at home, and she had no support. . . . she was dependent, and she was sheltered, you know, and she was tired." For Colón, unequal gender relations were another dimension of what was "wrong with the picture" and another dimension that sparked and informed her political activism.

The three youths' sense of injustice was combined with a sense of responsibility that was fostered by their families, the community, and by

Casa del Carmen, a Catholic social service agency. Ramos recalls, "We were part of that system over at Casa del Carmen, we participated in sports, we cleaned up, so we were into giving a little something back. We saw it in our parents." The nun in charge, he continued, "would require that our fathers and mothers would give something back, some volunteer time." Ramos concluded, "I think that we had an upbringing and an education that propelled us to take a leadership role. . . . Wilfredo came from that type of background and so did I, and our people were people that were already giving something back to the community." For Rojas, who had wanted to be a priest, "being involved in the Young Lords was an extension of us wanting to do things" for the community.

Aspira, a community organization dedicated to the education of Puerto Rican youth, fostered these activists' sense of identity and provided role models and organizing experience. Yet, the youths came into conflict with the agency's approach and its directors. Colón recalls, "Aspira was very conservative then . . . but you had progressive counselors who allowed students to meet and discuss things. . . . They had this young person . . . [who] would teach us about capitalism, about Puerto Rico, about the culture, the relation with the Americans, etc." Rojas found two role models at Aspira, Patricia DeCarlo, an organizer, and Baltazar Dávila, a counselor, "who was gay, and was not ashamed to be gay." He says, "Pat DeCarlo was probably one of the people that I really can credit with making me political. . . . Pat understood that we wanted change, and . . . that our mindset was different from the Aspira directors." Rojas and Ramos organized their high school Aspira clubs, which according to Rojas, "were about dancing, going out, and seeing the girls . . . and basically having a good time. We were teenagers." When Ramos wanted to name his club Ponce de León, DeCarlo suggested Pedro Albizu Campos instead. Ramos remembers the results, " . . . before you know it, all the Aspira clubs changed their names. . . . It was a great movement, and that kind of said to us this is what we were looking for—our own identity."

Ramos and Rojas, nonetheless, disagreed with Aspira's approach and left the agency. In 1969, the *Inquirer* ran the headline "Drive Started to Develop Puerto Rican Leaders." The article revealed a tension within Aspira over what constituted Puerto Rican leadership. Aspira's national director, Louis Nuñez, advocated an individualistic model of professionals who had escaped from "the slums." Instead of students feeling "despair over their dismal atmosphere," he wanted Puerto Rican professionals "to serve as role models so that the students will see there are some people making it." In contrast, the Pennsylvania director, Rafael Villafañe, stated, "Our goal is the development of community leadership. . . .

We want to guide students into higher education, but we also must make sure they commit themselves to returning to the community." His approach was collective, as students would "come back and help the Puerto Rican community solve its problems."[4] For Rojas, "Aspira was too conservative. . . . They didn't want to send [the youth] to college to come back and give something to the community but [wanted to] send them to college so they can make something and . . . get out of the ghetto. . . . That's not what I wanted to further my education for." Ramos criticized the clubs, saying, "Wilfredo and I belonged to our respective social clubs, and we were looking for more of an identity, who we are, and trying to do something." They tried combining clubs and bringing in "the guys that used to stay home and weren't streetwise" and "some of the junkies from our community." Rojas's club split, "I was young, vibrant, felt invincible, felt indestructible, and I really wanted to change the world. . . . Some of the people came with me, and we decided to form the Young Revolutionaries for Independence."

Their awareness of other social movements sharpened Rojas's and Colón's perceptions of the issues confronting Puerto Ricans in Philadelphia. Rojas traveled the country with the Office of Equal Opportunity evaluating youth programs. He says, "I was very inspired by what the African Americans were doing and the fact that they were forging ahead." While in California, his interests broadened: "I read about Ché Guevara. . . . I started to identify with Ché as a Puerto Rican, and what that did was instilled in me a willingness to fight for Puerto Ricans." He recalls, "I came back really hyped because I met a lot of interesting people." Colón worked with the United Farm Workers and the grape boycott in Washington state through the American Friends Service Committee. She explains, "I saw these people struggling, *y entendí que* . . . I'm more like you than the rest of these young white persons that pay to do volunteer work. . . . It was because I was poor, and the same problems that were existing there, existed in my home." She continues that she knew "[a]ll that was in Philadelphia but . . . I wasn't exposed to it in Philly. I would go to school, baby sit, come home. My parents weren't sophisticated."

For Colón, the trip fostered her political awareness and her independence, and the two were very connected. She had gone, in part, "to be independent because I was real protected, [it was] real strict at home." She says, "I had to sleep in the Chicago airport for three days, my first time out of my parents' home, and I had to become independent." When she returned home, she recalls, "I then realized the racism that I had gone through in high school." She attended a peace demonstration. "All of a sudden," she recounts, "we saw the American flag coming down and the Puerto Rican flag went up." She met the Young Revolutionaries for Independence and decided to participate.

Founded by Rojas and Ramos, the Young Revolutionaries for Independence paved the way for the emergence of the Young Lords in Philadelphia. They fashioned themselves after Cuban revolutionaries. Rojas recalls, "We walked around with battle fatigues and Fidel Castro buttons that we used to get from the Socialist Workers Party." Teachers objected to their attire and labeled them communists. Students protested, according to Rojas, "pushing for our student bill of rights, where they would allow us to wear buttons and bring in speakers that were controversial speakers. . . . One day we decided to go up—we wanted to meet the Young Lords." In New York the Young Lords explained their organization and their platform. The Young Revolutionaries came back to Philadelphia "on a real high about the Young Lords," switched from red to purple berets, communicated with the New York Lords via letters and telephone calls, and "decided that we wanted to affiliate with New York." Ramos became the captain of defense, Rojas became the lieutenant of education, and Colón became an active supporter. In August of 1970, the Young Lords' *Palante* newsletter announced the new branch: "The brothers and sisters in Philly realized months ago that a revolutionary party was needed to improve the conditions there and started acting to meet the needs of our people." By 1971, the national office deemed Philadelphia "one of our most effective branches."[5]

The Philadelphia Young Lords emerged as the response of Puerto Rican youth to their experiences in the city. They adopted the Young Lords' national platform because it addressed their concerns for the independence of Puerto Rico and the issues affecting their communities. Anticipating the accusation that the Philadelphia Lords were "just trying to copy the Lords in New York," Ramos wrote in *Palante* in 1970, "[t]hese people must realize that the oppression of Puerto Ricans in Philly is the same as the oppression in New York. The conditions in both of these colonies are the same. . . . The struggle is the same."[6] While they confronted similar issues, the branch retained its own distinctive stamp. Rojas characterizes the differences: "If we can put labels on the different chapters, you would say that Chicago were like street Lords because they came out of being a gang. New York were like college students who brought in some street people. . . . And in Philadelphia you had a bunch of Catholics—Catholics who got together, brought in some junkies along the way, and dragged in a few students." The Philadelphia Lords retained their ties to religious institutions—it was not surprising that the permit for their festival was issued to a Catholic nun. The early attentions of the police continued and the Lords confronted a repressive police force and city administration under the direction of Frank Rizzo. As Young Lords, Philadelphia's youth advocated independence for Puerto Rico and responded to the needs of their barrios.

INDEPENDENCE AND THE LOCAL COMMUNITY

The Young Lords bridged homeland politics—independence for Puerto Rico—with the issues affecting their working-class community. Their ideology linked the colonization of Puerto Rico with the oppression of Puerto Ricans in the continental United States, and their platform proclaimed, "We Want Self-Determination for Puerto Ricans, Liberation on the Island and Inside the United States."[7] Making these connections strengthened their sense of Puerto Rican identity and their political analysis of the larger forces affecting their lives. Strategically, however, this dual focus created tensions. Until 1971, their daily activities centered on their barrios, as they developed a grassroots approach to community services and demanded community control of existing social services. They promoted independence for Puerto Rico through political education. In 1971, they shifted their focus and established branches in Puerto Rico to promote independence. This shift raised tensions over strategies, priorities, and ideologies. This dual focus on homeland and barrio politics also created alliances and adversaries. Initially, clergy focused on the Young Lords' community work, dismissed their political ideology, and supported the group. The city administration and the police focused on the group's politics and opposed them. The Young Lords' confrontation with the city administration and the police forged a redefinition of Puerto Rican leadership that altered Puerto Rican politics in the city.

For the Young Lords, poverty became a crucial link connecting the homeland and the barrio. Rojas concedes, "We were trying to make the connection . . . a lot of people couldn't understand why we wanted Puerto Rico free when we didn't live in Puerto Rico, we lived in the United States." Ramos explains their response: "We were saying that independence was something that was good for the people, basically because . . . the status quo did not help the poor—did not help the poor in Puerto Rico, didn't help the poor in our community in Philadelphia." Similarly, Colón says, "We did talk about the independence of Puerto Rico, as being a colonized people, and so they saw the connection of being colonized in the United States—poor education, poor housing . . . and feeling the poverty that existed here and the reasons." Ramos describes their efforts:

". . . we had to do something about the poor in our community because we couldn't do anything about the poverty in Puerto Rico with the exception of saying that independence was an alternative for the poor and that we believed in it. . . . So we had to help the poor, and in doing so we put out our message of being in support of Puerto Rican independence." Because they "wanted to help our people," they focused on improving conditions in the barrios and relied on political education to promote independence.

This approach defined what it meant to be a Young Lord. Rojas insisted in a 1971 interview, "Brothers and sisters who prefer to sit around the office and not talk to the people, you know, get out there and help them where they're at in the streets . . . those brothers and sisters can't be Lords." The Young Lords ran two free breakfast programs, one at the Lighthouse for more than one hundred children and the other at St. Edward's Parochial School for more than eighty children. They had a continuous clothing drive. They arranged testing for tuberculosis and volunteered at Casa del Carmen's health clinic, as Young Lord Freddy Rosario asserted, "making it possible for our people to get what is rightfully theirs." They approached gangs through political education. Rojas recounts, "Our whole thing was political—we're brothers, we're Puerto Ricans, we're blacks—we shouldn't fight each other. The enemy is the system. We have to beat the system. These young guys weren't trying to hear that. They were about turf." [8]

For the Young Lords, social services became a vehicle for criticizing the "system" and for political education. Their platform called for "a Socialist Society . . . where the needs of the people come first" and for "control of our communities by our people and programs to guarantee that all institutions serve the needs of our people." Juan González, a Young Lord in New York City and political activist later in Philadelphia, describes the difference from preexisting social service agencies: "While those agencies sought assistance from the government for Puerto Ricans, the Young Lords *demanded* that assistance as a right." In doing so, they "broke with the more mainstream, less confrontational approach of earlier agencies." The Young Lords, according to one reporter, served breakfast with "a lesson about why the kids' parents can't afford the food boys and girls need in order to do well in school." The reporter continued, "The Lords believe this is the patent difference between their breakfast program and a bread line. The latter is a handout, the former is a vehicle for instilling political consciousness." [9]

The Young Lords provided services and demanded that existing agencies meet the needs of the community. Colón recalls, "Even in the Lighthouse, we faced the impact of the Young Lords." The Lighthouse provided social services and recreational programs. In 1971, the sports department elected three Whites, three Blacks, and no Puerto Ricans to its board. The *Inquirer* reported the response, "Five community leaders—all women— said yesterday they have enlisted the help of six Puerto Rican organizations in their fight for a voice 'in all phases' of the Kensington agency." Colón, a member of the Lighthouse board, asserted, "We're going to demand that the board enforce its directive that two Puerto Ricans be elected to the sports department." Ervia González, a community health worker, agreed, "We want representation at the Lighthouse, and we're going to see we get it." Ultimately, Colón resigned from the board but not before the Young Lords and the Black Panthers breakfast program had come to the Lighthouse.[10]

The Young Lords' approach to drugs illustrates their combining of political education, direct service, and demands on existing agencies. In October of 1970, they called a press conference to "declare war on dope pushers." Rosario explained their approach to drug dealers saying, "They do not understand that they are killing their brothers when they sell them dope. We will educate them." He was convinced that "[t]he big racketeers will keep sending their poison until all of our people are politicized and know that capitalism wants us to be junkies and mindless pawns." Challenging the association of Puerto Ricans with drugs, he continued, "Drugs were here long before any Puerto Ricans thought to live in this racist society." Ramos agreed, "The root of the problem isn't the small user in the ghetto. This heroin is coming from outside the ghetto, from white people. Why don't the police track that down?" While mounting this critique of "the system," the Lords rehabilitated addicts, some of whom became Young Lords. At the same time, Rosario charged, "The Anglos' government and hospital system does not see fit to support us in this struggle," and so the Lords vowed to be "a constant reminder to city hall that we Puerto Ricans are through begging!"[11]

By focusing on their community programs and dismissing their "radical" ideology, some clergy supported the Young Lords. Father Thomas P. Craven, director of Casa del Carmen, explained, "It is difficult to organize the whole community behind issues, and the Lords are trying to change that. . . . I think, recognizing their problematic ideology, that the Young Lords have a right to exist. . . . What I see in them are noble intentions." Similarly, Rev. Gerald Kelleher said, "I think they're great kids. I don't, of course, buy all their politics. But from a priest's point of view, its a lot easier to work with people who have ideals. What I like about them is that they're doing something; they're concerned." For Father Craven, there was also a personal dimension: "Just because young people whom I've known for a long time—and whose families I know—have been radicalized by a different ideology, I see no reason to stop being their friend or to break off communications with them." Casa del Carmen provided office space, while the Lords ran a clothing drive, provided interpreters for the health clinic, and joined in a procession against drugs. Rojas acknowledged, "We were very Catholic. So the thing was that there are these Catholic kids that grew up in the neighborhood, that were always tied to the Casa del Carmen, that are now asking us to take them in and get them an office for them to promote the breakfast program. Because we weren't really talking about revolution, we were talking about a free breakfast program." [12]

Despite their "religious fervor" and ties to particular clergy, the Lords were critical of religious institutions. Ramos criticized churches as "the biggest money-making organizations in the world," yet he explained the ongoing relationship: "I believe in what Christ built the church on, serving the people. . . . Individual priests have gone back to basic beliefs of serving people. That's why we haven't attacked the church." The Lords' mottos included "If Christ were alive today, he'd be a Young Lord" and "Every Christian who is not a revolutionary lives in mortal sin." Rojas recalls, "A lot of us studied the theology of liberation. We all went to church. It was a weird contradiction in that some of our other chapters were atheists, and we were very Catholic. . . . We really believed that Catholicism was about changing peoples' lives and fighting for the downtrodden." Yet, on November 5, 1970, the Lords took over the Kingsway Lutheran Church. Ramos reported in *Palante*, "It is becoming apparent that the church, like all other institutions in our community, is not there to serve the people and that the only way they can be made to serve the people is if the people start doing it themselves." They provided a legal information center, an interpreting program, and drug rehabilitation. Rojas reminisced, "What was interesting about this church takeover was that we had the consent of the priest." Like other clergy, Rev. Roger Zeppernick explained, "The Lords are involved in human liberation, and I see more Christian upbringing in them than I do Marxist-Leninist orientation." [13]

The Young Lords were also supported by their families. Colón believed, "So there were some people, some older people, that were supportive, who came around and understood. And mostly, it was family related, like my parents. They were supportive of me, you know, because I was a good kid. . . . They just figured 'she's very patriotic.'" Rojas felt he had several "families:" "When I needed a good Puerto Rican meal, I'd go back home, but my family was the Young Lords because we always hung out together. And we always respected each others families, so that I can go to Juan's

parents' house and they would feed me, or he could come to my house."
The support, for Rojas, rested on family ties and the issues: "Our parents
would support us because we were their kids, so whenever an event
happened they would come to meetings, they would come to protests.
They would be there because they were supporting their kids, and a lot of
the things we were saying was true—we were talking about an end to
discrimination."

While their community activities generated support from some, the
Young Lords' politics triggered the wrath of the city administration and
the police. Although police brutality affected the entire Puerto Rican community, the Young Lords' politics heightened the conflict. In August of
1970, the Young Lords were, as one article proclaimed, "Blamed by Police
for Unrest." The *Inquirer*, however, explained the cause of the "unrest" at
a local bar: "Police report the disturbance was touched off last Friday
night when white patrons . . . beat and ejected a Puerto Rican patron."
Racial incidents had occurred at the bar, as the White Roofers' Union
confronted racial change in the neighborhood where they held their union
meetings. The Puerto Rican community responded, "The Lords were in it,
the Bonets and their tape recorder were in it, nearly everyone living within
a three-block radius of the intersection was in it." What the newspapers
called a "weekend disturbance," Rojas recalled as "a rising up of the
people." When it was over, six people were injured including four police,
eight were arrested, and the bar was firebombed. The roofers moved their
union meetings to another part of the city, and the bar's owner hired a
Puerto Rican staff.[14]

The Young Lords were "blamed" for spreading "rumors" of police attacking Puerto Ricans during the "disturbance." Police captain Malcolm
Kachigian stated, "They [the reports] are nothing I can base a criminal
charge on . . . but I believe them because this is an anti-establishment
group." Ramos instead blamed "police harassment" and city councilman
Harry P. Jannotti and said, "He's trying to destroy the Young Lords
because we believe in self-determination for Puerto Ricans." Jannotti
responded, "He's lying, as far as I am concerned they were causing
trouble. . . . We haven't harassed them at all. . . . But we are going to go
after them." Maria Lina Bonet, president of the Puerto Rican Fraternity,
concluded, "There's no question that on Friday there was a lot of police
abuse and brutality." Residents charged that police had broken into several homes, used police dogs, and beaten a pregnant woman and several
youth. Bonet held a meeting in her home to address police brutality and
invited Captain Kachigian and Councilman Jannotti. Her solution was to
request a meeting with Police Commissioner Frank Rizzo and to circulate
a petition to have the bar closed. Although she agreed with Ramos about

the police brutality, Bonet advocated a conciliatory approach to resolving issues in the Puerto Rican community and objected to the Young Lords' politics. She denied the Young Lords permission to meet in the fraternity's building, exclaiming, " . . . those posters! I don't mind the Puerto Rican patriots, but *no one's* putting Castro and Guevara on *those* walls. . . . If the Lords ever really hurt this community, that's the day I'll go after them." [15]

For the Young Lords, this confrontation with the police was not an isolated incident. The national branch concluded, "[T]hey have undergone practically the heaviest attacks of any branch; there have been numerous beatings, false arrests, and several firebombs which have wrecked their offices." [16] Ramos reminisces, "We were scorned by the police. We were talking about community control of the police. We were objecting and protesting the gang warfare going on and the flow of drugs into the community. I mean we were addressing these issues when we were eighteen years old and as a consequence, we had our office bombed." When their office at Casa del Carmen was bombed, Rojas says, "A lot of us had to get out of a little window. And when we came out the police were laughing at us." Rojas was also arrested: "They arrested me, took me to the station, beat the shit out of me and never booked me—they let me go. So I was one of the people that testified at the hearing that I was falsely arrested." For Ramos, the most painful attack was that on his family. He explains, "They did a number on my parents, and on our families that was unbelievable. . . . My father had a nervous breakdown. . . . They just pressured him that they were going to kill me, they were going to kill Wilfredo." These memories led Ramos to conclude, "We, at a very early age, had to face a lot of reprisal, a lot of repression . . . in retrospect, we were way too young to take on all those responsibilities, but we had no choice."

In addition to spawning allies and adversaries, their dual focus on homeland and barrio politics also created strategic challenges. In 1971, the Young Lords opened branches in Puerto Rico "to unite our people on the island and the mainland with a common goal: liberation." This decision increased repression against the Young Lords, created tensions with independence movements in Puerto Rico, and fostered divisions within the Young Lords. Ramos, who became a member of the national staff in New York City in 1971, went to Puerto Rico in 1972. He says, "That's where the infiltration really became very, very concentrated and the split of the Young Lords eventually came. . . . It was the politics of Puerto Rico versus the politics of the big cities. . . . I took the side that said that we needed not to be in Puerto Rico. *La experiencia de nosotros*—our experience—was strictly a mainland experience, with Puerto Rican hearts and culture and history, *pero* outside of that, the way people moved and did things in Puerto Rico was different." Ramos believed that it was infiltration "that above all destroyed the Young Lords."[17]

In Puerto Rico, Ramos discovered, "We were definitely out of tune with the movement in Puerto Rico. . . . They were nice on a personal note . . . but in the movement, they didn't like us. The Young Lords were *muy atrevido*." Colón, who went to Puerto Rico through the American Friends Service Committee, was told "that when the Young Lords got there they were really heavily criticized." She described the independence movement in Puerto Rico as "very academic" and "very scientific" in contrast to the Young Lords and concluded in hindsight, "So the fact is going to Puerto Rico, talking all that stuff, is like Columbus discovering something that's been discovered." It was a jarring experience, as Ramos revealed, "People in Puerto Rico were very disrespectful to us. . . . It was shocking, yeah, because we thought that they would be proud of us because we were Puerto Ricans of the States that wanted very much to be a part of them."

Their experiences in Puerto Rico sparked a debate over whether to stress independence or Puerto Ricans in the United States. On June 6, 1972, *Palante* announced that Juan Ramos and others had "resigned their positions and have abandoned the Party's work in Puerto Rico." The Central Committee criticized the "faction" for advocating a focus on the struggles of workers in the United States: "The group says that U.S. imperialism is only a particular of the United States, that the general struggle in the U.S. is between the U.S. ruling class and the multi-national U.S. proletariat; that because of this, Puerto Rican workers in the U.S. should devote most of their time to struggles in the U.S. and not the national liberation of Puerto Rico." The Central Committee, in contrast, argued, "[T]he major conflict in the world today is of oppressed nations against the imperialists. The primary duty of workers in the U.S., as one of the major imperialists powers, is to support national liberation struggles against U.S. imperialism." Ramos was labeled a "right opportunist" and was "purged from the Party." The bridging of independence and local issues, which had given the Young Lords their impetus, became divisive.[18]

Although the linking of homeland and barrio politics was strategically difficult and contributed to the splintering of the Young Lords, this bridging had a lasting impact on Puerto Rican politics in Philadelphia. The Young Lords redefined Puerto Rican identity and Puerto Rican leadership. Ramos concludes, "We definitely made a big difference on the identity of Puerto Ricans in this city. I think that was probably our biggest contribution." For Colón, the impact was personal and political: "The Young Lords awakened and discovered that pride to what my culture was. I don't think I would ever have had that going to a Catholic school that was all White and living with parents that were not very sophisticated and who were just surviving." She also credited the Lords, as having "impacted even the leadership now to have that vision that you have to know who you are and where you came from to know where you are going." In June of 1971, the *Evening Bulletin* captured the shift: "A new wave of ethnic pride has been sweeping the Puerto Rican community here recently." Businessman Domingo Martinez was quoted as saying, "Before, people who made it didn't want to be called Puerto Rican, now they are proud of it. One of the things we won't sell at any price is our culture." And it was a short step from "ethnic pride" to demanding "respect." Rojas remarks, "A lot of folks thought that . . . we were crazy for challenging the system, but it wasn't a question of being crazy. It was a question of gaining respect." For one reporter, it was the presence of the Young Lords that "indicates in no uncertain terms that Puerto Ricans do not intend to be victimized for long." [19]

The Young Lords' ideology, while based on ethnic pride, was not narrowly Nationalist and instead opened the doors to discussions of gender and the possibility of political coalitions. Unlike other Nationalist movements of the era, including those in Puerto Rico, the Young Lords did not base their definition of Puerto Rican culture on a reassertion of traditional gender roles for women. They changed their platform from a demand that "*machismo* must be revolutionary" to "We want equality for women. Down with *machismo* and male chauvinism." There were limitations; according to Colón, "I think there was a lot of sexism within the Lords. . . . I couldn't really be in the leadership or a full-fledged member of the Lords . . . because I lived at home. I wasn't going to sleep with every brother, you know, call it 'sister love.'" Clearly, the platform was only a beginning. In addition, the Lords' demand for "Power to all oppressed people!" was inclusive. Their platform called for "self-determination for all Latinos" and for the "liberation of all Third World people," including "Black people, Indians, and Asians." In defining themselves as "revolutionary nationalists" who "oppose racism," the Lords asserted, "Millions of poor white people are rising up to demand freedom and we support them." In Philadelphia, they worked closely with the Black Panthers, especially on breakfast programs and against police brutality. They supported Mexican farm workers and the grape boycott and joined others in opposing the war in Vietnam. [20]

THE PUERTO RICAN COMMUNITY AND ITS POLITICS

The Young Lords' bridging of homeland and barrio politics challenged the established Puerto Rican leadership and fostered a realignment of Puerto Rican politics in the city. They redefined Puerto Rican identity and Puerto

Rican leadership, questioned the social service approach of Puerto Rican agencies, and planted the seeds for progressive coalitions. The Young Lords' confrontation with the police and the city administration drove a wedge into the long-standing affiliation of Puerto Rican leaders and Frank Rizzo, who was the city's police commissioner and later was mayor from 1972 to 1980. This wedge became a fissure and Puerto Rican politics shifted. Although the Young Lords Party dissolved, former Lords remained active in city politics, forming a Philadelphia chapter of the Puerto Rican Socialist Party and then the Puerto Rican Alliance. The concern with homeland politics that the Young Lords inserted into Puerto Rican politics remained, as former Lords and subsequent political organizations continued to grapple with the balancing of homeland and barrio issues.

While the Young Lords confronted police brutality, the established Puerto Rican leadership supported Frank Rizzo. The Concilio de Organizaciones Hispanas (Council of Hispanic Organizations) was the main Puerto Rican organization of the era. Concilio, which started as an umbrella organization for social and fraternal groups, became a social service agency funded through the Philadelphia Antipoverty Action Commission. In 1971, Ramón Velázquez became the president of Concilio. Rojas credited Velázquez for helping to bring Aspira to Philadelphia, and Rojas's club had met in his restaurant, but he explains, "Our break with him [Velázquez] was the fact that he supported Rizzo, and Frank Rizzo at that time used to beat folk with his billy stick, and he had a bad reputation in terms of dealing with the Black and Puerto Rican community, of police brutality." In a 1971 newspaper article, Velázquez explained his support for the Democratic candidate: "Rizzo is a second-generation Italian who worked his way up the hard way, he understands us." City councilman Angel Ortíz, in a recent interview, described Concilio's as "a hat-in-hand-type of leadership." He continued, "They would come into the mayor's office and deal with Frank Rizzo, they were very much pro–Frank Rizzo at that point. They were beholden, he gave them a few antipoverty grants and so on." Concilio was also criticized for factionalism and inadequate services. Even though she worked in social services, Colón retorted in 1971, "Work with Concilio—I wouldn't even bother. They're too established. They don't meet human needs." [21]

Rizzo became the issue that realigned Puerto Rican politics in the city. During his second term, in 1978 Rizzo tried to alter the city's charter so that he could run for a third term. Puerto Rican activists met the challenge. Former Young Lords had started the nucleus of the Puerto Rican Socialist Party in Philadelphia. Colón had held a meeting in her home attended by Ramos, Rojas, and others. They studied the party and decided to form a chapter. Ortíz, who came to Philadelphia from New York City in 1976 as an attorney with Community Legal Services, had been active with the PSP in New York City. In Philadelphia, the PSP began meeting out of his home and the offices of Community Legal Services. Initially, the PSP focused on independence but increasingly incorporated local issues. The PSP organized marches and demonstrations, started housing groups that opposed gentrification, and confronted police brutality and the police killing of Puerto Rican youth José Reyes.

Rizzo's referendum created a political crisis and a political opportunity. Ortíz recalls, "We were a small group of PSP individuals, and we had a lot of people that were affiliated and associated, but we needed to broaden it in terms of the struggles that we were having here. . . . A lot of Puerto Ricans are very much afraid of the word socialist. . . . So we were looking for a mechanism to do that. Frank Rizzo offered us another." Puerto Ricans forged a coalition, Puerto Ricans United Against Rizzo, worked with White liberals and African Americans, and mounted a voter registration campaign. Although a majority of Puerto Ricans had voted for Rizzo in both of his mayoral campaigns, more than 60 percent voted against him in the referendum. Ortíz explains the result saying, "The leadership broke down very clearly, the traditional leadership went with the mayor, and those of us that were Left, we went to make an alliance with the African American community." Rizzo was defeated.[22]

After the defeat of Rizzo, Puerto Ricans held a convention and formed the Puerto Rican Alliance. Again, the former Young Lords and PSP activists were involved, and Juan Ramos became the first president. Like the Young Lords, the alliance addressed homeland and local issues. Ortíz recalls, "It was known as a socialist, proindependence, political grouping. . . . It was a very clear, clear Left organization that was dealing with the democratic rights of Puerto Ricans, here in the island, here in the city." The alliance mobilized the community around housing, workers' rights, education, and police brutality, while protesting the U.S. Navy's presence on Vieques. They continued the confrontational style of politics, organizing squatters to occupy vacant housing owned by Housing and Urban Development, holding a spontaneous sit-in at Independence Hall and raising the Puerto Rican flag, and taking over Jimmy Carter's campaign headquarters in 1980. Unlike the Young Lords, the alliance entered electoral politics and succeeded. In 1984, Angel Ortíz became city councilman and in 1985 Ralph Acosta became state representative and was succeeded by Benjamín Ramos. Ortíz explains the importance of the Alliance: "We didn't control jobs, we didn't have community organizations, we didn't hire anybody, but at that point we had the people's support—we were the leadership that the community out there trusted, because we were fighting the establishment." In contrast, Ortíz stressed, "None of the other folks who came through traditional leadership have ever been able to get elected." Puerto Rican politics in the city had been realigned.

This shift in Puerto Rican leadership in Philadelphia was the result of Puerto Rican activism from the early 1970s to the 1980s. Despite the changing organizations, many of the activists, the issues, and the confrontational style of politics continued. Writing in the late 1980s, González observes, "[W]e have two of the most committed and politically progressive elected officials of any Puerto Rican *colonia* in the nation. . . . This is no accident. It is a direct result of the struggles of the past fifteen years." Similarly, Colón concludes, "The Young Lords were critical to any progressive movement in Philadelphia." Concerns with homeland and barrio issues were not mutually exclusive—attention to homeland issues did not prevent activism on issues affecting Puerto Ricans' daily lives in the United States. The dichotomy in immigration studies that marks the beginning of "adaptation" with a shift in focus from the homeland to the United States does not hold in the case of Puerto Ricans in Philadelphia. Instead, the focus on homeland and barrio issues reflected and contributed to the emergence of transnational communities and an emphasis on biculturalism in the U.S. This dual focus mirrored the ongoing colonial ties between Puerto Rico and the United States. This was a second generation that came of age during an era of political activism and ethnic revitalization. This was a community shaped, not only by its "minority" status, but also as activist and journalist Pablo "Yoruba" Guzmán noted by "our overwhelming preponderance in the working class."[23] These factors had a lasting impact on Puerto Rican politics.

7   *"¡Rifle, Cañón, y Escopeta!"*

A Chronicle of the Puerto Rican Student Union

"¡RIFLE, CAÑÓN, y Escopeta: nuestro pueblo se respeta; y si no . . . maceta!" ("Rifle, cannon, and shotgun: our people will be respected; or else . . . we'll crush you!").[1] That was the rallying cry of a new student group that appeared on the scene of Puerto Rican politics in the fall of 1969.[2] A slogan that embodied the militant—and militaristic—spirit of the times, the Puerto Rican Student Union (PRSU) was to voice this chant many times in marches, pickets, and other actions, on campus and off, until the group faded from the scene in the mid-1970s. Known in Spanish as La Unión Estudiantil Boricua, PRSU boasted solid roots and a fervent following among the first generation of *Boricua* youth to enter higher education en masse. Throughout its years of activity, the PRSU was to receive notice on several occasions in the New York and Puerto Rican press.[3] But it was among the student population that the group won respect and admiration for its uncompromising commitment to promoting self-esteem and opening the doors of opportunity for Puerto Ricans.

This chapter is an effort to document the story of the union. As both a member and observer of the organization, I will highlight the achievements and key failings of this episode in our community's experience. I will also consider its place in the history of Puerto Rican radicalism, and reflect briefly on the current experience of *Boricua* and other Latino students.

ANTECEDENTS

The precise origins of the first attempts to organize Puerto Rican university students within the United States is a matter of speculation. A new wave of *Boricua* enrollment was triggered by such 1960s programs as the City University of New York's (CUNY) SEEK (Search for Education, Elevation, and Knowledge) and College Discovery initiatives, along with the State University of New York's (SUNY) Educational Opportunity Program (EOP) and the several private colleges' efforts. These, in turn, were the products of a decades-long struggle throughout the country to make higher education accessible to low-income and minority youth. The onset of the CUNY open admissions policy and its predecessor experiments further increased the presence of Puerto Rican students on campuses. In 1969 there were some 5,500 Puerto Rican undergraduates in CUNY; five years later the number had tripled, amounting to 7.4 percent of all undergraduates.[4] College newspapers of that period confirm the degree to which students organized into clearly discernable *Boricua* groups in the 1960s and 1970s. Many culturally oriented and language-based groups and clubs existed in the mid 1960s. For example, I had the choice of joining an Aspira or a Spanish club when I entered CUNY in 1966.

The late sixties and early seventies represent a watershed in *Boricua* student organization and activism. The New York area in the 1960s witnessed a remarkable surge in university student activism that was part of a general upheaval in U.S. society. At the center was the protest against the war in Vietnam. A number of predominantly White student organizations flourished, including the Students for a Democratic Society (SDS) and the student arm of the Communist Party U.S.A., the W. E. B. DuBois Clubs. Outside of New York such groups as Student Non-violent Coordinating Committee (SNCC) organized Black students with leaders such as Stokely Carmichael, and the Mexican American Youth Organization (MAYO) organized Chicanos under the leadership of Willie Velásquez and José Angel Gutiérrez.[5]

Puerto Rican university students, such as Juan González who was active with Columbia's SDS, were known to be among the ranks of non-*Boricua* student groups. Arguably, most Puerto Ricans were cognizant of, and in many cases participating in, the events overtaking the universities. At Brooklyn College minority students were the subject of progressive students' efforts, when early in 1968, a group of radical White students demanded that the college open the doors to one thousand Black and Puerto Rican students. As a result, an educational opportunity program was approved by the faculty council of the college, leading to the admission of 192 minority students for the fall 1968 semester.[6]

Boricua student activity took a variety of forms prior to the emergence of a more politicized expression. In 1966, a group calling itself the Puerto Rican Student Movement (PRSM) was organized by Aspira club members and graduates who had enrolled in the CUNY system. PRSM was known to be politically traditional and advocated involvement in the electoral process, a view that was out of step with the growing militancy of the time. According to PRSU documents, PRSM dissolved because of an inability to attract a committed membership.

Another formation that existed during the pre-PRSU era was a group known as Puerto Ricans for Educational Progress (PREP). Comprising a network of students from well-known private colleges, its primary purpose was to recruit high school graduates to such schools as Princeton, Yale, and Manhattanville. However it too dissolved after a brief history. There were also a number of fledgling student groups in SUNY during the mid-1960s. But it was not until the spring of 1969 that the student movement ignited as years of exclusion came to a boiling point.

THE STRUGGLE FOR OPEN ADMISSIONS

One issue that served to merge the efforts of Puerto Rican students and their African American counterparts was the fight for open admissions in CUNY. This struggle also served to catapult the organization of Latino and Black students to a new stage and increase the number of participants. At City College, then considered the flagship of the City University, members of Puerto Ricans in Student Activities (PRISA) emerged as key players. Working together with Black students of the Onyx Society, they spearheaded the fight. PRISA student leaders included Henry Arce, Tom Soto, and Eduardo "Pancho" Cruz who together with many other militants, such as Guillermo "Willie" Morales (who subsequently would be associated with the clandestine Fuerzas Armadas de Liberación Nacional—FALN), forged a unity with Black students.[7] At other CUNY campuses similar coalitions fought for open admissions and raised other demands, such as the creation of programs for Black and Puerto Rican studies. Across such campuses as City College, Bronx Community, and Brooklyn and Queens Colleges students coordinated actions.[8]

It is difficult to identify which of the CUNY campus groups contributed most to the implementation of the university's open admissions policy. At City College, after initial skirmishes between minority-group students and Whites, a major strike and campus shut-down occurred in the spring semester of 1969.[9] Community groups from *El Barrio*, Harlem, and the Lower East Side and students from other colleges converged on the campus expressing moral support and—just as important—bringing food, clothing, and other resources. Among those present was Luis Fuentes, the first Puerto Rican superintendent of a school district in New York City. Among the initial actions taken by the students was to raise the Puerto Rican flag on a location normally reserved for the U.S. flag and to rename campus buildings in honor of Black and Latino leaders. One building was renamed Pedro Albizu Campos, another after Ernesto "Ché" Guevara.

The strike was coordinated by a commission of Black and Puerto Rican students who called themselves the "Committee of Ten." The committee was selected from the larger Black and Puerto Rican Student Community

(BPRSC). Its membership consisted of students who also integrated the Onyx Society and PRISA. Near the end of the semester, on May 5, 1969, students withdrew from the occupied buildings after the CUNY administration secured a court injunction.[10]

The struggle at Brooklyn College was equally militant. On April 18, 1969, students from the Black League of Afro-American Collegians (BLAC) and the Puerto Rican Alliance (PRA) united and invited radical Whites to meet with them. That day 150 Blacks and Puerto Ricans, together with 40 white students, conducted a sit-in at the college president's office. They demanded open admissions, the establishment of Black and Puerto Rican studies institutes, an increase in the hiring of minority faculty, and curricula adjustments to reflect the changing student demographics.[11]

Similar mobilizations occurred at Lehman, Queens, Bronx Community, and other colleges. And while CUNY was clearly the center of student militance, there were growing signs of a spreading nationalism and political activism beyond the CUNY system in public and private colleges within New York City and beyond. Paralleling the emergence of radical activity in the community, the Puerto Rican student movement was beginning to be a force. This was the context within which PRSU—the first significant intercampus organization—was to enter the drama of Puerto Rican history.

EMERGENCE OF A NEW FORCE

The impetus for an intercampus federation arose from political events on the island. In September of 1969, student representatives from various campuses met at Lehman College to consider ways in which to assist the University of Puerto Rico (UPR) students who were members of the Federación Universitaria Pro Independencia (FUPI). The New York students had banded together to raise funds for the UPR students who had been imprisoned for allegedly torching the Reserve Officers Training Corps (ROTC) headquarters at the Río Piedras campus.

Stateside students sent telegrams to the island government protesting the treatment of the students and distributed flyers and held press conferences to let the New York Puerto Rican community know of the situation. This would be only the beginning of a long series of confrontations between students and the Puerto Rican government. The crisis escalated on March 4, 1970, when police killed a student, Antonia Martínez, at an antiwar demonstration at the University of Puerto Rico.[12] A year later another riot ensued leaving 31 shooting victims and 169 people arrested.[13]

At first, it might appear ironic that island-based events would be the catalyst for uniting students into a citywide coalition. But such was the explosive nature and appeal of nationalism that it motivated New York City youth—many of whom had never lived in Puerto Rico, some of whom could not speak Spanish—to bond together in political activism.

My introduction to what became the Puerto Rican Student Union came in the fall semester of 1969 when I, along with a group of fellow students from CCNY, attended an information meeting held at St. Mark's Church in lower Manhattan. The meeting was called by the eventual leaders of PRSU, and the principal spokesman at the event was William Nieves, who was a CCNY student returning to the school from a year's absence. The gathering was impressive and emotional. The church was crowded with university students and community activists. The meeting left a lasting impression while raising our hopes that it would lead to unified student efforts.

The activities to support the UPR students helped forge a unity among the *Boricuas* in New York and at the same time sparked the formation of a permanent intercampus student organization. A document prepared by the union emphasized the need for student unity: "Since meeting to deal with the case of our brothers in Puerto Rico, we realized we had an urgent need to have a Puerto Rican student movement that not only is ready to mobilize when problems like these arise, but is a movement in constant action and that functions at the level of all universities in [the New York] metropolitan area." [14]

The intercampus meetings continued in the fall and were followed by a two-day convention that was held in *El Barrio*. This historic gathering was attended by more than one hundred students, representing fifteen colleges and universities. The second day of meetings was interrupted when the students decided to lend their support to *nuestros hermanos los* Young Lords who were in the midst of their takeover of a church and its transformation into the First People's Church. This encounter began a lasting relationship between the union and the Lords—one that would have major consequences for the student group.

From the convention came the formal establishment of the Unión Estudiantil Boricua. The founding members identified the following goals:

• To organize university-level students into a unified movement that would serve to defend their rights as Puerto Ricans.
• To jointly struggle with members of the Puerto Rican community in combating all the problems that were identified or confronted.
• To support the struggles of other minority-group members in the United States.
• To support the struggles of the Third World.

• And most of all, to achieve the independence and liberation of Puerto Rico.[15]

Once organized, the union was confronted with the usual growing pains of a new organization. Several members grew impatient and left to join the Young Lords, who already had an established reputation and great prestige among activists. However, a large working nucleus remained with the PRSU, and a storefront was rented at 440 East 138th Street in the Bronx, which served as a community agency and central headquarters. It was from this location that the PRSU involved itself in many community projects. From 138th Street, *la Unión* also coordinated numerous actions on college campuses. In contrast to radical student groups in the New Left, this was to be a student organization with roots in the community.

Among the first campaigns was our intervention in an upstate conference that was to recognize the achievements of the proannexation government of Luis A. Ferré. The conference was titled "Puerto Rico: A Story of Success." PRSU joined the Movimiento Pro Independencia (MPI) and Alianza Puertorriqueña (the Brooklyn College Puerto Rican student group), traveling three hundred miles to disrupt the proposed proceedings at Oswego, New York. Union members, along with others, seized the microphone, tore down pictures of Ferré, and replaced them with those of Pedro Albizu Campos.[16]

Thereafter, the union members joined demonstrations to support the Puerto Rican students at Buffalo State University who protested discriminatory practices against minority workers. At Bronx Community College, the union got involved in defending the first bilingual college program that offered courses in Spanish to primarily Puerto Rican students. The demonstrations led to a takeover of both the college and the Board of Higher Education, which ultimately saved the program.

The PRSU served as a key link between the student movement in Puerto Rico and the United States. Delegations were often sent to express solidarity with students on the island. One represented the PRSU in an anti-draft demonstration called "La Marcha de La Juventud Puertorriqueña en Contra del Servicio Militar Obligatorio de los EE.UU" ("The March of Puerto Rican Youth Against the U.S. Military Draft"). Together with the MPI, the Union participated in *la Brigada Manuel Ramos,* a volunteer brigade that organized opposition to strip-mining practices of U.S. copper companies in rural mountain areas on the island. Later, when the island of Culebra became a focal point for protests against bombing exercises by the U.S. Navy, PRSU was there too.

Puerto Rico was not the only destination point for political travels and solidarity-building. Delegations were dispatched to meet with other student movements throughout the United States, most notably to California at the invitation of the Chicano Moratorium, a Mexican-American student organization. Even international trips were undertaken: PRSU representatives also went to China, Cuba, and Vietnam.

On the community level, the union joined the Health Revolutionary Unity Movement (HRUM) and the Young Lords to help expose Lincoln Hospital's poor service delivery to community residents. In one incident involving the hospital, seven members of the union were brutally beaten and arrested by police.[17]

In the spring of 1970 the PRSU reclaimed an empty lot that was situated directly across the street from their headquarters. The lot was renamed "Plaza Borinqueña" and was used as a playground and center for cultural and political activities. To enhance *la plaza,* union members painted on the walls of surrounding buildings a huge Puerto Rican flag along with revolutionary slogans and images of *Boricua* patriots. Plaza Borinqueña became the sight of a memorable concert offered by the great Cuban band leader Machito. Excerpts from that concert were subsequently featured in an award-winning documentary on Machito that was prepared by Puerto Rican filmaker Carlos Ortíz. The images of *la plaza* captured on film offer the only opportunity to appreciate the massive task completed by union members. Years later, Plaza Borinqueña was replaced by a low-rise housing development.

Not long after moving into the 138th Street site, union members began to organize local residents. In the building housing the union, where a three month-old girl had lost her life because of insufficient heating, a successful rent strike was organized. Involvement in the community arena entailed the organization of "community cadre," noncollege youth who lived in the surrounding area. Because members of this group included several drug users, the union even started a detoxification effort.

In the late spring of 1970, the union again embarked on a joint effort— this time with the Young Lords and MPI to mobilize a large contingent of protestors at the Puerto Rican Day Parade. This was the beginning of annual demonstrations at the parade that brought together organizations with such agencies as Aspira. Hundreds, in some years thousands, of independence supporters would march up 5th Avenue to the cheers—and jeers—of the multitude. So many of us marched up the avenue, mostly in military garb, that we resembled a liberation army of Puerto Rican male and female youth. If only for the duration of the parade, one would sense the approaching independence of Puerto Rico!

In its first year, La Unión Estudiantil Boricua became immersed in a dizzying array of campaigns, projects, and controversies. The organization remained faithful to its originally stated objectives, which in retrospect were incredibly ambitious. Remember what we had pledged to do: combat all the problems faced by the Puerto Rican community, support other people's struggles, including those throughout the Third World, and achieve Puerto Rico's liberation. Quite a tall order for a group of inexperienced, full-time university students. But those were the times.

Driving the political commitment was a strong nationalist fervor that incorporated Marxian tenets. This is apparent in one of the union's principal programmatic documents: "The Puerto Rican Student Union has developed into a political movement that struggles to break the chains of this capitalist society. We understand that the real problems that our community faces are the fruit of the class struggle that we live. That Puerto Rico not only has to be free but also freed from the class oppressor, and that it is our responsibility to leave the universities and go out to our communities and awaken them from the sleep to which they have been subjected for so long." [18]

The PRSU was successful in bringing together a cadre of student leaders who represented the best available at the time. They came from several campuses in various New York City communities and had family roots in different parts of Puerto Rico. One was impressed by the inclusive nature of the leadership, comprised of both females and males, and by the manner in which consensus was reached on a variety of issues.

EXPANSION

Within a year of its founding, PRSU had attained rapid and successful development. It was solidifying ties to other organizations, particularly, MPI, the Young Lords, and El Comité. Their influence was such that when Juan Mári Brás, Secretary General of the MPI, conducted a political tour in the United States during the fall of 1970, he made sure to secure a meeting with the union leadership in their Bronx locale.[19]

The second year brought even greater visibility and expanding membership for the Union. A regular publication, *Maceta*, was issued, targeting educational and community topics. And a creatively designed button gave the student activists an effective symbol with which to recruit members and develop membership loyalty. The logo featured two clinched fists. One emerging from a depiction of Puerto Rico, the other from mainland tenements. On the base was the Puerto Rican flag with the bold letters "PRSU" superimposed. On the upper margin the words "Unión Estudiantil Boricua," in bold black lettering, appeared on a white field. Initially, the button was worn on a maroon beret that helped distinguish the union from the Young Lords, who wore lilac berets. The organization even had an official presence in the hallowed halls of the American Museum of Natural History. When, in 1970, the museum sponsored a multiscreen projection exhibition on the Puerto Rican community, a profile of PRSU was included. We had come a long way in so short a time.

Organizing activity proceeded without a slowdown. Efforts included a citywide conference designed to launch a phase of mass organizing; and mass organizing efforts were made as well on various college campuses where Puerto Rican students were still fighting for access, services, and *real* curricular reform.

THE COLUMBIA UNIVERSITY CONFERENCE

Having recruited student leadership from various colleges and established a community office and programs, the students began planning for a major student conference at Columbia University. The meeting was to take place on September 22 and 23, 1970, to coincide with the 102d anniversary of El Grito de Lares, the first armed uprising for the national independence of Puerto Rico. The planners included members of the Young Lords Party, marking the first genuine collaboration between the PRSU and YLP.[20] At the time the union had also begun a close working relationship with one of the most important community-based organizations, the United Bronx Parents (UBP). Headed by Dr. Evelina Antonetty, a longtime activist, the UBP provided support to the PRSU in its many activities, including the preparations for conference. The event, drawing more than a thousand Puerto Rican and Latino student activists from throughout the country, was an enormous success.

Participants from scores of colleges attended workshops on topics ranging from the politics of Puerto Rico to academic concerns. Issues addressed included opposition to the military draft, support for political prisoners (such as the five Nationalists and Carlos Feliciano), and such day-to-day matters as the financial struggle of students in higher education. The convention proposed the organization of "Liberate Puerto Rico Now Committees," whose goal was to build a solidarity network across U.S. college campuses. Plans were also approved to organize a massive march to the United Nations during the following month. It was agreed that on October 30—the anniversary of the 1950 Nationalist uprising in Jayuya, Puerto Rico—Puerto Ricans and their many supporters from other movements would assemble in front of the international center to denounce colonialism in Puerto Rico.

There was ample media coverage. But when Geraldo Rivera, who was just beginning his career in the news business, tried to film one of the sessions, a group of students forcefully repelled him. The youths viewed

Rivera as a representative of the mainstream media. Ardently antiestab-
lishment, they objected to being used in one of his broadcasts. Ironically
Rivera had previously defended both PRSU members and Young Lords
when he was a practicing lawyer.

The focus of the proceedings was the colonial status of Puerto Rico,
with an additional theme being the ways in which imperial domination
affects Puerto Ricans in the United States. Attendees were reminded that
they were responsible for carrying on the legacy of struggle, which dated
back more than a hundred years to El Grito de Lares. This crucial historical event announced the "birth of a new people," which has sustained a
continuous liberation movement—first against Spanish, then U.S. domination. Attendees were also reminded that colonialism's reach is extensive
because the educational system that misinforms and conditions our youth
in Puerto Rico, operates in our communities here as well. By implication,
Puerto Ricans in the United States and Puerto Rico are united in their
common oppression.

Plenary speakers included PRSU leaders Hildamar Ortíz and Diego
Pabón, Flavia Rivera of FUPI, and Young Lord leader Denise Oliver. Dozens of workshop sessions were programmed to cover the full gamut of
topics that interested students.

The conference concluded on its second day with students marching
from Morningside Heights, the home of Columbia University, to Plaza
Borinqueña in the South Bronx. There the various groups comprising the
Puerto Rican movement gathered to remember El Grito de Lares in what
was to become an annual event.

A month later, the conference saw a dramatic conclusion of its efforts,
as ten thousand people filed down the avenues of Manhattan from *El
Barrio* to United Nations Plaza. This was the historic march to the UN
spearheaded by the Young Lords and supported by the entire ideological
spectrum of the Puerto Rican movement: nationalists, socialists, communists, social democrats. More important, the mobilization attracted thousands of individuals, unattached to any organization or unconscious of
any ideology—regular folks who responded to the call for justice in
Puerto Rico. It was a high point for the movement, and PRSU was a crucial ingredient in its success.

The Columbia conclave was followed by concerted union efforts to
achieve its stated goals. Union members also strove to integrate themselves
into several local struggles, most prominently in the housing area. Students joined community activists on Manhattan's West Side where apartments were being left empty and rundown by landlords and developers in
the hopes of getting tax breaks to "upgrade" them and receive higher
rents. Meanwhile hundreds of families were living in the area in decrepit

housing conditions and saw an opportunity to improve their living standards in the vacant apartments. By moving in and setting up living quarters, they in effect appropriated housing that was being hoarded by absentee landlords. Thus was born the "squatters' movement." Along with other groups, PRSU helped to form "urban brigades" made up of students from various campuses. They centered their work on helping to rebuild housing on West 112th Street.[21]

THE ORGANIZATION OF CHAPTERS

PRSU leaders realized that the organization could not live by jumping from one citywide campaign or mobilization to another. For the organization to thrive, it meant building strong local chapters on individual campuses. Having gained prestige from its role in successfully pulling off the Columbia Conference and having been assigned the task of developing "Liberate Puerto Rico Now Committees," it embarked on a new round of organizing efforts at specific colleges. With ambitions of being a national federation, the union had to deal with the reality that many colleges already had Puerto Rican and Latino organizations. Such groups as PRISA (CCNY), LUCHA (Lehman College, New York University, and Manhattan College), PRIDE (Baruch), the Puerto Rican Alliance (Brooklyn College), and Unión Estudiantil Pedro Albizu Campos (Queens College) were well developed. Other collectives were operating at such places as Fordham, SUNY and in locations outside of New York. Many of these groups had been involved in supporting the open admissions struggle at CUNY, the Young Lords' church takeover, and political prisoner work; most had members who were affiliated with existing independence and Left organizations.

Nevertheless PRSU pressed on with the task of expanding its influence on a range of campuses, either by starting new chapters or working with existing forces. A discussion of a sample of experiences will give the reader a sense of the challenges faced by the young organization. As in 1969, CCNY—the alma mater of several Nobel Prize–winning writers and scientists—was a center of student activism. City College was to become a key base of operations for PRSU. Other standout campuses were Columbia, New York City Community College, Bronx Community College, and Lehman College.[22]

City College

At CCNY a group of PRSU activists approached the remaining members of PRISA to suggest the establishment of a union chapter. As a protagonist in the open admissions struggle of 1969–70, PRISA enjoyed a positive reputation, and loyal members quickly rebuffed the idea of a PRSU chapter in their place. But the number of CCNY students who had participated in the development of PRSU was substantial, and they outnumbered the remaining PRISA members. Whether through graduation, academic or financial difficulties, or political burnout after the 1969 CCNY strike, a number of key Puerto Rican activists did not return. A weakened PRISA hastened the development of PRSU in the fall of 1970.

The success of the Columbia University conference helped enormously to reenergize student activism at CCNY. A student there at the time, I sensed revived militancy and enthusiasm from a new crop of students fresh from high school and transfers from the community college system.

CCNY's chapter was founded and headed by William (Willie) Nieves. He had assumed a leadership role in the work of the headquarters in the Bronx and was to become a long-term member of the leadership Central Committee, which served to steer the activities of the entire union. Willie's energy and militancy was contagious. A role model to many, he had qualities and experiences that fostered respect and a strong following. Willie was well liked and although very serious and committed, he was sensitive and had a sense of humor. Almost everyone regarded him as a true friend. He was known for his nationalist feelings and although he had spent time in Cuba, he was not a Marxist zealot. Willie also had been a Peace Corps volunteer in Colombia. After visiting Cuba as a guest of the Cuban government, he was subjected to considerable harassment by the FBI. On one occasion FBI agents broke into his apartment only to find PRSU activist Carmelo Casanova. Carmelo was interrogated, and the apartment was searched. Geraldo Rivera, then a lawyer, provided Willie with legal assistance.

The PRSU chapter at CCNY was arguably the largest and most militant. However, this did not prevent members from graduating; most would eventually go on to become teachers, professors, lawyers, doctors, and other professionals. The chapter played an instrumental role in the development and growth of CCNY's Department of Puerto Rican Studies. CCNY was not the first CUNY unit to secure a Department of Puerto Rican Studies, although it had witnessed the most militant demonstrations of the 1960s for the establishment of such a department. Lehman, Brooklyn, Hunter, and Livingston College in New Jersey had actually created departments earlier.

This was because the 1969 strike resulted in a compromise solution. Instead of agreeing to a Puerto Rican only studies program, the administration set up a Department of Urban and Ethnic Studies (UES). Not until a new round of demonstrations, led by the union in 1970, did the college concede to the creation of a Puerto Rican studies department, which was established in 1971.

Before the demonstrations the members met regularly to discuss various issues and to solidify the work of its membership. In addition, regular political education (PE) classes were held in the assigned PRSU office at the aging Finley Student Center. Participants attended with their copies of Chairman Mao's little red book, *Quotations from Chairman Mao Tse Tung*. Members would address ideas contained in the book and complete the sessions with a criticism and self-criticism period. Criticism gave members the opportunity to focus on methods of work and to correct erroneous practices.

Discussions on the need for a Department of Puerto Rican Studies dominated the proceedings. Dissatisfaction with the existing UES department and agitation on the part of Prof. Federico Aquino helped prompt the union to take action. Aquino coordinated the UES Puerto Rican course work. The union was particularly displeased with a course on the history of Puerto Rico offered by the Department of History and the manner in which Puerto Rican themes were treated by members of the Romance Languages faculty.

The course on Puerto Rico's history attracted the attention of the many activists who had enrolled. An Argentine taught the course in the fall of 1970. The course included an impressive selection of texts, but the instructor avoided reference to the independence or Nationalist movements. This infuriated those of us enrolled and eventually led to a confrontation. After a loud shouting match at one session, the faculty member cursed at the students and, fearing reprisals, ran out of the room, with students chasing after him up the stairs. He finished the semester but was then replaced by a Cuban professor the following semester.

In February 1971 Union members finalized plans that called for a takeover of the Department of Romance Languages. On the February 18 at 6:00 A.M., a group of PRSU activists moved onto the campus and prepared for a possible confrontation with CCNY security guards or students. Previous confrontations between student groups had been serious. Back in the fall of 1970, non-Latino students challenged the union when it demonstrated or disrupted business-as-usual. This time the strategy worked as the university was obviously not interested in another violent confrontation and the media coverage that would attend a long drawn-out struggle with students.[23]

When the CCNY administration finally authorized the creation of the Department of Puerto Rican Studies, union members became full participants in setting up the new operation. With the assistance of students and Dr. Frank Bonilla, who was brought in from Stanford University to help design the progam, Professor Aquino developed the proposal that subsequently became the basis for establishing the first Puerto Rican studies department at CCNY. Subsequently Bonilla donated his consultant fee to the PRSU, which later used the funds to pay for a trip to Culebra where members joined the FUPI's campaign to end naval bombing of the island municipality. A related accomplishment of PRSU's activism was CCNY's agreement to open an office of Puerto Rican development, designed to increase Puerto Rican/Latino student enrollment and to bolster retention rates. PRSU helped select the first director of the department, Yolanda Sánchez, who was already a well-known and respected community leader.

Other Chapters and Campuses

At Columbia University chapter members engaged in the work associated with the first planned student conference. They also worked toward the development of course work in Puerto Rican studies. The contributions of the Columbia chapter were important to the overall success of the union. When the union closed its storefronts in the Bronx and Brooklyn, this chapter secured office space near their campus. They provided valuable leadership. In time, Emilio González, a chapter leader, would become a member of the union's Central Committee.

When assuming a position on the Central Committee, Emilio González provided the union with a strong Marxist orientation. Emilio was well read and was somewhat older than other members. He was devoted to the work of the union and was willing to share valuable insights. He was a fledgling leader of the Puerto Rican community who joined the staff of El Centro de Estudios Puertorriqueños when it was founded. In fact, a number of the Columbia chapter members were appointed to El Centro's staff as research associates and in other capacities.

At New York City Community College (now New York Technical College) chapter members also played an important role in the development of a Puerto Rican and Latin American studies program. Early in its history the program was directed by Prof. John Vásquez. When he vacated the position, the union members helped ensure the appointment of Monte Rivera, who had been active with CCNY chapter. Under Rivera's leadership the program ballooned into one that offered almost thirty sections of courses in Puerto Rican studies in the spring of 1973.

The fourth chapter was organized at Bronx Community College (BCC). BCC had extensive experience with *Boricua* student activism, especially at its original location at 184th Street and Creston Avenue. Bronx Community served as an important recruiting ground for students who would later transfer to senior colleges, such as Lehman and CCNY, where they continued the work of PRSU. BCC members were active in fund-raising activities, which helped to finance the PRSU office when it was moved from Columbia to 117th Street in Manhattan, opposite the Young Lords' national headquarters.

At Brooklyn College the Puerto Rican Alliance (PRA) had always been the leading *Boricua* group and had spearheaded efforts to create the Puerto Rican studies program. PRSU activists worked to establish a chapter, which coexisted with PRA for a while. Eventually, however, PRSU ceased to operate there as it was unable to displace the leadership role of the veteran group. Included among PRSU's accomplishments was the opening of a PRSU community office on the south side (*Los Sures*) of Brooklyn.

In addition to the chapters, a number of members, including those in leadership, came from campuses where chapters did not exist. At Hunter College, PRSU members worked within the existing Puerto Ricans United (PRU). Hunter College was also the last home of the union before it dissolved in 1976–77. At the time the union coordinated its efforts from the office assigned to PRU in the high school at 695 Park Avenue. From Hunter College the union prepared many of its last public documents. These included communiqués in support of the Department of Puerto Rican Studies faculty of Brooklyn College who resisted the forced appointment of a departmental chair in 1976.

Lehman College members were instrumental in the founding of the union and establishing its first community office. Several were part of the union's original Central Committee. They had experience in the struggle to strengthen Puerto Rican studies on that campus. In fact, the first Department of Puerto Rican Studies was started at Lehman, and the distinguished writer Dr. María Teresa Babín served as chair. At one point, the department was the largest of its kind as it also housed a bilingual college program that had been transferred from Bronx Community College. Despite the department's size and relative success, the union members were never fully satisfied with Dr. Babín's leadership. She was perceived as an "absentee chair" who spent too much time away from the college.

In addition to the chapters of the union and the smaller cells that worked in several colleges, the union had members who worked alone or in small groups on campuses, such as Baruch College, Manhattan Community College, Princeton, and Yale. Several union activists were high-school students who formed PRSU nuclei at Monroe High School and the High School for Art and Design.

THE DECLINE OF PRSU

After the peak period of late 1969 through mid-1972, the activity of the PRSU dropped considerably. The decline may have been inevitable, given the rapid takeoff and overexpansion. Certainly it had to do with the student base, a population characterized by instability and constant turn-over. Many members either graduated or left college or simply cut back on their activism to avoid becoming another dropout statistic. In any case, the organization found it difficult to sustain the momentum and enthusiasm of the early phase. PRSU continued to function in one form or another until 1976, but it never recaptured the initial burst of enthusiasm that made it one of the key components of the movement.

Another reason for its decline appears to have been the organization's close—some say too close—relationship with the Young Lords. During 1972 the union, despite substantial opposition from the membership, chose to merge with the Young Lords. By early 1971, the need to affiliate with a political party was promoted by many members of the union. PRSU considered possible affiliation with the Young Lords, the Puerto Rican Socialist Party (PSP, formerly MPI) and the Puerto Rican Independence Party (PIP). In the spring of 1971 at a general membership meeting held at St. Mark's Church, a commission made up of Willie Nieves, Emilio González, and myself was delegated to discuss a possible merger with one of the three parties. Emilio and Willie were members of the PRSU Central Committee, and I was part of a secondary leadership called the Field Committee. The three of us went to Puerto Rico where we met with the leaders of the PSP, YLP, and PIP.

In Río Piedras we met with Rubén Berríos and then PIP–vice president Carlos Gallisá. PIP was headquartered on Muñoz Rivera Avenue, where their offices had been subjected to drive-by shootings by right-wing groups favoring statehood for Puerto Rico. Consequently, a huge steel-plate wall was installed to protect those inside. I remember being gathered directly behind the protective wall discussing politics with the PIP leaders.

That same week we met with Juan Mari Brás and other members of the PSP leadership. PSP headquarters were situated in an old building over-looking the Plaza de Recreo (Public Plaza) in the heart of Río Piedras. Their offices were also vulnerable to armed attacks by bands of annexationists, provocateurs, or agents of secret police squads.

We met with the Young Lords in an apartment where Gloria and Juan González lived in the El Caño section of Santurce. In addition to Juan and Gloria, other YLP leaders were in Puerto Rico, having initiated the "*Ofensiva Rompecadena,*" a strategy to shift the YLP's focus from the United States to Puerto Rico.

Our assigned task was to bring back the results of our discussions to the membership and the Central Committee. It was apparent to me that Emilio González favored a merger with the Lords and that Willie Nieves seemed to lean toward the PSP. In the process each advocated for their point of view, making every effort to convince other members to support their choice. Indeed discussions about the merger went on for months. Ultimately the decision was made to merge with the YLP.

In the fall of 1971, José Cruz and I signed a lease to rent a loft in *El Barrio* that would serve as the PRSU headquarters, shifting from our original South Bronx office. The new locale was located on 117th directly opposite the YLP national headquarters. This may have played a role in the eventual PRSU-YLP merger that was agreed upon in early 1972.

Although there was substantial PRSU opposition to the merger, union members were nevertheless willing to make it succeed once the decision was made. Opposition to the merger came from those who believed that PRSU was significantly different from YLP; and union members did not always agree with actions taken by the Lords, such as the attempt to take the lead of the 1971 Puerto Rican Day Parade, which resulted in a serious clash with police. The merger was executed, but it was fragile.

In May of 1972 a crucial incident brought underlying conflicts to a head when Diego Pabón, a PRSU founder and former chairperson, was accused by the Lords of being an undercover agent. Union members were split; many were convinced of the allegations, but a sizeable number were not persuaded by the serious charges. Intense discussions ensued between the two factions. In the end the majority was sympathetic to the Lords. A large contingent who supported Pabón left the union and subsequently issued a paper explaining their action. Those who left saw the accusation as one of a series of unsubstantiated charges and feared that the real reason for Diego's ouster was based on differences over political strategy. For many this marked the beginning of the decline of PRSU.

The Pabón affair was not the first time that accusations had been made against a PRSU member. Previously Carlos Aponte, who was instrumental in forming the PRSU and later left to join the Lords, was accused of being a police infiltrator. Most PRSU members refused to accept this claim against Aponte, who was very much respected by his former colleagues. The actions against Pabón in 1972 seemed like a repeat of the controversy surrounding Aponte.

While in Puerto Rico, union members witnessed another sad incident. The YLP had been organizing opposition to a government plan to demolish housing in a poor neighborhood of "El Caño."[24] The objective was to "upgrade" the area with middle income development. With this and other campaigns the New York radicals had gained admiration and respect from local residents, who saw them as standing up for the disenfranchised. New recruits were joining the organization. One member in particular stood out because of his dedication and hard work. He had assumed responsibility for driving us to various locations where we sold

Palante, the newspaper of the YLP and which was a principal source of income as well as an organizing medium. Unfortunately he must have rubbed someone the wrong way because he was accused by the YLP of being a police "plant" and was expelled from the group. For most of us the accusation in El Caño was not believable, and it too left a lasting negative impression.

After the merger, PRSU's independent status began to erode as it became subsumed by the YLP. In July 1972 the YLP changed its name to the Puerto Rican Revolutionary Workers Organization (PRRWO), shifting to a more ideological Marxist-Leninist stance in the process. PRSU was then referred to as a "mass organization" of the PRRWO.[25] In practice PRSU leaders played a limited role within the transformed organization. As political debates intensified and rifts developed, many of the remaining members of the PRSU separated from the former Lords. According to Pablo Guzmán, the conflicts in PRRWO came as a result of a "movement path of dogmatic correctness" that put them on the "verge of acting like . . . a gang—of beating down anyone in our ranks who disagreed." [26]

From 1972 to 1976, PRSU was able to carry on its work on several campuses, as related above, but it eventually lost steam. The union never regained the citywide momentum and force of the early years.

Conclusion

Looking back at the history of PRSU invites some reflections on the state of student activity today. Indeed Latino student activism has surged in recent years. In 1993 and 1994 students at Cornell University staged demonstrations to protest the destruction of artwork that was on exhibit as part of a Latino heritage program. (The university had recognized Hispanic heritage with a display of paintings by Latino artists. The paintings were mutilated allegedly by White students.) At about the same time thousands of Hispanic students were involved as CUNY students took to the streets to protest proposed budget cuts that would affect all of CUNY. And in 1996, Latinos at Columbia joined Black and Asian students in demonstrations, which called for ethnic studies programs. In these, and other struggles, Puerto Rican youth have been prominent players.

Today, however, *Boricua* students are less likely than in years past to band together as a group independent of other Latinos. Even more significant they may have a less pronounced affinity to Puerto Rico and the issues that affect the island. Familiarity with Puerto Rican history and the liberation movement is less extensive than it was in PRSU days. These days Hispanic student groups tend to be comprised of representatives from various Latin countries, and this condition tends to diffuse or subordinate the question of Puerto Rican independence when it comes to setting the agenda of these groups.

More than before, *Boricua* students are born and raised in the United States and do not experience the nationalistic fervor that existed previously. Also, nonuniversity groups, such as the Puerto Rican Socialist Party, the Young Lords, and El Comité that were visible forces for independence then, no longer exist.

This is not to say that Puerto Rican nationalism does not exist among youth. It does. At the 1995 Muévete (Move Forward) conference, which was attended by a thousand Puerto Rican and Latino high-school students, chants of "*Viva Puerto Rico Libre*" were heard at a general assembly.

To take as only one example of the changed context, one has simply to look at SUNY–Old Westbury, arguably the cradle of the New York–based Young Lords Party.[27] In the current environment, it would be difficult to organize and sustain a specifically Puerto Rican group. The Latino population is very mixed with large Dominican and Salvadoran enrollments. There are students from every Latin American nation and Spain. The Puerto Rican enrollment is substantial, probably constituting a plurality but not the majority. The varied enrollment gives rise to a mixed social, cultural, and political agenda. This should not be perceived as a negative comment—it is simply the reality. In this context, political concerns arising from El Salvador, the Dominican Republic, or Puerto Rico are treated with parity in student discussions. It would be unrealistic to impose an agenda on a mixed group of students that focuses on the aspirations of one larger sector.

Alianza Latina, the Latino student group at SUNY–Old Westbury, is led by students who come from various countries. This subordinates the Puerto Rican. In addition many Puerto Rican students are born and raised in the United States and speak Spanish hesitantly. These two factors may contribute to a cultural rift, and as a result some Puerto Ricans do not involve themselves with Latino concerns. While Old Westbury may or may not be typical of other colleges with significant Puerto Rican and Latino populations, I would not be surprised to find that there exists elsewhere the same obstacles to forming *Boricua*-specific groups.

Some say that the gains of the past placate present-day students. For example today we find Latino faculty and administrators where there were none previously. Many programs in Puerto Rican studies have since evolved into Latino Studies, creating the impression that Latino, as well as Puerto Rican, concerns are being addressed by the academy. Also the increased enrollment of Latino and other students of color reduces the demand for access to higher education, which was the center of the struggle for open admissions some three decades ago.

In the 1960s the obstacles confronting university students of color were glaring. The issues they raised were clear cut: increased enrollment and financial support; a relevant curriculum; ethnic studies; and the need for faculty and administrators of color. The PRSU was a product of those times and served an important role. Today also Puerto Rican and Latino students coalesce with other groups to solve the pressing issues of the moment. Today's activists may not realize that they are following in the footsteps of those predecessors who helped create the very programs and institutions that are now under attack.

The union was a sociopolitical phenomenon, a movement, and a powerful force that was borne out of a constellation of factors that converged in the 1960s and 1970s. The militant Puerto Rican nationalism of that period helped solidify PRSU and other groups. That same nationalism and militancy fed the movements that led to the attainment of many of the institutions we fight to defend today. Only history will tell if a revived nationalism and cultural identity can once again ignite student activism.

JAN SUSLER

8   Unreconstructed Revolutionaries
*Today's Puerto Rican Political
Prisoners/Prisoners of War*

IN THE 1960s and 1970s Chicago's Puerto Rican community, like
so many other communities, was in rebellion, resisting the violence and
brutality of colonialism, racism, exploitation. Its young leaders sought not
only to battle against and expose these evils, but to help the community
take control of its institutions, to instill a sense of hope.

One place where the hopes for revitalization converged was Tuley High
School, which had a predominantly Puerto Rican enrollment. But with
an administration and teaching corps comprised mostly of non–Puerto
Ricans, there was a serious lack of communication and understanding between staff and students. Unhappy with the lack of attention and respect
accorded their children, parents and educators initiated a campaign for
reform.

> Tuley High School soon became the most visible scar on a community al-
> ready pocked by poverty and the problems facing Puerto Ricans. And as the
> community filled with the faces of its people, it also filled with accusations.
> Latin fingers, guided by years of pain and disappointment surrounding ev-
> ery facet of their lives in Chicago, pointed in frustration at the school. The
> school would finally unite the people. The school would give them a chance
> to win.
>   "This is a community of hopeless people," said the Rev. Joseph Fitz-
> harris, assistant pastor of St. Aloysius Catholic Church, the local parish.
> "Anyone who can afford to leave here, leaves. So the Tuley thing . . . well, it
> gave the people a chance to win something. And winning means hope." [1]

Among the leaders of the battle at Tuley were Carmen Valentín, a bilingual teacher and counselor at the school, and Oscar López Rivera, a Vietnam veteran and community organizer. With a broad community-wide
coalition, they sought to inform the school administration and the general
public of the needs of the school's predominantly Puerto Rican student
body. The coalition insisted on the replacement of Tuley's principal, who
they felt was insensitive and ineffective. Their initial efforts fell on deaf
ears, and their demands were rejected outright: "[Oscar] López emerged
from the meeting and told the picket line that 'no one in this city is aware

144

of the problems in our community and no one cares. But we will go back to our community now and find a way to make them aware of what is going on."[2]

Who could have guessed that these young, talented community leaders, frustrated and impatient with the violence of colonialism and poverty, would eventually go on to form part of the Fuerzas Armadas de Liberación Nacional (FALN; Armed Forces of National Liberation). Between 1974 and 1980, the FALN operated as an underground organization and claimed responsibility for armed actions against military, government, and economic sites mainly in Chicago and New York. Ultimately they were captured in a series of arrests during the early 1980s; they denounced U.S. imperialism and never wavered in their defense of the right to armed struggle. The judge who sentenced them to jail described them as "unreconstructed revolutionaries."[3]

Proclamations from the underground boldly challenged what they perceived to be the centers of U.S. power: the military and the multinational corporations that dominated life in Puerto Rico and, ultimately, Puerto Rican communities everywhere.

> Our attack against the property of the U.S. military [in 1978] represents in part a reprisal against the U.S. Navy. The Navy's continuous bombardment of the Island of Vieques represents an act of aggression and violates the security, wishes and interest of the people of Vieques and all of Puerto Rico. . . .

> We have chosen these multinational corporations as our targets [in 1977] because they best characterize and represent Yanki imperialism. These corporations are using underhanded and barbaric tactics to explore our natural resources, especially land and offshore petroleum and minerals such as copper and nickel. . . .

> In bombing the New York Hilton [in 1976], we strike against one of the corporations most responsible for *yanqui* colonialism in our country.[4]

Yet, a look at the historical moment might provide clues to the emergence of the FALN. It was a time when anticolonial, national liberation movements had prevailed throughout the world, and anti-imperialist movements were at war. Says Carmen Valentín's then-*compañero*:

> In Africa, Cuba, Ireland, Germany, China, in Puerto Rico itself, there were lots of forces that influenced her. Carmen was influenced by Cuba— she's a student of Cuban history. There were people all over the world in armed struggle—Italians, Germans, Irish, Nicaraguans, Salvadorans, North Americans in the U.S., etc. There was a worldwide movement that influenced thinking in Chicago. All of Central America was at civil war. . . . If it could happen in Central America, why not in Puerto Rico? They truly believed

that at that stage in history what they were doing would bring about a different result.[5]

Oscar López Rivera attributes his involvement, in part, to his experience in the U.S. Army in Vietnam, where, he says, "what I found was a humble and valiant people who resisted and rejected the only true invading force—the U.S. military and its allies. That spirit of resistance and struggle impressed me a lot. I also found that the Vietnamese people looked a lot like [those in] the Puerto Rico of my childhood, and that there was much in common between their reality and ours."[6]

He was an admirer of the clandestine movement in Puerto Rico: "The emergence of the Comandos Armados de Liberación (CAL; Armed Commandos of Liberation) in Puerto Rico was a source of inspiration and hope for me. . . . Probably I identified with its actions because of my experiences in Vietnam. There was no doubt in my mind that armed struggle played a primordial role in any national liberation struggle. I was impressed by CAL's action and its clandestine existence."[7]

In the mind of many *independentistas* the behavior of the United States with respect to Puerto Rico is a flagrant violation of ideals the United States claims to be essential. The very history of these United States— child of a violent anticolonial struggle waged by scraggly, impoverished, and disunited forces against the most powerful empire at the time—provides a stark contrast to U.S. domination of the Caribbean island.

> Ironically, even the American liberal heritage proved to be a factor causing the Puerto Ricans, and again particularly the better educated ones, to re-examine their Puerto Rican identities. They learned to apply the American ideals and values to which they were exposed in their classrooms and by the media to their own experience and to their own island. . . . American colonists were heroes who had justly fought for their country's independence. . . . World War II had been fought to defend nations from powerful aggressors and to free those who had already come under their yoke. In the post-war era, the United States had looked favorably upon the colonies of Europe breaking away from their mother countries. Both the Korean and Vietnamese Wars were officially depicted as efforts by America to ensure that these Asian peoples would have the right to determine their own national existence free from foreign domination. For many Puerto Ricans the inevitable question was: "Why shouldn't this historic ideal of America apply to Puerto Rico as well as Vietnam or Korea?"[8]

The cost of "breaking away from the mother country," when "mother's" name is the United States, proves very dear. In the arrests during the early 1980s, the U.S. government took Valentín and López into custody along with many members of the clandestine independence forces within the United States and Puerto Rico. They are among fifteen women and men from Chicago, New York, and Puerto Rico, who remain in prison serving the equivalent of life sentences: Antonio Camacho Negrón, Edwin Cortés, Elizam Escobar, Ricardo Jiménez, Adolfo Matos, Dylcia Pagán, Alberto Rodríguez, Alicia Rodríguez, Ida Luz Rodríguez, Luis Rosa, Juan Segarra Palmer, Alejandrina Torres, and Carlos Alberto Torres.[9]

Upon arrest, thirteen of these women and men declared they were combatants in an anticolonial war to free Puerto Rico from U.S. domination. They invoked international law, which provides that a colonial government may not criminalize anticolonial conduct and that captured anticolonial combatants are entitled to prisoner-of-war status.[10] They asserted that the courts of the U.S. and its political subdivisions had no jurisdiction to try them as criminals and asked to be remanded to an impartial international tribunal to have their status judged. Two of the political prisoners fought the government's evidence in pretrial motions and at trial, exposing rampant government intrusions into the rights of those being tried.

While the POW position has been recognized by international judicial bodies and other international fora, the state of Illinois and the U.S. government refused to recognize the prisoners' POW status and proceeded to try them for criminal offenses. The thirteen, however, persisted in their refusal to recognize the courts' jurisdiction. Remaining consistent with the argument that U.S. courts had no authority over their situation, they presented no defense and prosecuted no appeals.

The Trials and Sentencing

The various proceedings against the captured *independentistas* were marked by a virtual hysteria on the part of the media, law enforcement, and the courts. Many of the arrests were carried out in military regalia, replete with helicopters, snipers, and swarms of FBI agents.

In the earlier arrests the government sought, and the courts set, prohibitive bail. With the advent of "preventive detention," the government sought, and the courts ordered, no bail at all, and, in one case, set the record for the longest preventive detention. Awaiting trial, all the prisoners were held in the most punitive, restrictive, often unprecedented isolation unless and until some intervention occurred, from inside or outside the prison—hunger strikes by the prisoners, protests by the independence movement and supporters, lawsuits by movement attorneys, and monitoring by Amnesty International.[11]

Newspapers whipped the public—and potential jurors—into an anti-terrorist frenzy, sending a message to the judges and juries that the accused were guilty, and U.S. marshals, out in force tried to intimidate supporters.

The courts, open as a forum for the government's political agenda, facilitated an atmosphere of fear by permitting the government's use of such terms as "terrorist" and banning the defense from using such terms as "colonialism." They convened anonymous juries and cut back on traditional limitations on state power, particularly the right to be free from unreasonable searches and seizures.

After a brief encounter in the courts, the Puerto Rican revolutionaries were faced with the dismal prospect of long-term confinement in federal prisons. Their refusal to accept U.S. moral or political authority was repaid with sentences that rank among the lengthiest in the history of the United States in spite of public recognition that included an editorial in the *Chicago Tribune:* "Most of the incidents have involved bombs, fortunately so placed and timed as to damage property rather than persons. . . . But again the terrorists were out to call attention to their cause rather than to shed blood." [12]

Government statistics demonstrate that those who commit criminal offenses receive far shorter sentences than do independence fighters. For example, the national average sentence for convicted violent felons is less than eight years, with actual time served of less than four years in prison. [13] In comparison, the fifteen Puerto Rican prisoners are serving a collective sentence of 981 years, or an average of 65.4 years. This is about six times longer than the average murder sentence. [14] What does this mean for each individual case? Luis Rosa was nineteen years old when taken to prison. He will be 119—and the year will be 2088—if he is made to serve his entire sentence. Carmen Valentín will be 132; Adolfo Matos, 108; Oscar López Rivera, 113; Juan Segarra Palmer, 90; and so on.

Comparing their sentences to those meted out to anti-independence forces likewise proves their politically punitive nature. Former Puerto Rican police colonel Alejo Maldonado, an admitted assassin, is soon to be paroled from prison after serving less time than have most of the political prisoners/prisoners of war. This is a man who, according to press reports, participated in police death squads that involved kidnappings, extortion, trafficking in weapons, torture, and murder. [15]

In 1978 two young proindependence activists, Carlos Soto Arrivi and Arnaldo Dario Rosado, were killed in Puerto Rico at Cerro Maravilla. Although the extent of Puerto Rican police and FBI participation in the assassinations and ensuing cover-up has never been full disclosed, the five Puerto Rican police who were convicted received sentences of from ten to thirty years. The commander of the intelligence unit responsible for the murders was released on parole after six years in prison. [16] In 1976, Santiago (Chagi) Mari Pesquera was brutally murdered. Chagi was the son of Juan Mari Brás, a leader of the Puerto Rican Socialist Party (PSP) and then-candidate for governor. While many feel the crime has yet to be solved, a man convicted of the deed served only eight years in prison.[17]

Comparisons to recent cases involving police brutality in the United States lead to the same conclusion.[18] Sentences given to members of right-wing paramilitary groups and those who bomb abortion clinics and shoot at physicians likewise pale in comparison.[19]

The average time served in federal prison for murder is 5.4 years, in state prison, eight years.[20] Although none of the fifteen Puerto Rican political prisoners was charged with or convicted of murder, most have now served eighteen years in prison—more than twice the state average.

PRISON CONDITIONS

It is a violation of human rights that those who have dedicated their lives to the freedom of their people and to self-determination must endure prison, even for one day. The Puerto Rican political prisoners and prisoners of war have endured conditions that are designed to break not only their commitment to independence but to destroy their human spirit, conditions that violate even the minimum standards under international law.

Placement in prisons far from their families has meant long-term separation, contrary to the Bureau of Prisons' stated policy, which encourages maintaining family and community ties. Adolfo Matos, in Lompoc, California, rarely sees his daughters who live in New York. Lucy Rodríguez' son Damián can afford to see her only infrequently. Elizam Escobar's mother, who lives in Puerto Rico, can travel to see him in Oklahoma only once a year.

After more than seventeen years of imprisonment, many of the prisoners' parents have passed away. In spite of bureau policy permitting bedside visits and attendance at funerals, prison authorities have consistently refused to let the prisoners grieve with their families. They have continually ignored letters of support from ministers and elected officials. They rejected requests that Ricardo Jiménez see his mother who was dying of cancer, that Adolfo Matos attend his mother's funeral, that Carmen Valentín attend her mother's memorial service, that Elizam Escobar be present at his father's bedside and burial.

Officials have classified every one of the prisoners as a special monitoring and high-security case. Over the years they have refined their techniques, experimenting with special control units as in the case of Lucy Rodríguez at Alderson's Cardinal Unit, with Alejandrina Torres and other women political prisoners at the Women's High Security Unit at Lexington, and with Oscar López Rivera, at Marion and now at Florence's Administrative Maximum Unit. The government's restriction of sensory stimulation and human contact has been widely condemned as violating international human rights standards, but the practices continue in full force.

In spite of adverse prison conditions, the prisoners have remained active and involved. They work as teachers and tutors with other prisoners, conduct AIDS education, and participate in cultural programs. They maintain contact with the independence movement and write for events and publications. Many have become artisans in media ranging from copper etching to clay to textiles and beads. They read, study, and correspond. They exercise to try to stay fit. As they themselves have said, their unwavering commitment to the self-determination of their people helps maintain their dignity and sanity.

PAROLE

Parole is the conditional release from prison before the expiration of one's sentence and is available to those convicted of antisocial offenses. Indeed the majority of those who seek parole are released.[21] However this basic provision has not been made available to Puerto Rican political prisoners. Four of the prisoners have sought release on parole, approaching the process from various perspectives. The response from the government—regardless of what approach was used—was to apply a higher standard than most prisoners must meet by assigning these prisoners to a unique category to which only 1 percent of all prisoners are assigned and then to deny parole. Alberto Rodríguez, after serving twelve years of his thirty-five-year sentence, was told he will remain in prison until the expiration of his sentence. Dylcia Pagán and Carlos Alberto Torres, who at the time of their hearings had served more than fourteen years of their fifty-five- and seventy-year federal sentences, and Juan Segarra, after serving twelve years of his fifty-five-year sentence, were all told to serve an additional fifteen years before they would be considered for release on parole. The documents denying the prisoners parole expressly rely on their proindependence affiliations and activities.

THE CAMPAIGN TO FREE THE PRISONERS

In November of 1993, supporters of the prisoners' release submitted a formal application to the Clinton administration asking him to exercise the constitutional power of pardon and to grant their immediate and unconditional release.

There is rich precedent for their release. Throughout history, U.S. presidents have exercised the constitutional power of pardon to release those who acted or conspired to act against the government, including Confederate soldiers who took up arms in the Civil War and were convicted of treason, socialists convicted of organizing armed resistance to conscription during World War I, and, of course, the Puerto Rican Nationalists who fired on Blair House in 1950 and on the U.S. Congress in 1954. In the United States, as in other countries, pardons and amnesties have been effective, often in postwar situations, in promoting harmony and healing national wounds.

Since the initiative for a presidential pardon, public opinion in favor of their freedom has continued to grow as more people have become aware of their case. The range of support extends over the entire spectrum of the Puerto Rican society. In Puerto Rico, throughout the Puerto Rican and Latin American diaspora, and increasingly among North American progressives and the religious community, the plea for their release has intensified. The list of endorsers comprised a "Who's Who" of the Puerto Rican nation, including all three Puerto Rican members of the U.S. Congress, scores of Puerto Rican elected officials throughout U.S. cities, former governors of Puerto Rico, and leaders among all three major parties. The full range of cultural, professional, religious, and civil rights organizations has participated in this effort, inspired either by humanitarian or political principles. Delegations from the United States and from Puerto Rico meeting with White House officials sense an increasing receptivity to the pending petition. The pressure continues to mount, as the centenary of U.S. control over Puerto Rico approaches.

Some observers point to the U.S. government's contradictory posture in post–Cold War politics: "We . . . live in a different world where yesterday's so-called 'terrorists' are today's dignitaries, from the recasting of world leaders like the Palestine Liberation Army's Yassir Arafat in his reconciliation with Israel, to the Irish Republican Army's Gerry Adams, and the release and growing international stature of South African President Nelson Mandela. . . . [D]uring President Clinton's visit to Ireland [in late 1995], he pushed for the government to release Joe Doherty, a member of the IRA, who was extradited last year from the United States on murder charges against an Irish police officer."[22]

For many it is also contrary to the spirit of the times that the U.S. government continues to hold onto the principal remnant of its colonial adventures dating back one hundred years. The 1990s is the decade in which the United Nations mandated the end of colonialism. In spite of numerous UN pronouncements over the years in favor of a process to decolonize Puerto Rico, the U.S. government retains control over this vestige of the colonial era, in direct conflict with proclamations in support of national sovereignty around the globe.[23] And in spite of U.S. pressure on other governments to release political prisoners, the United States continues to hold its own political prisoners. Resolution of the question of Puerto Rico's status, currently an issue in the U.S. Congress, is affected by the continued imprisonment of these men and women. At the April 1997 public hearings held in Puerto Rico to discuss the island's future political status, a spokesperson for the Puerto Rican Independence Party expressed this sentiment:

> Finally, I want to urge the members of this Committee to exercise their good offices to encourage President Clinton to resolve a matter he has under his consideration at this moment, the adequate resolution of which would constitute a gesture of good faith which would validate the U.S. government's commitment to self-determination.
>
> The length of their [the prisoners'] sentences is absolutely disproportionate to the offenses for which they were convicted, and there is no room for doubt that political considerations dictated the excessive severity.
>
> I ask that you express to the President that for humanitarian as well as political reasons, he grant a commutation of these sentences, a matter about which there exists broad support in Puerto Rico, beyond political lines.[24]

Whether or not the colonial status of Puerto Rico is resolved, the U.S. has an opportunity to live up to its own history and the standards it imposes on the rest of the world and release these fifteen "unreconstructed revolutionaries," who are the living legacy of what some look at with nostalgia as bygone days. As author Julia Alvarez' fictional Dominican "butterfly" said, reflecting on her country's violent past littered with the deaths of her three revolutionary sisters, "I'm not stuck in the past, I've just brought it with me into the present."[25] Our own present brings with it a past that we share with the prisoners and that beckons us not just to reflection but to action.[26]

II. HISTORIES AND REFLECTIONS

PABLO GUZMÁN

9   La Vida Pura
A Lord of the Barrio

I HAD never done anything like this before. Twelve other guys, one woman, myself, and a small handful of people who, until moments before had been spectators, were about to set a barricade of garbage on fire. Garbage in the ghetto sense: rusted refrigerators from empty lots, the untowed carcasses of abandoned vehicles, mattresses, furniture, and appliances off the sidewalk as well as the stuff normally found in what few trash cans the city saw fit to place in *El Barrio*. We were taking on the sanitation department, although it wouldn't be long before firefighters and police became involved—not to mention John Lindsay's city hall.

It was a late Sunday afternoon. Somehow, after gathering the material on the corners of Third Avenue and 110th Street, we had managed to pile it across the wide avenue between green lights, catching the uptown traffic before it moved again. Many drivers cursed, a few were just curious. But though Juan tried explaining through a bullhorn, and though Sonia, Voodoo, David, Mauricio, and a couple of others began waving their purple berets to warn the first drivers to slow down, none of them were prepared when this instant barrier suddenly got torched. I was helping to flip a junked car into the blockade when I saw the gasoline being poured. It was ignited and more gasoline was poured as the flames shot upward. A couple of bystanders I didn't know amazed me with how quickly and professionally they stoked the fire.

When the fire trucks arrived, I should not have been surprised that they were met with bottles and bricks. But it was still unsettling. We had been trying for weeks to rally a crowd and could never draw one, though the week before we had some success on the steps of a church at 111th and Lexington Avenue when David unfurled a Puerto Rican flag. Now, however, this blazing protest had done more than get people's attention. We needed to control what was becoming a mob. Through his bullhorn, Juan González shouted: "The firemen are not our enemy! They're not the problem!" But the firefighters had already gone into reverse.

When the cops arrived minutes later, we had wanted to talk, to explain.

This chapter originally appeared in the *Village Voice*, March 21, 1995.

That we were making a point, and now we'd clean the mess up. All we had been trying to do after sweeping up the streets on previous Sundays was talk with sanitation about once-a-week pickups and nonexistent trash cans, and about how to decently treat people asking for help instead of blowing them off with "You spics get the fuck outta here, this space is off-limits. You gotta problem, talk to the mayor." But the cops came out of their cars swinging. We whipped off our berets and tried melting into the crowd. What really saved us, though, was the people on the rooftops, who instantly started hurling missiles from above. As we had prearranged in case of such an emergency, we ran in twos and threes to a spot outside *El Barrio* in Black Harlem. There, we sized up our first battle. I couldn't believe how my chest was pounding from the run. And the rush. About a dozen "civilian" participants had taken off with us, following the purple berets. This took us by surprise. Still, it was an opportunity. So in a playground we explained what we were about and enlisted our first recruits. It was the summer of 1969, and the first stateside organization of radical young Puerto Ricans was announcing itself—we hoped—as a political force.

RAÍCES/ROOTS

We called ourselves the Young Lords Organization. In June 1969, two small groupings from Spanish Harlem and one from the Lower East Side, consisting overwhelmingly of guys between seventeen and twenty-two, decided to merge. I was in the Sociedad de Albizu Campos, named for the leader of the old Nationalist Party of Puerto Rico. Primarily college students, we had begun meeting three months before. I had just returned from a semester of study in Cuernavaca, Mexico, completing the required "in-the-field" half of my freshman year at the State University at the brand-new Old Westbury. I left as Paul Guzman, a nervous only child of a Puerto Rican–Cuban mother and a Puerto Rican father, both of whom were born "here"—stateside. I came back to the states as Pablo Guzmán. The other East Harlem group consisted mostly of high-school dudes who met in an after-school photo workshop run by Hiram Maristany. The Lower East Side group was a mix of college and high-school aged guys who we later found out had already been penetrated by two or three NYPD Red Squad agents.

Immediately after the merger, Mickey, David, and I drove in Mickey's Volkswagen Beetle to Chicago. We didn't know at the time about the Brown Berets or La Raza Unida among the Chicanos and the Mexicans of the West and Southwest. But Mauricio and I had read in that week's *Guardian* about what the Chicago Panthers called a "Rainbow Coalition" they had put together. The Panthers had turned (or were trying to turn) two Chicago gangs, the Young Patriots (poor Whites with Appalachian roots) and the Young Lords (Puerto Ricans and Mexicans), away from 'banging and toward something more constructive. If there was already a Latino group in action, we reasoned, why not throw in together? The Lords' chairman, Cha Cha Jiménez, breezily gave us permission to organize as the New York chapter of the YLO. The affiliation with Chicago was where we got our purple berets—even though they claimed to be moving away from street life, the Lords weren't giving up their colors.

This whole gang thing was fairly jolting. Although to this day people think the New York group was a gang because of that name, we never were, and except for Felipe Luciano (one of the few New Yorkers who had been in a gang himself), we walked lightly around the Chicago boys. Nevertheless, it was a Mexican member of the Chicago Lords, Omar López, who came up with our slogan, *"Tengo Puerto Rico en Mi Corazón"*—"I Have Puerto Rico in My Heart." We loved it, and it soon spread throughout Puerto Rican circles. Only years later did we learn that it contained a slight grammatical error, a testimonial to the bad Spanish most of us "spoke." We were truly examples of Ricans raised in the states.

I wasn't yet nineteen. My folks would have freaked if they'd known what their only child—the altar boy from Our Lady of Pity who was supposed to use his Bronx science diploma and college scholarship to bust out of the ghetto—was really doing on his summer vacation. But it didn't come from nowhere—my parents and my grandparents, after all, had first instilled in me a sense that there was far too long a history of injustice in this society. "Only," as my father would say later at my trial, "your mother and I never thought you would actually try to do something about it. Not on such a scale, anyhow."

By the time of that trial, the Young Lords Party—we split from Chicago in April 1970 because we felt they hadn't overcome being a gang—had been targeted by Hoover's FBI as the Latino version of the Panthers and the Weather Underground. Although we never kept a roster, I tallied our New York membership at the end of 1970, and we had grown to more than a thousand, with storefront offices in *El Barrio,* the Lower East Side, and the South Bronx. We had branches in Newark-Hoboken, Bridgeport, Philadelphia, and Puerto Rico, active supporters in Detroit, Boston, Hawaii, in the military and in the prisons. We published a weekly newspaper, *Pa'lante.* We had organized workers, including medical professionals, in the city's hospitals and had a sizeable following on campuses across the country, where we often spoke.

Links with artists and rising entrepreneurs had broken the grip of two White DJs on what was beginning to be called "salsa" music and inspired a cultural boom reflected in songs by musicians like Ray Barretto and Eddie Palmeiri with a vision beyond "Hey Mami you look so fine." Unlike some on the New Left who specialized in trying to out-argue each other, we had a community base, leading ten thousand people in October 1970 on a march from Spanish Harlem to the United Nations demanding Puerto Rico's independence. We also had a reputation for taking the best the police threw at us and hitting 'em right back: pitched battles from rooftops and street corners that spanned days and nights were common through 1971. It may be hard for some to understand now, but back then, petitioning for change often meant the cops got turned loose on you.

By our sixth year, it was over. Partly because of destabilization by arrest and government infiltration but mainly because we were young and prone to mistakes—mistakes of leadership, of vulnerability to betrayal, and of the same movement infighting that we had once so despised. But before we dissolved, the Young Lords Party had left its mark:

- A new Lincoln Hospital was built in the South Bronx after we seized a facility that the city had run out of a condemned building for twenty-five years.
- We forced the city to use the lead-poisoning and tuberculosis detection tests gathering dust in some agency's basement after we liberated them and exposed epidemics in both diseases—which are now making comebacks.
- We pushed the Board of Corrections into reforming prison conditions just before the Attica uprising—which our sixteen-year-old chief of staff, Juan "Fi" Ortíz, witnessed as our representative on the negotiation team.
- We encouraged schools to teach Puerto Rican history. Some, at least, now do.
- We created a climate for the start of bilingual education. Never intended as a parallel track, but as a way of mainstreaming Spanish-dominant kids to English proficiency, it has since been sabotaged by educators who were against it from the beginning.
- We produced the first radio show by a New York–born Latino (myself, over WBAI).
- Ask any Latino professional in Nueva York who advanced in government or the corporate world between, say, 1969 and 1984, and you'll be told they owe part of their opportunity to the sea change in perception the that Young Lords inspired.
- We helped raise the understanding, first among Latinos and then the society at large, that Puerto Ricans possessed a culture on a par with anyone's.

Try to understand what all this meant to a generation of Latinos and others we came in touch with. Even Rudolph Giuliani's special adviser and running mate Herman Badillio, one of our early targets, has said, "A measure of just how significant the Lords were is that in the years since, no group has come along to provide that kind of leadership for our people." Of course, in 1969, when the Lords were coming up, "our people" were barely a step beyond neocolonialism. There were no "Kiss me, I'm Puerto Rican" buttons. Salsa concerts did not sell out Madison Square Garden. No borough had a Puerto Rican plurality. There was no Hostos Community College. WCBS's Gloria Rojas and J. J. González were the only Latinos reporting local news on TV. White racists had only recently been forced (by sheer numbers, sometimes reinforced by fists) to drop a "tradition" at Orchard Beach that "restricted" Puerto Ricans to two sections. Santana had not yet electrified Tito Puente's music. Al Narvaez was the only Latino with a regular byline at the *Times*. It was not taken for granted that there would soon be a Puerto Rican mayor of New York. That Oscar de la Renta and José Ferrer were Latino was overlooked by almost everyone but themselves. The idea of Goya foods as a "gourmet" product was unimaginable. There was no Puerto Rican legislative caucus in Albany. Freddie Prinze had not yet broken through.

Though there was a small Latino middle class, it was unknown to the "outside" world. Puerto Ricans were still classified on official documents as "other" or "White." Most of us in the states did not know who or what we were. We tended to identify, according to our skin color, with "being White" or "being Black"—and more than a few misguided souls ID'd with "being White" even when Mama Nature had us looking more like Aunt Jemima's baby. Certainly the organization stamped everyone involved. In almost everything I do today, be it compassion and discipline as a father or my fairness as a journalist, I am incorporating what I learned as a Young Lord. They were five and a half of the most exhilarating years of my life. Even the brief stretch in prison. You learn from every experience. Or you die. Some snapshots follow.

Jane Fonda and the People's Church

In September 1969, we had picked up on the Panthers' example of serving free breakfast to ghetto kids to illustrate yet another priority "the system" somehow missed. By November, the demand for the program was booming; we needed space. After scouting several locations, we found a Methodist church under our noses at 111th Street and Lexington Avenue.

What we didn't know at the time was that the church was empty six days a week because most of the congregation had fled to the suburbs, and that the pastor, who had escaped from Castro's Cuba, viewed us as his worst nightmare. But we found out that in December the church was having a "Testimonial Sunday," where anyone could stand and, uh, testify. Felipe, who had been vacillating about whether or not to commit to the Lords, finally gave in to our idea that he'd be the ideal chairman. He testified on behalf of the breakfast program, with eight or so other Lords present. But church officials had alerted the police, who were hiding in a nearby room and sitting in the pews in plain clothes, and when Felipe rose to speak, a melee erupted. At one point, a choir member in robes cracked a brass candelabra over a Lord's head. Everyone was arrested, and Felipe's arm was broken.

In the immortal words of Bugs Bunny, "Of course, you know this means war." We waited a couple of weeks for the heat to die down—and then, the Sunday after Christmas, barricaded the building, renamed it the "People's Church," and quickly set up our programs: free breakfast, health services, clothing drives, cultural events, Puerto Rican history classes. The cops posted hundreds of blue coats and helmets around the area, but by then Spanish Harlem was loyal to the Lords, and the cops couldn't stop the flow of supporters. For ten days, the church became a mecca for Latinas and Latinos who had been looking for just this. That's how the Philly branch got started—the word traveled that far. As Minister of Information, I soon figured out that the takeover was a godsend to the media, coming at the slowest time of the news year. Coverage was so massive that I decided to change my style—rejecting the bad Panther imitation of the first day of the takeover, I switched to clear glasses instead of shades, a more collegiate sweater, a touch of wit in the give-and-take. Ultimately, Ted Kheel and Herman Badillo, of all people, mediated a settlement that wiped out the symbolic arrests of early January that ended the takeover. The National Council of Churches made other space available. But not before Jane Fonda and her *Klute* costar Donald Sutherland showed up. Still in costume, they were stopped and frisked at the door like everyone else—I got to the door in time to catch Donald Sutherland "in the position," spread-eagled against a wall and getting patted down. It was a goof to see people from the neighborhood nudging each other for stardust ("Look, Jane Fonda!"). Absurd, and sweet. And Fonda surprised us with some on-the-mark questions ("Just what do you stand for? Who are you allied with?"). Later, as that night's activities ended and three hundred or so people were leaving, Fonda and Pia Lindstrom enjoyed a warm reunion ("Jane!" "Pia!") complete with *mucho* air kisses and hugs. Lindstrom, one of Ingrid Bergman's daughters, was a general-assignment reporter for WNBC, and the two obviously knew each other from way back. I loved watching but wasn't ready for Fonda coming over and asking—she was cool though, she made sure it was away from Lindstrom—if I could give Pia an interview. It was the second week of the takeover, and I had frozen media requests not wanting to burn us out. But . . . "Pia!" "Jane!"

The Mob Covers Our Contract

During the first half of 1970, after repeated demands from folks in *El Barrio,* we tried moving out the drug dealers. Not the small-time, nickel-bag-of-pot guys but the bigger heroin pushers. Frankly, we didn't have the resources to tackle it. But it was the neighborhood's number-one quality-of-life complaint. We couldn't ignore it.

Needless to say, many cops were part of the problem, and working with a few movement documentarians from Newsreel, we surreptitiously shot footage of cops doing business with dealers—shaking hands, putting goods in the trunks of squad cars, transferring the goods to their own cars. We brought the film to WCBS, WNBC, and WABC, and I got a lesson. They all refused to air it. Said they didn't use outside camera crews. When we offered to take their crews to the same spots, they also refused. That's when I first learned TV news bosses could be cardboard cutouts.

We told the dealers that maybe it would be in their interest to take their business elsewhere. They laughed. We started a campaign of getting loud around their favorite spots, blasting their cover with bullhorns, hassling their foot soldiers, leafleting, and generally being a pain. Then somebody in the neighborhood took it upon themselves to escalate matters. A couple of dope dealers slipped off a couple of rooftops, and at least one "business-man" was found early one morning swinging from a lamppost. Lynched. All this could have been because of some turf battle among drug factions, but given the timing, we obviously got the "credit." The good people in the neighborhood patted us on the backs when we walked down the street, and if we tried to demur, we met "knowing" nudges and a conspiratorial wink.

Other interested parties were less amused. A few of us soon got the word that the Mafia had put out a contract: five thousand dollars on four of the five Central Committee members and ten thousand dollars on Felipe. We decided that the best defense would be to go public. At a news conference we called to expose the contract, Chris Borgen of WCBS-TV asked whether we were saying "the Italian mob is after" us. "The Mafia," I answered, "is an equal opportunity employer. They work with every ethnic group in the drug business. The Italians are not necessarily the ones putting out the hit."

The next day, I got feedback from a highly unexpected source: my father. He was at the door of our storefront on Madison between 111th and 112th. My mother had helped out with our clothing drives, but my father never came by, though he had reluctantly given his support. We went for a walk through *El Barrio*. Two of the security detail assigned to the Central Committee in the wake of the contract started walking a bit behind; my father stopped and looked back somewhat scornfully. I waved them off, knowing he wanted privacy. "Those two are supposed to come between you and a mob hit?" he said sarcastically. "Including the woman?" "Hey, she kicks ass. You'd be surprised. There's women throughout the organization." There would have been a woman on the Central Committee if Sonia hadn't left because of family problems. By November, two women would be added to the top leadership. Now, if my old man knew about the Gay Caucus . . .

My father wanted to turn the corner in more ways than one. "About that business you were talking about on TV—I got a call from Pete." Pete and Orlando Moreno were two of my father's brothers. As kids Pete and Orlando had thrown in with the toughest elements in an East Harlem that was then more ethnically mixed. With Pete as the "brains" and Orlando as the "enforcer," they had become associates of one of the Five Families, subcontracting a numbers-and-coke operation in Spanish Harlem and the South Bronx. "Pete says his partners want to have a meeting with your boys to discuss this contract business. I suggest you do it. But I don't want you there."

"What, I'm not afraid—"

"That's the deal." His tone had changed. He cut me off sharply. "We're arranging the sit-down. But I told Pete to tell them that you're not to be there. If Felipe's there, they'll feel like they're talking to a boss. That's very important to these people. But I want you out." He looked straight at me. "Paulie . . . you're all I've got."

I let out a frustrated breath. We started walking again. My father's voice grew softer. "So, this is where you're living now?" "Yeah on 111th." He laughed. "This is what your mother and I left. And now you're back in the tenements. Remember when I would take you here for a visit? You would keep close to my leg, afraid. 'When are we going to go home?' I wanted you to see how tough it was out here, so you wouldn't come back. And now . . . we stopped again. He took my shoulders. "Paulie, your mother and I worry about you. But we love you. And we're proud of you *coño*. You're doing what my generation never did. And should have." He gave me a hug. I felt damn good.

The deal that went down was that the Cuban dealers who had put out the contract would withdraw in return for the Lords backing off. This was just as well. In response to our war on heroin, the cops were squeezing us from the other end, sending all complaints about robberies, muggings, and rapes to the Lords. We had to deal with the more serious of these crimes or lose standing in the community, but the burden was too much—the neighborhood needed police even if the worst of them demanded a piece of the action. We passed word through the mob that dealers had to stop hustling near schools and conducting street bazaars, claimed a small victory, and moved from our own Vietnam-style quagmire on to projects we could win.

My father called upon my uncles one other time. Just before I began my prison sentence, the word went out to Mafiosos in every federal prison to look out for "the Marino kid." It was weird, in places like Lewisburg, Atlanta, and the old West Side House of D in Manhattan, to have wise guys seek me out and ask if I needed anything. Weird but admittedly welcome.

Yoruba Meets the Spirits

Soon after we opened our first office, the Madison Avenue storefront, in September 1969, a Lord came up to me with a mysterious smile on her face. "Some people up front want to see you. They say they'll only talk to Yoruba." A few of us had taken nicknames, and mine came from the name of a mostly Nigerian tribe. Since I had been getting a sizable number of kook calls, I was leery: "Have they been screened?" But when I parted the curtain, all I saw was eight or ten people in African finery, a few carrying percussion instruments. The tallest man in the group approached me. "Yoruba?" he asked me. I nodded. "*Somos un círculo Santero.* We have come to honor you, to thank you for taking our name, and to give this place a blessing." *Un limpio.* A cleansing. It made sense. When the Yoruba were "brought" to the Americas, they carried with them their ancient religion, Ife, which took different forms on different soil: in Haiti, Vodun; in Brazil, macumba; down South, particularly in the Louisiana bayou country, one worked roots or saw the monkey lady; and in Cuba and Puerto Rico, the followers of the seven powers practiced Santería. Before any of us could really say anything, the chanting and drumming had begun. I was completely caught off guard. There was nothing in Mao's *Red Book* to cover this.

A woman in the group came up to me. In a near whisper, she said, "We knew your grandmother." Talk about a small world. My father's deceased mother was a Santería priestess—and her mother's mother was an African slave. "You have the same aura around you. We can see it." She gave me a warm feeling.

A couple of other Lords came to the office and were taken aback. "*Un limpio?*" one said. "What kind of metaphysical bullshit is this?" Calling something metaphysical was one of the harsher slams we revolutionary materialists could deliver. "Watch your language," I scolded. "Metaphysics had nothing to do with it. This is a legitimate part of our people's culture. And besides, it's got a good rhythm!"

"Where Are the Damn Guns!"

In early October 1970, two of our members, Bobby Lemus and Julio Roldán, were arrested basically for drinking beer and hanging out with some guys on a stoop one night. This was 1970, remember. The next morning, Julio was found hung in his cell at the "Tombs" (Manhattan House of Detention), the latest in a series of controversial "suicides" in jails and police precincts, often with autopsies returned that did not indicate unassisted death. We had been covering the issue in *Pa'lante*. Julio was a quiet, unassuming little guy of about thirty who joined mainly because he believed in independence. His main contribution was cooking at one of our communal apartments at East Harlem.

Surrounded by five thousand demonstrators, we carried his casket from the González Funeral Home on Madison Avenue and marched to the church on 111th that we had taken over a year before. We took it over again, suddenly, posting armed guards at the entrance and at either side of the casket. The standoff would continue, we said, until conditions in the prisons changed. It was the first time we had ever been connected with weapons. We caught even most of our own organization by surprise. Given the risk involved, and the infiltration we took as a given, we had to. The police, already at war with the "soft" Lindsay administration, were furious, but the mayor did not want a confrontation, and so he negotiated. The cops vented their frustration in other ways.

Very soon after the takeover, the Central Committee received reports from inmates in cells next to Julio indicating that he may have taken his own life. This created a debate that split the leadership. My view was that we should admit to doubts and cut our losses immediately. By this time Felipe was not part of the leadership, and indeed, soon he would be gone altogether. Meanwhile, a hard-liner named Gloria Fontanez, recruited from Gouverneur Hospital in the Lower East Side, had risen rapidly through the ranks. She argued that we should stick with our issue regardless of its actual truth, and the majority went along so as not to undermine the months of work we'd put into the UN march scheduled for October 1970. Because I continued to argue, I was suspended. In five and a half years of hard work, that is the only episode of which I am not proud—that and not doing more to get Gloria tossed out.

The march to the UN came off spectacularly, as it probably would have had we left the church earlier. But when the march was over with, we were still there. Negotiations were ongoing, however, and by God they budged: The Board of Corrections would institute sweeping reforms, and José Torres would get a seat on the board.

So now there was the matter of getting out of the church. Past the ring of cops waiting to bust us for the guns. The deal with the city included an amnesty clause that the city was sure would backfire on us. The cops would be allowed in to make sure there were no guns, and only upon their OK could we walk with no charges against us. Because the police had the place surrounded and had infiltrators inside, they were sure they were going to catch us sneaking guns out. And then, all bets would be off. On the appointed day, the police arrived, and at the front door I had the captain and his escort put up against the wall and frisked. "Sorry, Captain," I said, "but we agreed: no weapons. And that includes you. We don't want to say anybody planted anything, right?" The captain acquiesced, and because this occurred within view of reporters covering the "surrender," the image of the Young Lords telling a police captain to assume the position spread. The PBA (Policemen's Benevolent Association) and indignant editorialists called for his head, on a stake right next to ours.

The cops searched thoroughly and found nothing. To this day, I have had police veterans ask me how we pulled it off. Later that day, I had to break policy and get the story from the Lord in charge, David Pérez. "Never underestimate the power of the people," he said laughing. "The cops stopped everybody they thought looked like a Young Lord a block from the church. 'Where are the damn guns?!' one cop yelled at me. But we've spent the last year and change organizing this whole community, not just a part of it. They've been stopping everyone under thirty-five. We broke the weapons down and hid them under the coats of *las viejitas,* the little old ladies who look like your grandmother. Hey, those little old ladies were down."

Geraldo Rivera Saves My Ass

In April 1970, a seven-month effort by Juan González was to culminate in the takeover of Lincoln Hospital. Juan and his team had organized doctors, nurses, other health-care providers, and patients in Manhattan and the Bronx in revealing exposés of just how poorly the system works for poor folks. From lead poisoning and tuberculosis, we had gone on to report the wave of unnecessary hysterectomies performed on Latin women, organized disgruntled rank-and-file workers within 1199, "liberated" an X-ray truck, promoted preventive medicine, and tried to show the links between the pharmaceutical companies, the AMA establishment, hospitals, and insurance outfits that made up the multibillion-dollar health-care industry. But our immediate plan was to take over Lincoln Hospital in the

South Bronx and run it with the help of staff who were fed up with rats in the emergency room, antiquated equipment, meager supplies, and chronic personnel shortages.

Lincoln was a mess. For twenty-five years it awaited demolition, and for twenty- five years the city never funded the construction of its replacement. Getting spics a better hospital was the last thing on their agenda. I was from the South Bronx, and growing up I had heard the stories of a stabbing victim crawling two blocks to the catchment zone where the ambulance would take him to Morrisania (which would eventually be shut down as well). Apocryphal, perhaps, but it reflected Lincoln's street rep.

At dawn, we moved in, sneaking through windows and doors opened by doctors and nurses working with us. From inside, we told the guards they could go on a "lo-o-o-ong" break. A huge Puerto Rican flag was flown from the roof. The city was notified, and acute-care patients were transferred, but all other patients were treated by a reenergized staff. A phalanx of cops in riot gear sealed off the area outside, and the standoff was on. We held a news conference in the hospital auditorium, me in an Afro and white lab coat, and made our case against the city. Deputy Mayor Aurelio sent Sid Davidoff and Barry Gottehrer and their Latino "liaison," Arnie Segarra (who went on to become Dinkins's appointment aide). Negotiations began. By late afternoon, we had won: A new Lincoln would be built. And, of course, the participants would receive amnesty.

The cops were not going for this amnesty bullshit. And they could give a fuck that Lindsay was their boss—he was as hated as Dinkins. So a few blocks from the hospital, I was chased by four detectives in an unmarked car. I thought I had given them the slip, but a dog, a goddamn dog, came nipping after me and slowed me down, and I was collared. Just before they got the cuffs on, I pulled my beret from my back pocket and waved it to the onlookers. "Call the Young Lords!" I vainly cried out. Then my wrists got pinched tight, and my head was slammed on the car roof before I was thrown inside.

They gave me a few more shots, but I knew I was in for a serious beating back at the precinct. As spokesmen, Felipe and I were the biggest targets. On two occasions, cops arrested guys they mistook for me, breaking one's leg and another's arm. In Chicago, I spoke at a rally at the start of the Chicago 7 trial, and as I was finishing, word came that the cops were going to bust me. I managed to escape but learned later that once again the cops grabbed a look-alike and beat the shit out of him. I had been shot at by cops and nearly run over by a squad car in both Chicago and New York. And now my charmed existence had come to an end.

At the 40th Precinct, I was put in a "bing," or holding cell. Louie Perez, who had been assigned as my security when he left Lincoln, was already there. This Negro detective put on a show for his White comrades. They had taken Louie's nunchakus, the "karate sticks" many Lords used. "So, this is what you use against cops, huh?" the lackey said. "Well, let's see how it stands up against this"—and he patted one of the three guns he was visibly packing. His boys laughed, and I knew we were goners. "This is America, cocksucker." He was leaning in close through the bars. His hand was at the lock. "And you oughta be taught what happens to punks who want to mess it up for the rest of us." He was going for the key. Louie and I braced ourselves.

Suddenly, there was a commotion. Bustling sounds from below. Shouting, growing louder. Gerry Rivera materialized, with what seemed like half the precinct coming up the stairs behind him, Keystone Kops–style. He dodged a cop, leaped over a railing, dodged another, and got to our cell. "You OK?" he asked. I was ready to kiss his feet. "Yeah, yeah," I panted. "You just made it. Behind you, watch out!" He turned just before the first cop could grab him. "I'malawyerthesearemyclientsyoutouchany oneofusI'lltakeallyourbadges." Cops froze in mid air.

From an office, a supervisor emerged looking down at some paper. "Jesus! I just got off the phone with headquarters. Do we have some Young Lord here for the hospital thing, they're getting all kinds of calls from the media—" He finally looked up and took the scene in. "What the fuck is all this?" Gerry wadded through fifty or so cops and glibly explained. I had to laugh; he was a piece of work.

Gerry burst into our collective lives soon after we had opened the first office, interrupting a meeting with our lawyers to charge that we had no Latino representation, like, for instance, him, even though one of our attorneys was a Puerto Rican he knew personally. Appalled though we were, we admired his chutzpah. But when he tried to join we drew the line. "This is an adventure for you, bro," he was told. "You're not really into the ideology." Still, he had a lot of heart, and he loved the street battles— and the press conferences. Eventually he took advantage of a scholarship to the Columbia School of Journalism that I had turned down because it would have meant leaving the Lords. We wished him well. Once out of Columbia, he got a gig with WABC-TV and hit the ground running. And that's how the Young Lords Party unleashed Geraldo Rivera on an unsuspecting universe.

WHEN THE MUSIC'S OVER

The Young Lords Party began a couple of years after the Panthers, and while they were an inspiration, we also learned from their negative examples—one of which was, avoid going to jail because of stupid shit. So we never got wrapped up in legal battles that consumed precious resources, and most of our leadership remained intact—until my Selective Service case came up. When I had to report to the draft board, I did it with a flourish, in full regalia—beret festooned with various movement buttons, safari field jacket, combat boots, shades—accompanied by one male and one female Lord. Tore up my draft card and gave the requisite speech. The whole thing was silly, and the Central Committee would never have approved my Abbie Hoffman–style gesture. But a year later, when the government moved to prosecute, it got serious.

While I was out on a personal recognizance bond for my pending case, the Central Committee allowed me one last "present." I would be the group's representative at a celebration of the Chinese Revolution. In the People's Republic of China. This meant slipping out of the country when I wasn't even supposed to be in Brooklyn. I arrived in Shanghai in late August 1971 and left in early November. Traveling through China's cities was eye-popping, just a wondrous oversaturation in a completely different culture . . . and it also strengthened me for one last shot, when I returned, at returning the organization to its community base. By the time I went to China, the group that had been so welcomed by so many Latinos had taken a narrow, "movement" path of dogmatic "correctness." We were on the verge of acting like . . . a gang—of beating down anyone in our ranks who disagreed. This change was mostly because of Gloria and the clique around her—and those of us they were able to browbeat. Gloria "exiled" Juan González to Philadelphia, where I would be a year later.

While the organization was rightly grappling with how to advance toward an older, working-class base (and in the process maturing), Gloria & Co.'s definition of "working class" became, in practice, paradoxically elitist. When I came back from China, I was alarmed by the number of resignations. I had talked with many who had left and kept hearing the same thing: "Gloria . . . there's no democracy . . . too much bullshit . . . we've gotten away from the people." Juan "Fí" Ortíz and I tried to lead an internal campaign to open things up again without forcing a split. We saw what the fed-encouraged Huey Newton–Eldridge Cleaver break had done to the Panthers. The rank and file rallied to our proposals. But Gloria & Co. called our hand. Fí said, "In this case, bro, a split would be progressive. Fuck 'em." And even though we would have lost in the Central Committee, an overwhelming majority of Lords would have left with us. Many more would have returned. But I was haunted by the corpses of factionalism that littered the Left. Reluctantly, miserably, I abdicated my leadership of the internal democratic campaign and accepted yet another suspension for insubordination. Fí became the latest veteran to resign.

Soon Juan would be demoted. And in February 1972, I was "banished" to Philadelphia.

"How Many Ping-Pong Balls Can You Put Up Your Ass?"

I was charged with two counts of Selective Service violation. We decided to fight, to see whether we could set a precedent with a hung jury, which had never happened in a draft case. I was opposed to the Vietnam War and to the double system of justice based upon race, class, and sex in this country. But I was no draft "dodger"; I didn't go to Canada or accept China's invitation of asylum. Apparently, the government began to wonder about its chances. As the trial approached, they began offering deals: Just go to the induction center at Whitehall, we'll see you flunk the physical. No? How's this: We'll accept conscientious objector status. (Sorry. That should be reserved for genuine pacifists and others. As I said at the trial from the witness stand, I wasn't opposed to war. I would have fought in World War II. I was opposed to *this* war.) After a three-day trial, the jury deliberated for about forty minutes. When a juror cried during my testimony, I thought we had the holdout we needed. But the judge's instructions echoed the prosecutor's summation: "Did Mr. Guzmán report for induction or not?" Guilty.

Appeals took about another year. Then on May 30, 1973, I was brought in for sentencing. Similar defendants were getting six months or community service. But it was payback time. "Two years. Concurrent. Be grateful young man. It could have been more."

Nevertheless, I was lucky. Going in, my biggest fear was getting raped—and somehow, not showing that my biggest fear was getting raped. But prison was a wild pecking order. When you first come in, you get classified by other prisoners according to what got you busted. When the word got out that I was in for being a Young Lord, most guys steered clear. Some, out of respect for what groups like the Lords and Panthers represented. But many others because they were sure I was goddamn crazy.

Tallahassee was somewhere between maximum and minimum security. After six months in prison, where I observed my twenty-third birthday, my body was in the best shape it would ever be. There was nothing else to do. And, as with most places, you make friends. One day, one of the Cubans from Miami came up to me. "Hey man, I hear you're getting a visit this week. That's great man, me too. *Mira*—she's bringing me some stuff. *Perico. Me entiendes?*" Coke. The antenna went up. He went on, lowering his voice like we were going to be in on something together. "I'm bringing it in to sell, *entiendes,* but I figure there'll be enough to give the guys a taste. You know, *para nosotros.*" He took my silence as a sign to continue. "The stuff's gonna be wrapped in bags. Now how many Ping-Pong balls can you get up your ass?"

"Wha—*QUE FUE?*!

"I figure I can do six—"

"Whoa, *'perate,* back up. I'm out."

"What? How can you be like that man?"

"It's easy. Forget it. Ain't nothin' goin' up back there, you dig it?"

"Come on man, it's for the brothers!"

"Yo, fuck the brothers."

Word got around fast. Cats were coming up to me on the chow line. One guy just materialized next to me with a downcast look: "Come on, man. I'd do it for you." "*Pa'carajo.*" Another guy: "Yo, home, I thought you was down."

Practically every Latin shut me out of the crowd—not a good deal long term. Don't get this wrong: Back then, I got high. But this was stupid. And the perpetrator of this BS was one of the more unstable guys in a population not noted for Cool Hand Lukes.

Visiting day came. Also in the big loungelike room was a lower-level Colombo associate from Queens who made the trip down South with me. Call him Vinnie.

Vinnie sashayed over to where I was sitting. He thought this was a cool walk. He pointed over to the Ping-Pong champion.

"What the fuck is he doin'?"

"I know this is his, like, fifth trip to the bathroom."

"Guy's fuckin' obvious. You did the right thing."

"Yeah, but now, only two of the Latinos will talk to me."

"Fuck 'em."

He cruised back to his spot. Once the visitors had gone, they lined us up to reenter. And then it was announced. "Strip search!" The Ping-Pong champ was dead. With what he had up his butt, he was going to be firing bullets when they bent him over. Ping-Pong was coming up soon. He was sweating.

I whispered to Vinnie, "Come on, let's help this schmuck out."

"How?"

"We start a fight."

"Are you serious?"

And before I could answer, Vinnie shouted, "Are you serious!" and shoved me back several feet. "Damn right I'm serious!" And I knocked him back. We "grappled," knocking over a lamp and moving some furniture, before the guards came and grabbed us, whistling everyone else back into general population. Vinnie and I were questioned and held for about an hour and then released to a warm welcome. Ping-Pong was at the front of a crowd of Latinos and New Yorkers. "My man!" Guys cheered. "You too!" he told Vinnie. "You all right with the Latin brothers, amigo."

"Fuck that," Vinnie said. "Where's the blow?"

PUNTO/BUT NOT THE END

I was paroled on Valentine's Day 1974, after nine months. You need a job to qualify for parole. My old man used his garment-center contacts to get me into the warehouse of a Philadelphia dye factory. Had to join the Teamsters. With overtime, it was the most money I had ever made. I was still with what was now called the Puerto Rican Revolutionary Workers Organization, heading it's Philadelphia branch. Before my sentence, my suspension had been lifted, and I was a member of Gloria's "expanded" (read "packed") Central Committee. It was obvious that the organization was spinning its wheels. Not even a rectification movement would turn things around; there wasn't much left.

In September, Gloria ordered me to move back to New York. The only job I could get on short notice was as an assistant dishwasher at a day-care center in the Bronx, and I lost it within a month. Some serious bills were due, and I decided to bite the bullet and go for some "nonproletarian" labor. I sold an article to the *Voice*. By late December, there was no getting around it: We weren't the Young Lords anymore. I still wanted to organize but not with this crowd. I left. A week or so later, I returned home from another wasted day trying to find work—whenever I came close, the FBI would scare employers off. Somebody was already inside my apartment, a cop who had once been assigned to surveil us. "They think your leaving is a front," he told me. "That you're really heading up the underground wing. That you're going to run the FALN." I threw my keys on a table and laughed as I fell into a chair. Most Lords figured the FALN was either a COINTELPRO operation or close to it, because their targets were purely terroristic, organizing no one and scaring everybody; the month before, they'd set off a bomb at Fraunces Tavern. I think I convinced the cop I had genuinely left the organization.

A few days later, there was a knock on the door. The voice on the other side was a sister from the organization who I thought was cool. When I opened the door, two of my former buddies sprung on me, one with a gun to my head. The young woman ran down the stairs crying. "I'm sorry, Yoruba." They were all sorry. Said they were ordered by Gloria to get some books I had "stolen." "This is bullshit," I told them. "She's trying to play us against each other." It was like talking to zombies. But I got off light. By the spring of 1975, there were people being held and tortured. In a weird reunion, many of the original members got together at the new Lincoln hospital and sent Gloria & Co. a message that we'd put her lights out if the violence persisted. It was our last act. But more important, it got some of us talking to each other again. We had become quite estranged. Gloria had taken an organization that had captured the imagination of a large chunk of Latin New York with more than one thousand members and reduced it to about fifteen dangerous wackos.

So: Was it worth it?

Yeah. We were kids who succeeded wildly, raising ideas that have lasted. More college groups are asking us to speak about the Lords than ever. Sure, I wish we had overcome the dogmatic tendency within us that Gloria fed off. I wish I had helped Fí split the organization. It didn't happen. Many of us went into a funk about how it all ended. We didn't even speak to each other for a long time. But for too long we let that cloud over all the good we accomplished.

The main reason why so many kids, and quite a few adults, are asking about the Lords today is because they took a look around the current landscape. They see nearly three times as many Latinos in the New York area and even more of a middle class than there was in the Lords heyday. Yet they see that as a group we have not advanced. Politically. Economically. In education, housing, business, ownership, family stability, prison rate, mortality rate—by any yardstick we are getting clobbered. There is no independent Latino voice setting our agenda or holding the government, media, or corporate structure accountable. So what people are asking is, what would today's Lords do? Because they know that one way or another they'd be kicking ass. I have faith that this question will be answered. After all, when we started in 1969, there had been no precedent. Only a raging need. So—*Que viva los* Young Lords of tomorrow.

ESPERANZA MARTELL

10 "In the Belly of the Beast"
Beyond Survival

BEGINNINGS

WHEN I was four—the year was 1949—my whole world crumbled around me. No longer did the sun kiss my skin. No longer did the earth touch my feet. No longer were smells and sounds familiar. I was uprooted from my country. The sound of the monstrous thing they took me away in shattered my being. I could not breath. My tears were unseen. I am sure she, my mother, comforted me, but she was a stranger. Her smell was not familiar, not of flowers and fresh air, not of *yucca* and *yame*, but alien. I had not seen her for a year. Or was it forever. . . . Later I got to know that then-unfamiliar smell well—a smell of concrete and cold streets, of roach-infested buildings and locked doors, of isolation and confusion, of unhappiness. But later does not count when you are a child. Later is always now, and now was so painful. Now was so confusing. There was no understanding in the now, and the child cried—and in her sleep she still cries today . . . ask her friends.

The experience of being uprooted from my homeland has had the most profound impact on who I am today; and it is the basis for the deep, justified rage I feel. I am a person without a country. I do not fit there or here, but I carry a deep love for my birthplace, Puerto Rico—the place that could have been my home.

My mother, María de los Angeles Gaetan Martell, has also had a great impact upon me. She passed on to me her love of Puerto Rico through her stories of growing up in Bayamón. In our home, although quietly, Albizu Campos and the Nationalists were seen as patriots and were talked about with love and pride. My mother also passed on her courage, hope, and love for our people. Her adventuresome nature had her riding motorcycles in the forties, and when the economic conditions in Puerto Rico became bleak she left for New York without knowing any English. She was not going to let her two children go hungry; she joined the thousands of Puerto Ricans who were part of the mass migration to the United States in the late forties and early fifties.

I grew up in Manhattan on West 81st Street, where my mother still lives

today. Our home was always open to our community. When people came
from Puerto Rico, this was the place to go. They knew they could get
support, whether it was a meal, information on how to find a job, a
room, or just a place to rest. My mother took care of children and was
the neighborhood nurse. She had a room where she would detox addicts
cold turkey with herbs and love. She was part of a strong community
of women, and I was right in the middle of it. I was the community translator at the welfare center, schools, and hospitals. My mother worked as
a hotel maid for twenty-five years. There she learned how to make the
union work for her and taught me about the importance of being a union
member.

I picked up organizing and leadership skills out of necessity early in
life at home, school, and in my community. In the Police Athletic League
(PAL), at the age of eight, I got my first real training as an organizer
participating in the different PAL activities: art classes, tumbling team,
chorus, dancing, and cooking classes. I was also part of the after-school
programs in my elementary school, PS 87, and in JHS 44. When the
PAL program closed I joined United Neighborhood House and Goddard
Riverside Community Center (GRCC). I see myself as a real product of
the University Settlement House movement. They developed leadership
skills in poor working-class Puerto Rican and African American youth.
Fred Johnson and George Lockheart, two wonderful and dedicated counselors, had a great impact on my development. At sixteen, I was part of
the GRCC leadership training and the Citywide Youth Council run by the
Youth Board of the City of New York. We organized meetings, dances,
and trips and learned how to advocate for our rights as young people.
I was also close to a youth gang, the Enchanted Angels, and was part of a
girl's group called the Teenettes.

I began working at the age of fourteen as a counselor for the Summer
Youth Program and then at the Pioneer Youth Camp/GRCC in Rifton,
New York. This experience exposed me to progressive thinking and further leadership development. However working as a youth counselor at
University Settlement House in the Lower East Side at the age of nineteen
was where I began to put into practice my leadership skills. Since then I
have worked with every age group from nursery school to seniors, advocating and organizing as a social worker.

I have survived all the ills of growing up Puerto Rican and part of the
working class of New York City. I have experienced physical abuse, rape,
alcoholism, and a racist educational system—a system, that when it first
learned my name told me to change it. When I spoke Spanish, I was sent
to the principal's office, and when I said, "I want to be a nurse," I was

given cooking and drawing classes. This is just a small part of my story of living in the belly of the beast and going beyond survival.

Getting Political

I really believed in the American dream, a real patriot. I would even cry when I heard the national anthem, but the atrocities of the Vietnam War, the South, and the killing of President Kennedy turned me around. How could my country be doing these things? I began to look for answers; I became a civil rights and antiwar activist very early on. I went to my first May Day demonstration at age fourteen with Dr. Janet Karlson, a White Harlem activist, a communist, and the mother of my friend Kathe. My first real political act of defiance against authority was deciding not to salute the American flag at graduation from Julia Richmond High School in June of 1963. A group of my fellow students and I were protesting the hosings, killings, bombings, and general terrorizing of Blacks in the South. The school administration threatened not to give us our diplomas, but we stood firm and protested anyway. That same summer I was in Washington, D.C., when Martin Luther King Jr. gave his "I have a Dream" speech. I, along with thousands of others, was wading in the Lincoln Memorial pool, standing up against racism and economic injustice.

After graduating high school I was a functional illiterate with a general diploma, and I attended Washington Irving Evening High School to get the academic credits required for college. There I organized against the war bringing the Berrigan brothers (they are still Jesuit priests) to speak in support of Lt. Howard Levy, a doctor who refused to serve in Vietnam. I went to the W. E. B. Du Bois Club meetings in the Lower East Side, the youth group of the Communist Party of the United States. I was even asked to join one of their study groups but did not because I found the members too dry and too white. Once at City College I got involved in organizing evening students during the student strikes of 1968 and 1969. I was on my own now and worked full time, always finding ways to be politically active and to dance. I was a serious *salsera*. I was at the Pentagon demonstration in 1968 putting flowers into the soldiers' bayonets and running from their tear gas. I was also at Woodstock working in the first-aid tent and dealing with mostly white youths who had OD'd on drugs.

For a while I was even going to the Movimiento Pro Independencia (MPI) meetings—not really understanding what the group members were saying; I was bored but felt it was important for me to be there to develop myself. I was determined to learn and understand what was going on in Puerto Rico and with Puerto Ricans in the United States. I needed to know my history, but it was all in Spanish, and I was just relearning my language. Most of the time I did not feel I belonged, but the MPI meetings were open so I went. At the time I believed it was because I did not speak the language that I felt so uncomfortable, but now I understand that it was the class, language, and even color discrimination that existed in the group. Maybe the discrimination was not intentional, but it was enough to make me feel uncomfortable. Most of the members were intellectuals from the island with minimal understanding of Puerto Ricans in the United States and with little or no interest in our situation. They seemed more interested in working with their white European-American counterparts than with us. I did not allow myself to be discouraged and found some very supportive people. Such *compañeras* as Genoveva Clemente, Ana Marta Morales, and Rosa Escobar saw our potential and believed that Puerto Ricans in the United States had an important role to play and nurtured many of us. As an artist I was also involved in the Puerto Rican cultural movement made up of poets, musicians, and other artists. I developed close friendships with Pedro Pietri, Dylcia Pagán, Sandra María Estéves, Tato Laviera, Joe Falcón, and the late Carlos Osorio and Jorge Soto, among many others. I have never been a person who joins groups or activities without really knowing what I am getting into, so I did not join any organization. I was learning from different people and groups, experimenting with and experiencing the movement on all its levels.

CUBA

Things changed when in August of 1970 I got the opportunity to go to Cuba with the Venceremos Brigade. Cuba was the center of revolutionary activity for the anti-imperialist movement. I had supported the Cuban Revolution since the mid-1960s, even though I had some questions about Communism. The youth movement identified with Ché Guevara on a deep, personal level. To us Cuba and Ché were one. When he was assassinated in 1968 I was heartbroken. He was our symbol of hope, of the possibilities, of revolutionary love and courage. How dare they take him away from us—first Malcolm, then Albizu, and now Ché. I cried at the loss and became even more committed.

In 1969 I joined the Venceremos Brigade, an anti-imperialist organization that since 1968 had been taking mostly young white people to Cuba to help build the revolution and to see for themselves how socialism was working. More than five hundred youths from every nationality and from all over the country went to challenge the U.S.-government travel ban to Cuba that violated our constitutional rights. Along with Cubans and other international work brigades we planted citrus trees in the Isle of Youth. This was a powerful educational experience that I will never forget, especially the camaraderie and support.

For two and a half months we worked, played, studied, and traveled around Cuba, working shoulder to shoulder and learning from revolutionaries from all over the world. The most impressive were the Vietnamese, who at a time when the U.S. government was bombing their homeland, showed us love and respect. The *compañeros* from Angola were the same. Whenever we asked what we could do to support them they all said the same thing: "The only way you can help us is by making revolution in the United States, put pressure on your government to stop the bombings, to stop the economic blockades, to stop the CIA infiltration." This trip to Cuba transformed and saved my life. It gave me the hope that I still have today. I, as part of a worldwide working class, a person of color, could make a difference, could give leadership, and could help transform the world. This is why, to this day, I am an active supporter of the Cuban Revolution.

El Comité

Before I left for Cuba, I had been active in supporting El Comité, a community group based on the West Side of Manhattan that was started by a softball team made up of ex-gang members, factory workers, and Vietnam vets. I had grown up with most of them, and we were close friends. Federíco Lora, one of the founders, had been my friend since the age of twelve and married my second cousin Carmen. El Comité was family; we were all from the neighborhood and had strong ties. As part of the squatters' movement in the West Side of Manhattan, El Comité had taken over a storefront on 88th Street and Columbus Avenue. The squatters' movement was the organized response of the poor, working-class, multinational community to the city's Urban Renewal Program or, as we called it, Herman Badillo's "Urban Removal Program." In Vietnam the government was bombing villages, and in New York it was destroying good, low-income housing to build high-risers for the rich. For us it was one and the same. We organized with "Operation Move-In" in the fight to take back our community.

The week I left for Cuba I gave Federíco my most prized possessions: my Puerto Rican flag (it was hard to find one in those days), all the Marxist books from the study group I did not go to, and books on Puerto Rican and Latin America in Spanish that I had not read. By the time I got back from Cuba El Comité was a full-fledged revolutionary organization. Although I would like to think it was my gifts that made the difference, El

Comité was a product of the era. The times were hot; things were happening real fast. We were witnessing a worldwide revolution; there were liberation struggles in Asia, Africa, Latin America, and right here in the United States with the Black Panther Party and the Young Lords Party. All these organizations were anticapitalist and socialist in nature. Their political programs and their newspapers reflected the writings of Malcolm, Marx, Lenin, Ché, Mao, Regis Debray, Ho Chi Minh, Giap, Camilo Torres, and many other revolutionaries. Imperialism was being challenged head-on in Angola, Cuba, Vietnam, and in every corner of the world by young people who had nothing to lose. Here in the United States we equated socialism with ending racism and poverty in our communities. We believed we could make it happen, transform the capitalist shit around us. The gains we made were many in education, health care, jobs, housing, etc. We did have an impact on this country's thinking and opened up opportunities for many in media and government. For those of us who took up our people's legacy of struggle, the revolution was now and state power was right around the corner. We were working-class youth who had said "¡*Basta Ya!*" (Enough!) and were living our lives as political activists, working to transform everything around us with revolutionary theory and practice.

I arrived back in New York from Cuba on October 28, 1970; I had become a vegetarian, had moved into a women's collective, and was ready to join an organization. By this time I had already dropped out of college (not to return until 1994). Of course my first choice of organizations to join was the Young Lords Party. They were all over the newspapers. While in Cuba we followed the church takeover in *El Barrio*. I marched with more than ten thousand people in the Venceremos Brigade contingent on October 30, 1970, to the UN demanding Independence for Puerto Rico. I was pumped and mustered up the courage to make the most important decision of my life—to join the Young Lords Party. I went to their office on 111th Street and Madison Avenue, opened the door, and the smell of pot hit me. I said my *hólas* (hellos), looked around, bought their newspaper, *Pa'lante*, and left. You see, my younger brother Angel Rafael was struggling with his drug addiction at the time. Many of my friends had died from drugs or were in jail. There was no way I could rationalize substance abuse within revolutionary politics. I drank from the age of fifteen to twenty-two and stopped drinking because I was becoming an alcoholic. I had chosen to live a drug-and-alcohol-free life and was active with the antidrug movement. I believed and still do that we cannot organize our community if we are using the substances that are being used by the government to control and kill us.

Although I was a Young Lord at heart, I could not join them. But I was still committed to joining a revolutionary organization. MPI was out because I was "too New York." The Black Panthers' ten-point program did not address the independence of Puerto Rico. My only option was El Comité. Their political program was similar to the Young Lords' and included an antidrug policy, but I took it slow. I first began work on organizing *Unidad Latina,* the community newspaper published by El Comité. Ironically it was Richie Pérez from the Young Lords who trained me by building on my skills as a layout artist. Being at the central office of the Lord's Party in the Bronx was an unforgettable experience, and since then Richie and I have continued to collaborate in social justice work.

It was not until January of 1971 that I became a full-fledged member of El Comité and part of their steering committee, with Federíco Lora, an ex-U.S. Marine from the Dominican Republic, and Americo Badillo, an ex-Jesuit from Puerto Rico. I was in charge of outreach and community organizing and worked as assistant editor of *Unidad Latina.* I was twenty-four, full of energy and revolutionary fervor, and felt I could do anything. I accepted the challenge to be in leadership not really understanding why I was chosen and doubting my ability. I walked in fear; my level of insecurity and self-doubt was high. Clearly, I was a product of capitalist society, and although I fought internalized oppression and colonized mentality tooth and nail, that capitalist society still had a hold on me—but I participated in leadership anyway. Looking back I can now understand why I was chosen to be in the steering committee. I was already a seasoned organizer who had technical skills and a clear commitment to revolutionary struggle. And how many poor, working-class Puerto Ricans had hands-on experience with the Cuban Revolution? I was also a woman, and El Comité had made a commitment to develop women's leadership. As a member of El Comité I helped train many people in community organizing and raised political consciousness all over the city. I was an anti-imperialist, a revolutionary Nationalist moving toward socialism, trying to make a better life for myself and my community. I believed that we needed to dismantle capitalism to survive as a people and organized toward that end. I still do!

In the early years El Comité was involved in different campaigns in the neighborhood and citywide. We were known as a militant, principled, and dedicated organization that did what it set out to do. We focused on the quality of public education, the need for bilingual programs, housing, health care, re-education of our community, the independence of Puerto Rico, and the release of the Nationalist prisoners. We were part of a multinational movement that was developing in this country and worked together with the broader community to make change. The West Side was a hotbed of struggle. All along the streets and avenues (Columbus and

Amsterdam) groups were setting up storefronts in vacant buildings because absentee landlords were letting the buildings lay idle and waiting for the real estate market to skyrocket. There were lots of creative groups working with the community. There was a women's center run by white radical feminists. Asians, under the leadership of Yuri Kuchiyama, organized "Chickens Come Home to Roost," another community-based political group. A popular karate school, run by Sensei Gerald Orange, trained women and people of color in self-defense. Two other storefronts included Ana Marta Morales' Café, the *Nueva Canción* cultural center featuring Latin American protest music, and the "Broadway Local," a community newspaper and food shop run by hippies. Even the middle class were opening up their brownstones for political activity. *"Casa Betances,"* Nelson Canales's home, was one of these places and so was Ruth and Eli Messenger's home.

Unidad Latina was the first political publication of El Comité. It began as a bilingual, local community paper and grew into a citywide publication. We talked about our day-to-day struggles and taught our history in our paper. At first Federíco Lora was the editor and did most of the writing, but as we grew we used the paper to train everyone in the organization in all aspects of journalism and communication skills. We used it as an organizing tool and as a way to relearn our language. Every Saturday we would go all over the city, to every Puerto Rican and Latino community, knocking on doors selling our paper, educating and recruiting new members. We had the latest news from our local struggle, from Latin America, articles on our history, poetry handwritten by Federíco, and political drawings by our local artist. We also made connections with the worldwide, working class revolutionary movement. By 1972 we had expanded and even had an office. Americo Badillo took over the paper to make it more professional and political. He and I had class differences that came out in the work. As he said many times, he was from *"la gran burguesía"* ("the big bourgeoisie") of Puerto Rico.

In March 1971 El Comité organized a conference at the All Angels Church, at 112th Street in *El Barrio*, demanding the freedom of the Puerto Rican Nationalists. This was our first major effort that, I think, established us as a serious Puerto Rican organization. We worked closely with Frank Vergara and other students from the Borough of Manhattan Community College. Frank became a leading member of the organization and is still active today. Close to one thousand people attended this conference. Family members, representatives from the Nationalist Party, from every Puerto Rican organization here, and many from the island spoke. There had not been an activity of this magnitude since the arrest of the Nationalists in the fifties. El Frente Unido Pro Presos Políticos Puertorriqueños, a coalition of the different organizations and individuals, was formed to coordinate the work for the release of more than nine political prisoners in U.S. jails. One of our first actions was a mobilization to Washington, D.C., in 1972. More than two thousand people attended. We had began the process for the release of the Nationalists, which was finally achieved eight years later.

Housing was one of the areas in which El Comité did its best work. We worked with "Operation Move-In," the 112th Street squatters on Amsterdam Avenue, and housing organizers in the Bronx and Lower East Side. We would move families back into buildings that the city and landlords had closed. We even took over the newly built high-rise buildings. The film *Rompiendo Puertas* (*Breaking and Entering*), made by Third World News Real, provides a portrait of the full impact of the times. (If you are quick you might get a glimpse of my Afro. It was also our policy not to be filmed. The credit and any publicity had to go to the community, not the organizers.) In November of 1971 we pulled off the "Thanksgiving Day Turkey Offensive." In one of the buildings we were organizing, the tenant's association had been negotiating with the slumlord for months. There was no response. It was a cold November, no heat, no hot water; the landlord would not make any repairs, and the city was not taking any action. We agreed that if the tenants could not have a thankful Thanksgiving, neither would the landlord. We rented a bus and with all the tenants went out to Queens and picketed the landlord's home on Thanksgiving Day. It did not end there. We had our own silk-screen shop, and the night before we silk-screened one hundred posters of the landlord wearing a Ku Klux Klan hood—his name and "KKK" were printed all over the poster. Thanksgiving morning, before dawn, we plastered the poster from the top to the bottom of his office building as well as throughout the entire neighborhood using hot, homemade glue. It worked—he responded to the tenants' needs with speed. The organizing work was labor intensive, but we had the will, commitment, and energy that was needed to do it, and we did.

People ask what were the differences between the Young Lords and El Comité. First of all I think El Comité's members were older. The average age of a Young Lord was the late teens; El Comité's members were in their mid-twenties with more life experience behind them. Most of the members of El Comité were workers with families; even the few who were students were working. Many had experienced the Vietnam War. Some had been organizing in their community for years. El Comité's members were anti-drug. We were a smaller organization rooted in our local community struggles and had more of a family focus. We were also extremely consistent and followed through for years with all our struggles. We were more grounded in reality and knew change took time, organization, and patience. We promoted that all our members learn basic skills: reading, writing, Spanish, history, and further schooling for those who wanted it. In the early period, to prevent co-optation, we had a policy that our members could not work in government or poverty organizations. Our connection to Latin America and Puerto Rico was strong. We had members from Argentina, Cuba, the Dominican Republic, Mexico, and other countries. We were able to deal with the tension between organizing for national liberation and our democratic rights in the United States with better balance. The organization was exposed to serious revolutionaries from other countries and from the United States who took us under their wing and pointed the way, and we were open to learn from them.

In the spring of 1972 we began an intensive study to understand our history, Marxism, and organizing. In the beginning this was difficult because many of us could not read well enough to understand the concepts. Some of us could not read at all. We used films and drawings, read out loud, and did one-to-one study. I remember being in a study group and reading Lenin's *What Is to Be Done* in Spanish. The group met three times a week. In the mornings I would go to my study group, and in the afternoon I would go to my tutor, Félix Cortéz, who was a Columbia student, a poet, and a squatter. He would go over everything in English and break down all the words and concepts I had not understood. This was the way many of us prepared for the discussions on the transition the organization was going through.

In October of 1972 I left El Comité. In retrospect I can say that it was because I disagreed with the political direction the organization had chosen to take, but at the time I simply thought it was for personal reasons, not understanding that the political is the personal. The position I supported was that El Comité continue to study Marxism but remain a community-based organization. However, after the period of intensive Marxist study, I agreed with the rest of the membership and in August of 1972 El Comité became a Marxist-Leninist organization. The members of the organization at that time were the late Iris Vergara, Max Colón, Americo Badillo, Nancy Miranda, Orlando Colón, Noel Colón, Maria Collado, Federíco Lora, Carmen Lora Martell, Manny Ortíz, Pete Rentas, Victor El Gato, Nelson Gómez, Hawk, Lillian Jiménez, Frank Vergara, Julio Pabón, Lourdes García, Nilsa Gutierrez, Emilio Morante, Elogio Ortíz, Arsenio Butch González, and a few others. Many of the original members from the softball team had left the organization by this time. The new members, even though they came from working-class backgrounds, were mostly students.

On the final day of our transition meeting, although most of the members felt I had not developed enough politically and was too "street" for the position, I was still chosen to continue in leadership as a member of the new Central Committee. Basically, I was chosen for my organizing skills only. I tried to work under the new structure for two months but could not. It was too hierarchical, centralized, and rigid for me. We had lost the collective, flexible, humanistic feeling. There was no more compassion, no balance between the political and the personal. I was overworked and no one cared. Criticism was used to beat people up and not to help them grow. I left emotionally devastated because of the criticism and feeling alienated, rejected, and alone with deep hurt and anger. I had lost my "family"; I became another casualty of the times.

It was a difficult time for me, but with the support of Federíco Lora, comrades from other organizations, and such good friends as Diana Caballero, I continued my political work. I worked with El Frente Unido in support of Puerto Rican political prisoners, with the women's movement in support of the national liberation of Vietnam, and with the Puerto Rican cultural movement demanding programming on public TV, including such programs as *"Realidades."* I was an artist-in-residence at El Taller Boricua and worked with the original group that fought for the creation of the Center for Puerto Rican Studies. I was also active with the Puerto Rican Solidarity Committee. I continued working in coalitions with El Comité and would align with them on many issues because I had similar politics—not surprising given that I had helped to form the basic politics of the organization. I think this is why so many people to this day believe I was a long-term member of El Comité–MINP.

THE LATIN WOMEN'S COLLECTIVE

In 1975 I was invited to attend the Second Women's Conference in support of Vietnam in Toronto, Canada. I had attended the first conference in 1971 and was part of the national organizing committee, a multinational group. Olga Sanabria of PSP, Eli Morales of MPD (Movimiento Popular Dominicano, a Dominican revolutionary organization), Dr. Helen Rodríguez (a leader of the campaign to prevent sterilization abuse), Carmen Lora of El Comité–MINP, Concha Mendoza of the Antonio Maceo Brigade, Genoveva Clemente, and myself made up the Latinas who attended from New York. For the conference we put together a presentation that was to become the political framework for the creation of the Latin Women's Collective. Around the same time I had been discussing with Federíco Lora the need to begin a Puerto Rican women's organization to train sisters in leadership skills for El Comité–MINP and for the movement in general. It all came together in the summer of 1975 when Eli Morales, Carmen Lora, Genoveva Clemente, Ana Juarbe, Sandra Trujillo, Blanca Vázquez, Lillian Jiménez, Elina Roman, and others begun the organizing process for the Latin Women's Collective. We had worked together in different movements and were coming together for the first time to organize women from a working-class perspective. This was very important to us because as women of color we wanted to separate ourselves from the white feminist movement, which we felt was racist and ignored our needs. We researched our situation in education, health, labor, and we studied Engels's *The Origins of the Family and the State,* revolutionary women's organizations in Cuba, Vietnam, and other countries, women's organizations in the United States, and women leaders in our communities here in the United States, Puerto Rico, and Latin America.

We wanted to create an organization that was reflective of our needs and those of the community—for women by women with working-class politics. Our slogan was *"Liberación De La Mujer Através De La Lucha Obrera,"* ("Women's liberation through the working-class struggle"). We believed that working-class women historically had been the backbone of most political and community organizations, but they never took or got the credit for their hard work. To be leaders we had to develop writing, speaking, and analytical skills and the courage to take up the struggle against sexism within us and our community. We took the challenge, and the Latin Women's Collective was born. We combined the personal and the political, applying critical thinking to all aspects of our lives. It was about internalizing our politics and living them actively in our hearts. We wanted to know why it was so difficult for women who had been in the Left for so many years to speak and be the powerful leaders that they were openly. We looked at the political, historical, cultural, and individual barriers. We learned to be assertive with support from our sisters and to transcend our tears and shake the fear. We were determined to let go of centuries of internalized oppression that many women had perpetuated by saying "I cannot do it," and allowing men to lead. We conducted basic training in how to speak, read, write, research, run meetings and how to organize different types of activities and how to think critically. We measured our success by the women from the collective who became active leaders in our community.

The organization grew in members, and at our peak close to sixty women attended our monthly meetings. We got incorporated, opened a storefront in East Harlem on 115th Street, institutionalized March 8 as International Working Women's Day, published a newsletter, *La Semilla,* worked with women from the community, and developed a real support network for our members. We were a volunteer organization with a steering committee made up of representatives from each of the working committees. In the beginning of the organization there was a balance in the steering committee because there were representatives from different organizations and nonaffiliated members. But as the organization took root, some of the participating groups left. El Comité–MINP began to recruit from the collective, pulling out the more developed members and continued to use the collective to further develop their own membership, including even white women. This left a political void in the Latin Women's Collective. The new, less-experienced members of El Comité–MINP who were students wanted to turn the collective into a social-service organization.

I left the collective in the summer of 1978 after a long struggle within the organization to restructure it politically and organizationally. There were those who wanted to strengthen our anticapitalist, anti-imperialist perspective and those who wanted to "mainstream" the organization. They said we needed to become more democratic and have the members more involved in decision-making. To this day I do not know what that meant because the steering committee of the collective was made up of two representatives from each committee and meetings were open to all members. We did everything collectively and could not make any policy decision without the approval of the general body. I believe that under the guise of democratizing the collective what members of El Comité did was change the working-class politics of the organization. If we look at the history of El Comité–MINP, we can see that at the time this so-called democratization was going on in the collective its leading members were leaving for Puerto Rico, and there was a similar struggle within El Comité–MINP. After I left, the other leading independent forces also left, and six months later the collective closed its doors. For me it was a learning experience that I carry with me always. It taught me a great deal about coalition work within organizations. Even with the contradictions within the organization I feel it was a great success because many of the women who worked with us are still actively organizing working-class women in our communities here and in their homelands. We were able to change the quality of life of many women and their families and many are still pursuing this kind of organizing today.

REFLECTIONS ON EL COMITÉ–MINP AND THE LEFT IN GENERAL

As I make the following observations keep in mind that I was no longer a part of the heart of the organization. In the mid 1970s El Comité changed its name to El Comité–MINP, and the paper's name to *Obreros en Marcha*. Its work continued to grow and flourish. The group played an important role in the development of the New Communist Movement in the United States and in the struggle for the national liberation of Puerto

Rico. It was also known and well respected for its democratic-rights work all over the city. Many of their members began to get involved in mainstream politics. El Comité–MINP was a product of the times and just like all the other Left organizations they were also consumed by the system. Although it took longer with El Comité–MINP, it closed its doors in the spring of 1981.

As the U.S. human rights movement grew and became more militant in its opposition to racist and antipoor, anti-working-class domestic and foreign policies, the FBI intensified its domestic surveillance and counterinsurgency programs aimed at the Black and Latino community. From the late 1960s on, the U.S. government's counterintelligence program, COINTELPRO, attempted to destroy radical dissent in the United States by murdering, framing, and incarcerating the movement's leaders. Others, such as Guillermo Morales who was a member of the FALN and currently living in Cuba, were forced into exile. COINTELPRO intimidated, co-opted, and frightened many of our people away from militant radical solutions. The government, along with the media, intensified its misinformation campaign by making capitalism attractive and selling false hope. Many people began to believe that our social and economic problems could be addressed within the capitalist system and joined capitalist parties. How wrong they were! Without the militant fight, the capitalists took back many of our democratic rights one by one.

Beside the government attacks some of the other factors, in my opinion, that led to the closing of El Comité–MINP were: 1. Many of the founding members with distinct working-class politics left for Puerto Rico leaving a political vacuum and creating a class imbalance in the organization. The new leadership was made up of mostly students with more conservative politics. They wanted to mainstream the organization and move into Democratic Party politics. 2. El Comité, just like the rest of the Puerto Rican Left, prematurely became a pre-party formation. The Young Lords became the Puerto Rican Revolutionary Workers Organization in 1972, and MPI become the Puerto Rican Socialist Party in 1971. History has shown that the groups read the times wrong and moved faster than the people, and in the process destroyed their organizations.

When El Comité–MINP became a pre-party organization and began to work with the party-building movement they also opened up to multinational membership, but those that joined were mostly European Americans. I know that El Comité addressed the issue of racism from a theoretical framework, but I do not think they took up the question of how internalized racism and white-skin privilege can divide an organization that does not deal with these issues. I believe it is the responsibility of European Americans to take up actively the inner struggle against their racist attitudes within their own community as they fight for social justice in a multinational organization. This is one of the many ways they can be true allies to people of color.

Of course there was also the issue of homophobia, which the organization was having a hard time addressing. The Puerto Rican movement has had a history of gay and lesbian leaders in the movement for national liberation. Some of these leaders have felt that the only way they could maintain their position in the movement was by staying in the closet. Although El Comité–MINP had a progressive position on the issue of gay and lesbian rights, they were not able to create a safe and supportive atmosphere for their gay and lesbian members/leaders to be open. These unsupportive attitudes reinforced the internalized homophobia of the gay and lesbian leaders. It seemed that the organization believed that the effectiveness of their organizers would be compromised if the community knew they were gays and lesbians. In my experience this has not been the case in general. Many times I have found our community to be open and supportive of gay and lesbian activists. What has been important to the community is the person's ability to organize, not their life style. The responsibility of an organization is to educate the community and to promote unity in diversity in its organizing and not to censor itself. We need to challenge all backward thinking.

The decline of the international socialist movement also affected El Comité–MINP and the Puerto Rican movement in general. Many people lost hope, not knowing what to do next. They stopped believing that the working class could win and became cynical and disenchanted, with many turning to drugs and alcohol. They did not understand that this was part of the dialectical process of growth, development, and change.

When we look at what caused such a viable organization as El Comité to close its doors after ten years of exemplary organizing, we find a combination of external factors, the state, the changing political climate, and the internal sociopolitical, cultural factors, such as not being able to deal with the contradictions that are created between class, race, gender, and sexual orientation. El Comité–MINP stands with the history of the Puerto Rican Left in New York. There have not been many Puerto Rican Communist organizations in New York City with the long trajectory of struggle like that of El Comité–MINP. I hope that one day the organization's history will be written, fully capturing the range of perspectives that made up its experience. Documenting this history is key to the growth of our community and movement.

In looking at the Puerto Rican movement as a whole and the positive contributions that we made in the seventies and early eighties, first we need to point out that we built on our legacy of struggle. We stood on the shoulders of such Nationalists as Betances, Albizu, Lolita Lebrón, and such communists as Luisa Capetillo, Jesús Colón, Bernardo Vega, Julia de Burgos, Juana Colón, Evelina Antonetti, Antonio Corretjer, Genoveva Clemente, Gerena Valentín, and many others. We were able to reclaim our culture, history, and language and pass it on to the younger generation of Puerto Ricans. It was through our generation's efforts that the door of hope and possibility was opened. Our African/Taino music, art, and dance began to be heard throughout the public schools. Puerto Rican museums, colleges, and cultural centers were created. The women's role as leaders in the Puerto Rican movement was also key. We were able to link the community, labor, and women's-rights struggle with our day-to-day fight for human justice. We established coalitions with other Latinos, African Americans, Asians, Native Americans, and European Americans, fighting back against our common oppression and becoming stronger.

We had some victories in bringing about open admissions at City University, initiating bilingual education programs, strengthening community control of the schools, opening community health centers, winning the fight for low-income housing, creating affirmative action programs, and strengthening the unions. We were also able to free Puerto Rican political prisoners Carlos Feliciano, Eduardo "Pancho" Cruz, Humberto Pagán, Martín Sostre, Humberto Cintrón, numerous grand-jury resisters, and the five Nationalists (who were released in the fall of 1979) because of all our efforts. It did take us nine years from the time we made the commitment to free the five Nationalists, but we were consistent in our efforts and made it happen.

Puerto Ricans in the United States were more accepted by the Puerto Rican Left on the island. They began to take us more seriously, and some of them began to see us as part of the national liberation struggle. Even with all our setbacks we still have a viable movement today. It is slowly regrouping, learning from its mistakes, and with a new vision it is moving toward the future with more commitment and determination.

Many of the same issues that contributed to the dissolving of El Comité–MINP affected the movement overall: COINTELPRO, the decline of the international socialist movement, racism, homophobia, leading members leaving organizations and not believing the that working class could win. We can add to this list a few more issues.

Many of our best communist organizers joined the Democratic Party. They said that we needed to work within the system to change it, but clearly they were co-opted. What else can it be called when former leading members of Communist organizations are now head city negotiators using all their Marxist training to deny health, education, and welfare to the working class and acting as apologists for capitalism?

Sectarianism and infighting also devastated our movement. Groups that believed they had the correct political organizational line would not work with other organizations or would say one thing and do another. There were also the emotional and physical attacks of comrades by comrades to the point where people's lives were threatened and some comrades were seriously hurt. The accusations of agent infiltrations had everyone paranoid and left us with low levels of trust. To this day many will not even talk about their experiences, harboring anger and resentment.

Our idealism and political immaturity also affected us. We were not able to see beyond the current situation and did not have the vision to ride the waves of change and hold onto our dreams; we fell into pessimism and forgot our history of struggle and that creating change takes time and patience.

I will never forget this time of my life. I learned a great deal and also made some very good friends. I now have been politically active for more than thirty years. I have worked in different types of organizations dealing with all kinds of issues and people, inside and outside of my community. What I bring to this organizing work, whether it is a parent's association meeting or the solidarity movement, is a commitment to class struggle and dialectical thinking. Many people who considered themselves communists in the 1970s, the same people who carried Marx, Lenin, and Mao in their back pockets, today ask me, "Espé, when will you grow up?" In contrast to them, I did not become a communist until the 1980s, even though I had strong working-class politics. As I said before, I need to know what I am getting into before I join anything. It took me years of study to understand, to accept the science of historical dialectical materialism; of course, I still have questions, but that is my nature to question everything. To those who ask whether I have grown up, I say, "Yes, I've grown up; into a communist!" And I hope to become even more committed.

Since the 1980s I have worked with the National Congress for Puerto Rican Rights, the International Working Women's Day Committee, the Puerto Rican Committee Against Repression, El Comité de Afirmación Puertorriqueña, the Mumia Abu Jamal Coalition, and other antiracist groups to stop police brutality, racial violence, and the death penalty. I continue my work for women's rights and alternative healing. The well being of my community is at the forefront of all my work. In all the issues with which I deal, I always raise the liberation of Puerto Rico and the freedom for our prisoners.

In recent years our work has gone against the current; we have been challenging the apologists for the Democratic Party who told us that direct action does not work anymore and those who said communism and the movement for social justice is dead. We are out in the streets demanding what is ours, raising consciousness and creating a new movement. We continue to build alliances, posing alternatives for young people looking for answers and the truth. I have found that it is important to be consistent if we want to make real change and not despair. We need to always look for alternatives and believe in a deep way that we are going to win no matter what the setbacks.

The work to free the Puerto Rican political prisoners and prisoners of war has to be a top priority. I approach this work both from a human rights and a national liberation perspective. There are many people who say that we cannot combine issues, that we should only look at the humanitarian aspects of the amnesty campaign to free the Puerto Rican political prisoners—that we will get more people involved in the campaign if we only talk about the prison conditions, their poor families, and the exorbitant number of years they have been in jail. This is what I call the "*ay bendito*" (poor me) syndrome. This is all good and well, but the state is not making a separation. These patriots are in U.S. jails because they believe in the independence of Puerto Rico, our right to self-determination, and the right to armed struggle. The few prisoners that have gone in front of the parole board with exceptional records have been told that they must renounce their political beliefs in one way or another. Each of them were denied parole when they held to their position. I am of the belief that you cannot separate the issue of the human rights violations from the struggle for national liberation. It is important to be honest with people by clearly painting the whole picture and letting the people decide how they are going to support the release of the prisoners. With the truth, we decriminalize the struggle for the independence of Puerto Rico. As a colonized people, we have the right under the United Nations charter on decolonization to pick up arms, and this comes from my beliefs as a revolutionary pacifist. Camilo Torres was a Latin American priest who, back in the 1960s, saw the need to engage in armed struggle to end the power of the elites who were terrorizing the Colombian peasantry. I am sure it was the most painful thing for him to turn to revolutionary violence. But what else can one do? Even the War Resisters League, a leading pacifist organization, now supports the release of the Puerto Rican prisoners.

In the last few years the organizing for the release of the prisoners has taken on more momentum. The work of ProLibertad and the Amnesty Campaign to Free the Puerto Rican Political Prisoners combined with efforts in the legislative and religious communities have been very effective. We have taken the campaign to the community. In the summers of 1995, 1996, and 1997 more than eighty ProLibertad volunteers could be found collecting signatures at the Puerto Rican Day Parades, festivals, and even at beaches. To break with our fear of the state and to stop the isolation of the prisoners, we ask people to send postcards to the prisoners. This has made the prisoners more real and gotten them more involved with the struggle for their freedom and with the community. We need to hear the prisoners' voices and engage them in the process for liberation actively. ProLibertad is creating a book of poetry written for the prisoners, a video, a freedom quilt, and it is conducting training in organizing skills. Now we are organizing to commemorate one hundred years of U.S. colonialism with demonstrations to the United Nations and in Washington, D.C., joining in the international call for the end of colonialism and for the freedom of our political prisoners.

We Will Be Free!

Two decades from now I will be in my seventies and hope to be active still. I want to be a Doña Adelfa Vera or a Rosa Escobar, Puerto Rican working-class women who became stronger in their convictions and actions as the years passed. By their example, they have passed on years of experience. Now it is our turn. Together with our youth we will find ways of freeing ourselves from internalized oppression and be the powerful people that we are. Capitalism and colonialism will lose their hold on us. We have the power to transform ourselves. I was able to rise from the depths of capitalism and so can all of us who want a better world for ourselves and the generations to come. It takes time and patience to build a movement and sustain a revolution in our hearts and minds. But I know we can do it because we have been doing it. We do have the collective power within us to transform our lives and save our planet. We just need to believe that we will win! As my good friend the poet Susana Cabañas says in the last lines of her poem *"Elegía a Julia de Burgos"* ("Elegy to Julia de Burgos"):

> Yo rehuso convertirme en otra estadística.
> Seré yo y será borinquen
> Libre!

> I refuse to be turned into another statistic
> I and *Borínquen* will be
> Free!

11 Our Movement

One Woman's Story

I WAS born on Wilkins Avenue in the South Bronx and grew up in a succession of New York City neighborhoods. When I was still an infant, my family moved to Washington Heights in Manhattan; we lived there, on 178th Street and Amsterdam Avenue, until I was nine years old. I have good memories growing up there. My father owned a candy store next door to our building at 500 West 178th Street. There were lots of kids on the block and in the summer, after dinner, we would organize "Ring-O-Leave-E-O" games that would last until nightfall. Sometimes we'd have about twenty-five kids hiding out in different apartment buildings spanning three city blocks. We'd huddle under stairs, in the cellars, until the leader found us, and we were out of the game. I remember at summer's end, sitting on the stoop with my two friends, Maria and Connie, watching the bigger kids going off to school with their new book bags and starched clothes, wishing we were going too. Being the youngest of four kids, I was always anxious to get older so I could do what my brothers and sister Philip, Ruben, and Vicky did.

It wasn't until I started first grade at Incarnation, a Catholic school, that I realized the world was not so innocent as our play times on 178th Street. There was a gang from the Bronx, the Fordham Baldies, that was terrorizing Puerto Rican and Black girls by cutting off their hair. Several girls had been attacked, and I remember how afraid I was because I always wore my hair in a ponytail. Things got so bad that Incarnation released us early from school one day because word was out that the gang was going to attack our neighborhood. My mother had to come to school and pick me up; no child was released without an escort. I went straight home and stared out the window waiting to see if the gang came. It turned out to be a false alarm. There were a lot of gangs back in the fifties. My older brother Philip told me about the Irish and Italian kids that went after the "spics" and "niggers." Gang fights were as common then as they are today, the difference being that in the fifties the weapon was a knife, now it's a gun.

My father died at the age of fifty-five of heart failure, just as our application for a public housing apartment was approved. Mami, my two brothers, my sister, and I moved to the Soundview Projects in the Bronx and lived there for seven years. I'll never forget the day we viewed the apartment—it was paradise to me. There were trees, lots of open fields, and flowers. It all seemed so clean and beautiful. Yes, in those days you could say that about a public housing development. We were all excited and told Mami that she had to take this apartment. My mother was so devastated with my father's death, alone at thirty-eight years old with four kids, all she could think of was that this apartment meant having a roof over our heads that she could afford.

Soundview was then a strong community of working-class families. My friends were Black, Puerto Rican, and Jewish, and we all went to the same schools through high school. Foremost in my mind was that I would no longer have to go to Catholic school. Soon after moving in, a Franciscan father from the Holy Cross Church in Soundview visited our home. He said he came to see about my registration in the fourth grade and to let my mother know that she would have to make a one-hundred-dollar contribution to reserve my seat. I always thought that my mother decided to enroll me in PS 107 because there was no way she could come up with one hundred dollars. It was only later, as an adult, that my mother told me that the Franciscan father followed her into the bedroom and made a pass at her. So that incident and the money were the deciding factors in which school I would attend.

Already disillusioned with the church, I stopped attending Sunday mass by the time I was eleven years old. When Papi died, the church would not say a mass for him because before marrying my mom, he'd had a previous marriage. All I could think of was that they never let that get in the way of taking his money for our tuition or Sunday offerings. Yet the church with all its gold and silk, seemed so hypocritical to not allow my mother and family this religious right.

By the mid-sixties life in Soundview became less safe. Heroin had moved into the poor and working-class communities, and along with it came robberies and violent crime. Mami worried herself sick all the time because she couldn't watch over her daughters. Both of my older brothers enlisted in the Armed Forces, leaving my mother, sister, and me to constantly be looking for *un sitio seguro*, a safe place to live, as my mother would say, so she could go to work at 6:00 A.M. and return at 6:00 P.M., without having to worry too much about her daughters being home alone. Soundview was no longer a paradise.

We moved so many times that the joke in the family was that Mami was really a gypsy who couldn't settle in any one place for too long. Even now in retirement, Mami is still moving, so now we say, when the "Santini Itch" takes over (for the Santini Brothers Moving Company), there's no stopping her.

In search of our *sitio seguro* we moved to Tremont and Burnside Avenue in the Bronx, then back to Washington Heights for a while. These were working-class communities in transition; ethnic Whites were leaving as greater numbers of Blacks and Puerto Ricans were given apartments, but the neighborhoods and public schools were still very diverse ethnically with an always growing number of Blacks and Puerto Ricans. I completed college while living at home with my mother because I knew that was her dream. She worked long and hard and was proud of her children. We had all graduated from high school and started working as soon as we turned sixteen, but she wanted us to do something more for ourselves. *Los sueños de todo padre y madre, que sus hijos vivan una vida mejor que ellos—con más seguridad financiera.* The dream of every parent, that their children live a better life than they had—with greater financial security.

BECOMING POLITICALLY CONSCIOUS

By the time I was twenty-one years old I was in my senior year at City College of New York (CCNY). My older brother and I belonged to a collective of eight young Puerto Ricans, most of whom worked in Aspira of New York as counselors. We called ourselves Puerto Ricans For Self-Determination (PRSD) and published a monthly newsletter called *El Atrevido* (*The Bold One*) featuring articles about different struggles unfolding in the city and tri state area. We started out meeting in my brother's living room and having two and three hour discussions on articles and books that we would assign for reading. Only two of us were women, and neither of us spoke up very much in the beginning. I was overwhelmed and intimidated by our meetings. This was all new to me: discussing capitalism, socialism, colonialism, class struggle, and liberation movements. But, my brain was a sponge, soaking up all the information. I fervently listened to these young Puerto Ricans, filled with a love for our people and a passion to see our community uplifted.

It wasn't long before Mariana and I started writing articles for *El Atrevido* too, although with less frequency than the men. When it was time for production and mailing of the newsletter, everyone participated equally.

After about a year of working together, we began to discuss whether we should remain a small collective or join one of the two leading radical groups in New York City: the Young Lords Party or the Movimiento Pro Independencia (MPI). We spent about two months reviewing documents of both organizations to see which came closer to representing our concerns and political interests. We respected both groups and thought that each played an important role in organizing our communities, although we understood that each had a different membership and ideological thrust.

As a college student, first at Bronx Community College, then at CCNY, I had met members of the Young Lords. The Puerto Rican Student Union (PRSU) was well organized at CCNY, and my close friend Pat was working with the Health Revolutionary Unity Movement (HRUM), a health workers' organization. Both groups were an outgrowth of the Lords' efforts.

The MPI had been founded in 1959 in Puerto Rico and had always had a small group working in New York City. Several of the other members of our collective knew about MPI from their student days at the University of Puerto Rico and through colleagues at Aspira who were members of the organization.

Unfortunately, by the early seventies there were already growing tensions between the Lords and MPI. The Lords were mostly U.S.-born or U.S.-raised Puerto Ricans while MPI was predominantly made up of island-born Puerto Ricans. Both groups prided themselves on being the representatives of the working class and mistrusted the other group's claims to being the vanguard of the movement. The issue of language— whether we all had to speak Spanish—was a constant source of conflict. Because much of the MPI leadership came from the well-educated middle class of the island, their Spanish was impeccable. Those of us born in the mainland did not always speak Spanish well, hence the development of such terms as Spanglish and Nuyorican to describe second- and third-generation, U.S.-born Puerto Ricans. For some, this description was worn proudly, in defiance of those among us who felt superior. For others, it was cause for confrontation because it denied us our right to a national identity, which geographic boundaries could not erase.

I have always seen myself as falling somewhere in between; I learned to speak Spanish and English at the same time so I had a good command of both languages. I grew up listening to salsa, soul and jazz, eating rice and beans, pizza and bagels, and going to Latin or disco clubs. Multiculturalism, diversity—the buzzwords of today—were always part of my life and culture. It was what made me proud to be a Puerto Rican New Yorker.

The Lords saw the island-born Puerto Ricans as imposing their "right to leadership" on U.S.-born Puerto Ricans. And, of course, as in all cases where more than one group tries to organize the same constituents, there were plain old turf and power struggles, along with personality clashes.

These are my own perceptions of some of the problems that kept the Puerto Rican movement from working together, and it was a weakness that we did not overcome during my time in the MPI-PSP (the MPI became the Puerto Rican Socialist Party, PSP in 1971). In fact, I believe our community remains divided along these very same issues. So little changes in ten or twenty-five years. Language continues to divide us. Puerto Ricans and other Latinos born and raised in the United States, who primarily speak English, are seen by some as less Latino. Spanish is sometimes used as a litmus test for authenticity. In school, on the job, and in the community, the English-dominant Puerto Rican is sometimes seen as a competitor who will be given greater advantage.

The sixties were a time of motion, disturbance, organizing, and anger over the racism and sexism that pervaded our society. It was a time when we, as young people, began to question and confront the system. And while we thought that we were the ones to be leading the real struggles against oppression and colonialism, ours was an extension of the hundreds of years of class struggle and organizing that many others before us had taken up. I was strongly influenced by the Civil Rights movement, the opposition to the war in Vietnam, and the women's liberation struggle.

As a high-school student at James Monroe in the Bronx, I discovered and joined Aspira, where I learned Puerto Rican history. Aspira was initiated in 1961 in New York City by Dr. Antonia Pantoja, a Puerto Rican woman who founded several of the leading Puerto Rican education and social service agencies during the War on Poverty era. Dr. Pantoja has been a constant force for our community's empowerment, and she recently received the Presidential Medal of Freedom from President Clinton, the highest award bestowed on citizens. She is the first Puerto Rican woman to receive this award. Aspira was dedicated to promoting education and leadership among Puerto Rican youth. Today, it continues to serve Latino youth with chapters in several major cities. The organization validated my feelings of pride in speaking two languages, loving our music and foods, and learning about my parents' homeland. Throughout my ten years of schooling, I had never involved myself in extracurricular activities, except to sing in the chorus. I became the president of the Monroe Aspira club, and my girlfriend Ileana was the vice president. No longer was I the "quiet" student with "so much potential," as my teachers said. Now I was running meetings, organizing students, attending leadership workshops. My very first trip to Puerto Rico, in the summer of 1967, took place with the Aspira club members who had been selected from various high schools throughout the city. Isaura Santiago, until recently president of Hostos Community College in the Bronx, was our group counselor and chaperon.

I felt the need to involve myself in the struggle somehow because there were too many things happening in the United States and around the world to just watch passively on the news or read about in the paper. Racism and discrimination touched my life at an early age, and by the time I was in high school I saw the need to fight against it. The images of Black people being hosed down and attacked by police dogs in the South and Vietnamese villages being bombed enraged me. At home, it was us, the "spics" and "niggers" who were attacked by White gangs or discriminated against by landlords who thought renting to us meant "there goes the neighborhood."

TWELVE YEARS OF RADICAL ACTIVISM

By the time I was in college I knew I had to make some choices. At any rate, in the summer of 1971, we made our choice: the Puerto Ricans for Self-Determination decided to join MPI. We thought MPI articulated a clearer organizational and political link to the struggles in Puerto Rico and the United States. It also had a membership that was much more representative in age, educational level, and class background than most people realized. We had members like Marcianito and Salas, who were well into their fifties and sixties. Then there were others like Ché and Shelley, who were in their late teens. We were factory workers, professionals, people born in the United States or Puerto Rico, from all the different Puerto Rican communities—Williamsburg, the South Bronx, *El Barrio,* northern New Jersey. There were labor organizers, intellectuals, college students, whole families.

We joined the MPI In June. The Puerto Rican Day Parade was approaching, the largest annual gathering of Puerto Ricans in the United States. I wanted to march with the Young Lords in the parade because they had decided to take the front of the march to raise their issues and demands right there on Fifth Avenue. As I stood watching on the sidewalk while the Lords contingent gathered, the police were mobilizing in Central Park at the entrance on 59th Street and Fifth Avenue. The police were out in force, on foot, on horseback, in their riot gear. They attacked the Lords, they beat them, they hauled them off to jail. Our community's response was mixed. Some understood the attack as a real show of police brutality and force; others said the police had been provoked by these young radical communists who spoiled a day of celebration and pride. For me it marked the beginning of twelve years of affirmation of the need to devote myself almost full time to bringing about some form of change in this country and in seeing Puerto Rico *Libre* (free) from U.S. domination.

From 1971 to 1973 PSP steadily grew, both in Puerto Rico and on the mainland. On 14th Street near the historic Union Square, we had our central headquarters known as Misión Vito Marcantonio–Casa Puerto Rico. It was an open loft space located in one of the central hubs of Manhattan, bordering the Lower East Side, the Village, and the Gramercy Park area. The space had a small store, Librería Puerto Rico, that featured books on Puerto Rican history, culture, posters, and artifacts. Every New York City train line converged at 14th Street, making for easy access to our chapter offices throughout the city. The streets were always packed with people. School kids coming from Washington Irving High School, Tad's Steak House was just below us, and at night the Palladium Theater just a few doors down had live music concerts and dance performances. The famous Luchow's Restaurant was nearby too; rumor had it that this used to be a gathering place for Nazi sympathizers during the 1930s and 1940s. We never did confirm this. Klein's Department Store across the street attracted the working poor from every borough, while scores of commercial businesses stretching from the east to the west side of 14th Street marketed their wares to hundreds of shoppers every day. Today, Luchow's and Klein's are no longer there.

Union Square has been the site of working-class rallies, protests, celebrations, and festivals since before the turn of the century. I remember speaking there before a women's rights rally, as a PSP representative. The crowd cheered me on as I spoke about the need to preserve and protect women's reproductive rights, called for the freedom of the five Puerto Rican Nationalist prisoners, (Lolita Lebrón, Oscar Collazo, Irving Flores, Andrés Figueroa Cordero, and Rafael Cancel Miranda), and demanded independence for Puerto Rico and social justice for Puerto Ricans in the United States. But I was terrified, my knees were shaking, my stomach was all twisted. I swore they could see how nervous I was.

Every Friday night the PSP sponsored *charlas* (forums); sometimes films or *música de protesta* was the feature. Anywhere from twenty-five to a hundred people would gather in that second-floor loft, engrossed in intense political debates and discussions. It didn't matter that in the summer there was no air conditioning and if you put the big floor fan on, you could barely hear the speaker or film, or that the heating system usually broke down during the coldest winter days. There was always something going on at Casa Puerto Rico, from early morning to late at night. As the organization grew, this became the offices for our full-time organizers, the place where our bilingual newspaper was born. I worked out of these offices for a couple of years myself.

For me this represented a time of developing my skills in speaking and understanding Spanish, of intellectual growth, in socializing not only with Puerto Ricans of all ages and backgrounds but also with other sectors of the Left. As organizers and leaders in the PSP we had to be ready to appear before a group of five or five thousand people at any time and deliver our revolutionary message. I did this often in Spanish or English. Sometimes I led political education groups as part of the training of new members. Other times it was a presentation in celebration of *El Grito de Lares* or May Day. We organized annual summer outings—*Jira de Verano*—in Arrow Park, or had "Oldies but Goodies" dances to raise funds. We even developed some "love ties." Quite a few marriages and families got their start in these settings.

In 1973 the PSP held its first congress in the United States. An influx of new members, many of whom were born or raised on the mainland, had turned the discussions and debate more toward the struggles taking place in our mainland communities. The leadership of the PSP in Puerto Rico had become more aware of the need to incorporate the reality of Puerto Ricans in the United States into the organization's strategies and tactics.

Certainly, the Puerto Rican Left was on the rise as a mass movement. In addition to the Young Lords, there was El Comité, another organization that emerged from housing struggles on the West Side of Manhattan. I think it's fair to say that these three organizations, PSP, the Young Lords, and El Comité, formed the core of the new Puerto Rican revolutionary Left.

The 1973 MPI-PSP congress was held on April 8 at the Manhattan Center on West 34th Street. At that conference, it adopted a political program—summarized in a published document titled *Desde Las Entrañas* (*From the Belly of the Beast*)—and transformed itself from a mass-based, proindependence movement to the Puerto Rican Socialist Party (PSP), a Marxist-Leninist, working-class organization dedicated to the struggle for Puerto Rican independence and for socialism both on the island and on the mainland.

The U.S. branch (La Seccional) was established with this dual focus. We continued to organize throughout the United States with the objective of organizing a chapter (*núcleo*) in every Puerto Rican community in the United States. New York City had the most local chapters, but we eventually built strong bases in northern and southern New Jersey, Hartford and New Haven, Boston, Worcester, and Springfield, Chicago, Philadelphia, even as far west as Los Angeles and San Francisco.

Throughout the cities where the PSP was organized we were involved in many different struggles. We played an important part in the student movement to save Hostos Community College in the Bronx. We organized Puerto Rican workers in the steel plants of Gary, Indiana, and migrant workers through ATA (Asociación de Trabajadores Agrícolas); we were involved in housing struggles in Boston that later gave birth to Villa Victoria in the South End. We fought against the proposals to barricade the

Puerto Rican community in Hartford and for tenants' rights in New York City. We organized antirepression campaigns and mobilized to free the five Nationalist Puerto Rican political prisoners. And while focusing on these individual actions, we also worked to raise awareness about the colonial situation of Puerto Rico within our community and among broader U.S. progressive communities and movements. We constantly grappled with establishing priorities, but we never quite mastered the task.

I eventually came to serve in the leadership of the organization as head of finances for the U.S. branch and later as organization secretary. I visited PSP chapters throughout the United States and came to know hundreds of *compañeros* and *compañeras* in the organization. I met many of the dedicated, courageous, and gifted organizers and activists in the Puerto Rican community who were found in our ranks. These "militant" and "affiliate" members, as they were known then, built strong chapters in the community, workplaces, unions, and schools. We sold *Claridad*, the official newspaper of the organization since the days of MPI that had been published in Puerto Rico since 1959. By 1972 we had begun to publish our own U.S. supplement the *Bilingual Claridad*—which lasted for more than ten years. My paper route was always in the Bronx, either the West Bronx or sometimes Soundview. Running into my family was the only thing I worried about. My father's side of the family was very conservative and some were prostatehood when it came to Puerto Rico's status. One of my cousins saw me and my older brother marching in the Puerto Rican Day Parade with the PSP and booed us, with his thumbs turned down, to the end of the block. He stopped coming to our family gatherings and distanced himself almost completely from my mother, brothers, and sister. I couldn't believe that politics would divide anyone in my family, especially cousins that I had grown up with. So I always made it a point to keep my political views separate from the people that I loved—especially the ones that didn't agree with me.

The financial support network that the PSP built with its *cotizantes* was yet another impressive achievement. *Cotizantes* were supporters throughout the United States whom the membership visited monthly to collect their donations in support of the organization. These supporters were the lifeline and sustenance of the PSP—hundreds of individuals and small businesses that supported the struggle to end U.S. colonial domination in Puerto Rico and who wanted to advance the struggles for better conditions in the United States.

Members worked very hard and made many sacrifices for their beliefs. Many worked full time at day jobs to earn a living and on evenings and weekends dedicated long hours to build the PSP. Others gave up jobs to work full time for the organization. It wasn't always easy. People with families went through some really hard times financially and emotionally. When I got married in 1974, both my husband Andy and I were full-time organizers for the PSP. We were really lucky when the two of us got a paycheck at the same time—which was not often—and not very much money. We often couldn't pay the rent and sometimes had to flip a coin to see who would use the last token to go work at the party headquarters. Things got so bad that we had to sneak out of the apartment one night in one of those "midnight moves," owing three months of rent that we knew we could never make up.

Even single people suffered. Some would get ill from the long hours, bad eating habits, and sheer stress. In addition, the tension and exhaustion sometimes built up resentments and anger in later years after the person left the organization. It was often difficult to maintain a healthy balance between the political and the personal sides of our lives. In retrospect, I realize that people's motivations for joining any organization are not always sound ones. Certainly, in the day-to-day pressures and conflicts, we hurt ourselves and one another. Only later did I realize that this is a fact of life for all workaholics; the Left does not have a monopoly on the problem.

The PSP started to organize mass events after the 1973 congress. The first was the *Acto Nacional*—National Day of Solidarity with the Independence of Puerto Rico—on October 27, 1974. Together with the Puerto Rico Solidarity Committee and other groups, we mobilized close to twenty thousand people and filled Madison Square Garden.

In 1976 the United States celebrated its bicentennial anniversary of the signing of the Declaration of Independence from British colonialism. To counter the celebrations scheduled for Philadelphia on July 4, the PSP spearheaded a coalition of Left and progressive organizations.

Throughout the United States, the July Fourth Coalition represented a broad range of grassroots movements, political organizations, and liberation struggles. More than fifty thousand people marched through the streets of Philadelphia, ending with a massive rally of speakers representing scores of issues and political organizing efforts throughout the country. A similar activity was organized in San Francisco.

I was the New York coordinator for the July Fourth Coalition assigned by the PSP. I think this was a real turning point for the organization. The building of our own base and of a mass movement of Puerto Ricans in the United States was placed in serious jeopardy when we began to concentrate so much of our efforts on these mass mobilizations. These were moments of great visibility and impact in our communities and even among progressive sectors in the United States. But they also presented great problems. Many of our full-time members were spread so thin working within these broader Left coalitions that our own organizational base was weakened. There was strong dissension among the base of local organizers throughout the United States over whether we should place so much emphasis on these kinds of all-consuming events. Local organizers wanted to spend more time dealing with local issues that affected the Puerto Rican community where they were—housing, education, health, employment. The leadership of the PSP in Puerto Rico and some of the central leadership in the U.S. branch wanted to escalate visibility around the issue of independence for Puerto Rico by organizing massive protests of the Puerto Rican community, in the belly of the beast. There was an agonizing tension between organizing in solidarity for independence versus organizing around day-to-day problems confronting the Puerto Rican community on the mainland: the "dual priority" became impossible to implement.

The incredible growth of the MPI-PSP between the years of 1970 and 1977 led many of us to believe that the "revolution was around the corner." We believed, with Juan Mari Brás (general secretary of MPI-PSP from 1959 to 1981), that "we will see independence and socialism in our life time." But the change in the political and social climate during the late seventies taxed our enthusiasm; there was greater repression and less support for radical groups and even for liberal thinking. Political organizations were weakened by those who infiltrated our ranks to sew dissension and mistrust. Internationally the problems that socialist countries were confronting posed other deep questions for socialists in the United States. In 1980, the election of Ronald Reagan was a setback for Left and progressive movements in general.

Armed actions in Puerto Rico and on the mainland divided Puerto Ricans and gave the United States and commonwealth governments an opportunity to mark *independentistas* as "terrorists." In our own ranks, differences of opinion led to heated debates and even factional splits over such questions as electoral political participation, armed struggle, and the right relationship between independence and socialism as strategic goals.

There is a lot of research describing the FBI's covert actions against progressive and radical movements in this country. COINTELPRO was one such action designed to disrupt, divide, and ultimately annihilate the radical organizations of the sixties and seventies. Not only is this recorded in official government documents, released under the Freedom of Information Act, but some activists of that period have vividly described what occurred. Elaine Brown, in her book *A Taste of Power*, recounts her experience as a leader in the Black Panther Party. Iris Morales, in her film *Pa'lante: The Young Lords,* talks about how her organization was affected by this government operation. The phone taps, infiltration by police agents, visits to people's jobs or homes by federal agents were all designed to frighten families and create havoc in the movement. In the late 1980s, *Claridad* published the names and printed photographs of hundreds of police agents who had infiltrated the MPI-PSP and Puerto Rican independence movement.

We were afraid of being hurt, of winding up in jail, of having our futures ruined. Our families too were frightened. Mami kept asking me why I was so involved in issues around Puerto Rico when I hadn't even lived there. She attended some of our political events, read *Claridad,* and contributed financially to the organization as a *cotizante.* She agreed with many of the things we said. She had been told by a landlord that an apartment was rented when it wasn't. She had done factory work for the lowest wages with no health benefits, vacation, or sick days. She sometimes worked ten and twelve hours a day to provide for her four children and still could barely get by on her income. She pawned every piece of jewelry my father ever gave her to make ends meet. Nonetheless, her youngest daughter was involved in things *"que podría traer peligro y problemas,"* that could only lead to danger and problems. So she worried about me.

The PSP had a profound effect on my capacity to analyze political, historical, and social phenomena. Being a PSP member was the perfect extension of the learning process I had begun in Aspira. The ongoing discussions on the interrelationship of Puerto Rican and U.S. history with global issues helped to anchor a growing sense of my own identity. Too much of the way that history is taught in school is disconnected from the people's response to the changing economic, social, and political reality. When I began to rediscover U.S. and world history through the labor struggles, liberation movements, and periods of social upheaval, I could make the connections with the Civil Rights movement, the peace movement, and the struggle for independence of Puerto Rico. These early years of training in a political movement continued to shape my view of the world and the need for social justice even after I became a social worker in the field of public health.

CONFRONTING SEXISM

As a young woman joining the organization, I struggled throughout with *compañeros* whose machismo did not decline with increasing political consciousness and education. For some the rhetoric on promoting and following the leadership of women was impressive, but in practice and on a personal level they failed miserably. As the PSP grew rapidly on the mainland, the party leadership in Puerto Rico wanted to assure that the U.S. branch stayed true to the party line when it came to political direction and focus. We had many political commissars coming from the island, especially when we were preparing for some major campaign or mobilization. They were always men. On one occasion, it was my night to serve on security duty in our main office. Break-ins of offices of Left organizations were common, with the Black Panther Party experience being the more recent and obvious example of that. My partner for the night was one of the visiting island leaders, who at midnight still had not arrived to cover with me. I called his house, and he was sleeping. When I asked if he had forgotten about his assignment, he said no, and then flat out refused to come. I did my security assignment alone that night. The next day in a meeting of our U.S. branch committee, I demanded that he be censured for his action. I insisted that the leadership of Puerto Rico couldn't pull rank and shrug off work that was assigned to them while they were here in the states. This was just another example of the male chauvinist attitude in our ranks. When women in the party were giving the orders or questioning performance, it wasn't taken seriously. The response was classic—most of the men quickly said, "Oh no, this kind of thing is unacceptable, we'll have to take the criticism to the *compañero* and remind him of his responsibility." No one wanted to discuss it further.

Puerto Rican society and culture are largely based on a patriarchal, male-dominant structure. It is therefore of no surprise that elements of sexism and machismo are ingrained in family life and other social systems. The PSP was no exception. Eventually I reached a prominent leadership position in the organization but not without constant confrontation and challenges from the men.

The story of our women as leaders in the movement is barely known. Books and films usually project a male-dominant view. But we were there, throughout the organization. Our leaders came from all levels of the organization: from bottom to top. They were the women who organized at their jobs, in the schools, the ones that took up many of our struggles in the community. They even included some who were projected as the spokespersons for the PSP, *dirigentes de la Seccional.*

The women in the organization were constantly being confronted, their leadership always tested. To many in Puerto Rico, I was viewed as *la feminista nuyorquina* (New York feminist), too influenced by the U.S. feminist movement and not to be taken seriously. Why should we focus on the issue of sexism when we were dealing with a movement that emphasized class struggle and an end to colonialism? Within the Seccional, I was seen as being too sensitive to "women's issues." Why must I always criticize the men? My response: the men were often patronizing and invalidated the role of women and their contributions.

In the PSP a group of us organized a woman's caucus; in fact this is what most of the women in Left organizations did. We studied the writings of the Russian leader, Clara Zetkin on the "women's question." We read about revolutionary Cuban women—Haydée Santamaría, Vilma Espín—and the role they played in toppling the Batista government. Our struggle was around machismo as manifested in the organization, in our culture, and in our personal lives. I led many study groups just of men where we discussed sexism, machismo, and the principles of a socialist society where gender discrimination would be abolished. For the most part, the men just listened, swallowed hard, and after I left joked about the experience and resumed their business as usual. Years later, some of these men would tell me that they were intimidated by me because they knew I wouldn't let them get away with a thing. That's when I laughed and thought, oh, that's why I didn't get asked out on many dates!

Women with children and women who were married were seen as a liability. They were not promoted because their family responsibilities were seen as a weakness, limiting their activism. On the other hand, men with children had no limitations because it was taken for granted that their wives would take care of the household. For the PSP and the Left in general, women were a weaker link in the struggle, their leadership constantly doubted.

The mystique and aura surrounding the revolutionary were built on the *male* figure. The woman as revolutionary and leader was rarely understood, accepted, validated, or promoted. Therefore her projection both at the time and in the recording of our history is woefully absent. We tried to change the definition of leader itself, but we weren't always successful.

This dynamic seemed to play itself out differently on the island and in the states. The men in the states seemed to display a more covert sexism, probably because they did not want to be ostracized by the women in the MPI-PSP or by other movement women. Publicly they denounced sexism and the oppression of women, but they often used that rhetoric as a shield they could hide behind to project themselves as a more advanced *hombre nuevo*. When it came to their personal lives, many of them talked the talk but couldn't walk the walk.

On the other hand, the men in Puerto Rico practiced a more overt sexism. They felt no compulsion to appease the feminist movement, which they viewed as an aberration spawned by the *yanqui* radical Left. Some might say that at least they were being more honest than their counterparts in the states, but the result was the same: both abused their power and authority to exploit women in the organization. Sadly, the rhetoric of the male revolutionary became a tool to sometimes gain sexual favors and a cheap labor pool for the tasks the men didn't want to do.

The underestimation of our women as leaders was evident in other ways as well. The woman was expected to be the "work horse," the one who paid attention to the details and implemented the plans; the man was cast as ideologue, analyst, and thinker. But the strategist, as in military jargon, is male. Search your own imagination. Who is the "real revolutionary?"

In the real MPI-PSP, of course, women often performed the role of ideologue, analyst, and visionary; they dealt with the details and provided leadership. Their contributions were great, but they were minimized and too often removed from the HiStory of our movement and struggles.

LOOKING AHEAD

I left the PSP in 1983 because I did not think we were effectively organizing Puerto Ricans in the United States. I believed that the leadership in Puerto Rico had weakened its position on the strategic importance of building a movement in the United States—a position that it had never fully embraced regardless of what it said publicly. I felt a need to do more work around the issues that were devastating our communities in the United States. I wanted to have a greater impact on our youth and see them infused with the passion to learn, to struggle, and to create a better future for themselves. Drugs, HIV/AIDS, high dropout rates from school, violence and deteriorating living conditions were draining, killing Puerto Ricans. The PSP was not talking to the community about how we could collectively work toward eliminating these problems *now*.

But there were many lessons and experiences gained by those of us who were involved in an active and militant way. I always describe this experience to my friends and family, and now my children, as a positive experience overall in my life.

One of these experiences is captured in the idea of *compañerismo,* the comradery, trust, and collective spirit that I often felt during those twelve years. I believe this mutual solidarity and support can be found only when a group of otherwise disparate people unite in the pursuit of a goal that transcends their own self-interest. It's like a bonding of minds and purpose that creates strong relationships among people who barely know one another, who often have little else in common. When I traveled to Chicago, California, the New England area, I often stayed in people's homes, people who I was meeting for the first time. I shared unforgettable moments with hundreds of Puerto Ricans, other Latinos and non-Latinos, whose hospitality and warmth were limitless. Our fight for social justice, an end to racism, sexism, and colonialism made us *compañeras.* Certainly, I cannot say that we all loved one another or that we never had problems. But the deep conviction of working toward a common goal—together—has an incredibly powerful force.

That sense of *compañerismo* clashes with the competitive, materialistic, individualistic values instilled in us in our schools, at our jobs, where we live. Making it to the top, at whatever the cost, and the emphasis on consumerism are cornerstones of "American freedom and democracy." These conflicting value systems tug at the very heart of the Puerto Rican reality.

Of course, this whole intense experience makes me not only reflect about the past but also contemplate the future, especially the future of our community and its organizations. I come away with many thoughts about how things will have to change if the Puerto Rican community hopes to flourish and preserve all the good of our culture and tradition.

Still now, women continue to be in the forefront of the issues that most affect our community and our lives. Women often force our community to take a position on HIV and AIDS, drugs, domestic violence, education. With their pulse on the community, women continue to transform ideology, analysis, and political thinking into action.

This is one struggle that women must continue to lead on political, legal, and social fronts. Our women, historically, have been strong, hardworking, pivotal players in the political and social struggles here and in Puerto Rico. Yet this fact receives little public acknowledgment, nor is it adequately recorded in our history. Nonetheless, women must continue to play a role in leading these struggles—whether it be on human and political rights issues or on issues of harassment and discrimination in the workplace, to reproductive rights and ending the violence toward women in society. Women must begin to record this history so that our children will learn to think differently about the roles of men and women in society.

In addition, the Puerto Rican community needs to create opportunities that unify us around a common purpose, a common goal. This is a change that I have struggled to make myself. Since the early 1980s I have shifted from political organizing around ideologically radical positions to working with community groups that serve communities of color. When I began to see the numbers of Puerto Ricans, especially women, that were infected with HIV and the rise in the number of Puerto Rican children placed in foster care, I was overcome with a sinking sense of despair. I realized that Puerto Ricans must collectively come to terms with the alarming changes in demographics and family structure that these epidemics are having on us. The far-reaching goals of Puerto Rican independence and socialism in the United States I saw as simply too removed from these pressing issues. It's not that I don't support these goals as ideals we should ultimately strive for; it's just that they don't give me a "handle" with which to organize our communities. This is unfortunate, but it is our reality.

I went from being a full-time political activist during the 1970s to working for elected politicians. In 1988, I joined the staff of David N. Dinkins when he was borough president of Manhattan. When he was elected mayor of New York City in 1989, I directed his Office of Health Policy. Being part of the first administration headed by an African American mayor was an exciting and challenging experience. Many of the skills I picked up during my earlier life came into play here. In effect, I went from being a "radical" to working within the "system." I left the mayoral staff in 1991, by then realizing the enormous opposition to progressive policies, both outside and even inside the administration. Here too I saw women constantly challenged and undermined by the upper-echelon government officials and bureaucrats.

Unfortunately, I feel that both experiences—my years on the Left and my years in "the system"—show that each side was flawed in its ability to respond to the many needs of our community. The Puerto Rican Left would not concern itself sufficiently with economic, social, and gender inequalities. In the final analysis, our elected officials had to answer to the financial moguls, the party machinery, and a racial politics that just wouldn't let a Black man run the city. Political expediency took precedence over long-term commitment to building communities and investing in a healthy, productive, and educated population. The city's financial crisis in the early 1990s became the excuse for avoiding fundamental social change.

My experience has taught me something about the persistence of inequitable gender relations. Although I won't minimize the ideological differences between the experiences of Left and electoral politics, both are embedded in a male-dominant structure, one that ultimately leads to the same failures. We have a long way to go before we transform these relations. But of one thing I am sure: until men accept women as their peers and leaders, *neither* strategy—radical nor electoral—will succeed in changing conditions in our community.

In recent years I have devoted myself to working around such issues as infant mortality and domestic violence. I continue to cross paths with many of the women from the PSP. Ironically, I began to work with a battered women's organization in Boston, named after actress and former PSP activist, Myrna Vázquez. Tragically, Myrna died following heart surgery in 1975 at the young age of forty.

The issues that I feel passionate about remain the same: the struggles of women as equal members of society, giving our young every opportunity to become healthy adults, removing the racial and economic disparities that keep our society divided—these are the changes we need to make.

The Puerto Rican community has to instill this sense of hope and passion for struggle in our youth. And as a maturing generation we have to do better in mentoring and advising the younger leaders that are coming up. We need to support and acknowledge the good work that is done by so many political and service organizations. We must also insist that they maintain the highest standard and integrity in their work. But, the destructive bickering, competition, gossip, and *caudillismo* that moves us further away from developing a strong Puerto Rican community have to end. Too often we lack the broader vision that our institutions must be built along *several* fronts. No one person or organization will be able to resolve all the problems we have. It takes courage and confidence in the strength that we bear collectively that makes our actions over time reap greater rewards. Our young people are especially astute in sniffing out those so-called leaders whose real agenda is self-promotion. They are not fooled. Young people only become more cynical and disengaged from the political process if that kind of leadership dominates.

Organizations come and go, but our community's struggle perseveres. I left the PSP in 1983. In the early 1990s, the organization decided to transform itself again, merging with other forces to create a new entity, the Nuevo Movimiento Independentista (NMI). In some ways it had come full circle, returning to its roots as a broad coalition, as in the MPI days. Only time will tell if the organization achieves greater success.

In the meantime, social and political realities have not changed for Puerto Ricans since 1971, when I was twenty-one years old and saw the need to be a part of the movement. No matter what, I will keep contributing to our struggle in the ways I think most productive. I'll always keep in mind that our children need to be taught their history, and that *la lucha continua,* the struggle continues.

IRIS MORALES

12 ¡PALANTE, SIEMPRE PALANTE!
The Young Lords

A CHILDHOOD AS "GO-BETWEEN"

MY PARENTS came to the United States during the Puerto Rican migration of the late 1940s. My mother came from the northwest town of Aguadilla to work in the garment industry as a sewing-machine operator. My father, a sugarcane cutter from Sabana Grande, worked as an elevator operator in several New York City hotels. They met and married in the United States and raised four daughters. As the oldest child, I became the translator for my parents, serving as the bridge between the Puerto Rican culture and the American way of life. Other family members would bring letters they received from North American institutions asking me to translate from English into Spanish and write any required English response. Neighbors would regularly ask my mother's permission for me to accompany them to the Social Security office, the worker's compensation or welfare office, or any other place where English only was spoken. Often when on a translating trip at the hospital or local school with my mother or a neighbor, another person—a Spanish-speaking stranger—would also require and request translating assistance.

The role as "go-between" helped in my later radicalization because I got to see institutional practices up close. I got to feel the disdain and injustices with which people, bureaucrats, and institutions responded to Puerto Ricans. I experienced the mistreatment and humiliation. It seemed that all the institutions—from the local school to the Social Security office to the hospital emergency room—were willing to experiment with and throw away our lives. I felt the disrespect and the lack of understanding of people who are poor, who speak another language, and who are of a different skin color. These experiences with institutional racism were imprinted somewhere in my consciousness. Later when I read about the racist practices of U.S. institutions in other communities or countries, I connected with it and thought, yes, I have seen them do that. Yes, I know how the holders of power exploit poor communities. Those early experiences were invaluable in becoming a political person and being able to maneuver the system to survive.

LEADING UP TO THE YOUNG LORDS EXPERIENCE

My political awakening began while I was in high school. I learned that the U.S. government forced Native Americans to live on reservations and interned Japanese Americans in concentration camps during World War II. Through some school friends, I attended youth meetings of the Student Non-Violent Coordinating Committee (SNCC) and the NAACP (National Association for the Advancement of Colored People), and I marched in demonstrations against the Vietnam War.

After graduating from high school, I became a tenant organizer with the West Side Block Association, a neighborhood storefront set up by a group of Columbia University students. We went knocking door-to-door, talking to people about housing problems—everything from lack of heat and hot water to vermin infestation. We represented tenants in court and conducted rent strikes, organizing people to fight for decent and humane living conditions.

Later when I entered City College, I joined ONYX, the African American student organization; there were no Puerto Rican or Latino organizations on campus. I studied African American history and especially the teachings of Malcolm X. As the number of Puerto Rican students increased on campus, we organized the first Puerto Rican group called Puerto Ricans in Student Activities (PRISA).

During this time, I was also working as a teacher in the Academy for Black and Latin Education (ABLE), a storefront school on 105th Street and Columbus Avenue. Several African American men from the neighborhood created the school; we had attended school together and knew the neglect of the public school system first hand. ABLE was an alternative way for young people to complete their high-school equivalency diploma. But as we taught our classes, many of our students, who were addicted to heroin, nodded out in class and were unable to learn. When we searched for treatment services, we found none. St. Luke's, the local hospital, was completely unresponsive to our concerns. As a result, ABLE organized a takeover of the hospital administrative offices demanding services. Out of the takeover, ABLE successfully negotiated the first thirteen hospital beds in the city to specifically treat drug addition among adolescents.

Around this time I participated in cultural activities at the East Wind in Harlem and at the Gut Theater in *El Barrio* where I met many emerging poets, writers, and political leaders of the day. Although impressed with the artistic and intellectual vibrancy of the cultural movement, I was disappointed with those who justified the second-class position of women of color as a positive cultural legacy. Also in *El Barrio*, I connected with the Real Great Society and joined a bus load of Latinos and Latinas and

African Americans on a trip through the Midwest to the Crusade for Justice Conference in Denver, Colorado, in 1968. It was there that I first met Jose "Cha Cha" Jiménez and other members of the Chicago Young Lords.

Cha Cha, a soft-spoken and unassuming leader, told us that the Young Lords were originally a street gang that developed in Chicago during the 1950s to protect neighborhood territory. Cha Cha, a member since 1959, had been in and out of jail for petty offenses. In jail, he met Fred Hampton, the leader of the Chicago Black Panther Party, who introduced him to political ideas. They talked about the movement for Black liberation and discussed building unity between Blacks and Puerto Ricans. When Cha Cha got out of jail, he returned to his neighborhood and organized the Young Lords to protest the city's urban renewal plans that would have uprooted the Puerto Rican/Latino community. It was 1968, and the gang, while protesting urban removal, was transformed into the Young Lords Organization (later the Young Lords Party). They designed a button with a map of Puerto Rico and the slogan, *"Tengo Puerto Rico En Mi Corazón"* ("I have Puerto Rico in my heart"). They went door-to-door promoting community control and self-determination for Puerto Ricans and pressured institutions to respond to the concerns of the surrounding Latino community. The Young Lords Organization set up "serve the people" programs and united with the Black Panthers and the Young Patriots (a radical hillbilly group) to organize the Rainbow Coalition. From the streets of the second-largest Puerto Rican community in the United States, the Young Lords Organization was becoming known as fighters for the equality of Puerto Ricans.

The winter after the Denver conference, I traveled to Cuba where supporters from every country in the world gathered to participate in the tenth anniversary celebration of the Cuban Revolution. While I was in Cuba, my fellow Latino and Latina and African American students at City College took over the university demanding open admissions and African American and Latino/Latina studies. From the Cuba trip, I returned to Harlem University where the takeover was still in progress.

Within six months, I was working with the Young Lords in *El Barrio*. Joining the Young Lords was a natural progression of the activism I had been involved in and the ideology for liberation that I was developing.

THE YOUNG LORDS' ACHIEVEMENTS AND CONTRIBUTIONS
Puerto Rican Pride, Political Militancy

At a significant historical moment, Puerto Rican youth entered a national and worldwide movement that said, in no uncertain terms, the status quo must change. Inspired by liberation struggles worldwide, in the United

States, and in Puerto Rico, the Young Lords militantly and proudly stood up for the Puerto Rican community. It was a stand against economic exploitation, social injustice, and colonial dependency that resonated throughout the communities in the United States. It was a call for revolution!

The Young Lords said, "We're tired of injustice, and we're not going to take it lying down." That was the first step toward a very simple, popular appeal, reflected in the garbage offensive. The squalor of the barrio was the most visible and physical manifestation of oppression and neglect. Streets overflowed with garbage because the people of *El Barrio* were not a high priority for New York City sanitation services. When the Young Lords swept the streets and set fire to the garbage throughout the summer of 1969, they pressured the sanitation department to clean up the barrio streets. From East 110th Street, the garbage offensive spread to other blocks in the neighborhood and established the Young Lords as street fighters willing to confront the police and government authority to get results.

On another level, we reclaimed our identity, our heritage, our place in society. Although we were living in the United States, we declared, "We're Puerto Rican and proud." We were now here in mass numbers, and our generation asked, "Where do we go next? Our mothers have worked in sweatshops; our fathers have been dish washers. We want better jobs and doors opened to quality educational opportunities." We were trying to figure out our situation without too many role models.

SERVE THE PEOPLE: THE BASIC IDEOLOGY

In the fall of 1969, the Young Lords began to work with welfare mothers and expanded activities to provide free breakfast for children and free clothing programs. As the programs grew, they required more space. Looking around *El Barrio,* the Young Lords assumed that the local churches would want to help. Since the First Spanish Methodist Church on 111th Street was not used during the week, the Young Lords approached the pastor requesting space. Not knowing that the reverend was a Cuban refugee, the Young Lords tried to convince him to open the basement facilities for the free breakfast program. He adamantly refused. One Sunday, the Lords went to church to address the congregation directly. When they got up to speak, a signal was given to the police, who were stationed throughout the church. Bedlam broke out as police attacked, beat, and arrested members. The incident gained strong media attention—"Young Puerto Ricans ask Church for Food Program for Children. Thirteen Arrested" read the headlines.

About three weeks later, the Young Lords occupied the church, named it the People's Church, and set up "serve the people" programs. We ran free breakfast and clothing programs, provided health services and community dinners, set up a liberation school, and on New Year's Eve held a revolutionary service to herald, the "People's Decade." We proved that programs to serve the barrio community were possible when there was political will. Thousands of people passed through the doors of the People's Church, attracted by the spirit and clarity of purpose. We explained our programs and recruited hundreds of supporters. But the church's pastor continued to deny the use of space. The Central Committee of the YLO negotiated with the police, and at the end of eleven days, the police moved in. They arrested 106 Young Lords and supporters who, with raised fists and singing "*Que Bonita Bandera,*" filed out of the church into the waiting police wagons.

Puerto Ricans watched closely. Some were frightened by the militant rhetoric, but the Young Lords won the hearts of the barrio community. The People's Church drew national media attention to the miserable living conditions of the Puerto Rican people in this country. It became a political landmark proclaiming the dissatisfaction of the growing Puerto Rican population in the United States. A new generation of young Latinos and Latinas challenged the system, boldly demanded respect, and popularized the idea of "serve the people."

THE MEMBERS WERE THE STRENGTH OF THE ORGANIZATION

The militant spirit and commitment to work directly in the community attracted many of the best organizers. Activists who had participated in the Civil Rights, Black liberation and cultural Nationalists movements joined. Others were community organizers with experience fighting for education, jobs, housing, and health issues. Some united from the student protest movements including the Columbia University and City College takeovers.

We were convinced that we could make the world a better place for all of humanity. After all, the richest country in the world had resources to provide food, clothing, housing, and health care for everyone. It was unconscionable to have so few with so much and so many people with so little. We believed that the most disenfranchised segment of our community, the most oppressed—the street people—would play a revolutionary role because they had nothing to lose. For us, "community" included these people, who today are considered part of the "underclass." We identified completely with the most oppressed sectors because we came from those sectors.

The Young Lords had popular appeal because the issues that we were talking about were issues that we had lived. Most members were Puerto

Ricans born and/or raised in the United States in working-class and Spanish-speaking homes. The majority had attended U.S. public schools and were very familiar with other U.S. institutions. Young African Americans also joined and made up about 25 percent of the membership. Other Latinos—Cubans, Dominicans, Mexicans, Panamanians, and Colombians—also joined. One member was Japanese-Hawaiian. Young Lords were veterans of the street fights in the 1950s, former prison inmates, recovering heroin addicts and alcoholics. We were college students and high-school youth no longer in school. Young Lords were also young factory and hospital workers and mothers. Some were veterans from Puerto Rico and the United States who had fought in Vietnam. The Young Lords were committed men and women in their late teens and early twenties who had experienced racism and exploitation in the United States. We learned to work together and developed bonds that have lasted a lifetime.

The strength of the Young Lords Organization was in transcending our differences and understanding the power of collective action. The Young Lords raised consciousness through bold public actions that focused on the exploitation suffered by our community. Even those who disagreed with our tactics had to agree the injustices we pointed to were clear. The Lords' Information Ministry skillfully used the mainstream media to get our message out beyond our communities and across the United States. Through the *Pa'lante* newspaper, first published in 1970, and the "Palante" radio program on WBAI, young Latinos and Latinas also discussed the major political events of the day—not just those taking place in the local community but about national and international current events as well.

The organization touched people of conscience in our community. Not many organizations do that. Often people vehemently disagreed with the Young Lords. Today we could identify a dozen organizations that have put out position papers on this or that. Who knows, who cares? The Young Lords engaged a generation, and from that a movement and people were inspired to do other things. That was a tremendous contribution.

PEOPLE'S HEALTH: A POLITICAL PRIORITY

People's health was a political priority for the Young Lords right from the beginning. "How can children go hungry in the richest country in the world? Children cannot learn in school if they do not have breakfast," we said. The breakfast program was about the nutrition of children, about having a healthy body in order to have a healthy mind. Subsequently, the Young Lords created a comprehensive health program advocating for preventive care and developing innovative programs around drug addition, lead poisoning, tuberculosis, and anemia.

Every Saturday, Young Lords, accompanied by a group of medical students, went knocking door-to-door talking to families and collecting urine samples from their children. The testing exposed the high incidence of lead poisoning in our community. Landlords used cheap lead-based paint for tenement walls, and young children unknowingly put the chipping paint in their mouths and suffered brain damaged. Journalists wrote about it, and officials passed legislation requiring the removal of the paint.

Similarly, the Young Lords exposed high levels of tuberculosis when conducting door-to-door testing in the Bronx and *El Barrio*. We tried to get city administrators to bring a tuberculosis detection X-ray truck into our communities, but they refused. One day in June 1970, we liberated the X-ray truck, named it the "Ramon Emeterio Betances Free X-ray Truck," and brought it into East Harlem. The driver and technician stayed in the truck and helped us take X-rays. Over the next three days, we tested hundreds of people.

We believed that institutions in a community have a responsibility to that community. Lincoln Hospital in the South Bronx was a dilapidated building that had been condemned twenty-five years earlier. The community called it the "butcher shop." Although the city kept promising a new facility, they never got to its construction. With the Health Revolutionary Unity Movement (a group of hospital workers, doctors, and community members), the Young Lords rallied for community-worker control of Lincoln and formed the Think Lincoln committee. When a young Puerto Rican woman, Carmen Rodríguez, died from a botched abortion, the Young Lords organized protests that brought attention to the deplorable hospital care for Puerto Rican and African American women.

In July 1970, the Young Lords occupied Lincoln Hospital for one day. The demands to the hospital included immediate funding to build a new hospital; door-to-door preventive health programs in the community; no personnel cutbacks, and child care for workers and patients. A second Lincoln Hospital takeover took place later that year, and fifteen people were arrested. It resulted in the hospital administrators agreeing to the creation of the Lincoln Detox Program, which would serve hundreds of people addicted to heroin. We believed in community control of institutions; and in spite of the personalities and big egos, we understood the importance of collective action. In 1976, the city built the Lincoln Hospital that now stands at 149th Street in the South Bronx.

FREE PUERTO RICO NOW!

While working in local communities, we raised consciousness about the United States' colonial domination and exploitation of Puerto Rico. Uniting with the Puerto Rican Socialist Party, El Comité, the Puerto Rican Student Union and other groups, we made sure that the colonial status of Puerto Rico got on the agenda of progressive movements across the United States. In 1970, the Young Lords and the Puerto Rican Student Union organized a student conference at Columbia University specifically to create "Free Puerto Rico Now!" committees in every school and college campus. A thousand students from throughout the major northeastern cities attended. As a result of that work, we also mobilized ten thousand people in 1970 to march to the United Nations calling for the liberation of Puerto Rico and an end to police brutality.

PRISONERS' RIGHTS

Also, from the beginning, the Young Lords made a commitment to work with brothers and sisters in prison. We communicated regularly with Latinos in prisons who wrote us describing inhumane living conditions, and we set up the Inmates' Liberation Front. More than once, brothers showed up straight out of jail to the Young Lords office "reporting for duty."

When the Attica rebellion took place in 1971, the inmates specifically requested that the Young Lords participate as one of the prisoners' representatives negotiating with authorities. A former Attica inmate, José "G. I." Paris, and seventeen-year-old Central Committee member Juan "Fí" Ortiz represented the organization in the historic negotiations. With other progressive organizations, the Young Lords organized support demonstrations in communities throughout the city.

Young Lords also participated in organized campaigns to free political prisoners Martin Sostre, Eduardo Pancho Cruz, Carlos Feliciano, the five Nationalist prisoners, and the Black Panthers.

WOMEN'S LIBERATION

The Young Lords Organization raised consciousness about feminism and women's rights. The initial Central Committee was all-male, including Felípe Luciano as chairman, David Pérez as minister of defense, Juan González as minister of education, Pablo "Yoruba" Guzmán as minister of information, and Juan "Fí" Ortiz as minister of finance. With the consent of the Central Committee, women members organized a caucus to discuss "women's issues" and study the thirteen-point program of the organization.

To us, point thirteen, "We want a socialist society," meant the liberation of both women and men. As we met and talked, our indignation at our second-class status grew. We worked just as hard as the men; we also put our lives on the line, and we wanted our voices as women reflected in the ideology and activities of the organization. The Young Lords would have to concretely address the oppression of Latinas and machismo. We prepared a list of demands that were presented to the Central Committee.

First, we wanted women represented in the top leadership. The Central Committee appointed Denise Oliver as the first woman to the Central Committee in 1969; with her participation, we gained a strong feminist advocate in the leadership. A year later the Central Committee added another woman, Gloria Fontáñez, to the top leadership. We also wanted all other leadership levels and all ministries to include women. The Central Committee responded by appointing women to the national and central staffs and to the defense ministry. Some brothers said, "The women are not as politically developed as the men." Our response was, "Women will develop within struggle. Put women in leadership."

We also demanded that the thirteen-point program and platform of the Young Lords be changed. Point ten read, "Machismo must be revolutionary and not oppressive." We responded that machismo could never be revolutionary. That is like saying, "Let's have revolutionary racism." It is a contradiction in terms. The Central Committee rewrote point ten and moved its position to number five. It said, "We want equality for women. Down with machismo and male chauvinism." This point was the only change that the Young Lords ever made to the program.

The Young Lord women won an important victory. However, we knew that it was not enough to say, "We want equality for women." We were not interested in just a paper victory. Significantly, the Central Committee agreed that machismo or abuses of women would be grounds for discipline, suspension from leadership, or even expulsion from the organization. Most of the leaders were disciplined or suspended for machismo at one time or another.

Accountability was extremely important because many organizations practiced only lip service when it came to feminist ideas. We insisted on child care so that women could attend meetings and be politically involved in the movement. It is still the case, and it most definitely was then, that women are the primary child-care providers.

We insisted that every issue of the *Pa'lante* newspaper reflect the struggles of women and include articles written by women. Women wrote articles about women's oppression and machismo, about workers' struggles in hospitals and factories. We also wrote an initial article exposing the mass sterilization of Puerto Rican women. We reported on a conference in Canada, which we attended to express solidarity with the women of Vietnam.

With these principles in place, more women joined the organization. The internal struggle strengthened the participation of women and gave voice to Latinas across the movement. We considered ourselves feminists but distinct from the White women's liberation movement, which believed that men were the principal enemy. We were critical of that movement for purporting to speak for all women when it represented primarily White, middle-class women. It never successfully addressed the concerns of women of color and poor women. In fact over time, the demand for affirmative action in some industries became synonymous with creating job opportunities for White women but leaving people of color behind.

We organized the Woman's Union, a mass organization for Latinas, working directly around women's issues, such as child-care and health concerns. In *El Barrio,* the union tried to establish a much-needed child-care center, but the project got mired in New York City regulations and bureaucracy. The Women's Union published its own newspaper, *La Luchadora.* It wrote about the three levels of oppression faced by Latinas—as women, as workers, and as Latinas. The paper reached out to all Latinas—homemakers, factory and hospital workers, students, and also women who made a living on the streets as prostitutes. *La Luchadora* also provided information and took positions on such critical health issues as the need for birth control information, the right to an abortion, and the battle against the forced sterilization of women. The Woman's Union held meetings and conducted political education classes and activities with Latinas throughout communities and schools and led the way for other Latina organizations that subsequently developed.

DEALING WITH INTERNALIZED RACISM

The Young Lords believed that to create a new society, we had to deal with internal contradictions among the people, such as domination based on gender or race. The organization unmasked and exposed the existing racism among Puerto Ricans and Latinos. There was much denial about the existence of racism in Puerto Rico, even in the independence movement. Yet examining the economic and social structure of Puerto Rico or Latin America showed that White, European descendants held the upper positions of power and privilege. Further, they excluded and systematically exploited people of African and indigenous descent.

The Young Lords also challenged the hypocrisy in our culture that accepted the racist ideology inherent in such sayings as *"hay que mejorar la raza"* ("to better the race") and *"pelo bueno, pelo malo"* ("good hair, bad hair"). The organization opposed white supremacy and cultural genocide—the devaluation and destruction of our culture. Instead we celebrated our African ancestry and culture; members wore large Afros, and some assumed African names. We fought "colonized mentality," the psyche of inferiority resulting from U.S. colonial domination of Puerto

Ricans and consistently presented these ideas in the *Pa'lante* newspaper and other publications, such as the pamphlet entitled, "The Ideology of the Young Lords."

YOUNG LORDS OUTSIDE NEW YORK

Outside New York, Latinos and Latinas were inspired by the ideology and actions of the Young Lords and sought to connect with the organization. Defense Minister David Pérez was in charge of visiting interested groups. He traveled to other cities, assessed the groups' work, conducted political education classes, and developed relationships. In this way, the organization established solid branches in Newark, Philadelphia, and Bridgeport and developed close political ties with groups in Boston, New Haven, Jersey City, Hoboken, Cleveland, Detroit, and other cities. The branches followed the thirteen-point program, conducted "serve the people" programs, and organized at the community level for Puerto Rican/Latino concerns in their city. They all faced direct police harassment, firebombings, and repression—often more severe than what was experienced in New York.

SHORTCOMINGS AND WEAKNESSES

Youthfulness

Though the youthfulness of the organization was a strength, it was also a major limitation. Certain mistakes made by the Young Lords were simply the result of lack of life experience and perspective. Also, with initial successes and growing recognition, a youthful arrogance and failure to understand organizational vulnerabilities developed. Accordingly, destructive forces were able to capitalize on this lack of experience and maturity.

The organization's rules of discipline required that members work "twenty-five hours a day, eight days a week." Membership on this basis could not be sustained over the long term. Because of the full-time commitment, people with full-time jobs and/or families could not easily participate. Therefore, the membership base remained primarily youth, students, and the unemployed. Yet, the organization paid little attention to personal development issues of the youth members, such as getting a formal education or job, developing relationships, childbearing, and parenting.

Centralism and Democracy

A more serious problem had to do with a faulty decision-making process, and this was related to our militarist structure. We followed the theory of "democratic centralism," attempting to balance centralized decision-making with democratic participation by the membership. Centralism was necessary to discuss the strategy and tactics involved in various takeover actions and activities that required maximum security and trust. However, at other times there was little democracy. In practice, the Central Committee made all decisions and set the direction of the organization. The first leaders founded the organization, and they decided who else would join leadership. There were no elections. Emphasis on strict adherence to Central Committee directives frequently stifled member creativity and initiative. Charismatic leadership sustained the organization initially but not over the long term.

At different points in the organization's history and as early as 1970, there were various internal crises expressed as conflict against a particular leader or the struggle for the inclusion of women. These were really part of a broader struggle to democratize the organization, to have members' voices and by extension, the community, really heard in the decision-making process.

Unfortunately, the organization never achieved a balance between democracy, individual freedom, and collective accountability. As the organization evolved from the Young Lords to the Puerto Rican Revolutionary Workers Organization in 1972, there was a deceiving appearance of democracy; but the opposite was true. There was a total lack of democracy. A few individuals decided and established the politics of the organization expecting all members to follow.

When members raised differences of opinion with ideology or tactics or leaders, they were often subjected to name-calling and labeled "opportunists." The Central Committee even falsely accused some members of being police agents. During the Puerto Rican Revolutionary Workers' phase, the ruling group maintained control by accusing everyone who disagreed with them of being agents and collaborators. The accusations lost credibility and allowed real agents to continue to operate in the movement unexposed.

The Move to Puerto Rico

The Young Lords sought to define the relationship between Puerto Ricans in the United States and Puerto Rico. Initially, the Young Lords promoted the "Divided Nation" theory. This was the position that Puerto Rico was a divided nation with one-third of Puerto Ricans living in the United States and two-thirds living in Puerto Rico. From that position flowed several political consequences. Among them was the decision that the primary struggle of Puerto Ricans in the United States was the liberation of Puerto Rico. In March 1971, the Young Lords launched "*Ofensiva Rompecadenas*" ("Break-the-Chains Offensive") directing resources and attention to Puerto Rico. The U.S. branches were considered the base area necessary to keep the Puerto Rico branches in El Caño and in Aguadilla operating. The military slogan was, "Prepare the base, to defend the front."

As *"Ofensiva Rompecadenas"* unfolded, members both in Puerto Rico and the United States questioned the expansion. In April 1972, all the members in the Aguadilla branch resigned and the Central Committee accused them of factionalism. In the United States, many of us concerned about the decreasing attention to local community organizing activities were at a loss about what to do. When Minister of Information Pablo Guzmán, after returning from a trip to China, wrote a paper outlining how to get the organization back on track, we supported it. The paper argued that the move to Puerto Rico was a mistake and that we had to get back to organizing poor and working Latinos in the United States. It rejected the divided nation theory, concluding that Puerto Ricans in the United States are an "oppressed national minority" and that Puerto Rico is the nation. Several Central Committee members and some national staff members, such as Richie Pérez and myself, supported the paper, and we all agreed to launch a rectification movement. We were excited about the possibility of revitalizing the organization and took advantage of the fact that the Central Committee members who would object were out of town. When they returned to New York, they were furious.

After a critical meeting, the Central Committee adopted the position paper. However, they also agreed to discipline the supporters of the rectification movement for "violating democratic centralism." As a result, some of us were sent to branches outside New York, a move to divide the dissenting group. That is how I got to Philadelphia in 1972.

The move to Puerto Rico was a disaster for the organization and the biggest mistake it ever made. The group lost its relationship to the Puerto Rican community in the United States. Simultaneously, the organization became increasingly dogmatic as members spent most of their days in endless debates about Marxist-Leninist-Maoist philosophy. Isolated from reality of the Puerto Rican/Latino community, the organization became irrelevant.

Leaving the Organization

I resigned from the Central Committee of the Puerto Rican Revolutionary Workers Organization in 1975. By then it had disintegrated into a small group run by Gloria Fontánez, a self-proclaimed "proletarian leader." She surrounded herself with an unthinking clique who did her bidding, including intimidation and violence against those members who disagreed with her.

I was back in New York after having spent two years in Philadelphia.

As part of the branch there, I first worked as a sewing-machine operator in several men's clothing factories. Later I was a hospital worker and organizer. Gloria Rodríguez, a dedicated organizer from New York, was also a leader of the branch. Most of the brothers were from the North Philly streets. Although the branch was in decline by 1972, we organized against the rampant police brutality and racism for which Philly and so many other urban cities are well known. We united with other groups, especially the Black Panther Party and I Wor Kuen, an organization of Chinese-American activists. We produced a newsletter, *Abuso*, and organized students at Temple University and women in the community.

The year in New York before I resigned, there was little community work taking place, no "serve the people" programs, no more door-to-door health testing, no community education classes, no more Women's Union. Most of the early Central Committee members were gone. Membership had dwindled. A few organizers were abandoned in factories and other workplaces. The passion, commitment, and hard work of the Young Lords was replaced with ideological squabbling. I was totally demoralized. The organization I joined five years earlier was dead.

The Role of Government Repression

COINTELPRO, the FBI's counterintelligence program, was set up to destroy the African American liberation movement, the Black Panther Party, and progressive organizations, such as the Young Lords. Police agents within the organization worked to intensify the differences and natural contradictions that existed among us. Using Nationalism and disagreements about political strategies, they sharpened divisions and created factions. Intimidation tactics and beatings silenced opposition. They replicated this scenario across the United States.

The U.S. government's surveillance and repression against the independence movement started with the invasion of Puerto Rico in 1898. For decades after, the government launched jailings and massacres of proindependence activists, including the Nationalist Party and its leader, Don Pedro Albizu Campos. As the Puerto Rican community grew in the United States, the government extended its repressive activities to activists living in the United States. In 1960, the New York FBI field office circulated a memo to its San Juan and Washington, D.C., offices instructing agents to initiate a counterintelligence program against proindependence activists in New York. The FBI's articulated goals were clear. Create disruption and discord, demoralize activists, and cause defections from the movement. The explicit strategy was to exploit factionalism—a fault that they identified as endemic within proindependence groups. Those marching orders were given to FBI agents who also played that role within the Young

Lords. Unfortunately, the full story of police and government involvement within the Puerto Rican movement in the United States has yet to be told and documented.

PUERTO RICO'S FUTURE

In 1998, the United States marks one hundred years of colonial domination of Puerto Rico. I continue to believe that Puerto Rico should be independent, a free country, and I support the right of the Puerto Rican people to self-determination. Within the United States, we have a special responsibility to continue to struggle for Puerto Rico's independence and for the freedom of political prisoners who are still in prisons for fighting for a free Puerto Rico.

Models of Leadership

Not everyone who commits to progressive movements as a young person necessarily sustains commitment for a lifetime. Leadership is determined by practice, by what a person does. Many leaders separate their politics from their personal lives. Yet politics has to translate into one's life in order to truly transform society. "Leaders" who work with youth and who have children must provide for them—financially, emotionally, and with time spent with their children. Leaders have to set an example.

We must reevaluate our notions of leadership. Unfortunately, today's ideas of leadership are still quite patriarchal and elitist. The definition of a leader is still the lone charismatic male heading a hierarchal organization. Collective leadership models to include working people, women, youth, gays, and those who are most marginalized need to be developed.

MAKING THE DOCUMENTARY *¡PALANTE, SIEMPRE PALANTE!* THE YOUNG LORDS

In 1988, a group of former Young Lords met. Some of us had not seen each other since the disintegration of the organization in the mid-seventies. As we reflected on our experience, we expressed concerns about what we saw happening with Latino and Latina youth—the internal violence, the deep sense of hopelessness, and the lack of purpose. We talked about how important the study of our history had been to our development and planned various activities to connect with young people. I volunteered to work on a committee to produce a video about the Young Lords experience, and as often happens, I inherited the project.

The initial work consisted of proposal writing. Fund raising was difficult because grant makers were not interested in political projects or Latino/Latina history. Also I was committed to telling the Young Lords' story the way that we experienced it. History books are generally written by those in power, and I knew it was important that we be the protagonists of this story. As I conducted interviews with former members, I looked for consensus about facts, beliefs, activities, and lessons learned. This approach made fund raising more difficult because many funders wanted a traditional "objective" documentary with the expert outsider commentary.

Over a six year period, the project received research and production grants from the New York State Council for the Humanities, the Paul Robeson Fund, and the Aaron Diamond Foundation. In 1996, *POV/Point of View*, the public television documentary series, granted funds and technical assistance to complete the project and set a broadcast date.

An important funding source was the Latino/Latina youth community. For more than two years, I screened and presented a work-in-progress to student and community groups. Those presentations gave me the opportunity to engage in discussions with Latino/Latina youth across the United States, and the feedback was invaluable to the finished work. Also many young activists joined me to complete the project doing everything from research to original music. Among them Vanessa Roman continues as the distribution coordinator of the documentary. Through these exchanges, we successfully established relationships with the documentary's intended audience.

In the fall of 1996, *¡PALANTE, SIEMPRE PALANTE! The Young Lords* was broadcast nationally on public television. That night, 750 people gathered together to watch the broadcast and celebrated the screening with poetry, hip hop and *bomba* music, and *plena* performances at the Borough of Manhattan Community College in New York.

DIALOGING WITH TODAY'S YOUTH

History and Identity

Young Latinos and Latinas today face a complicated world of poverty, single-parent homes, segregated and low-quality public schools, drugs, violence, prison, and lack of jobs. They have grown up familiar with AIDS, homelessness, police brutality, and the criminalization of Latino/Latina and African American youth. Subjects of a fast-paced, highly consumer-oriented society, they buy and wear fashion styles that advertise the logos of companies that often do not employ people of color. Increasing numbers of Latino/Latina youth struggle to hold down jobs while attending college, knowing an education is important to a future in a globalized economy. Latino and Latina young people are major consumers of television and film, yet they rarely find positive representations. The Latino/Latina community continues to be marginalized.

A cultural and political renaissance is happening among Latino/Latina youth, and they are engaged in renewed interest and exploration. Young Latinos and Latinas are seeking information about history and the role that Latinos have played in this country. Books are still scarce; videos are almost nonexistent. Youth are also interested in the activism of Latinos in the 1960s and 1970s. The Young Lords experience, especially the early period—very dramatic, militant, defiant—is appealing to young people who are rebellious.

Young Latino/Latinas are struggling with issues of identity, class, and race. Second-, third-, and fourth-generation Puerto Ricans in the United States, many who do not speak Spanish, ask, "Am I Puerto Rican? Am I American?" When one parent is Puerto Rican and the other African American or Dominican or Irish, they ask, "Where do I belong?"

There are questions that interface with class. In the 1960s, we were primarily working class, all of us. Today the children of a middle-class sector ask, "Am I really Puerto Rican? My parents are Puerto Rican. We ate rice and beans, but we were not poor," assuming that to be Puerto Rican or Latino means only to be economically disadvantaged.

Latino and Latina youth are insecure about the future. Will there be jobs? Many are setting up small businesses for economic survival, others because they want creative independence. Health and environmental concerns also raise the level of insecurity about the future.

Color issues persist. A portion of the documentary addresses the struggle against racism within the Latino community, and it resonates deeply with youth who experience racism as a continuing major internal problem. Studying our African ancestry and promoting our culture is very important to young Latinos and Latinas.

Latino/Latina youth are also grappling with what it means to be Latino as the community grows to include people from all Latin America and the Caribbean. Young people struggle with maintaining national identity while simultaneously developing Latino unity. There are bonds of affinity as well as tension and conflict. Clearly, we need varied organizational forms and multiple tactics to build a mass Latino movement for social and economic justice.

Finally, young people ask many questions about what motivated individuals or what motivated a generation to take the actions taken in the 1960s and 1970s. Of course the related question is, how to motivate people to take political action today.

BUILDING LENS: The Latino/Latina Education Network Service

¡PALANTE, SIEMPRE PALANTE! The Young Lords led to the creation of LENS—the Latino/Latina Education Network Service, a nonprofit organization that owns and distributes the documentary throughout the United States. It has been enthusiastically received by youth, community organizations, and educational institutions. The reception confirms the importance that young people assign to documenting our history and disseminating our stories.

LENS is dedicated to using the visual medium as a positive way to open dialogues about social and political issues. With *¡PALANTE, SIEMPRE PALANTE!* as an educational and outreach tool, LENS works directly with Latino and Latina youth. The focus is to motivate young people to develop their talents for social justice and community empowerment.

THE STRUGGLE CONTINUES

I am pleased to see the resurgence of activism and organization-building that is underway in our community. We have to use our knowledge and resources to continue to struggle for economic, political, and social justice. We need to organize for universal health care, food, clothing, and shelter for everyone, for quality education and jobs. We have to create conditions to allow the full artistic, spiritual, and intellectual development of all of us. Learning from our past to continue toward the liberation of humanity, our struggle continues.

CARLOS GIL

13 Artist, Writer, and Political Prisoner
An Interview with Elizam Escobar

ELIZAM ESCOBAR is an artist, writer, and political prisoner currently incarcerated in El Reno Federal Prison in Oklahoma. Sentenced to a total of seventy-eight years, Elizam is one of fifteen Puerto Ricans imprisoned for belonging to the clandestine movement for the independence of Puerto Rico.

GIL: Please tell us a little about your upbringing, relationship with your parents, and family life in Puerto Rico before you came to the U.S.

ESCOBAR: I was born in Ponce, "officially" on May 24, 1948, but "really" I was born a day before or after, or who knows. What happened is that my aunt went to inscribe me [in the Office of Demographic Registry], and, as the time to do so had passed, in order to avoid paying a fine, she did it a day after I was born. That means I was born the twenty-third. Nevertheless, when my parents have told me the story they can't agree: one day, two days, after, before, etc. Maybe it was a bad luck omen. In any case, at first this confusion about dates bothered me. Later I took it as a sign of good beginning: a false registration and the uncertainty of not even knowing when one was born. Can you imagine.

My whole immediate family was also born in Ponce. My father, Eliphelet Escobar, died in 1991. Even when we assured payment of all the expenses of the trip, hotel, meals, etc., and of the security guards, they refused to let me go visit him in the hospital or attend the funeral. For security reasons, they say, and because I represent a danger to the community. However, the contrary would be correct: with me, they couldn't be more secure in Puerto Rico, and the community, including the mayor of Bayamón, who you know is a statehooder, sent letters so they would let me attend. I was able to speak with my father for the last time only because my brother connected a series of telephone wires to the room where

This interview is based on an original version published in the Puerto Rican Spanish-language journal *Postdata* (no.10–11, 1995). The interview was conducted by correspondence from February to October 1995. The editors thank *Postdata* for permission to reprint this interview.

he was—in intensive care, where there were no phones. It was even more difficult because the phone I was calling from was right in the middle of the hallway of the unit where all the prisoners continually meet or pass through. Without any privacy, I had to bid my father farewell. The next day he died. My mother says he was just waiting to talk with me. My mother, Deadina Ortíz, is now seventy-two years old and is active in the campaign for our freedom. She is an exemplary mother. After me comes my sister, María del Rosario, who has three children: Tata, Tutin, and Ester Mari. And then, my brother, Eliud, who has a son, Elizaín, and a daughter, Elicelis, and he's married to Elizabeth, who is also an exemplary mother. I have a son, who you already know about from the photos in the exhibit *Transfixiones*. Elizer Escobar-Matsoukas is his full name. He is twenty years old and in his third year studying music at the State University of New York. He is of the "cosmic" type: from me he gets something Taíno, African, and Spanish-Galician and, who knows, maybe a little Arab—from his mother, half Jewish and half Greek. He was born in New York City in Columbus Hospital—the same hospital where Albizu [Campos] recuperated. So he, too, is full of premonitions. He was only five when I was arrested. The first time he came to see me in prison almost a year later in Pontiac (one of the Illinois state prisons about two hours from Chicago), it had a big impact on him. He couldn't even kiss me. Little by little this passed, and when the guard announced that the visit was over, he started to cry. Another year passed between this visit and the next. They had moved me to a prison pretty far from Chicago. His mother, Niki, and I had been divorced before my arrest. She has been very good. We have always been friends, and she has supported our relationship. Since 1984, we see each other at least once a year. My parents always brought my son, and now my *compañera* Jan. In all, he has been very strong. Well, to finish the answer, I have more than twenty cousins, some in the United States, others on the island.

GIL: Elaborate some more on your childhood and adolescence. For example, the schools you attended, your first loves, your neighborhood and friends. What music did you listen to? Were you a member of a church?

ESCOBAR: I spent my first ten years in Ponce. My parents were raised on the same street, Miramar in Barrio Segundo, four or five houses apart. After they got married, they moved a few times until, for economic and family reasons, we returned to Miramar Street to my paternal grandfather's house. Then he went to New York, and I didn't see him again until he came back in a coffin some years later. From Miramar Street we moved to Lomas Verdes, Bayamón. Also for economic reasons. My father worked construction, was a master plumber; and it was there, in the north where there was a lot of work. I didn't want to move away from my friends. Saying good-bye was hard. I think it was in 1958. I remember because I had a bicycle that was a '58, with two headlights in front, that my parents bought me as soon as we got to the new neighborhood. It was a completely different world: from a working-class barrio to a "middle-class" urbanization. It was as if I'd moved to another country; from a dry place with a terrible sun to one that was green, muddy, "cold," where it rained buckets and where there were all sorts of night songs: *coquís,* crickets, *chicharras,* etc. I remember that when the family would come from Ponce to visit us they could hardly sleep at night. But, aside from this little "trauma" of moving, my childhood was the experience of a happy and stable home. This is my impression. Bayamón was experiencing a sort of economic boom. Urbanizations and shopping centers began to appear everywhere. Bayamón sewed itself with cement, and the least that there was were Bayamonites.

The first social class conflicts I began to experience were in school. There weren't any schools in Lomas Verdes yet, so we had to go to school in town, to Muñoz Rivera by the public bus. There, the kids from the public housing project, Virgilio Dávila, and its surroundings, initiated me as soon as I arrived. There were only a few of us because Lomas Verdes was still under construction. They hadn't even finished the first section, and the house we were living in was rented until they finished the house my parents bought. Well, they invited me to fight a blond kid with a German last name. Imagine! What a headache! But since I'd come from a barrio in Ponce, I was already used to fighting. In fact, I think television had already had an influence—with its cowboy movies, like Bob Steele, whose hat never fell off even when he fought or crawled on the ground or in gullies, its films of Pedro Infante, and episodes of "Flash Gordon," etc. In Ponce, as soon as television arrived—I was about six or seven—we got one. So, I told them I'd fight—it's not like I had a choice—and we went behind the school to throw some blows at each other. I think the blond kid had less of a desire to fight than I did. Later, another fight, at a higher level. I lost, but gained their respect. You should realize I'm talking about when I was around ten years old. The older kids fought almost every day. It was an adventure to go to school. But I made friends with a lot of kids from the projects. I went to their homes, we'd go to the river together, etc. Later, when the schools opened in Lomas Verdes, my last years of childhood and the first of adolescence were focused on my street, with all the kids who came from all over the island or New York, and a Boy Scout troop founded by one of the neighbors who'd come from the U.S. In the troop we learned everything: swimming, camping, planting, milking cows, first aid, life saving, etc., in addition to competing, breaking rules, and making "scouting" a party. In the *camporees,* we were the bubonic plague. Pretty audacious.

I think I was about thirteen when I took catechism classes to become a member of the Lutheran church of Lomas Verdes. I took it to heart. So much so that I still have the impression of how ridiculous my friends, my family, even the minister, made me feel.

My mother was Catholic, and my father, I think, Baptist. They were married in the Catholic church; but in Lomas Verdes, the Lutherans began to hold services in homes, and my parents participated. They became members. Then, when the membership had grown pretty large, they built a modern church. That's when I took those classes. Ironically, I lasted longer in church when I wasn't a member than when I was. I think not only because I became "disillusioned" with my catechism classes and what it led to, but also because I was embarrassed to have the other kids see me going to church. So, gradually I stopped going until the minister gave up on me. I "liberated" myself from religion, though not from the Christ figure or the idea of God, at that age. The idea of God ended little by little in my years at the university. The figure of Christ continues, in my own way, in spite of Nietzsche, or maybe with Nietzsche.

In that same time, we had a lot of parties in people's houses, and everyone came even if they weren't invited. The music in vogue in my early teens was the "Mashed Potato," the "Twist," and Cortijo and his band. Some of us would go to Alfred D. Herger's teenager matinee. That was more or less where Puerto Rico's "new wave" began. But in general, I listened to all sorts of music. As for my father's music, I had to either listen to it or get out of the house. I found it insufferable: Rafael Muñoz, Daniel Santos, Dippiní. When I was just a kid, I liked all those singers: Felipe Rodríguez, El Indio Araucano, Los Hispanos, etc., but as a teenager, they seemed ridiculous to me. In addition to what I've already mentioned, there were also the beats that would later be called salsa, doo-wop music, rock and roll, the Beatles, Dylan, Serrat. When I was twenty and thirty, I began to appreciate the older music. I went to Cervantes Saavedra High School in Lomas Verdes. I was there for only two years because I graduated in the summer, having been influenced by various friends and because I didn't want to leave behind a girlfriend who'd graduated. I started at the university in 1965, which I think was too early and without being appropriately prepared.

GIL: How did you become involved in politics? What reading did you do? What were the prospective referents (what you aspired to)? And finally, how was the world then (in the sixties and seventies)?

ESCOBAR: My initiation into politics was as a direct "observer" in 1950, as a young child, during the Nationalist insurrection. My mother's brother, Arturo Ortíz, was killed in the police's first confrontation with the Nationalists in *El Barrio* Macaná in Peñuelas. According to my father, we were coming from Berto's barbershop, coming up by lower Miramar. Halfway there he stopped and took me into his arms as the police were shooting into a house that was apparently closed up. A few hours later, my father found out through the neighbor who lived in the house next to that one, that it was him [Escobar's father] the police were looking for. The police left without finding anyone.

I used to have a recurring dream where I saw people who had been shot dead, laying in the gutters. Clearly, Miramar Street. I would simultaneously see, from a hill or a tall place, a shoot-out taking place around the horses of a carousel. From there it would go to the bed of a moribund woman who would caress me and who looked at me with tenderness and sadness. I never "understood" this dream until my father told me the story during a visit in prison; and my mother clarified that her sister, Tata, died of a heart problem she'd had for a long time, right around the same time as Arturo died. He died in October, only eighteen years old; she was twenty-six and died in November of 1950.

I also remember the PIP [Puerto Rican Independence Party] caravans, when I was a kid, but I didn't become active until the so-called plebiscite of 1967. In Cervantes, there was a FEPI [Federation of Proindependence High-School Students], in '63 or '64. But I was never very interested. My sister was a member, but I wasn't. I felt the ideal and defended it more from the ethical point of view, but the public aspect didn't attract me — maybe because I was a little shy or because in reality nothing political like that interested me. When the MPI [the Movement for Independence] started its campaign in Bayamón, some PIP members, like my father, joined them. Thus, I knew people from the MPI, its periphery, and youth from the FUPI [Federation of Proindependence University Students]. By 1967 I was already good friends with some of them, and thus I joined the antiplebiscite campaign. That same year I also joined the FUPI at the Río Piedras campus. From that moment I began my radical militancy, although truly, more pushed on by friendship than because of any political vocation; more from anger and indignation than from having any aspirations of being a leader. In the same way, if what threw me into direct struggle was my friendship with the comrades from Bayamón, what made me decide to pursue humanities and fine arts at UPR [University of Puerto Rico] — in addition to the fact that what I wanted didn't exist, and in addition to following another friend of mine from Lomas Verdes who was in fine arts — was that I didn't want to add to my student militancy studying at social sciences, which was the "center" of political activity on campus. It would have been intolerable.

In those same years, the FUPI split. I stayed in the so-called "factious" side. They took leadership, momentarily, until the MPI intervened and kicked them out or they left, I don't remember which. A lot of the factious FUPIs went to work with Ana Livia Cordero's *Proyecto Piloto* [pilot project]. Others, like me, visited them, and we would meet, but basically we remained unaffiliated for some time. In my case, [remained unaffiliated] until I met the folks from the Socialist League at UPR and Pepito Marcano and began to work with them.

But before the militancy, I want to tell you that I had come into contact with the literature of the Cuban Revolution, the guerrilla movements in Latin America, and Black Power in the United States, but especially literature from China. These were my first Left and Marxist-Leninist readings. Later, in a strike at the Humanities Department, the professors organized independent classes, and in one of them, organized by George Fromm, called, I think, "The ideas of Karl Marx," I took my first course—though in pretty much of an outline form—in Marxism. It only lasted a few weeks but provided me with an introduction to the classics. The next "course" was when I joined the Socialist League. But, since it was such an intense, ardent, and active moment in the student struggle at Río Piedras, as in all the main cities in the world, I didn't do a lot of reading that wasn't for academic courses or study groups on Marxism and politics.

GIL: Tell us about your migration. For example, what made you go; how did you deal with the language, the climate, the atmosphere?

ESCOBAR: The time arrived that I had to abandon my studies without having finished. Political, personal reasons. In my case, the militancy but also a major conflict between the discipline required by the [Socialist] League, and my style, or, better put, my propensity to a certain bohemia. I worked construction with my father as a plumber's assistant. Then I was offered a job as an art teacher. I worked for a few months in the summer. Unemployed, and separated from my first wife, I decided to go to New York with a job offer as a counselor in one of the Puerto Rican studies programs. I went but didn't get the job because supposedly they'd cut the funds—I suspect other reasons—and ended up not as a counselor but a street sweeper and sign painter at a community program in Brooklyn.

I'd already been to New York the summer of '64. I went again in '69 or '70—I don't remember exactly—to go with my pregnant wife to Mount Sinai Hospital because she was having complications due to the Rh factor in her blood. At the same time, I was participating, with other members of the League, in a fraternal activity with the Progressive Labor Party. So I already knew something about New York. I didn't have problems with the climate, and with the language it was an issue of improving with practice. The atmosphere, social as well as political, went well with my way of being. As an aside, when I remarried I went to Puerto Rico with my wife and son, and I visited Corretjer and Doña Consuelo. They told me that I was the only Puerto Rican they knew for whom New York had served him well. I don't know in what sense they were saying it, but it seemed strange to me. Anyway, New York was a great experience for me, but not everything went well.

GIL: What else did you do besides the community work in Brooklyn? How did your cultural and political work go?

ESCOBAR: I was able to continue my university studies in New York through a bilingual program that included finishing my bachelor's degree and getting a teaching certificate in New York. I did all this. I worked in elementary schools and then in a high school in *El Barrio,* or Spanish Harlem. In the year before my arrest, 1979 to 1980, I worked as a graphic artist and art teacher with the Association of Hispanic Arts.

Since I came to live in New York—we're talking about the beginning of the decade of the seventies—I integrated myself into the work of the Progressive Labor Party, a communist organization that had developed as a split from the Communist Party of the United States as a consequence of the ideological conflicts between the Soviet Union and China. I think, if I'm not mistaken, that the PL was the first organization in the United States to follow the Peking line, and then, when others began to approach Maoism, was the first to make a consistent criticism of Maoism. But in addition to its ideological positions, it had, by the end of the sixties, a solid group of Puerto Rican and Black leaders. It also had one of the very few Left publications that was bilingual. They were also the first to break the ban on travel to Cuba. And they dominated the last years of the university organization, Students for a Democratic Society, with their line of a worker-student alliance. Their antiracist struggle has been one of the most consistent and radical. With them I learned a lot and worked in various areas of organization, in cultural work with a guerrilla theater, on magazines or exhibits, including being a member for a time of the party's "official" musical group. I played the congas and sometimes sang. I always worked on the newspaper making cartoons. In the work with my high-school students, I organized a group from several Latin American countries, into the Antiracist Committee. I also worked in the community on the West Side, where I lived most of the time. But in PL, as in almost the entire U.S. Left, the struggle on the ideological level surpassed overwhelmingly the real struggles. I was really saturated with this. I'd had enough. Also I began to realize the difference between the ideal internationalism they promulgated and the inevitable prepotent register of their real internationalism, with good intentions but in the end with that mix of naïveté and typical arrogance of Yankee culture. So by then, '74, '75, their relationship with the Socialist League had decayed and ceased, but I stayed with them a few more years and at the same time continued my friendly ties with the league. The Progressive Labor Party worked directly in the centers of production and the communities and had broken with other Left organizations and national liberation groups. For these reasons, I didn't have much of a relationship with the independence movement in New York—only occasionally, and even then, on a social or cultural basis. I would go to Casa de las Americas, Casa Betances, or I'd see *independentistas* in celebrations or at art exhibits at places like El Museo del Barrio.

PL stopped supporting the independence of Puerto Rico. My position in the party became more and more unsustainable and conflictive, not only because of their position but because there was no real space for debate about this and other points. My membership no longer made any sense, and I left the organization, but we stayed on friendly terms. It was around this time that I began again to participate in activities of the independence movement and in the campaign for the release of the Nationalist prisoners and when I decided to join the Puerto Rican clandestine movement that operated in the United States.

GIL: What led you to make this decision?

ESCOBAR: I don't think it was because, as some in PL said, that I, like all Puerto Ricans, was still very Nationalist. The answer is much more complex and goes beyond the ideological. In fact, as I've already told you, I was a little sick of the U.S.-style ideological struggle and of defending political lines which I couldn't identify with like I used to. Better still, I understood the conjunctural importance of the clandestine movement as a symbolic force capable of invigorating the psychological aspect and self-esteem of a people or a struggle that many diagnosed as a "lost cause." But also, in the concrete, very concrete, aspect, of defending in practice the right to our self-determination and independence, to self-defense and to respond to the repression that existed in those years. All this was more important and unpostponable. And all this is part of the struggle against colonialism, and I was realizing that in the name of a proletarian internationalism from the imperialist country had initiated another process of mental colonialism, of inequality, impositions and of spiritual as well as intellectual poverty. Thus, joining the clandestine movement was also a form of necessary catharsis to be able to survive, existentially and politically, at this stage. It was that or become a hardened bohemian.

GIL: Tell us about your trial, arrest, conviction, imprisonment. How did your family react?

ESCOBAR: On April 4, 1980, a group of us composed of five women and six men were detained by the police of Evanston, a place north of Chicago. In the beginning, the police thought we were a group of Iranians, but by the following day, the headlines in the press spoke of the arrest of leaders and members of the FALN [the Armed Forces for National Liberation]. Among us were three people who had been forced to go completely into clandestinity and who were on the FBI's famous most-wanted list. Carlos Alberto Torres, for example, was number one on the list at the time of our arrest. The FBI, or the *"fibiolos,"* as the comrades of that time used to call them, maintained that the Puerto Rican clandestine movement was the main "domestic" security problem in the United States, its Achilles' heel—especially the FALN, which operated in the continental territory of the United States. The news spread rapidly, and by the following day, if I'm not mistaken, the community and the movement in Chicago mobilized to Evanston to express its support.

In Puerto Rico, Pepito Marcano told me he read the news and called my father to prepare my mother for the story. Immediately, my parents went to New York to my apartment. The FBI had turned it upside down. My mother was hospitalized for several days in New York. She's suffered from tachycardia since she was young. Then they went to Chicago, where they had to go through all the security requirements to be able to see me for barely a few minutes through a glass. Their support has always been unconditional.

All the arrested comrades were born or raised in Chicago or New York except me. In their communities, they had a history of struggle for civil and human rights. In Chicago, for example, they had collaborated to forge one of the most prestigious alternative centers of culture and education in the Puerto Rican community. They were convinced—having lived with the racist and cultural prejudice in the metropolis—of the necessity to use a more effective method of struggle to create consciousness and reach the deaf ears of the system and colonial authorities. They had understood, simply, the colonial root of the problem as well as the root of the colonial problem, there as well as here. To know these Puerto Rican sisters and brothers from the other side of the nation was a powerful experience—because of their dedication, boldness, intelligence, and valor. Some of them had never even been to the island.

Once we were identified and accused, we were subjected to two trials: first, at the state level and then the federal level. The principal federal charge was seditious conspiracy, and the trial began when we were already serving our state sentences—mine was eight years for conspiracy to commit armed robbery and possession of an unregistered gun. These same charges were brought against us again in the federal case. This constitutes double jeopardy, but it's legal if it occurs in two different jurisdictions. Seditious conspiracy means agreeing to use force against the lawful authority of the U.S. government to overthrow it. In our case, this offense is inappropriate and ridiculous and contradicts the U.S. Supreme Court decision that Puerto Rico is not part of the United States, in addition to the fact that its authority over Puerto Rico, in terms of international law, is not legitimate. Anyway, when Puerto Ricans oppose U.S. authority over us, we are challenging a foreign power. Thus there is no offense, and we can't be found guilty of seditious conspiracy. All the additional charges were violations of the domestic law which comprised this conspiracy.

As soon as we were taken to court, we declared that we were combatants in an anticolonial war of liberation against the U.S. government, which illegally occupies our country, and our belief in the right to combat and resist colonialism by all necessary means, including armed struggle to defend our territorial integrity, national unity, and independence. This inherent right was recognized since the seventies by the General Assembly of the United Nations, due to the fact that colonial powers acquire and maintain their domination by military force. Since the anticolonial beginnings of international law, which were established for the first time in the UN charter, specifically derive from the independence struggle of the Algerian people, who carried out their struggle in the colony as well as in France, the colonial metropolis, the right to resort to all necessary means includes the right to make a war of decolonization attacking the colonial power on its own turf. This right to a "second front" is particularly legitimate for Puerto Ricans given the fact that almost half our population has been literally forced to leave their country because of U.S. expropriation of natural wealth and to emigrate to the metropolis in search of work and then subjected to a continuous colonial oppression and discrimination in the very territory of the colonial power.

As a collective decision, we claimed the status of prisoner of war, based on international law, the declarations of the UN and the Geneva Accord and its protocols. We refused to recognize the jurisdiction of the U.S. courts in our case, and we refused to participate in the trials, demanding an international trial or in a neutral country. Suffice it to say that none of this was even considered by the courts, but it's interesting that some of the judges admitted that Puerto Rico was a colony but insisted that what was on trial were violations of U.S. domestic law. Thus, to double jeopardy we add the double standard that the federal authorities have kept using against us—recognizing our case as a highly political one—and at the same time branding us as common criminals. All this is reflected in the "special" treatment we are given in prison. On the one hand, the accusation of seditious conspiracy is of a political nature and used almost exclusively against Puerto Rican *independentistas* in the twentieth century. On the other hand, the immediate objectives were to criminalize our struggle, labeling us as terrorists and lunatics. Thus the trials were conducted in an atmosphere of antiterrorist hysteria, obtaining guilty verdicts even when the evidence against some of us was very scarce, and the prosecutors distinguished themselves by crass procedural violations in a trial without opposition.

The charges and sentences imposed in my federal case are as follows: Seditious conspiracy, count one—twenty years; count two, armed robbery of a rental truck (the same as the state case)—twenty years consecutive to count one; count three, possession of an unregistered weapon (the same shotgun)—ten years consecutive; count four, carrying four weapons during the act of committing seditious conspiracy—ten years concurrent; count nine, interstate transportation of twelve weapons—ten years concurrent; count ten, interstate transportation of a stolen car—four years consecutive; and count thirteen, interstate transportation of a stolen vehicle—five years consecutive. The total: sixty years consecutive. All our sentences ranged between fifty-five and ninety years. The average sentence in our case is 70.2 years. In 1980, our average sentence was nineteen times higher than the average sentence handed out that year, and more than seven times higher than the average for violent cases. Between 1969 and 1985, the highest average sentence for everyone convicted of homicide was 22.7 years; for rape, 12.5 years; and for weapons offenses, 4.1 years. This is the general picture of my conviction. I've been a prisoner for more than eighteen years straight, and my mandatory release is in the next century, in 2014. I'll be sixty-six years old by then, unless the campaign for our release gets results before then.

Now, as a final point, I want to clarify an issue of a political and ideological nature with respect to the position of prisoner of war, which has been very polemical within the independence movement, even though now our position is recognized almost unanimously, and with respect to how to approach the judicial process within the colonial context in which we find ourselves. For me, beyond its legitimacy based in international

law, the UN, Geneva, etc., the position of prisoner of war can be implemented in diverse ways, including by defending oneself against charges
without criminalizing our struggle, as, for example, Filiberto Ojeda did it.
Its political aspect is worth more than its juridical character aspect. Many
comrades, emphasizing their defiant attitude and condemning the judicial
system as an instrument of colonial domination and legitimization, place
the political where the legal should be and the legal where the political
should be. They thus end up affirming what they claim to negate and make
the work of the prosecutors and courts much easier. The courts, in whatever society we know of, are instruments of class legality and its concept
of justice. They offer, to a greater or lesser extent, certain resources at the
service of the parties. Without naively believing in a neutral and disinter-
ested justice, it is possible, if the criteria of the merits of each particular
case is considered, when this is possible or necessary, to minimize the
damage. This interpretation and attitude pierces through the supposed
antithesis of antilegalism versus legalism and posits the matter from the
perspective that the courts are only political/juridical structures which
comprise another specific area of struggle and before which specific methods and tactics must be used, avoiding dogmatism and without falling into
individualist opportunism.

GIL: In the beginning, how did you manage prison? What was prison?

ESCOBAR: Before, at the end of the sixties, I spent a day in jail at La
Princesa when I refused the military draft the first time. Other times I've
spent the night in jail, in Puerta de Tierra and in New York in the Tombs
and Rikers Island. But I'd never gone in knowing I was going to be there
for a long period of time. Psychologically, at the beginning, with an eight-
year sentence in the state of Illinois, things weren't so terrible since you
were basically facing doing half the time, in a hostile environment, but
with a lot of support inside as well as outside the prison. The hard part
came later when the federal government condemned us. Then, the time in
the state prisons was just a preamble to the life that awaited us in the
federal system. But, in institutional terms, there is a world of difference
between state prison (although the difference of each situation in each
state is also sometimes considerable) and federal prison. In the state, the
control on the part of the jailers is less sophisticated, but, especially in
maximum security prisons in which I spent the first three years, life is
harder and there are minimum opportunities and programs. There was
hardly any work. I spent almost twenty-two hours a day locked in the cell,
which was for two people, the first three years. Security for us was extreme, and they didn't want to give us any kind of work. You could shower

three times a week. The rest of the week we would bathe in the water from the sink above the toilet. The food was awful. One ten-minute phone call every month. They would go with the phone from cell to cell, and you never knew what day it would be your turn or if you would find someone at home. On the other hand, having visits was easier, less complicated and controlled than here in the federal prison. But the worst of all—apart from being a prisoner obviously—was the lack of privacy and the deafening noise I encountered when they put me in the first open-population unit where I was going to live. I thought I would go crazy because the noise, especially at night, was insufferable. This was because the cells were the "classic" type, that is, three walls without a window and an open wall with bars, and the prisoners could have televisions and radios in the cell, and the unit was four floors with four galleries on one side and four on the other, all exposed. Imagine when all those televisions and radios were playing at the same time. Finally, as with everything in life, you get used to it until you don't even realize it. But the lack of privacy has never ceased. And although I've been able to overcome certain aspects, this situation conditions and determines all the others. The world outside closed little by little until what remained were images and effects, and a spacious mental world began to open. Little by little I recuperated as I began to elucidate what the real possibilities were in terms of what could be done and what was worth the trouble.

GIL: What is your routine like in a normal day?

ESCOBAR: There is a certain routine, but it has its variations. I get up at six in the morning. Breakfast is now from 6:00 to 7:00 A.M. I almost never go. I drink instant coffee in my cell. I don't smoke. I quit over five years ago. A New Year's resolution in '90. Then I try to watch the news on CNN at 6:30. Then, at 7:00, I call Jan before starting to work in the showers. That's my job. By 8:30, when I've normally finished, if I haven't eaten breakfast out, I almost always make instant oatmeal mixed with granola. Then, I try to study or write until lunchtime. On Fridays, in the morning, I wash my clothes and sheets. At 11:00 they call for lunch. We could say that half the time I go, and the other half I cook my own lunch or dinner. I haven't eaten red meat since '91—another New Year's resolution. And since about that time they installed microwaves where you can cook. I've become an expert in prison cooking. At noon they close the compound. People go back to their jobs. Depending on who my cellie is, that is to say, the guy I share the cell with, on his schedule, I decide on my routine for after 12:00. Now, I go to the hobby shop at midday to paint.

I can be there until 3:00 P.M. Then, everyone returns to their units for the 4:00 count—you must be standing and with your door open. It's been about a year and a half that I've been living in a new unit with an internal air circulation system, without windows that open, and without fresh air. After the count, they have mail call—letters, newspapers, etc. Dinner is now between 4:15 and 5:00 or until they're done serving all the units. The compound is open until 9:00 P.M. Here, now, at 9:00 it's still daylight. Also, this is one of the few federal prisons where there is no controlled movement after the 4:00 count. I go walking in the yard or running or doing exercise after watching the news at 5:30. Or I go back to the hobby shop to paint or stay in the cell reading or writing. At 9:00 there's another count, and they close the units. At midnight, at 3:00 A.M., and at 5:00 A.M. there are counts. They come to wake up my cellie at 3:30 in the morning to work in the kitchen so my sleep is interrupted at that hour. I almost always go to bed at 11:00 or 12:30 at night. Over all, I am thinking all the time, which you're not supposed to do too much or ever.

GIL: What facilities are available to you in prison, and how do you get material to paint with?

ESCOBAR: As for written correspondence, I use regular mail. There are telephones available from the morning until 11:30 P.M. on weekdays and on weekends until 1:00 A.M. This is due to the time differences that exist between different zones in the United States and because on weekends they lock us up a little later. Regular letters and phone calls are subject to being read and calls are taped. On both sides of the communication, with the exception of special legal calls and special mail—legal, to government functionaries, official press. We have no electronic mail available to us. There are typewriters in the legal section of the library. We aren't allowed to have typewriters like before in the state prison. Nor can we have televisions or radios that aren't transistors with earphones. There are television rooms that also serve as the new chapels. Reality of realities. There's a photocopier in the library we can use. You buy a card that costs five dollars. Each copy costs ten cents. There are vending machines with sodas, cake, and candy. Also with cards. There's a commissary that sells food items, hygiene items, some medicines that they used to give you which now you must buy, exercise clothes, tennies, watches, lamps to read at night, etc. Here, like in the army, one department steals things from the other, and like all prison institutions, there is a black market and drug trafficking. As for art materials, you have to buy everything through catalogs of companies previously authorized by the institution—brushes, canvas, drawing paper, paint, stretchers, liquid gesso, oil, varnish, etc. All services count as "privileges" and can be suspended temporarily at any moment.

GIL: Is there something you've stopped believing? Something you affirm yourself in? Something on which you have changed your point of view? For example, in politics in Puerto Rico, the situation of international communism, your theoretical positions with respect to Marxism . . .

ESCOBAR: As a matter of principle I continue defending our right to self-determination and independence as historical and national imperatives, prerequisites to be able to begin to organize our society in the manner we believe most convenient within the limits of the historical context. Statehood or a "commonwealth" colony will always depend on the other, on the other's permission, and will always be approached depending on how this would benefit the United States or whatever other potency replaces it in the imagination of the colonized and those pariahs who profit from the situation. It doesn't matter how it's seen, from the most sophisticated or modern/postmodern theory you may find, you arrive at the same conclusion: there is no escape from the direct-classical-colonial condition without achieving our own sovereignty, no matter how relative it might be. And that is only the beginning. Worse things can always happens, of course, but nobody can promise the future or happiness. Utopia is a constant movement without transcendental guarantees, and with respect to society, it's constrained by all the previous struggles, knowledge, errors, constructed subjectivity, up and down, dreams, etc. But there are things that must happen first to validate the processes. Only in a colony like ours could the contrary be posited. For me it's clear: first, the power of decision. Then, if the decision is suicide, I think suicide is a dignified decision if it's taken freely. As an individual and as a member of a collective, I prefer freedom even if I have to pay dearly.

But beyond the issue of principles, the immediate problem that's before us is how do we approach this objective? What do we do? And here my points of view, opinions, and judgments, of necessity, are limited because obviously I'm pretty removed from what's happening there. I'm not an empiricist or anything like that, but I don't have all the sufficient elements since my knowledge is based solely on information I get from reading, analyses, debate, the symptoms here and there, or conversations I have. My reflections on the political process are on the general aspect, on my particular experience before as well as after prison. For example, I can relate to the Hostosiano National Congress and its positions of unity respecting diversity. But in the particular, in knowing really how things are done internally, in how this organism really functions, I can't say or pass judgment because my situation simply prevents me from doing so. But my support, if it's worth anything, goes to every unitary effort which understands that without difference no unity is possible, healthy, effective, or real. This also applies to other broader efforts, beyond the political parties and beyond ideological differences. Over all, I think we must keep seeking alternatives that pierce through the dialectic of traditional political parties, bureaucratic practices within these structures as well as state and governmental apparatuses. If I were out, I'd continue my combinatory praxis I've forged theoretically in prison, of infusing political direct discourse and praxis with the symbolic forces of artistic activity and applying the same process of liberation to the liberation movement. Maybe this sounds trite or like a fairy world of artists and intellectuals who think that revolution is like a poem or a theoretical treaty. But I believe in revolution as a process that principally grows from inside, and that no illuminated group can translate for others or impose from the outside. Nor do I believe in "collectivism," which, in the name of the people, the people as demagogy, annuls the individuality of its components. Or in the name of social class, ethnicity, race, sexual gender, nationality, or whatever category. What's important at this level is the construction of an open subjectivity, that sees in the process of liberation real immediate possibilities in the long or short run but connected to the dimensions of time by the present.

GIL: And on the situation of international communism? Marxism?

ESCOBAR: Well, let's go back to my subtext of the Progressive Labor Party as an entry to approach this thematic. PL's analysis is that the former Soviet Union, Eastern Europe, and the People's Republic of China went back to capitalism many years ago. That capitalism, not communism, is what's failing all over the world. The theory of revolution by stages, first socialism and then communism, failed and didn't arrive at communism but returned to capitalism. Thus, the task is to struggle directly for communism, which is a system of social equality. It means the abolition of national states, which are expressions of capitalism. It means sweeping away fascist repression; the abolition of racism and the construction of multiracial unity; abolishing sexism; equality without profit, without money or salaried slavery. And finally, communism means that the party directs society.

The issue here isn't the analysis or meanings attributed to communism as negation of the negation of capitalism and communism's categories that have passed through the moment of socialism. The problem here is how to arrive at these goals and thus, the issue of the party. Negri and Guattari posit a similar position in relation to capitalism-socialism-communism from the European experience as of a new subjectivity emerging in the Paris of May of '68. But they do it against the Leninist tradition. To be frank, I don't know if a party would be necessary if communism so neat and ideal could take place, or, to the contrary, if it would be idealistic to think that society could be directed without a party or something equivalent to a party which wants to give the final blow to the state apparatus. Or, as you would say, maybe the party is a dead metaphor. I think so. The problem is how long its real life-death will last?

For me, and for another kind of less pretentious Marxism, uncertainty is a permanent human condition, although, of course, relative. Scientific Marxism—enthusiastic in modern rationality, in fanatic confidence in science and reason, in the centrality and domination of the human subject in relation to nature or the environment—doesn't sufficiently take into consideration the problematic aspect of human existence. Marx and Engels, for example, in their correspondence, not only make continuous pronouncements of disenchantment and mockery with respect to "party men" but also point out the irony of revolutionary processes. On this point, the theory of Sartre's fusion group is illuminating. Finally, the party man is always an instrumentalist, and his teleology makes him an ideological prisoner of his own mystification, of his own fiction, because it makes it difficult to know (recognize) himself.

Today a lot of people talk about a global return to religion, to the mystical, as a consequence of the crisis of rationality. The era of Hellenism may have a lot of characteristics in common with our era. That's my opinion as a chaotic student. The citizen, the slave, were toys in the hands of omnipotent state power. The resignation and submission to an impersonal state power unites in the birth of an internal, spiritual freedom. From there, from his privileged status and wealth, Seneca wants to abolish existential slavery "spiritually." Then, accused of conspiring against Nero, he commits suicide. While Epictetus, who like Seneca, is a stoic but coming from real slavery, not only wants to console his human condition but that of others. Epictetus, as a Hellenic postmodern of the liberating tendency, explains man as an actor in a play written by an unknown author. In our "Hellenist" era, we also see the growth of resignation and the consolation of the masses—man, seeking these remedies, in extreme cases, but generalized, of the fundamentalist religions or in addiction to the artificial paradises of drugs and television. Discourses proliferate, establishing easily and conveniently the end of all difference as radical alternative to the status quo, the uselessness of all efforts in this direction, the reduction of democracy to elect professional politicians as representatives of their constituencies, and the myth of the irreversibility of the capitalist system.

But even knowing all these things, it's easy to become apathetic, either because of disenchantment with these same failed alternatives or because the exhaustion of society is crushing. Here in prison, for example, you realize that most of the employees have no vocation and no preparation for their jobs and work as little as possible. They know the system isn't functioning except as an interlude where criminal activity continues by other means and becomes strong and perfected through the exchange between prisoners of diverse communities and countries and experiences.

So this is about leaving the world to the direction of a group of empty-headed economists who have devastated our planet, or look for real, viable alternatives to break with all the fears and taboos and false limits they impose on us and we impose on ourselves. For me, Marxism still has, among the theories, epistemologies, or current methods perhaps the best explanatory power and continues to be a key force for transforming our contemporary societies. If this weren't so, capitalism itself wouldn't have apropriated its discourse, sometimes camouflaged, sometimes indiscretely. But always to manipulate. Nevertheless, we must pursue rethinking Marxism and enriching it with new practices and theorizations of bordering and alternate camps, even camps foreign to it. We cannot, we should not, indulge in the luxury of imposing more limits on ourselves than those that already exist. That is contrary to the revolutionary spirit and the best traditions of Marxism.

ANGEL A. AMY MORENO DE TORO

14   An Oral History of the Puerto Rican Socialist Party in Boston, 1972–1978

A HOT SUMMER IN 1972

ON TUESDAY, July 18, 1972, the *Boston Globe* reported that "sporadic trouble continued last night in Boston's Puerto Rican Community for the second straight night. Two stores were bombed and looted by a crowd of 300, mostly young people, who gathered in Blackstone Park on Washington Street, South End."[1] The following day another newspaper, the *Record American and Boston Herald Traveler*, reported that "roving bands of Puerto Ricans fired sniper shots, looted some stores, and firebombed a police cruiser and another car as Blackstone Park erupted for the third straight night. The park anchors Boston's largest Puerto Rican district. The guerrilla-like forays set off a three-alarm fire that sent 25 elderly persons fleeing in panic from an apartment building. . . . police estimate the militant mobs numbered perhaps 200 persons, most of them youths. . . ."[2]

The trouble began the previous Sunday, at the annual Puerto Rican Festival in Boston's Blackstone Park where twenty-seven people were injured and more were arrested. According to police, the sultry weather led to frayed tempers strained after a week of celebration. But many of the South End's Spanish-speaking residents contended that police behavior in quelling a fight at the festival only aggravated the situation. Witnesses claimed that the police used poor judgement when they rushed into the park scattering thousands of people, including many families with young children. Several Puerto Ricans present during the riots indicated that the police employed "excessive force, assaulted bystanders and used obscene and racially abusive language Sunday night."[3] Luis Palmarín, a resident of the South End said, "[T]he cop arrested me when I tried to stop him from beating a man who was bleeding badly. . . . [H]e threw me in the car, grabbed a soda bottle from the floor, called me a 'spic' and hit me in the face with the bottle. I couldn't do anything. I couldn't see his badge number."[4] Among those beaten by the police were Rev. Ernesto Serino and Edward Campbell, an official at the U.S. Justice Department. Campbell, an African American, had been assigned to Boston to mediate disputes between police and community residents. Reverend Serino, director of the Cardinal Cushing Spanish-Speaking Center, said that "the police came into the park as if they were faced with a full scale riot. They came in cruisers from all directions, zoomed to a halt and dashed out of their cars. . . . Nobody even remotely attacked them at all. I suppose when some of them arrived later . . . some bricks and bottles might have been thrown. But this was after some police had already plowed through the crowd." [5]

After three days of rioting and turmoil Boston's mayor Kevin White met with representatives of the Puerto Rican community and agreed, among other things, to investigate charges of police brutality and abuse against the demonstrators. White said that if specific incidents of police abuse were found they would be addressed, but he added that isolated cases should not be taken as an overall indictment of the police department. [6] The demands were presented to the mayor by Antonio Molina, head of a local Hispanic civil rights organization. As an example of the anti-Latino sentiment within official circles, Molina had charged that city council member Albert (Dapper) O'Neil told riot police to "club the maggots and the leeches out of the park." [7] According to one source, the situation was a landmark event for Latinos causing them to reassess their status in Boston and to mobilize for political power. In the aftermath of the confrontations with police, "frustrations of longstanding were . . . causing many of the Spanish-speaking community to gather and recite to one another all the grievances that they have experienced: unemployment, slum housing, discrimination, racism." [8]

By the morning of Friday, July 21, 1972, the *Boston Globe* in an editorial praised both the efforts of the Puerto Rican community and the city government for agreeing to deal formally with the issues that had created the atmosphere for the riots. The paper also raised several socioeconomic concerns affecting the Puerto Rican community that could no longer be ignored. There was a lack of Spanish-speaking police officers, which during the festival, made it impossible for Boston police to deal with a very tense situation. Deeper problems lay at the source of the conflict: poor housing, high drop-out rates from schools, cuts in welfare and unemployment at a staggering 32 percent. Contributing to these factors was the isolation and despair that defeats the desire for ethnic dignity. [9]

IGNITING AN ERA OF POLITICAL ORGANIZING

The incidents in the summer of 1972 became a turning point for many in the Puerto Rican community because those events generated a sense of cultural solidarity that crossed traditional political party lines throughout Boston's South End. Puerto Ricans, from both the Right and the Left, were mobilized as a force to defend what many considered a serious aggression to the dignity of the community by law enforcement authorities. But there was a larger context, too. Since the late sixties, Puerto Ricans throughout U.S. cities had been escalating their political involvement as a result of rising pressure from the independence movement on the island and militant political groups in urban centers here.

Among those who began to coalesce locally were a number of community activists from the South End joined by a core group of graduate students who were actively involved in the Puerto Rican community. Daisy Díaz, Natividad (Naty) Pagán, Ramón Feliciano, Jorge and Ada Palmarín, Harry Pérez, Ema Rodas, and later Jaime Rodríguez and Tito Mesa, comprised the group of community activists. Student activists, mostly pursuing graduate degrees in Boston-area universities, included Edwin Quiles, María Morrison, Roberto Marrero, Nelly Rivera, and Rodolfo Rodríguez. This essay records the oral history of their experience as members of the Puerto Rican Socialist Party (PSP), the leading radical group to emerge from the community during the 1970s.[10]

It is clear that the confrontations at the Puerto Rican Festival and the ensuing protest had spurred radicals in the community to think more strategically about what to do in the future. By the summer of 1972, there were many groups, including some community agencies, engaged in community work in Villa Victoria. Villa Victoria was the center of the Puerto Rican community in Boston's South End. During the previous three or four years, the community had fought hard to acquire the land previously known as Parcel 19.[11]

MARÍA MORRISON: This was part of the Puerto Rican struggle to gain access to fair and decent housing. It had been a long and tedious process, and fortunately we had won that battle. Many of those who carried the banner came from New York, but the real battle was fought by the community of people living in the South End. There were others that had come from the island and had acquired their political experience from working with the Puerto Rican Independence Party (PIP). In addition, there were many young and energetic college students from Harvard, Boston College, MIT, and Boston University who came and helped. Moreover, there was a group of progressive community residents who met to discuss a political agenda for the incipient community. It was during this process that the 1972 summer riots occurred. After the riots, a group of us met in different places to discuss the outcome of the incidents in the park. I remember that several people—like Daisy Díaz, Natividad (Naty) Pagán, Roberto Marrero, Nelly Rivera, Ema Rodas, Harry Pérez, Sonia Marrero, Jorge Palmarín, and Rodolfo Rodríguez among others—met at Ema's place, and it was there that we were introduced to Jesús López and

José La Lúz, who were members of the Puerto Rican Socialist Party (PSP) from Hartford, Connecticut.

ROBERTO MARRERO: I recall that we met to explore the possibility of organizing the community against city hall and condemning the police brutality that had occurred at the Puerto Rican Festival. Both José and Jesús discussed with us several community-organizing strategies that could be implemented. At the time, we were not organized. They insisted that we had to organize if we wished to accomplish our objectives. One strategy was the distribution of the newspaper, *Claridad*, throughout the community.

MORRISON: There were many persons in the greater Boston area who had heard about and were interested in *Claridad*, especially college students and people who came from New York. It was also agreed to publish a leaflet explaining to the community our position regarding the riots. Jesús suggested that we take some time to discuss among ourselves several options, including the establishment of a *núcleo* [chapter] of the PSP in Boston.

Subsequent meetings among the group discussed the pros and cons of different approaches to organizing. Having such a well-known newspaper as *Claridad*, with its connection to a respected political organization on the island, was an appealing factor for the activists, and it eventually convinced the group to formally set up a PSP chapter.

MARRERO: . . . on the one hand, there were those of us who wished to bring the PSP to Boston because we felt the need to organize and mobilize the community against the issues that have already been mentioned; but on the other hand, there were others who felt that perhaps it was too soon to organize ourselves as a party. Some people argued against the party discipline, its commitments, and many other unresolved issues; others felt that before we could decide to establish a *núcleo,* we had to find out how strong was the community support.

MORRISON: A group of us took to the streets to sell and distribute *Claridad*. As more and more people read the paper, we found that many became interested not only in the problems affecting the Puerto Rican community in Boston, but they also asked questions about problems affecting their relatives in Puerto Rico and in other Puerto Rican communities across the continental United States. In addition, there were many others who voiced a strong interest in fighting in support of Puerto Rican independence.

MARRERO: One thing that helped us was that while we sold the paper we also had an opportunity to talk to the people, and they asked many questions about issues affecting both Villa Victoria and Puerto Rico. As time went by more people bought the paper, and many others brought their concerns to us. It was evident for all of us that we were winning the people's hearts as well as their trust. This in itself was seen as a major victory for the organization because many of us did not live in Villa Victoria at the time. I must say that this process became quite burdensome to many of us because most of us were full-time students trying to make the best out of our limited resources. At that time, only Daisy, Naty, Harry, Ema, the Palmaríns, Ramón Feliciano, Sonia Marrero, and María Morrison lived in Villa Victoria. It was important for the organization that we tapped more people to get involved with community issues since many of us lived in Cambridge.

STRUCTURE, PRACTICE, AND STRUGGLES

By 1973, the basic structure and membership had been established, and the organization began a whirlwind of campaigns and struggles that was to last for several intense years. Most activities were carried out as part of a coordinated nationwide (in Puerto Rico and the United States) plan in which all PSP chapters were involved. But local *núcleos* also were engaged in specific issues pertinent to their environment. As in most cities, the central group of activists was made up of a modest number of *militantes* (militants) and *afiliados* [affiliates], but this core element was able to influence and mobilize a much larger periphery of *simpatizantes* [sympathizers] who attended broader activities, such as marches and demonstrations. They also provided financial and moral support; and of course were regular subscribers to *Claridad*. Former members described the early stage of the Party's development.

MORRISON: Besides me, the founding members were Natividad Pagán, Daisy Díaz, Roberto Marrero, Ema Rodas, Harry Pérez, Ramón Feliciano, and Jorge Palmarín. The first president was Ema Rodas, and Harry Pérez was press secretary. It was the later's responsibility to distribute and sell *Claridad*, the party newspaper. In addition, Harry Pérez was also charged with composing a local leaflet to inform [people of] Puerto Rican issues. We established membership dues and devised a strategy to increase our membership. With the help from both Hartford and New York, we organized into several study groups. Everyone from the community was invited to participate in our group discussions. One of these groups was devoted to the study of Puerto Rican social history and its problems; another one discussed Marxist theory; and another one analyzed community issues. The goal of our *núcleo* was to involve ourselves in the social issues affecting the community. By doing this, we would be able to attract more people to the cause of the independence of Puerto Rico and international socialism.

MARRERO: The crisis generated by the disturbances at the festival gave us an opportunity to prove ourselves in Villa Victoria. A lot of the local leaders and *pioneros* [pioneers or "old guard"] were able to grasp our enthusiasm and youthful energy in support of the community. Also, many found the information from *Claridad* filling the gap since the local media did not show any interest in reporting news from the island.

JAIME RODRÍGUEZ: . . . at that time we had about eight or nine active members. But I must tell you that these people had the energy of more than one hundred persons! I am talking of those holding the *carnet rojo* [red membership cards held by militant members]. In addition, we had about ten *afiliados* that constantly supported our work. Although our group was small, we were very well organized, and everyone in the community cherished our party discipline. We had to have discipline if we were to accomplished all the work that was required from our *núcleo*. At the time, many in the community, including the *pioneros*, were not happy with a PSP presence in Boston. They tried to undermine our work by telling folks that we were troublemakers and anti-American. [This was the] truth . . . in some aspects . . . but we made very clear to the community that we were fighting on their behalf.

The first thing that we did [to build community support] was to sell *Claridad*. . . . all of us were required to sell the paper; we gathered in *La Placita* [the community square] every Saturday morning and went out to distribute the paper. At first, people were afraid to talk to us or to buy the paper, but after months of interacting with us every Saturday morning at the same place and time, people opened themselves to us. The reason was that they knew that they could trust us because we listened to their demands, and [they] saw us actively fighting on their behalf. Everyone in the party, *militantes* and *afiliados,* as well as many others, took this commitment as a sort of a "missionary work."

BUSING AND BILINGUAL EDUCATION

In the early and mid-1970s the city was rocked by the controversy over busing. In 1972, a group of Black parents, supported by the NAACP, sued the Boston School Committee for condoning a segregated school system. This was followed by extensive legal maneuvering and massive protests by proponents and opponents of desegregation. Finally in the summer of 1974, Judge Arthur W. Garrity decided in favor of desegregation, ordering the school system to institute mandatory busing starting in September of 1974. Most Latinos were sympathetic to African American demands for equal access, but ironically the largest Puerto Rican community was situated in an already integrated enclave—the South End—of minorities, including Latinos, Asians, and Blacks. These parents, including many supporters of the PSP, did not want to have their children forced to attend White-dominated schools. Consequently, they organized to have the special needs of bilingual students protected.[12] Nelly Rivera recalled the complexity of the situation and the role of the PSP and other progressive Latinos in the process.

NELLY RIVERA: The party was fully convinced that the issue of busing and student integration was going to negatively affect Puerto Rican students attending Boston public schools. The issue here was that, with busing in place, many of our students would have to leave the community base, where there was already a critical mass in place, to be dispersed to other school districts throughout the city. Both Progressive Black, Puerto Rican, and Chinese parents were against busing because we had already integrated our schools in the South End. Many parents in the South End thought that busing would cause negative effects in their children's education because many of the White schools, located in neighborhoods like South Boston, were not academically equipped to handle the needs of minority children. In addition, we all knew that many of the White schools were not any better than the schools that we had in the South End.

    . . . the crucial issue for us was the fate of the bilingual education programs at our local schools. This became an issue because the Boston School Department had mandated that all bilingual students attending public schools had to be placed in a designated bilingual classroom in each school. The rationale was that every bilingual child, regardless of age or grade, would be placed in a single classroom in each school, instead of each grade having a bilingual classroom. This, of course, was not accepted by the parents.

TITO MESA: . . . we complained loudly about the brutality and abuse that our children were subjected to as a consequence of busing. Blacks and Latinos were not liked in South Boston and other White conservative neighborhoods. We had fought both racism and discrimination in the schools and in the work force. But ours was a strong voice because we went all over the city defending the rights of Puerto Ricans as well of other oppressed people of Massachusetts.

RIVERA: The party helped organize the community around this issue. Naty Pagán worked for the school department, and she was able to keep us abreast of the day-to-day operations. . . . [M]any people and party sympathizers got involved around this issue. The outcome of this struggle was the establishment of the *Comité de Padres* [Parent's Committee] who went to court to propose an amendment to the desegregation plan in order to allow the implementation of bilingual programs to proceed as mandated by the Bilingual Education Act (1973). Judge Arthur Garrity, who presided the case, allowed the *Comité de Padres* to enter the case as *amicus curiae*. The case was won by the parents. The party saw this as one of our greatest victories as well!

OTHER COMMUNITY STRUGGLES

Participants discussed the organization's involvement in other issues ranging from labor organizing to solidarity work during the mid-1970s.

RODRÍGUEZ: This was a very active period in the community because many important issues were taking place at the same time. Tito Mesa, who had come to Boston from Honduras in 1973, joined the party and was charged with the task of worker organizing. Jorge Palmarín and Tito Mesa organized the workers of Villa Victoria, and they succeeded in forming a labor union, which today is still very active. There were many marches and demonstrations in support of workers throughout the city that the party supported or helped to organize. In addition, the struggle to support bilingual education was very strong. The PSP organized many demonstrations at the bilingual department in Boston to support, not only the implementation of the program, but also the appointment of Puerto Rican and other Hispanics as teachers and school personnel.

MESA: During these three years [1973–75] the party grew, and we had persons working for us at colleges and universities, labor unions, public schools, and at the community level. During 1974, María Morrison became the president of the Boston *núcleo*. María was also a founding member of the Comité de Solidaridad con Puerto Rico [Puerto Rican

Solidarity Committee]. The committee's membership was predominantly Anglo liberal-progressives who were engaged in the struggle for the independence of Puerto Rico. The party also fought against the commercialism and venality that the Puerto Rican Festival exhibited at the time. I remember that we asked the festival's leadership for the right to march during the parade, and we were turned down with the pretext that we were "a subversive organization" and so on; well, we fought for our right to march and we won. I recall that we marched under the theme: *"Parada un Día y Hambre todos los Días"* ["Parade one day and Hunger every day!"].

Another important accomplishment was the party's expansion to other areas of Boston, such as Dorchester and Jamaica Plain, as well as to the city of Cambridge. From 1973 to 1976, the PSP had an impressive growth both quantitatively as well as qualitatively. I also believe that this was the period where the party was able to muster a lot of community support, directly or indirectly. We had people placed in many important positions. We had supporters from Harvard University and from the arts community as well.

AT HARVARD TOO

The PSP had a very active committee working in Harvard University under the leadership of Prof. Richard Levins, who had taught biology at the University of Puerto Rico, Río Piedras. Levins had been a member of the Movimiento Pro Independencia (MPI; Movement for the Independence of Puerto Rico) and had participated as well during the transition from MPI to PSP. Víctor López-Tosado, a graduate student at Harvard during this period, described the activities of the PSP in this most famous of ivory towers.

VICTOR LÓPEZ-TOSADO: I came to Boston in 1974 to pursue graduate studies at Harvard. At the university there was a study group chaired by Richard Levins. It was a study group whose purpose was to study Marxist and socialist philosophy. Prior to my arrival in Harvard, I was informed about the *núcleo* in Boston and I also knew several *compañeros* that had relocated [from Puerto Rico] to the Boston-Cambridge area to work and study. The Harvard *núcleo* was independent from other *núcleos*. Its role was to apply the political theories that were discussed in our group sessions into the praxis of community work. This is how I got involved with the Puerto Rican community in Villa Victoria. One of my first tasks was to sell and distribute *Claridad* as well as to do propaganda work. Each party member had different tasks to do during the week. For example, there was a *componente* (committee) in charge of housing, another one in charge of education, culture, and university work. In addition, there were ad hoc committees assigned to specific areas.

THE CULTURAL FRONT AND ATHLETICS

Another component of the party's work related to the cultural area. This became a very important medium because it involved many people and it served as one of the most successful ways of attracting the people from the community. Along with many others, Annette Díaz was actively involved in this dimension.

ANNETTE DÍAZ: During the years that the PSP was active in Boston, I recall that the party contributed actively to the development and implementation of many cultural activities that took place in Boston. The purpose of these activities was to generate funds for the party. You must not forget that most of the active members of the party were college students so money was always a problem. So the activities served both to get the community involved with the issues of day as well as to provide the party with a modest income. During that period, Roy Brown and El Topo came several times to Villa Victoria. Lucecita Benítez performed in a wonderful show at the Strand Theater. Vicente Castro, a Puerto Rican teaching at Harvard's Loeb Center, organized a community theater or *teatro popular* [people's theater] at Villa Victoria under the name, "*Virazón.*" Although this group was not affiliated to the party, many of its members and supporters were members of the party. Through "*Virazón*" many community residents had an opportunity to engage themselves in the theater and train themselves as actors and also work as part of the production staff. The content of the plays reflected on the one hand, the struggle for the independence of Puerto Rico and on the other, the struggle for international socialism. Sometimes, the plays that were held reflected the struggle of the community at a given moment. The important thing to remember is that a lot of people were attracted to the theater through our efforts. It was a great time to be involved.

We also contributed to the establishment of the "*Areyto*" cultural program at IBA.[13] The "*Areyto*" program provided community children with activities revolving around the culture of Puerto Rico. "*Areyto*" also had the first silk-screen workshop, which enabled us to print posters and t-shirts. Members of the PSP worked [here], and . . . our artists were able to produce some of the best *serigrafías* (silk screens) and *carteles* (posters) in that shop. Later on, Tito Estrada, a party affiliate and artist, left IBA and established his own *taller* [workshop]. Our messages were displayed throughout the community and the people's response was very positive.

ONE OF THE most interesting ways in which the organization reached out to community people was by organizing a softball team. People did not have to be a member of the party to play on the team, and by all accounts it was a pretty good club. It is unlikely that Karl Marx or Albizu Campos had this method of political organizing in mind when they originated their respective theories of struggle. Nevertheless the team became one of the most well-known signs of the PSP in Boston and was an effective way to maintain the organization's presence in the community.

RODRÍGUEZ: . . . at the end of 1973, the party established a softball team under the name "*Claridad.*" I was selected as team manager, and everyone in the community was welcome to become a team member. In fact, most of the players were not members of the PSP but wore the colors of the party. I believe that the team stole the hearts of many in the community.

PABLO NAVARRO: This was an excellent team. When I came to Boston in 1974 from Puerto Rico where I had been a professional athlete for many years, the first thing that I wished to do was to join the team. I had known the team for quite some time because prior to my move to Boston, I had served as a staff reporter for *Claridad*. We played against very good teams, and they considered us an excellent club. The games were always full of people, and most of us enjoyed the games and the community support. Another positive thing that occurred at the games was that we were able to sell *Claridad* in great numbers. I believe that was part of the trust and confidence that people gave us.

CRISES AND SETBACKS

Although the PSP became a well-known political influence in the Puerto Rican community, the party confronted several crises that contributed to its eventual demise in Boston and other cities. Former members offered several reasons for the decline.

NAVARRO: I believe that the pivotal force that accelerated the fragmentation of PSP, not only in Boston but in Puerto Rico and other mainland communities, had to do with the direction that the PSP took in 1976 to 1977. To do justice, we must accept the fact that at the *núcleo* level there was always a conflict between those members who held the notion that the party's exclusive mission was to fight on behalf of the independence of Puerto Rico and the implementation of world socialism; and those who held that, although there wasn't any conflict with that goal, if we wished to fulfill our objectives we had to bring the struggle to the community level—otherwise we would not be able to gain the support of our people. There were those of us who understood that our commitment had to go first to the fight against police brutality, the lack of adequate housing, discrimination, the absence of good schools as well as many other community concerns. So there was always this tension that was aggravated by the constant flow of directions that came from San Juan that attempted to tax our limited resources on behalf of some sort of crisis occurring in Puerto Rico. In the case of Boston, this was crucial because most of our members were college students who did not live in Villa Victoria or in the community. In addition to this, the turnover rate in membership was high because once students finished their studies, they left Boston. Very often, it was difficult to fill the gap.

RODRÍGUEZ: In 1976, the PSP organized a national march and rally in Philadelphia during the American bicentennial celebrations. We met under the theme *"Bicenterario sin Colonias"* (Bicentennial without Colonies). To make this event successful, we had to mobilize thousands of people from all over the country. This effort exhausted a lot of our resources and energy. After Philadelphia, many members returned with burnout symptoms. It took some time to recover from this event.

MORRISON: Another issue that divided the party was the decision of the PSP in San Juan to participate in the Puerto Rican general elections of 1976. This meant that after years of preaching electoral abstention in the "colonial elections," we now received instructions from San Juan and New York that we had to help register people to vote in the elections. Most *compañeros* of the Boston *núcleo* opposed this action because most of us were not in a position to participate in that process; besides, our commitment was with the Puerto Rican community here in Boston not in Puerto Rico. This process divided our group even more because the members who would soon be returning to the island understood that this was an important issue to pursue. The outcome of this debate was the loss of a significant amount of members that opted to leave the party rather than to invest time and energy in the election registration effort.

NAVARRO: The sad history is that we were all made to believe that the independence of Puerto Rico was just around the corner. All of us engaged ourselves in all sorts of personal sacrifices and deprivations in order to achieve that goal. I have to admit that my personal life, as well as that of many party members, was deeply affected as a result of our commitment to the PSP. My activism affected both my family life as well as my studies at Harvard. I also wish to point out that during my tenure as a party member in Boston, I had serious doubts as to the number of copies of *Claridad* that were sold. I do not believe that we sold that many copies.

I also feel that we, as a group, were inclined to be quite intransigent, ideologically speaking, with those people who disagreed with our party line. We were always right, and they were always wrong. The truth is that we were young and full of optimism, but again you cannot run a political organization with only a few individuals. The party had an active membership anywhere from ten to fifteen *militantes* and another ten or fifteen *afiliados*. It was not easy to be a member of the PSP. First of all you have to devote all your time and energy to the party; secondly everyone was watching your moves (on the one hand, there were party members, and on the other hand, community people); thirdly there was not too much time for social activities except for the official Friday PSP party, which tended to be an extension of the same group; finally, your entire personal life was directed by the party as we were constantly reminded that we had to set the standard or the model for everyone in the community to follow. After a few years, you could not escape the stress.

CONCLUSION

This brief account of the PSP's experience in Boston has been constructed primarily from individual interviews with key members of the organization. Perhaps one day a full-fledged history will be written drawing on a broader base of documentation and oral histories. We know from other sources and personal knowledge that the PSP attracted many other activists, such as Mauricio Gastón, a well-known housing organizer.[14] It became a center of influence beyond the Puerto Rican community, forming alliances with many Left and progressive movements in the area. In later years, many of its former members were instrumental in organizing the Latino community in support of Mel King's historic run for mayor under the banner of the Rainbow Coalition.

The participants in this oral history have mentioned several of the contributions of the organization and its members: the development of cultural awareness and grassroots theater projects; advocacy for parent involvement in the school system and for bilingual education programs;

organizing against racism and discrimination in the workplace; and defense of housing rights. This was promulgated all within the context of an anticolonial movement.

It is the consensus of most who shared their impressions that the PSP's decision to galvanize most of its resources in support of the electoral process in Puerto Rico sent a negative signal to its mainland *núcleos*. Many *compañeros* became disillusioned with the sudden change of goals and objectives, and it was evident that the party would not survive with its new mission. By late 1976, after the "Bicentennial without Colonies" campaign and after the November elections in Puerto Rico, some prominent PSP members had left the party in Boston.

Although other members moved into leadership positions and worked hard to keep the organization intact, there was a feeling among the group that things were not going to improve anytime soon; there was a visible decline in activity among members and in the support of sympathizers. By 1979 it was basically all over. The party went into disarray. Many members and former members felt neglected, rejected, and even double-crossed by the Central Committee of the party. Some members tried different ventures; still others tried to go back to their studies, their families, and their lives.

In retrospect most former members feel proud of their past work with the PSP. As the years go by, some have chosen to remember and reflect about the glories of former days gone by; others have opted to remain silent. There are still many others that are active in both their communities and politics both on the mainland and Puerto Rico. Many still continue to work for Puerto Rican independence.

Above: Since the 1930s, the Nationalist Party led by Don Pedro Albizu Campos garnered support among Puerto Ricans in the U.S. In 1969 a pro-independence contingent at the New York City Puerto Rican Parade was led by City College students (PRISA) dressed in traditional nationalist cadet colors and wooden rifles.

Below: The Young Lords Party at the New York City Puerto Rican parade in June 1970 was well-received by the many thousands of onlookers. The Young Lords and other radical groups often had to challenge parade organizers to exercise their right to march in the parades.

MÁXIMO COLÓN

CARLOS ORTIZ

Above: The campaign to free all Puerto Rican political prisoners united the entire Puerto Rican Left. Here members of the MPI-PSP, the YLP, and the Carlos Feliciano Defense Committee demonstrate in New York City in 1971.

Below: On May 16, 1970, Puerto Rican *independentista* Carlos Feliciano was arrested in New York City for alleged bombings and possession of dangerous weapons. Defended by attorneys William Kunstler and Conrad Lynn, he was acquitted of all charges. Feliciano was tried on similar charges in Manhattan and acquitted in July 1975 (shown above).

Above: In April 1969, Eduardo "Pancho" Cruz (front left) led the student takeover of City College of the City University of New York which sparked the struggle for Open Admissions and Black and Puerto Rican studies programs. In 1971, Cruz was imprisoned on charges related to the Puerto Rican independence movement. Also shown are William Morales (second from left), later imprisoned for his activities with the FALN, and Julio Rosado (far right) who was imprisoned for his refusal to testify before a Grand Jury investigating the FALN.

Below: In September 1974, the PSP staged a rally in Newark, New Jersey, defying a ban on demonstrations in the aftermath of an uprising sparked by police brutality during a Puerto Rican festival. The rally was addressed by Amiri Baraka, then leader of the Congress of African Peoples and renowned figure of the Black Arts movement.

Right: With more than 3,000 supporters in attendance, the Puerto Rican Socialist Party established a branch in the United States at its First Congress on April 8, 1973, in New York's Manhattan Center.

Above: On October 27, 1974, more than 18,000 Puerto Rican and North American supporters filled Madison Square Garden in New York City for a National Day of Solidarity with the Independence of Puerto Rico. Key speakers included, among others, Juan Mari Brás, Angela Davis, Chief Philip Deer (American Indian Movement), Dave Dellinger, Jane Fonda, Arthur Kinoy, Geraldo Rivera, Antonio Rodríguez (CASA), Irwin Silber, and Piri Thomas.

Below: The Struggle for democratic rights led to the development of broad based coalitions, such as Acción Boricua, organized in New York City in 1975 to fight projected budget cutbacks. Pictured (from left to right) are Richard Garza, Socialist Workers Party; Honorable Judge John Caro; José E. Velázquez, Puerto Rican Socialist Party; Frank Bonilla, Center for Puerto Rican Studies; and Evelina Antonetti, United Bronx Parents.

BOMEXÍ IZTACCIHUATL

CLARIDAD

Above: In May 1976, the student body of Hostos Community College in New York City protested plans to close the only bilingual college in the U.S. The Puerto Rican radical movement played a key role in mobilizing student and community support to save the college.

Below: A Bicentennial Without Colonies! On July 4, 1976, the PSP (New Jersey & Pennsylvania chapter shown above) spearheaded a coalition of progressive and anti-imperialist North American organizations that rallied over 50,000 people in Philadelphia and San Francisco in opposition to the official government celebrations.

Above: In June 1977, the New York City Council approved comprehensive guidelines to protect women from sterilization abuse in the city's hospitals. Led by the Committee to End Sterilization Abuse (CESA) under the leadership of Maritza Arrastía and Dr. Helen Rodríguez, protests like these were instrumental in achieving these reforms.

Below: As a result of a conference initiated by El Comité-MINP in March 1972, the movement was unified in support of Puerto Rican political prisoners. As shown in this 1978 rally, the United Nations was often the setting for pro-independence demonstrations and for the release of political prisoners.

CARLOS ORTÍZ

CARLOS ORTÍZ

Above: Victory at last! The Puerto Rican Nationalist prisoners were freed by President Carter after years of vigorous international campaigning. Shown here at a welcoming rally in New York City upon their release in September 1979 are (right to left) Oscar Collazo, Lolita Lebrón, Irving Flores, and Rafael Cancel Miranda.

Below: Visited by both Presidents Jimmy Carter and Ronald Reagan, Charlotte Street became a symbol for government abandonment of urban areas. On the eve of the Democratic Convention held in New York City in 1980, Puerto Rican workers took the lead to protest years of broken promises.

BLANCA VAZQUEZ

CLARIDAD

Above: The National Congress for Puerto Rican Rights has consistently led the struggle against police brutality and racial violence. In 1996, the family of Anthony Baez, slain while in police custody, organized a "We Demand Justice" march in the Bronx, New York.

Below: Then and Now! The present campaign to free Puerto Rican political prisoners mirrors similar campaigns during the 1970s. Shown above is a 1973 demonstration in Washington, D.C., during the Nixon Presidency.

A recent demonstration at the White House demanded the release of Puerto Rican political prisoners. Despite thousands of petitions and requests from all sectors of the Puerto Rican public, the Clinton administration has refused clemency to many who were sentenced to long prison terms without parole on charges related to their pro-independence activities.

PHOTO CREDITS

Michael Abramson is a photojournalist who chronicled the development of the Young Lords Party since its inception in 1969. Along with the Young Lords, Abramson published the book, *Palante: Young Lords Party* (New York: McGraw Hill, 1971), now a classic work on this movement.

CLARIDAD is a pro-independence weekly newspaper published in San Juan since 1959. In 1972, it began publication of a bilingual supplement that covered the activities of the independence movement in the United States. Special thanks to Edwin Molina for access to the *CLARIDAD* photo archives.

Máximo Colón's photos were featured in the newspaper *Unidad Latina*, published by El Comité-MINP in the 1970s. His photos have been exhibited in New York City, Washington, D.C., and recently in the documentary, *!PALANTE, SIEMPRE PALENTE! The Young Lords*.

Eduardo Cruz was a student leader during the 1969 takeover of City College of New York and a former political prisoner. He is now a practicing defense attorney in New Jersey.

Bomexí Iztaccihuatl, a former member of the MPI-PSP, began his career as a photojournalist working for the *CLARIDAD* bilingual supplement. He presently edits *BATU*, a cultural and sports magazine in the Bronx, New York and is chairman of the pro-independence. Andrés Figueroa Cordero Foundation.

Carlos Ortíz is an award winning journalist who has chronicled the independence movement, the South Bronx, and the Latin music scene. His works include independent films for public television, including the award winning film on the life of salsa composer and band leader, Machito. His photos have recently been featured in the Broadway production, *The Capeman*.

Blanca Vázquez is a member of the Justice Committee of the National Congress for Puerto Rican Rights and editor of CENTRO, the journal of the Center For Puerto Rican Studies at Hunter College of the City University of New York.

Special thanks to Maritza Arrastía, Nena Negron, the Center for Puerto Rican Studies, and the National Committee to Free Puerto Rican Prisoners of War and Political Prisoners (NCFPR/POW&PP) for their assistance in this project.

III. COMMUNITY AND SOLIDARITY STRUGGLES

HUMBERTO CINTRÓN

15 Poet, Writer, a Voice for Unity

An Interview with Piri Thomas

I CHUCKLED at the thought of it. Piri Thomas is not interviewed. He is encountered. He does not respond to questions with answers. He responds to stimuli with evocations. For Piri Thomas is not just writer, poet, and playwright; he is orator, actor, dancer, musician, commentator, and performer. He communicates with his fingertips, eyebrows, and shoulders. He grunts and hisses. He laughs and screeches and roars. He whispers and sighs. He spins and sweats and drums and cries.

He emotes.

His words are "bullets" or "butterflies," and he demonstrates both with candor. He has written several books since *Down These Mean Streets,* and though none of them have received the same critical acclaim, his popularity has never abated. The first Puerto Rican writer in the United States to gain such recognition, Piri Thomas is a legend in his community. He has carried this responsibility with dignity since being launched from the mean streets to the literary world—a living literary icon who persists in a world where those mean streets have evolved from zip guns to Uzis and where a holler and quick feet have been replaced by cellular phones and sleek sport cars.

He lives in the verdant hills of Berkeley, California, a far cry from the streets of *El Barrio.* A white picket fence and trim lawn surround his home—a Dick and Jane image from elementary school textbooks at PS 72. Few who dreamed that dream ever lived it. Piri has. But wherever he goes, *El Barrio* goes with him so he chooses his bullets and butterflies with care. He has traveled the world on missions of peace and justice. He has shared his thoughts with heads of state and the literary elite alike.

Once, when we met after several years and were catching up on our lives, I slipped into street talk and said to him, "Oh, man I got all kinds of shit going on." He stopped me cold. "Don't use that word, bro. Whatever you're doing is not 'shit.' If you talk about it like that, you'll think about it that way, and that's what it will amount to. Your work is too important to be defined by a four-letter word from the streets."

This chapter appeared originally in *Forkroads* (fall 1995). The editors are grateful to David Kherdian, the journal's editor, for permission to publish this interview.

Simple wisdom. A clear message. Piri cares. It is that caring spirit that drives him to create, to perform, and to inspire others. Whether he is in the auditorium of a university, in a neighborhood center, in a prison cell, or at home in his studio, there is certainty in one thing. The ivy-covered walls, the clapboard siding, the steel bars, or the picket fence may surround him, but they will never confine him. He takes two words, "truth" and "justice," tucks them under his evocative wings as ballast, and takes off on one of his "flows." You never know where he's going or when he's coming down, but you know you're in for an exciting ride.

CINTRÓN: Piri, tell me a little about your background and what influenced you to become a writer.

THOMAS: We are all influenced by others sometimes, whether we like it or not. That's why it's very important to have the wisdom to be influenced by those who can bring good energy [wisdoms] that one can recognize immediately. I, like others, like yourself, Humberto, grew up in a mean world. I was born in Harlem Hospital—the only hospital in East Harlem that would accept Blacks and Browns. We lived in three worlds: home, school, and the streets. The world of my home for the most part was polite and courteous, spiritual and full of wisdom; strong medicine if one chose to listen. In school, it was the hope that you would be assigned a teacher that cared enough to not put you down. To tell the truth, most of my teachers were kind, but others only saw it their duty to teach you to count to one hundred and learn enough English so you could push the garment-district wagons or become supers, porters, and janitors and assistant's assistant to the assistant *lavaplatos* [dishwasher], as found in one of Pedro Pietri's brilliant poems "Puerto Rican Obituary."

Bueno, after my beautiful mother, Dolores (Doña Lola), passed on when I was fifteen years old, I was on my own, but instead of allowing Mami's spiritual wisdoms to guide me, I got caught up in the survival of the streets where most anything goes, a reality of not having; and surviving was a twenty-four-hour special. So I made some big mistakes here and there that landed me in prison. But I knew in my heart that I meant to survive, but with grace. In prison you learn or you burn. I was determined not "to serve time," but rather make time serve me, to educate my mind, to eradicate it. I proceeded to get myself together while in prison; reading and writing, all forms of creativity, helped me do just that.

CINTRÓN: You talk about writing in prison, but it was many years later before you published *Down These Mean Streets*.

THOMAS: I got out of prison for Christmas 1957, and *Down These Mean Streets* was published in 1967.

CINTRÓN: What motivated you to start writing? How much of your writing was done in prison? How much after you came back to the streets? I'm not clear chronologically.

THOMAS: I started writing in prison. Although I had failed English in the school system, as a child somebody had recognized my potential—a teacher in Babylon, Long island, where we had moved when my father had hit the *bolita* [numbers] for a little money right after the war began. And this teacher had recognized that I had a talent for expression because when I wrote a composition she assigned, I spelled out how much I loved her and her brunette hair and her hazel eyes. However, I did not dig her pronouns and adjectives and all that shit, you know, because I didn't know what she was talking about. So after she sent the papers back to everyone she called me to her desk, and there was this written note there on the paper, and it said, "Son, your punctuation is lousy, your grammar is nonexistent. However if you wish to be a writer some day, you will be." And then it said, "P.S. We both love my wife." Signed her husband.

I learned two things from that. I learned that there was somebody who recognized a beauty in me, and I also learned that it could be dangerous to mess around with somebody else's wife.

I always had a gift for gab. We used to play the "Dozens," insulting each other in rhyme. But I didn't begin writing in earnest until I got to prison, and I realized that first I had to complete my education. So me and Indio, a beautiful Puerto Rican brother who was in for drugs, decided to take the high-school equivalency test. We studied and studied, and we took the test. When the test results came back we had both passed with dynamite marks. I was so proud; you know, getting that diploma was my first great feeling of achievement because when the certificate came it did not say Comstock State Prison. It said University of New York. I could present it with pride.

So then I began to write, and the words that I could not spell I wrote phonetically. I began to write my feelings. I began to make my inner journey, to find out who I was and where I came from. Because outside there was no rest, no pause, it was 150-mile-per-hour-survival. So I went back into time to see the scenes and relive the feelings all over again. To be with my family again because that's what kept me going in prison. I would time travel. I would go out there and walk the streets with my *familia*. And when it got too heavy for me, I put my arms around myself in the darkness of my cell, C513. I would hug myself very hard. I'd kiss my arms just so that love wouldn't die. And I began to write about the cruelty . . . the inner sense of the beauty, the whole thing. I wrote a thesis, studying psychology on my own in prison, about what was going on in my mind, and before I knew it I had poetry flowing out of my soul.

I went before the parole board. They hit me with two more years. I thought I would go crazy, but my writing helped me to overcome the rage that was building up in me and kept me from being a walking time bomb. I determined that if I had to die I would do it on my feet and not on my knees. That was how it was for me. And although prison is a tough pill to swallow, I had to deal for control because too many brothers in prison, and I'm sure the sisters, too, were becoming psychopaths or vegetables because of the damage to their feelings. And so I wrote and I wrote, and I ended up with a manuscript; I was like a monk writing beautifully, looking after my penmanship. Every word was a work of art. Those two years passed quickly, and this time I got my parole.

There was a chaplain inside who I called the "White-Haired Saint." He never preached to us; he was a friend, someone you could have confidence in. He was also someone I learned from. With him I studied theology, like the *Book of Daniel* and *Revelations*. All the energies . . . Buddha, Confucius . . . I absorbed whatever I could understand. . . . So when I finally came out of prison, I had a doctorate in the art of living. Anyway, I gave him the manuscript and said, "Claude [the chaplain], will you see this gets out?" Because I knew that if they opened it and saw what it was, they would destroy it. He said, "Don't worry." He took it. Then when I had gone through the gates, he came over and said, "Here, you forgot your writings."

When I got out, I started to work. I did all kinds of work. My first job was in the garment district; I was a handyman. I also had a part-time job at Macy's. Between the two, they nearly worked me to death. I got married to Daniela Calo in 1959, and we had two children, Ricardo and San-Dee. I didn't want to go back to the gravity of the streets so I joined my Aunt Angelita's Pentecostal church, Iglesia Rehoboth, on 118th Street between Lexington and Third Avenue. From the church I began working with gang kids, where I met a brother, Ricky Leacock, a great vanguard documentary filmmaker. And he introduced me to Angus Cameron, an editor at Alfred Knopf. Cameron was of Scottish background, a fine naturalist, and he respected humans, not for their color but for what they were as humans. I went home for my manuscript after he made an appointment for me, but when I got home I couldn't find it. So I asked, "Where's my manuscript?" and was asked in return, "Woo, was that important?" The children had got into it and wrinkled it up a bit, and somehow it was thrown into the incinerator by mistake. The only copy. I felt the tears jump into my eyes, and I fled into the bedroom. We were living in Brooklyn at the time, twelve stories high. I sat down on the bed and looked out the window, and all of a sudden a feeling within me rose and said, "*Mira, no te pongas con eso . . . lo escribiste una vez . . . lo puedes escribir otra vez . . . y mejor.*" ["Look, don't let it get to you . . . you wrote it once . . . you can write it again . . . only better."] I'm telling you this so you know what it is to have a will of strength . . . a spirit . . . that is always there because otherwise you'll die.

Out of that was born *Down These Mean Streets*. Up to that point, I had called my work *Home Sweet Harlem*. Once, when I got the manuscript back from Angus Cameron, someone had written on it, "A man who himself is not mean, can walk the mean streets." I liked those words, "mean streets." Later I found out that Angus [who had written those words] had been quoting from Raymond Chandler, who had also known some mean streets.

Fortunately, I was able to remember practically every word of the manuscript, and I wrote it better. I could remember every word because life is about feelings . . . good, bad, or indifferent, and the feelings of those experiences had been branded indelibly into my soul. All I had to do was tune into those feelings, and they were transposed into the present time with all the emotions and feelings of that particular time. Everyone can do it if they don't doubt themselves.

CINTRÓN: Talk to me about jail, social injustice, and literature.

THOMAS: Let me tell you something about prison, my friend, because it was behind bars where I first realized that the cruelest prison is the prison of the mind. That's where one—inside or outside—can really do some hard time. The political prisoners, they are free of the prison of the mind since they believe in their cause. I decided that I wasn't going to live in prison. I was going to live with my mind free inside, to stay in tune with the right feelings and energies. I did not wish to be behavior-modified and programmed. So I said to myself, "Listen, Piri, they only got your body, bro, they ain't got your mind."

In prison you can't appear to be scared, you must wear your face *cara de palo* [wooden face] so no one can read anything. And I chose those I wished to be with; after all, in prisons there are pecking orders based on crimes committed, with rapists, junkies, and crooked cops doing time in that order.

I learned from some of the humans in there. There was this young, White guy, a graduate of Princeton University, who, with his girlfriend, murdered her mother for the insurance money and left her in the bathtub covered with plaster of paris. He once said I was a conglomeration of a manifestation, and I asked what did that mean. He said conglomeration means you are many things, and manifestation is what comes out of it.

I observed and learned. I met brothers in prison with minds as beautiful and bright as brothers Malcolm X, George Jackson, Jeronimo Pratt, and Mummia Abu Jamal, or sisters Dylcia Pagán, Carmen Valentín, and Alejandrina Torres among others. Brothers and sisters who stood tall and walked with a sense of dignity, not with arrogance. Those were the ones that drew my attention. And I was a healer. People would go into depression—and I would do my best to raise their spirits, knowing that if I lifted them up, I would be uplifted, too. I fought hard at times to keep from falling into depression. There are all kinds of prisons, but as I said before, the worst can be your own mind. Street logic imprisons your mind. You know, for all its horror, prison for me turned out to be a painful blessing. I was in a place where I would either die or be refined.

One time in prison, faced squarely with the reality of being locked up, I felt as if I could go insane. But my spirit rose above it, and my soul grew stronger. A brother, nicknamed "Young Blood" had turned me on to read the book *Young Blood* by John Oliver Killens, whose words reawakened in me the feeling that I, too, could write. Years later I would meet John Oliver Killens, a beautiful Black brother. He was an excellent teacher—my brother and my dear friend. John was an attorney by profession but a writer by choice of heart and soul. I could relate to his fine works, like *The Cotillon* and *And Then We Heard Thunder*—about racism and a riot between Black and White American soldiers in Australia. I was inspired by Killen and Ralph Ellison and the writings of many others as well. I read A. J. Roger's *Man and Superman* and *The Power of Positive Thinking* by Norman Vincent Peale. I was reading anything and everything that could help lift my mind up out of the horror of the reality I was living in. I found wisdom in the scriptures, in the holy *Koran,* wherever I could find it, including some on the walls. I told myself, "I was not born a criminal from my mother's womb. I was born a beautiful child, just like any other child, into a criminal world, with all of the horrors of injustice constantly going on."

CINTRÓN: Was there anything to read by Puerto Ricans at that time?

THOMAS: As a child in the thirties in "Nueva Yawk" only [there were only works] in Spanish. It would have been great to have books about our history in those days. There are many fine writers out there, like Pedro Juan Soto, who wrote about the New York Puerto Rican experience in

Spanish, a book called *Spiks*. Why don't they mention his name as one of the fine pioneers? And Juan Antonio Corretjer, who said, "*Aunque naciste en la luna todavía—puertorriqueño eres*" ["Even if you were born on the moon, you are still Puerto Rican"]. The system was and still is intent on assimilation. I used to ask, "Mami, do we have any heroes?" In school I would ask about Puerto Rico, and I was told, "It's a nice place to visit as a tourist." I wanted to know if we had heroes like the colonists—the men and women who fought against England for dignity and independence. I learned eventually that Puerto Rico was and continues to be a colony of the United States, whose large corporations benefitted from cheap, available Puerto Rican labor. So what was new in the world?

CINTRÓN: What effect did *Down These Mean Streets* have? What effect did publishing it have on your life?

THOMAS: I would say that the effect was tremendous. I was catapulted to national attention, which led to speaking engagements around the country, including the University of Erlangen in Germany. But, overall, it has been an uphill struggle for Puerto Rican writers in the United States to get mainstream recognition and publication.

Not everyone was glad for me. Mami always said, "People don't have to kill you with hate; envy will suffice." I was in the barrio visiting an old friend, and a dude comes up and starts looking at me kind of bad, so I smile and ask, "Hey man, what's the matter, why you look at me so bad?" He pointed a finger at me and said, "Hey man, you were born in the barrio. Man, I was born in the barrio. Man, you was in a gang. I was in a gang. Man, you were into drugs. Man, I was into drugs. Man, you were into stickups and went to prison. Man, I was into stickups and ended up in prison." "So?" I asked softly, shifting my weight into a fighting position. "So, you didn't leave a fucking thing for me to write about." I shook my head sadly and said, "Now that's a fucking cop-out. How many books have been written about the Lone Ranger and Tonto, not to mention Tarzan and the apes? You mean to say that out of all our people's combined experiences, I've written it all? Man that is a cop-out." I saw the brother again some years later; he had gone back to school and graduated with a degree in social work.

Mami said we all have powers in us—one is of darkness and the other of light—and it's up to us to choose. Mami said, "It's OK to make money, *hijo*, but don't let the money make you." I, who have been in prison, have a high sense of principles learned from Mami and Papi, too. It was when I forgot their wisdoms that I grew ice cold to feelings, and I had to struggle to come back to the warmth of light. I'm always talking about honor and dignity, and some brothers have asked, "How come you always talking about honor and dignity, bro?" And I say, *Vaya,* bro, lest we forget and sell our souls." So these are among the feelings of grace that are a source of strength for me.

CINTRÓN: Tell me what it has meant to you to be Puerto Rican and to be a writer.

THOMAS: Not too many Puerto Ricans in the United States were being published in those days. That word "Newyorican" hadn't been coined yet. It was coined on the Lower East Side, but I never identified too much with Newyorican because I felt it kept me stereotyped to one place. I felt I was a bird. I hated tags, man. I have been in the struggle for justice with people who were of different political persuasions—the Left or moderate or liberal. I said to them, "I will struggle by your side for peace and justice, but I don't want to wear side-blinders so that I cannot see the situation on a scale of 360 degrees. It's not 'My country, right or wrong.'" Hell, I didn't get rid of one slave master of the mind to get another slave master of the mind, not even if the master speaks my tongue. I'll fight for justice by myself if I have to. But thank goodness I've never had to.

Because of this attitude, the Puerto Rican Socialist Party dropped me as not being disciplined enough. But that and more will be in the sequel to *Down These Mean Streets,* which is titled *A Matter of Dignity.*

As Puerto Rican writers in the U.S.A., we have made some progress. There is Felipe Luciano (who stopped writing but should get back to it some time), Pedro Pietri, Sandra María Estéves, Judith Ortiz Cofer, Nancy Mercado, Nicolasa Mohr, Tato Laviera, Victor Hernández Cruz, Martín Espada, Aurora Levins Morales, Mayra Santos, Maria Arrillaga, Miguel Algarín, Papoleto Meléndez, Jack Agüeros, and many other beautiful poets and writers from the island and from the metropolis. I believe that those of us who struggled in the early days opened the door for those wonderful writers. And how many more are out there, with their stories waiting to be told?

But you know, when we so-called Newyoricans go to Puerto Rico, by and large we are rejected. Only now are some bridges beginning to be built, and the ties are in our shared African heritage. Because the power structure of official Puerto Rican Culture with a capital C leaves out a real integration of the African roots into Puerto Rican culture. The indigenous and the African are mentioned, but then Spanish influence is given preponderance over other cultural forms. So it is fitting that the rejects of official Puerto Rican culture seek out unity with the rejected Puerto Rican culture in the United States.

CINTRÓN: You seem to move easily between fiction, autobiography, poetry, and plays. How do you explain that?

THOMAS: It's very simple to me. To me every child is a poet, and every poet is a child. Every child is born with a 360-degree circumference of creativity. Only we're inhibited by outside influences that cast doubts upon what we can do and tell us that we have to be a specialist in this or that field in order to have respect. And I have felt that words are words are words are words are words, and they are just like musical notes. You can take musical notes to make salsa; you can take musical notes to make blues; you can take musical notes and make a samba. I am a musical instrument. We all are born out of sound of rhythm and feelings and flows, and when we speak our essence can flow out like a song. My essence as Piri flows out this way. And if we don't look at it that way, it's unfortunate because we lose the joy of doing and the ability to create, to tune into the flow. If you doubt your ability to do this, you won't be able to do it. Hey, doubt kills! You doubt your creativity, and then you kill yourself when you say, "I can't do it." The only doubt that I really want to have is that I continue to doubt injustice. Because I'll always doubt that. But I will never doubt my creative energies, and I will allow no one to doubt for me. I can always feel another person's doubt on me. I dislike it, and I say, "Will you kindly doubt for yourself, I didn't ask you to doubt for me."

CINTRÓN: Your first book was called *Down These Mean Streets*, and you later wrote a play called *The Golden Streets*. Now symbolically there seems to be a conflict here. Can you tell us about *The Golden Streets* and how it contrasts with the mean streets you came from?

THOMAS: Ladies & Meesters, did you ever hear about the Puerto Rican dude getting off the *Marine Tiger*, the banana boat, and walking into a strange, alien world with his cardboard suitcase in hand, checking out the scene? He comes upon a five-dollar bill, and he kicks it out of the way. His buddy says, "What the hell you doing, that's a five-dollar bill." And he replies, "Hey man, I heard the streets here were paved with twenty-dollar bills. I ain't going to stoop down to pick up no lousy five-dollar bill." To *los pobres* [the poor] from all over the world, to the immigrants of all kinds, America was always the "Golden Streets." Even when people got pushed into the ghettos of "Nueva Yawk," hey, at least they were there from the hope of being able to fit into the so-called American melting pot.

My mother Dolores Montañéz was born in Bayamón, Puerto Rico, in Cerro Gordo, which bilingually means "fat mountain," and my father came from el Oriente de Cuba, Santiago. They both came to this country looking for better living conditions. Well, you know what they found! Hot-and-cold-running cockroaches, king-sized rats, and horror, hunger, and discrimination running free. And promises that never came to be. But they rolled up their sleeves and went to making a fortune of maybe eight dollars, nine dollars dollars a week; and in our home, poor as it was, my God, everything was clean. Dignity has no price. Just because you're poor doesn't mean you're bereft of your sense of dignity and honor.

And the assimilation that went on with us was terrible. They had no right to assimilate me the way they did—they took my name, Juan Pedro Tomás Montañéz and turned it into John Peter Thomas. Who ever heard of a Puerto Rican named John Peter Thomas? That's why I call myself Piri because that's what my mother called me—"*Mira, Piri, Mira, Piri,*" and it wasn't till years later that I found out that I was like a boy named Sue. Piri is a woman's name, and that's beautiful to know in honor of Mami, who taught me our language, which I wasn't allowed to speak in school. I remember one day in school when I didn't understand what the teacher said about our homework, I asked my friend in Puerto Rican Spanish, "*¿Qué fue lo que dijo esa vieja?*" ["What did that old lady say?"]. The teacher suddenly jumped on me and loudly admonished, "Stop talking that *burwburwbuburugubu.* You must speak English, you're in America now. How else do you expect to become president of the United States if you don't speak English?" Heh, heh heh. I think my young mind said, "Hell, she's got more faith than I do."

And out in the streets there were the looks, there were the words. They couldn't decide whether I was a nigger or a spic so they called me both. But in spite of all the wrongs going on, I was a very happy kid. I used to smile at everybody, even at those who didn't smile back. My father, Juan, had to tell me, "Son, you have to learn who to smile at. You have to learn how to smell *caca* [shit] twenty miles away. And know the difference between that and flowers since *La caca* comes in all colors and walks on two feet." Wisdom from the barrio ways! My father was Juan Tomás—Johnny they called him. He was a fine baseball player, a fine athlete, very beautiful in his flow.

Although the pull to assimilate us was great, it seemed that at the same time society really didn't care for us, especially the darker-skinned ones. One Christmas Eve, after hearing stories about Christmas in Bayamón or Santurce or Mayagüez or the La Perla slum or the Llorens-Torres Housing Project, I asked my mother, "If Puerto Rico is so great, why are we living here?" Mami rubbed her thumb and forefinger together denoting "economics"—those who flooded here were the poorest of Puerto Rico, descended from a people conquered for five hundred years. First there was

Spain; then the island was given as booty to the United States after the Spanish-American War and was then ravaged by the carpetbaggers who rushed in to make a fortune. Anyone who had any chance at all to make it down there, they stayed. The bourgeoisie of Puerto Rico came to Nueva Yawk for a quick look and then split back to their rolling green hills of their *Isla Verde*. I did not get to see Puerto Rico until I was thirty-two years of age. But I knew all about it because the family were always into conversations about Puerto Rico and *la familia*. Mami always spoke about her sister, my Aunt Catín and her husband, Lolo Castro, a minister as well as businessman. We were told about young Tío Angel Luis who was studying to be a lawyer. Stories were told and repeated about everyone and everything—stories that described the feelings, the beauty of the island they came from. And I kept putting together the places from where they each had come until it formed the complete island in my mind, and I felt its warmth.

The title *Golden Sheets* was meant to highlight the contradictions of the situation. Drugs like cocaine and heroin were eating the young in the forties. Somebody was making gold out of all that misery. Somebody was pouring the drugs into *Los Barrios*—we weren't growing poppy seeds. And all this-can-make-you-happy advertising for firewater of all kinds, including rum, Five-Star Pete (prune-juice wine). Pouring drugs on a population is nothing new. It's a means of keeping a people subjugated. Japan kept China conquered with opium. Native Americans met the same fate. Not only were alcoholics made out of many, but they were also given blankets supposedly for warmth, but which were contaminated with the deadly small pox virus.

It is a horror that there are humans who believe so ice cold like this. They believe that there are only two kinds of people in this world: those who rule and those who are ruled. And that's really ice cold! My being a writer gave me access to individuals and lifestyles representing different classes. Some people invited me so they could study me, not realizing that I also was studying them. In some of those instances, I saw ice cold that surpassed in evil whatever I had seen in prison. It was more like the mentality that produced fascism, capable of the evils committed in places like Dachau and Auschwitz, where I saw victims of the aftermath of World War II as a sixteen year old in the Greek Merchant Marine on the SS *Doris* sailing under a Panamanian flag.

In tense situations I was always able to send out energies that I wanted others to feel. I learned to do that very well in prison. 'Cause in prison if the guards had ever read the rage in me, they would have killed me dead. Because I hated racism. The only thing that kept me from hating all those that were White was that once as a young boy I said to my mother, "I hate all Whites!" "How dare you?" Mami scolded me, "Why do you want to make the innocent ones pay for those who are racist? You must learn to smell the look."

CINTRÓN: Most writers, when they make public presentations, read their own literature. Tell me, Piri, how come you often recite other people's stuff?

THOMAS: Because this is the way I can help pass on the truth of others, their beauty, their wisdom, the sum of our experiences. I have a gift of being able to read the poetry of others. I love to read their work back to them and mirror to them their own feelings. I tune into their feelings and their beacon of soul-flows. I enjoy it because I learn from other sisters and brothers of all the colors. When I was younger I wanted to be original, but one can only add to the original of what was there in the first place. Poems are made by children like me, but only nature can sprout a tree. We all just add a little more flow of extra beauty.

CINTRÓN: You use the word "flow" in many different ways. What are some of the meanings?

THOMAS: To me "the flow" is that which creates without one having to "consciolize" and "thinkalize" and "workalize" and "what am I gonna doalize." When you get beyond what I'm going to write about, then you're in the flow. "The streets got kicks man, like as a bargain shelf." The flow. You're dealing with flow. The feelings must come first; the intellectualizing follows. But the feelings should always be sincere without the weight of justification for whatever wrongs have been committed. Most children are born with the power of the flow meant to be utilized for good; but others, like Hitler, put it to use on a negative course. He could mesmerize people into rages as well as being silent party to the horrors committed in the name of a super race. Like most things on earth, power can be used for good or evil. That's what I mean when I speak about "flows." There are good flows and demon flows. Take your pick.

CINTRÓN: You were raised with a multicultural background. Tell me more about it.

THOMAS: *Sí,* I sure was. My parents were squeezed in between the Irish, the Italians, the Jews, the Blacks, and the Chinese—everybody was represented. We didn't have Puerto Rican movies in those days, only Hollywood and Mexican movies, with a Black film here and there. In those days, movies were our day-care centers. The Spanish-language movies were from South America. Mexico had lots of revolution movies and lots of romantic ones, too. Since I could understand them I could move through the different colors of the barrio through movies.

I consider myself *Un Negrito,* and I also have blood of the Taino as well as the blood of the conquerors, the Spanish, and other Europeans along the way.

Let me tell you a story. One time I had to take a bus ride to go ship out of Norfolk, Virginia. I was about seventeen years old. When we got to the Mason-Dixon line our bus driver got out, and another bus driver got on, and the son of a gun was a deputy sheriff bus driver with all the rights to carry a gun. And the first thing he said was, "Okay, all colored in the back. All the coloreds in the back." And people got up, and I had to decide what to do, and I said, "Hey man, I ain't colored, you know, I'm Puerto Rican." He said, "I don't care what kinda nigger you are, boy. Get your ass in the back or get off this damned bus *now*." That day I learned that as far as racist Whites were concerned, I was more brother with Blacks than I was with that driver. I sure hoped not all Whites were like him. I looked at his gun and remembered that discretion is the better part of valor. So I got up, and I said to myself, "I'll file this one in the front of my mind."

CINTRÓN: When did you really begin to be aware of racism in its broader sense?

THOMAS: Let me start at the age when Papi hit the numbers, and Mami saved some money, and we moved to a foreign country called, Babylon, Long Island. I couldn't stand Babylon. That was the home of the KKK. I was the only little *grano de cafe* [coffee bean] in a sea of white milk. My brothers could "pass," my sister could "pass." "*Nosotros los puertorriqueños somos así, podemos ser desde negro hasta amarillo*" ["We Puerto Ricans are like that, we can be anywhere from black to yellow"]. I got tired of being asked if my sister was really my sister. So I went back to my barrio at the age of fourteen and was sleeping on rooftops and street steps and in backyards. I knew better than to wear out my welcome in the different homes that let me in so I rotated them. They knew that I was practically an orphan. Sometimes, even with your parents still alive you could be an orphan in that sense. I loved my family, but I could not bear the horror of my daily experience. My dignity didn't allow somebody to look at me and call me a nigger. Actually, the first time somebody called me a nigger I ran to the library on 110th street right off Third Avenue and looked it up in the dictionary. "Niggardly" it said, and it turned out to be an Australian word, and it meant to be stingy. And I went looking for the guy to punch him in the mouth because I wasn't niggardly; Mami had taught us all how to share.

Ah, the mothers. We all had block mothers man; every other mother could be our mother because the mothers gave permission, and every father could be our father because the fathers gave permission. We were taught respect; we bowed our heads to authority. But when we bowed our heads to the school-system teachers, they thought it was a sign of servility. They didn't realize it was a sign of respect. You bowed your head. Japanese do it; Chinese did it; all the humans that have respect and beauty in their hearts do it as a sign of respect and humility. But the system persisted to create the generation gap between the parents and the children, and the gender gap between the fathers and the daughters and mothers by other means.

So it was in prison when I began to look at all the injustices objectively, saving my emotions for the creativity. I learned that all of us, although we are similar; we are like fingerprints and cultures, not quite the same, so we should get to know each other, born of respect, speaking tongues of honor instead of with forked tongues. People can justify anything, including dropping the bomb on children and giving themselves medals for it. The children of Earth, from all the Sowetos of the world, have never been given a straight chance. Only a few have ever been allowed in the running. The majority of children of color have been left out of a system whose top priorities are building weapons of war that will be obsolete in a few years and spending billions on other things besides the welfare and quality education of all children. But on goes the spending of billions and billions on everything except the children—cutbacks on the poor being the order of the day. It's outrageous, the hypocrisy, while black children, brown children, red children, yellow children, white children, multicolored children are dying because of the undisguised hypocrisy.

CINTRÓN: You obviously have beliefs in higher powers and life after death. Please tell me more about your thoughts on religion.

THOMAS: And as far as religion is concerned, my beautiful mother, Dolores, was a Seventh Day Adventist. After she passed on there was my second mother, Momma Bishop, who was an *espiritista*. My father was a deathbed Catholic who would only see the priest when he was ready to kick the bucket. In prison I studied different religions and asked myself, "Why can't we just put all the religions together and take the very best out of each and blend them with each other instead of constantly being at odds with each other?" Why can't we spell God, "Good"? G-O-O-D? Why can't we recognize God as a smile on the face of a child that is not being wasted. Children's minds wasted by all the violent crap shown on TV. There could be the good side of people portrayed in the movies and on TV instead of the constant showing of negative sides so people can say, "See, look what kind of fucked-up minds ghetto people got. Look, they want to kill cops." That's part of the propaganda they're feeding the neo-Nazi skinheads, KKK, and all the rest of the haters who are looking forward to a race war in this country. Check out history. It's happened before; it's happening now in former Yugoslavia. It's not called "genocide" anymore; it's now called "ethnic cleansing." What a horror! I say we all should be prepared to ward it off by building networks, finding common ground for a struggle among all colors; also there must be those who are for peace and justice, freedom and equality. White people who believe that dignity belongs to everyone. We have to learn how to communicate with each other, not as colors, sexes, preferences, or geographic locations, but as earthlings, born of earth and universe—*vaya*, how dare anyone call a child a "minority"?

CINTRÓN: What helped you cross over from prison life to a literary career?

THOMAS: There were many things and many people who helped me along the way. But I give most of the credit to my darling beautiful wife who passed away, Betty Elder. That was her professional name. Betty Gross Thomas, a fine attorney. She rose to specialize in international law for human rights, peace, and justice. I had the honor of traveling all over with her—to Geneva, Switzerland, for United Nations meetings. I learned so much. She opened up a whole new world for me of Bach and Beethoven, sounds of classical music and multiethnic music. This *Negrito* from 108th, 110th, 104th Street. My own brothers, sometimes they say to me, "Hey, what are you doing with a White woman?" And I say, "*Negrito*, I didn't fall in love with her color. I fell in love with her soul. She's the finest." I've been very blessed because when she was ready to make transition (way before her time), she said, "I know you will need a woman, and I want you to know it's all right with me." And so when her spirit flowed, I said, "Darling Betty, remember what you said about my needing another woman. Well, you do the choosing. For if I go out cruising I'm gonna come out losing because I'm sure to make a mistake. *Vaya*, sweetie, you choose the one that is to be for me."

Betty and I had met Suzie Dod in Cuba in 1985. She arranged trips to Cuba and Nicaragua in the early 1980s—very efficient, a real lover of peace and justice and the whole flow. This young woman had been born in the United States of Anglo-Saxon parents and since the age of five months was raised in Puerto Rico where her parents were missionaries. They worked in the mountains with the people in a project of social and economic as well as spiritual development, preaching the word while bringing scientific knowledge, modern conveniences, and health care to areas not yet reached. From the age of five months until she was seventeen years old she lived in Puerto Rico. Spanish was her first language all those years although she spoke English at home. Suzie Dod—Jennifer Suzanne Dod, Suzie we call her—came to study at Lewis and Clark College in Oregon searching for her other identity. But she basically was an immigrant returning to her own land, and she never felt right in the United States. She still feels very Puerto Rican in many ways. When she opens her mouth in Spanish she is Rican. She was raised where I was supposed to be raised. It's wonderful because her *alma* is Puerto Rican, just like my soul.

CINTRÓN: How is your Spanish now?

THOMAS: I almost lost my sense of Spanish because the assimilation had been so strong. When I was growing up at first I was thinking Spanish to speak English, and it got to the point that I was thinking in English to speak in Spanish. And it wasn't until I went to Puerto Rico at the age of thirty-two that I decided, "Hey, I'm going to get it all back. Every bit of it back." But while I was in Puerto Rico as long as I didn't open my mouth I was Puerto Rican, but as soon as I opened my mouth everybody said, "*¿Aja, tú eres del norte, verdad?*" ["Aha, you're from up North, right?"]. But, I've earned my way back, and I can think in Spanish and English all at the same time.

CINTRÓN: What do you think is the biggest obstacle to unity among the various Latino writers and artists?

THOMAS: We have been brainwashed by materialism and the obsession of being "*el quítate tú pa' ponerme yo*" ["get out of the way so I can take your place"]. We don't kill each other with hate as much as we do with envy. What we need is a unity of "we," and then we can present a united front against injustice.

Who said the barrios can't have their wise humans? Who said the barrios can't have their philosophers? Who said the barrios can't have their art, their painters, their writing, their poets? Who says that we cannot be all that? Does it only count on a level that because you have money then you're respected? Because you have pieces of paper, degrees, and so forth? When creativity and wisdom is such a natural freedom? Horse Shit! They had me into all that bag, and as a street kid I learned, "Fuck you all." I said, "I'm gonna take it from you just like they do in the gangster pictures and them robber barons and all those people who stole their way and made it big and later became humanitarians, philanthropists who seek to buy their consciences with blood money." I live with principles. I'm a man who came out of the streets, of drugs and eye droppers and all the rest of the shit. I went to prison, and I paid my dues. And I got a right to rise above all that. I am not going to live in the errors. And what people don't forgive me for the past, I forgive myself. I paid the dues and damned if I'm going to live my life with guilt.

CINTRÓN: How do you see the future?

THOMAS: I see the future—two sides of the coin. We either live in a truly democratic society or suffer the hell of a world order ruled by a cruel fascist system. In short, we will inherit the final solution. Those who are not considered members of a so-called superior race will vanish up in smoke from the face of the earth. We of all colors must unite—it's as simple as that. We must learn to respect each other. The power of the earth is in the hands of six hundred or seven hundred families. All the minerals of the earth, all the wealth of the earth, everything of the earth. They are the self-appointed gods. They have the power of life and death over us economically as well as in might. I heard of Nazi Hitler when I was a kid, of a new world order, and recently I heard Bush with his mouth opening up and talking about "a new world order." I said, "Whooah, hey an order for whom?" I can't stress enough the importance of unity among all the colors. The handwriting is not on the wall, its on our *culítos,* on our behinds, on our "tushes."

Listen, I have been accused of many things, among them of being a communist. *Vaya,* people don't have to be communists to know they're getting screwed. I've been to the ideologies. I been to the commercialized religions. I been to the politics, and man, they seem to be in the same pew. So I have stayed with the children. They have truth. Thirty-seven years I've been with the children. And before that I was with the children because I was one of the children. Which I still am in my way. And as a poet once wrote, "One hundred years from now it will not matter what my bank account was, the sort of house I lived in, or the kind of car I drove. But the world may be different because I was important in the life of a child."

16 Puerto Ricans and the Community Control Movement

An Interview with Luis Fuentes

Introduction by James Jennings

As a student in the late sixties I participated in several struggles on behalf of Black and Puerto Rican communities in New York City, including efforts in support of the Young Lords in Harlem as well as attempts on behalf of establishing Black and Puerto Rican studies in various colleges of the City University of New York. But it was what is known as the "Community Control Movement" in New York City that was most instructive to me about the nature and relationships between social change, race, ethnicity, and power in our society. As important as were the struggles of the Young Lords, as well as those of students and faculty attempting to democratize public higher education, it was the activism of Puerto Rican parents in the Lower East Side neighborhood of New York City that represented one of the most serious and sustained challenges to the social, economic, and cultural status quo in this city.

Led by such educators as the city's first Puerto Rican school district superintendent, Luis Fuentes, this coalition struggled intensely with city government leaders, the Union of the Federation of Teachers (UFT), and the media, insisting that parents should share authority to help determine the broad policies molding public schools. Many of the candidates running for the school boards mandated by the New York decentralization law (1968) and representing the coalition known as Por Los Niños (For the Children) were defeated in the face of massive resistance and resources from politicians, public bureaucrats, and civic leaders. This coalition of parents and community activists, however, forced a debate upon New York City that ultimately resulted in greater attention to the needs and well-being of Black, Latino, and Asian children.

The expansion of bilingual education occurred in many places throughout the New York City public school system as a result of the struggles of the coalition in the Lower East Side. The idea that the linguistic and cultural backgrounds of children was an important part of effective pedagogy in the public schools became more salient as a result of the coalition's activism. Another idea that has become more accepted today, and reflected in the parents' coalition in the Lower East Side, is that parents must be treated as critical partners in the public schooling process. Thus, over a period of a few years, and despite some electoral setbacks, this coalition of Latino, Black, and Asian parents helped to change thinking about public schools and how to make those schools more effective in educating children in urban settings. Today many education reforms, such as bilingual education, parental participation, professional development for teachers, and school accountability to community interests, are generally accepted and institutionalized in urban school systems, in part, because of the demands of struggles like that of parents in the Lower East Side in the late sixties and early seventies.

The Community Control Movement unfolded in the poor and working-class neighborhoods of Harlem, Ocean Hill–Brownsville, and the Lower East Side neighborhoods of New York City. While these neighborhoods were predominantly Black, and in the case of the Lower East Side, Puerto Rican, the movement to hold accountable public schools was supported by a racial and ethnic cross section of people. Although such newspapers as the *New York Times* and the *Daily News* led the charge in describing the parents' struggle as the work of Black or Puerto Rican militants, this was actually one of the most multiracial and ethnic neighborhood struggles in the history of New York City. This episode in the struggles of Puerto Ricans in the city was also an optimistic one.

Parents were motivated by visions of effective and democratic schools that would reflect concern for all people. Based on my own conversations with, and observations of, the parents and community activists during this period, I would offer that it was this sense of humanity and optimism on the part of parents that led them to challenge those educators and administrators who reflected, or acquiesced, to racism, to cultural arrogance, and a pervasive and systemic lack of concern for the well-being of the children entering the public buildings under their control. This is a lesson that should not be overlooked by those interested in expanding and strengthening the pursuit of social justice in our society.

Some characteristics of social movements generally include the involvement of masses of people, challenges to the institutional arrangements supporting the wealth and power status quo, and the introduction of new values, ideologies, or worldviews. These components were all present in these neighborhoods during the struggle for community control and parental participation. Yet few have examined this struggle as a form of social movement. This important episode and set of events in the history of Blacks and Puerto Ricans in this city has generally been overlooked in terms of its ideas, leaders, the parents, the community, and certainly the significant accomplishments of this struggle for access and excellence in urban education today. Actually, many of the seeds of Puerto Rican activism in other places were laid with the struggle for community control of schools as well as by the leadership of such educators as Rhody McCoy in Ocean Hill–Brownsville and Luis Fuentes in the Lower East Side.

During this period, I continually sought to link my academic work to Black and Puerto Rican community-based struggles. Thus in order to complete a paper for one of my courses I decided to interview Luis Fuentes, the district superintendent for the Lower East Side and one of the recognized leaders and supporter of this movement. He also happened to be the first Puerto Rican district superintendent in New York City. This particular interview actually represents a follow-up to a meeting I had with him in 1971.

In our meeting (which took place in 1995), I found Luis Fuentes to be accessible and one of the most perceptive and committed educators that I have ever met. After serving as district superintendent in New York City, Luis Fuentes joined the faculty at the School of Education at the University of Massachusetts at Amherst in 1977. Here he has mentored and worked with many students who are now serving in leadership positions across the United States. He retired from the faculty in 1992 and is currently a faculty associate at the William Monroe Trotter Institute at the University of Massachusetts Boston. He is also teaching elementary-school children in Hartford, Connecticut. He has been an important role model for many people in all these professional capacities.

I asked Dr. Francisco Chapman, a highly respected Dominican urban educator and author, to assist me with this interview and in formulating the questions posed to Dr. Fuentes. Dr. Chapman was also an active participant of the struggles described above. He played an influential role in organizing students to support the demands of the parents in the Lower East Side neighborhood. Dr. Chapman, therefore, has a keen sense of linkages between the Community Control Movement in the Lower East Side and other Puerto Rican–based and Latino struggles occurring during this same period. Some of these linkages are discussed in this interview.

There are at least three articles that we would recommend for further reading about this episode in the history of Puerto Rican activism in New York City: Luis Fuentes, "Community Control Did *Not* Fail in New York: It Wasn't Tried," *Phi Delta Kappan* 57, no. 10 (June 1976): 692–95; James Jennings, "Community Control: A Grassroots Response," *Journal of Education* 161, no. 4 (fall 1979): 73–87; and Louis Kushnick, "Race, Class, and Power: The New York Decentralization Controversy," *Journal of American Studies* 3, no. 2 (1969): 201–19. It should be noted that Dr. Luis Fuentes is currently completing a full-length manuscript describing and analyzing the Community Control Movement in Ocean Hill–Brownsville and the Lower East Side.

AN INTERVIEW WITH LUIS FUENTES, CONDUCTED BY JAMES JENNINGS AND FRANCISCO CHAPMAN

INTERVIEWERS: How would you describe the Community Control Movement in New York City?

FUENTES: I would describe the Community Control Movement as a response to the call for school integration. The school system in New York City wanted to remove Black students and other minority students from their communities in order to achieve what they called "integrated" schools. Basically youngsters were being taken out of their community schools and placed in predominantly White schools. Parents, recognizing the source for potential problems, felt that the schools closest to their residence could be worked upon and improved instead of allowing their children to be shipped to other schools outside of their own communities. In effect, the main characteristic of this struggle had to do with a community response to forced integration.

INTERVIEWERS: What were the demands of parents and community representatives regarding the public schools?

FUENTES: Essentially, the parents wanted schools that were productive. They wanted their children's schools to be as productive as the schools that they had attended either in the South or in Puerto Rico. They wanted these schools to be responsive and to have teachers and administrators who were accountable to the community and to the public. After all, these were "public" schools and the parents and children were "the public."

INTERVIEWERS: What issues precipitated a call for the community control of schools in the Lower East Side neighborhood?

FUENTES: The population in that area was predominantly Puerto Rican, Asian, and Black. The parents wanted to bring quality education to the public schools. They weren't as concerned as the administrators with the notion that if their children sat next to a White child, they would magically learn more. The parents were convinced, however, that if their child sat next to another student, no matter who he/she is, through an effective teaching corps and a responsive learning system, their children's education would be vastly improved. They wanted to have more programs in the schools that were favored by the community, such as a greater understanding of the Black culture, a greater knowledge of the Latino and Asian cultures. They also wanted bilingualism to be instituted in the schools.

INTERVIEWERS: Who were the individuals who emerged as leaders of the struggle for community control of the schools?

FUENTES: The leaders were the parents. Most of them were poor people, a significant portion on AFDC [Assistance to Families with Dependent Children]. But it was interesting how many fathers participated in that struggle! Although the movement, and its leadership, was dominated by women, many males did emerge as leaders as well. Interestingly these were people who previously were not engaged in the schools. But based on issues of the accountability of teachers and the responsiveness of the school system, they came forward and spoke out and became leaders and dedicated activists.

INTERVIEWERS: What was your role as a school district superintendent?

FUENTES: My job was to implement the wishes of the community school board. This school board very much favored bilingual education for all students, not only bilingual education but also cultural education as well as the improvement of reading scores of all the students. It was also my responsibility to bring in educators who reflected those concerns and to hire teachers who shared the aspirations of parents to see their children succeed. Essentially, my role as a superintendent was to provide the kind of leadership that would cause these things to happen.

INTERVIEWERS: What motivated the people in the Puerto Rican community to participate in the struggle for community control?

FUENTES: That's a difficult question to answer, in a sense. Some people were motivated by ignorance while others were inspired by a number of programs that were already in place. By ignorance I mean intolerance—or a fear of other minority groups. A lot of Puerto Rican kids felt put down and oppressed by youngsters from other communities or from other cultures because of their lack of language and commonality. The other reason was a growing desire to do something about human relations, and this is where bilingual education came in. We helped youngsters to gain self respect and knowledge of the language the majority of students spoke, which in this particular instance in the Lower East Side was Spanish. Later on, after the initiation of the Spanish-English programs, we found out that there was a great need for Chinese-English programs. And so Chinese was introduced in a district plan.

There is no question that the parents who participated in the struggle were motivated by a need to see their children feel comfortable about being who they are and speaking their language. This does not mean that they did not want their children to learn English. I've never met a Puerto Rican who didn't express the need for learning English. From the beginning parents wanted to make bilingual education a part of the school systems.

I am sure that some people will be surprised that I personally was opposed to bilingual education initially; this was because in 1967, I didn't know anything about bilingual education. I don't know how many other people knew anything about bilingual education, but I hadn't been taught that way. I had been taught English when I went to school, and the whole notion of now having another language spoken in the schools did not particularly appeal to me. I came to the New York City school system after having attended the schools there throughout my entire elementary and high-school career. I became a school principal through an effort known as the "Community Control Movement." Once I got involved in the job of school principal, I realized that I was there to work with what the parents wanted, and the parents wanted to experiment with the introduction of a curriculum in Spanish in the school system. At the beginning, I lent myself to it reluctantly. But after six months I became an ardent supporter because I saw what it did for the children—it brought them out, it made them bloom. For the first time they were talking in a language they knew and were accustomed to.

This also represented an extension of the home into the school. Thus we could now use the home as a teaching resource to make our schools more effective. For the first time parents were able to communicate with teachers—about their own children! Until then there were so few Spanish-speaking teachers that parents were closed out or shied away from participating in the schools. Bilingual education opened up the system for the Puerto Rican community. Those that tasted it, liked it and wanted to see it continue.

INTERVIEWERS: How were voter registration drives of parents planned and organized?

FUENTES: We were successful in registering, for the first election, more than two thousand parent voters who had not been registered before. The turnout for voting on election day proved what parents could do. More people showed up in the Lower East Side in District 1, the smallest district in New York, to vote than all of the other districts in New York City put together. So it worked. We were successful in getting representatives from both parties—one Republican, one Democrat. Following the process of registered parents, a Republican has to be present when a new voter is registered, and a Democrat has to be present as well. We teamed people up to get them registered.

The first time out we had about two thousand people voting. I would say that was one of our greatest achievements. We were able to politically indoctrinate these people since they had never voted before. Thus we ran a very successful campaign in getting the support that we needed.

Unlike the Union of the Federation of Teachers, we didn't have big bucks. They were able to advertise their candidates more. Our candidates represented the community, and Por Los Niños was the slate. Their candidates were exclusively White, middle class, with no actual ties to the schools other than that their relatives had jobs in the schools as teachers. Our candidates were all parents of children in the schools. We felt that our slate, which represented the community, was truly representative of what we aspired to do in the schools.

INTERVIEWERS: How were registered parents mobilized to turn out on election day?

FUENTES: Well that was not an easy process. You can have a million people registered, but it all comes down to who votes on election day. If people are registered and don't come out to vote, that's not good! Many of the people who did the registering took on the responsibility of getting people that they had contacted to come out and vote. Cars were provided. Victor Gottbaum, the head of the largest union in New York City, and his members provided transportation. These were taxi drivers, hospital attendants, lunch room workers, all kinds of people provided transportation for the people they wanted to vote. These individuals were stationed throughout the district. Some people knocked on doors to remind others to vote. They even escorted the people, waited for them, and walked them home. Others worked telephones to remind people. Still others worked the streets, bodegas, bars, etc.

During that first election we were successful in registering quite a few people that had never registered to vote before. I would say that we were even more successful in getting them out to vote. We used other techniques too. A truck was loaded with a group of musicians, and the parents from the PTA marched behind the truck. The truck traveled throughout the entire school district playing music. They wound up in an open-air auditorium, and there a lot of rally speeches were given. But getting people to come out was a result of the music, traveling through the neighborhood à la the pied piper.

Incidentally while the people were marching and the music was playing, they were distributing Chinese fortune cookies with the message: Vote Por Los Niños, in English, Spanish, and Mandarin. On the side of the truck there was a huge sign that read, "The Fuentes Bank—Vote District One, Vote District One." Those were just a few of the things that were done.

A number of well-known Hispanic performers were also invited. They not only performed but spoke to the community about the importance of registering to vote and coming out and voting on election day. There were a number of things going on that we haven't had an occasion to talk about in the past. The performers who came out were all professional people— Jose Torres, Machito, and Tito Puente. Even Herman Badillo, who the night before the election said he wouldn't support any slate, came out and supported the parents' slate. This kind of unity was a model for what we were trying to achieve educationally in the Lower East Side.

INTERVIEWERS: What was the impact of the participation of parents and community activists on the students and young people?

FUENTES: The fact that parents were, for the first time, directly involved with what was going on in the schools had a tremendous impact on young people. It motivated them to want to learn, especially since many of the people that we were hiring were the kinds of people who demanded of them that they learn. Anytime you have teachers who are able to communicate with parents, and parents who are willing to communicate with teachers, you have a complete circle, which makes it a lot easier to get young people to be motivated and want to learn.

INTERVIEWERS: Did the leadership of community agencies, neighborhood organizations, or other unions support the parents during this period?

FUENTES: There were many community organizations that supported us. In terms of unions, we had the largest union in New York City supporting us—that was the union of working-class people. We also had the support of students from various universities. People of all colors shared our deep concern for what was happening in the schools and saw this as an opportunity to contribute toward changing the status quo.

One particular group that stands out in my mind was LENA—a group of little old Jewish ladies from the Lower East Side who devoted a lot of time and energy to our cause. They were phenomenal! That group stands out in my mind simply because it represented and reflected what the struggle of the parents was all about. There were other groups as well. Being put on the spot to try to name one or two is difficult. I wish I could name them all; but there were *so many* that rose to the occasion that it would be almost impossible to remember and name them all.

INTERVIEWERS: How were events, ideas, or opinions communicated among the participants and supporters?

FUENTES: Major efforts were made to review and discuss every event before it took place. We made sure that parents were very well informed and kept up to date with what was happening in the schools. We held community school board meetings that were supported by the community. Ideas were presented at these open meetings. The board was open, and votes were taken right in front of the public. Everyone's opinion was respected. Most of our meetings were conducted in three languages: Spanish, English, and one of the Chinese dialects. Yes, there was a great effort made to communicate with parents and to get everybody's input into all of the things that we did in the community.

INTERVIEWERS: What kind of tactical debates arose among the supporters of community control?

FUENTES: One of the debates that I remember is the one that has affected me the most. At one time, some people felt that I might be the person standing in the way. I wasn't an elected official; I was only appointed by a community school board. These people felt (rightfully so) that I was being used as a pawn by the opposing side—that is, the union. Other people felt I was "the debate" and that to eliminate me from the debate between parents and the left would strengthen the UFT's position for no gain. I would say of all the strategic or tactical concerns or debates that was probably one that, after my first year, seemed to draw the most attention.

Some of the things that resulted in greater administration/unification had to do with how we worked with the parent groups. Every school was represented by a parent group and met either with the superintendent or on their own at least once a month to share their ideas. We had an opportunity to take over our own kitchens, and parents supported it because for the first time we would be serving rice and beans, ham hocks, black-eyed peas, turnip greens—the full range of things represented in the community's cultures, including Chinese foods. That appealed to the parents tremendously, taking over the operation of our own food preparation.

Through the setting up of that operation, parents came closer. They had a voice in what their kids would be eating. That paid off because not only did they get the foods they wanted, it gave us a chance to plan with parents and work with them to show them how these really were *their* schools. Later when the issues changed, it was easy to have the support of parents because we had worked together on something basic, like feeding their children and gaining their trust. When the issues changed and the focus came down to concerns about hiring and firing and the appointment of principals, the parents were given the final choice. Opposition only came from the UFT, who had a different idea about who should be hired or fired.

INTERVIEWERS: Who were the major players resisting the parents, and why did they choose not to support the parents and the idea of community control?

FUENTES: The major resisting force was the Union of the Federation of Teachers, who tried to generate the perception that all the teachers were against us. The truth of the matter is that there were many teachers who supported the parents. The UFT felt threatened by the emergence of vocal and organized parents. The administrators' association, which was predominantly White, had also expressed vociferous opposition to the demands of the parents. Thus we had a situation where two supposedly antagonistic sectors, management and labor, had a common interest in stopping the parents' movement.

The UFT came into being because it claimed that the association of administrators was dominated by the management. So they broke away from it and started their own union for teachers. The CSA (Council of Superintendents and Administrators) was their formidable enemy—but then came the Black and brown people and that changed their point of view. They united to resist this system. They joined forces to stop the movement by Black and brown parents to gain control of the schools. Both of these forces resisted what the parents wanted. Both of these organizations were simply frightened by the idea of parents running the schools.

The truth is that parents really didn't want to run the schools; they knew they couldn't. They knew that they had to have professionals. However, what they wanted was to develop a system of people working together, which until then didn't exist. It was always either the teachers working alone or the administrators working by themselves, and parents not having much input with either of these groups. What the parents wanted to see was a blending of the three groups—teachers, administrators, and parents—to work toward the betterment of the kids. Instead of being welcomed as apple pie is welcomed in any American tradition, they were met with resistance by organized administrators, the UFT, and the mainstream media. There are many *New York Times* articles, for instance, where the parents are referred to as hooligans or militants or troublemakers.

Both the teachers' union and the CSA gave the impression that they were afraid of what parents might want to do with the schools. They didn't want to give them a chance to attempt to try to do anything because up until that time these two unions had opposed each other. The administrators had been at odds with the teachers. Someone even said, "Their low expectation for parent control parallels their low expectation for our children." They were frightened and threatened because the parents were beginning to talk about hiring their own superintendents and hiring their own teachers. They knew that parents were concerned about the fact that many administrators and teachers did not represent the Black community, nor the Latino community in any of these schools. Parents also felt that there was an absence of gender equity in the public school system because there were many more men as school principals than there were women.

INTERVIEWERS: What has been the impact of the struggle for community control for urban education today?

FUENTES: Choices! Parents now have a lot more options than they used to. If you want your child to attend a school district other than the one you live in, fine. If you prefer that your child goes to a neighborhood school, that's fine too. It's a matter of options and choices. If you want your child in a bilingual program, that's an option. If you want your child to learn about African American education, that's a very good option, and these kinds of options are open to all people. Essentially, I would say that this idea and its acceptance today was at least one of the results of that struggle on urban education today.

INTERVIEWERS: Were there any linkages between parents involved in the struggle for community control and student or labor groups?

FUENTES: Well, to tell you the truth, I'm not familiar with any formal linkages. There were linkages, and I think it was more from a labor group's and student group's willingness to support the effort of parents. It wasn't that parents sought them out for help; it was them who came and asked the parents to let them help out. The attitude of the parents was: "This is our struggle, if you want to join us, welcome."

Frankly I don't think they cared as to what your political position was. I do know, however, that one mistake was made by a newspaper editor from a Puerto Rican leftist newspaper who remarked that the parents were "socialists." They put him on the spot immediately. They let him know that they didn't see themselves as socialists. Rather they saw themselves as parents who were concerned about their children's education and were taking the necessary steps to rectify the problem.

INTERVIEWERS: How did Puerto Rican nationalism influence the Community Control Movement in the Lower East Side in terms of programmatic demands, styles, or slogans?

FUENTES: I wish I could say that was an underlying cause for the emergence of the Community Control Movement. But that was not so. It would be ridiculous, however, to say that it played no part at all. I think it did, but I also think it was subtle on the part of the Nationalist groups.

I have to also say that we were let down in one particular instance by an organizing Nationalist group when we attempted to participate in a Madison Square Garden meeting of all the socialist groups. They were close to what was going on in the Lower East side, just ten blocks away—we were on 14th Street, they were on 34th Street at Madison Square Garden. Many of the parents tried to influence that group to march in our neighborhood and to make an appearance or to lend a hand of support to the movement from the Lower East Side. But we were shut out. The group failed to see the importance of what was going on there.

It was short-sighted of them, frankly. But Puerto Rican Nationalist sentiment increased, and one newspaper obviously increased its circulation in the Lower East Side as a result of the parents' struggle. A lot of people were going around yelling, "*Puerto Rico Libre*," even young people who didn't know what that meant or what it implied. The Community Control Movement expanded their ideological horizons.

You can't say that we were totally aloof of the influence of that struggle—and a struggle that still continues. But putting it in the perspective of what was going on in the Lower East Side, I would say that the Madison Square Garden meeting was a flop because the participants were not connected to our struggle. Some political activists also missed out on listening to what parents had to say. Parents were looking for ways of improving not only the schools but police, sanitation concerns, and unemployment. Political groups gave lip service but did very little to turn things around.

INTERVIEWERS: Are there any contrasts or parallels between the Community Control Movement in the Lower East Side and the Young Lords?

FUENTES: I would say that there are a lot of similarities. You're talking about two groups, both representing oppressed people. The Young Lords saw themselves as young people, most of them brought up in this country, who were going nowhere—at least that's the impression they had. But after [their participation in] the Lords many became attorneys and journalists. The Lower East Side is made up of Black, Puerto Rican, and Asian youngsters who saw themselves in the same dilemma—not being able to hack it to get through high school. I think in this respect there was a distinct parallel to the Young Lords' movement.

There was an even greater parallel in some of the things that they wanted for our community. The people in the Lower East Side wanted and got free breakfasts—so did the Young Lords. In fact, it was the Young Lords who initiated the free breakfast program in the Lower East Side. So I don't want to take that away from them, but a lot of credit has to be given to the parents who also joined with the Young Lords to make it happen. These are the parallels and the linkages I see between the two movements. Both groups were looking for greater opportunities, equity, justice, a better opportunity to learn. In that respect they had a lot in common. The Young Lords were struggling for the same thing. They wanted more community involvement in what the police were doing. They wanted better sanitation services, and, in that regard, they showed the positive nature of their role as opposed to what the political system felt they stood for.

INTERVIEWERS: Where are there linkages between the struggle for community control in the Lower East Side and political issues in Puerto Rico?

FUENTES: I don't think there were, except that being the politically wise people that politicians are—and I'm not excluding Puerto Rican politicians—it became a good place to provide themselves with a platform. And a lot of Puerto Rican aspirants to political positions did use many of the opportunities that the community opened up to plug themselves to win the esteem of the Puerto Rican community. I don't think that there were any close ties. I think in both groups it could be said that just like in other parts of New York City and outside of New York City, the Young Lords, Black Panthers, and all of these movements were part of the general mood of the country at that time—to move away from poverty. But the linkages were not fully developed. I think credit has to be given to the Black movement for social justice and civil rights. The rest of us simply followed. All of the other struggles were just a part of the fundamental Black movement for social change, and one struggle inspired others.

In terms of direct contact between the politics in Puerto Rico and the politics of the Lower East Side, those were not pushed by the community. They were pushed by those people who represented the political groups in Puerto Rico to gain favor for themselves. But the parents were not fooled by any of this; they were pretty sophisticated to what was going on. Basically the consistent position of parents was, "If you want to join us and join our struggle, fine. But you're going to have to do as we tell you to do. If you're going to carry your own agenda, forget it, we don't need you." So the parents were pretty well aware of the fine line, and they didn't want to deny anyone the opportunity to participate. On the other hand, they were not going to be controlled either.

INTERVIEWERS: How did your participation in the Community Control Movement change you?

FUENTES: Change me? I think it liberated me (laughter). I was always a team player for the years that I taught previously in Long Island, in Florida, in Georgia. But I always noticed that parents were very much involved in those school systems. I didn't see that same kind of opportunity for parents to participate in the New York City schools. So the movement to me took on the shape of opening the doors for parents. I felt from the beginning that there wasn't any job that parents couldn't be involved with and that they couldn't tackle.

For me there was a fundamental change that took place. When I saw those parents beginning to get the opportunity to be involved in what their kids were doing, they changed me too—I like to think that the movement liberated me in a sense. I became a team player again, but for a different effort, for a different audience, for a different group. I was no longer working for the system; I was working for the parents and for the children.

INTERVIEWERS: What is Luis Fuentes doing a quarter of a century after his participation, sacrifices, and leadership in one of the most important chapters in Puerto Rican history in the United States?

FUENTES: What am I doing? I'm doing what I've always done, I'm teaching. Except that after sixteen years of teaching at the University [of Massachusetts, Amherst] and sixteen years after serving as superintendent in the Lower East Side, I've gone back to teaching in the front lines. I'm involved with the public school system of Hartford, Connecticut, where I teach kindergarten, first grade, second grade, third grade—grades that I had never taught before. I've taught all of the other grades from the fourth grade up. So for me this is coming full circle. And it's amazing how much I am learning from these kindergarten kids. They're teaching me things I never dreamt about. I'm impressed by the effects of bilingualism as it's being conducted in that school system and the effect it's having on our young people and our community.

I see a lot of superstars coming along, something that I didn't see a quarter of a century ago because the movement had just started. But through bilingualism, I see young people who are outstanding in English and outstanding in Spanish. I'm convinced that people who are bilingual are far more intelligent than people who are monolingual, or at least they put those skills to work. Through these skills, they are able to interpret language better, and that pleases me very much to have been a part of what it took to make those changes in this country.

Someone from the School of Education at the University of Puerto Rico once told me, "I think you have turned out more Puerto Rican doctorates and masters than any other professor we know." I don't know if that's true or not, but just the thought of it makes me feel good.

Let me add to that while we're talking about Puerto Ricans. I have never restricted my efforts to working only with Puerto Ricans as a graduate professor—I'm happy and have received recognition for this recently, and it made me very proud. The Vietnamese community bestowed an honor upon me that I was very proud of. As a matter of fact, I've received numerous awards from Black groups, Black professional groups, ever since I got involved in the movement for quality education for all. Those kinds of awards make me feel happy because they're a testimony of what the public schools ought to do—that is, to serve all of the children not just one particular group of students.

I also have had numerous White students who have graduated with doctorates under my supervision and guidance—I'm proud of all of them too. I feel that in some ways I have contributed significantly to the movement that started in the Lower East Side, where people demanded and exercised choices. I hope that kind of demand and struggle never stops in this country. I think the minute we get away from choice, we're running back into the kind of anarchy that exists in every public school system where the employees are in control.

We now have parents involved, and we have kids involved in what's going on in the schools. That's probably the best thing that has ever happened to public education. People are finally working together, or at least are trying to work together, and it's something we can all be proud of. The real heroes of the movement are people like Georgina Hoggard, Henry Ramos, Father Powis, Reverend Oliver, Carmen Torres, Carmen Rodriguez, just to mention a few, and, of course, the parents who stood up and fought for what they believed in—and won!

LUIS APONTE-PARÉS AND JORGE B. MERCED

17 *Páginas Omitídas*
The Gay and Lesbian Presence

En español o en inglés es el rotundo maricón o el eufemístico gay, el pseudo-cientificista homosexual o el burlón loca, el metafórico pájaro, o la diminutiva mariquita, el májico fairy o el promiscuo puto, el pantomímico pato o el cromá-tico lilo, el nombre otorgado y recibido, el bautismo callejero y libresco, el mote, apodo, gentilicio, injuria, epíteto, santo y seña del deseo, pasaporte de la identidad sexual, nombre de pila del otro ha sido otorgado sin consulta y con escarnio, letra marcada en la memoria, afrenta sonora, cuando no escrita, que persigue a la criatura denominada como un apellido que no es ni materno ni paterno, un apellido propio impuesto por el otro, sin otro vínculo de sangre no sea el de la herida abierta por el nombre y que no logra cicatrizar ninguna explicación.[1]

In Spanish or in English it is the manifest faggot, or the euphemistic gay, the pseudoscientific homosexual, or the disdainful queer, or the metaphorical bird, or the diminutive *mariquita,* or the magic fairy, or the promiscuous *puto,* the pantomimic *pato,* or the chromatic *lilo,* the name granted and received, the streetwise and free baptism, the call name, nickname, name of origin, injurious slander, noun, saint and sign of desire, passport for sexual identity, first name of the other that has been granted without consultation and with abhorrence, marked letter in the memory, resonant insult, when not written, that persecutes the denominated creature like a last name that is neither maternal or paternal, a proper last name imposed by the other, without any blood ties except for the open wound that the name engenders and that no explanation could ever heal.

INTRODUCTION: Out There

FOR YEARS there has been a steadfast presence of Puerto Rican and Latino lesbians and gay men in the Puerto Rican Day Parade.[2] Casual observers of New York City's Gay Pride March would notice the seemingly large number of Latinos marching each June. A visit to the Lesbian and Gay Center would confirm the large number of Latino faces visiting there everyday. New York City's changing demographics suggest that by the 1980s and increasingly so by the 1990s, Latinos should comprise a large proportion of New York City queers. If the number of Latino queers were to correspond to the number of Latinos in the general New York City population, one out of every four queers would be Latino. With such a potentially large membership pool, why in 1995 are there so few Latino-centered gay (men) organizations? Why are there so few Latino faces in the "mainstream" gay movement? Why has a Latino gay movement been so difficult to build?

Although a full examination of the issues raised by these questions lies beyond the scope of this article, we argue that their answers can be uncovered in the intersection of historical trends with important events occurring in both the Puerto Rican and Gay communities. First, during the fifties and early sixties, homophile organizations, as they were known then, were made up of conservative middle-class White men, that is "people of age, profession, and means."[3] Their worlds were distant from those of Puerto Rican gays. While Mattachine Society homosexuals debated whether homosexuals were a "minority" in the *Mattachine Review,* young Latino homosexuals were arriving in New York, learning the language, and beginning to deal with their sexuality within the context of the Puerto Rican family in the barrio. Life was so asphyxiating and economic options so limited, that as soon as they could, many left their ethnic enclave.[4] Others, like Ray (Sylvia) Rivera, went straight to 42nd Street to hustle, "determined this time to move out of Viejita's apartment for good."[5]

Second, at the birth of the "modern" gay movement, the Puerto Rican community in New York was undergoing traumatic transformations. In retrospect it is now understood that the Puerto Rican community rapidly lost economic ground during the seventies as the city's economy was restructured away from manufacturing into the new service economy. The losses threatened the very existence of a young community with few resources and a weak social and institutional infrastructure. In the ascending gay community, on the other hand, middle-class White men were developing the skills and adapting to the new demands of the emerging postindustrial city; although by no means universal, same-sex, White men couples generated large disposable incomes.

Third, the birth of the gay movement coincided with a *resurgimiento* (reappearance) of Puerto Rican, Chicano, and other Latino consciousness aimed at dismantling cultural stereotypes by deconstructing and reassembling new identities: from Hispanic Americans to Chicanos to Nuyoricans, for example. Latino gayness was not central to the formation of this identity, an identity still in construction today. The center of gravity of the "consciousness" in New York City was located in the cultural and community-development arenas. The cultural arena emerges when a new generation of New York–based artists claim an independent space in the geographies of Puerto Rican culture by, among other things, placing New York City barrio-living at the center of their experience and asserting the use of English, Spanish, and "Spanglish" as part of their artistic discourse. This period of cultural renaissance and affirmation was the birthplace of such institutions as Museo del Barrio, Taller Boricua, Nuyoricans' Poets Cafe, the Puerto Rican Traveling Theater, and many other similar institutions throughout the city. The community-development arena gathered a new intelligentsia—the activists of the period, many of them professional lesbians and gay men, who chose to prioritize struggles between their personal liberation and the search for justice for their communities, and who developed educational, social, and human-services instruments of community development too numerous to list here.

Fourth, while the gay community was challenging the political establishment and organizing itself as an ethnic minority with accompanying political agendas, the Puerto Rican and Latino communities were being excluded from the Liberal and Democratic Parties. The political tradition of the Puerto Rican community in New York City, furthermore, had been for many years linked to the island's political arenas and historically immersed with the radical politics particularly surrounding the issues of colonial status, nationalism, and socialism.[6] During this period a new breed of politicos emerged, and Puerto Ricans became more active in electoral politics. These politicos were less progressive, and differing little from radicals, they would not include lesbian and gay issues in their agenda because their hands were full trying to regain lost ground while pandering to their national origin. Fifth, in the sixties and seventies the Puerto Rican community was being displaced wholesale from neighborhoods in New York—particularly in Manhattan, the epicenter of the gay movement—producing a deterritorialization of a people and their culture, a process whose impact has yet to be fully understood. At the same time the gay community was appropriating urban territory by building strong enclaves in lower Manhattan, what Castells has called an "alternative city" of sorts, that would provide them a stable space, a *place* in which to develop their own institutions.[7] After all, as one key leader of the movement once stated, "We have the built-in advantage of automatic integration: homosexuals can be born into any family, work at any job, and have any background whatsoever, and *succeed in any field*," a pronouncement most Puerto Rican gays could not make.[8] And last, the complexities that arise between Latino immigrant communities and the construction of a Latino gay identity have not been researched. The Puerto Rican diaspora—which emerged within a colonial context, across different geographies, and through circular migratory patterns—needs to be examined also in order to understand this construction. Thus connections between queer movements on the island or elsewhere in Latin America and New York activists remain obscure.

As a result of these transformations, the seventies and eighties were a period when the Puerto Rican community's will to survive was tested to the limits. This was also a key period in the development of the modern lesbian and gay movement's institutional infrastructure. Some in the White radical gay movement were asserting their muscle by seeking to "transform American society, not gain admittance to it."[9] Others, who were more conservative, were demanding a "place at the table," a space in the cultural discourse of the nation—a demand that empowered White males have always been able to make in U.S. history.[10] Early organizational meetings, furthermore, excluded the likes of Ray (Sylvia) Rivera, a Stonewall witness. As one of the founders of the Gay Activist Alliance said, "the general membership is frightened of Sylvia and thinks she's a troublemaker. They're frightened by street people."[11] Thus even those "street people" (which usually meant people of color like Puerto Ricans) who wanted to participate were excluded from the early leadership positions. Puerto Ricans remained outsiders, observers, and denied a *place at the gay table,* and thus they were excluded from full partnership in the institutional development of the lesbian and gay movement.

During this same period Puerto Ricans, other people of color, and women were struggling for their right to an education and a decent home, something most White men took for granted in U.S. society. In 1969, the year of Stonewall and Woodstock, the Young Lords Party—articulating a revolutionary rhetoric and demanding basic human rights, including the right to work and a decent home—was founded in East Harlem. The contrasts between the Puerto Rican and White gay communities could not have been greater. The distance between their separate needs and aspirations were seemingly continents apart.

To these factors have to be added the persistent racism and sexism within the gay community, paralleling the racism and sexism of general society. Being gay to most meant "white, middle class, youthful, nautilized, and probably butch," with no room for Black or Latino gay men within the "confines of this gay pentagon."[12] Dominated by White men, the gay movement was and has been unable to shed its race-specificity, gender, and class biases. Institution-building has been "market-mediated: bars, discos, special services, newspapers, magazines, phone lines, resorts, urban commercial districts."[13] Thus "the institutions of queer culture have been dominated by those with capital: typically, middle-class white men."[14] Indeed much of gay activism was predicated on that privileged status as she or he sought "not to transform an oppressive society but to tinker with it in order to reclaim—as an out, proud gay man or lesbian—his or her rightful position of privilege."[15] Early attempts at a radical movement through the establishment of the Gay Liberation Front, modeled after Third World struggles, calling for the "overthrow of patriarchy, white supremacy, capitalism, or all three as the means to end oppression of homosexuals," failed.[16] Thus the gay movement did not establish the necessary linkages to the struggles of women and people of color in U.S. society, in fact making the "other" all but invisible. By building an identity exclusively around sexuality and developing a political agenda that either excluded or subordinated other types of oppressions, lesbians and gays built a movement narrowly constructed around its primary subject.[17] "In disregarding the concerns of people of color and our agendas," it effectively dismissed Puerto Ricans and other Latinos as subjects of this movement.[18] Although generally an "invisible queer," the construction of "the Latino" among some White gay men was and remains one of "otherness" and the objectification of the *lumpen macho*.[19]

This chapter focuses on the development and accomplishments of the first Puerto Rican queer organization founded in 1987 in New York City, Boricua Gay and Lesbian Forum (Boricua). The history of *Boricua* allows us to examine the difficulties and barriers encountered by Puerto Ricans and other Latinos in building the institutional forums to speak to both the Latino and gay communities, past and present.[20]

LATINOS AND GAYNESS

"One of the students said, 'I thought homophobia meant fear of going home after a residency.' And I thought, how apt. Fear of going home. And of not being taken in. We're afraid of being abandoned by the mother, the culture, la Raza, for being unacceptable, faulty, damaged. Most of us unconsciously believe that if we reveal this unacceptable aspect of the self our mother/culture/race will totally reject us."[21]

In *Latino Voices,* a national Latino survey of the perspectives held by Puerto Ricans, Mexicans, and Cubans in a number of important political areas, respondents were asked to rank who they disliked the most among the following groups: the Communist Party, the Nazi Party, the Ku Klux Klan, gay and lesbian groups, Black Muslims, English-only, Atheist organizations, or other group. Mexicans and Cubans ranked gays and lesbians fourth most disliked (after Communists, Nazis, and Ku Klux Klan). Puerto Ricans ranked gay and lesbian groups third most disliked, in a close heat with Communists (21.5 to 22.7 percent), while only 10 percent disliked Nazis.[22] "Respondents expressed little tolerance for members of the disliked group holding office, public office, teaching in schools, or holding rallies."[23] These responses should not surprise anyone, particularly because self-professed ideology of respondents was moderate to conservative. In fact, just 29 percent of Cubans rated themselves as slightly

liberal, liberal, or very liberal, to 28.5 percent of Puerto Ricans respondents and 28.7 percent of Mexicans.[24]

There is a very limited body of systematic or scientific studies on
attitudes of Latinos toward gays and lesbians.[25] Conversely there is an
emerging literature examining sexual behavior of Latinos, particularly in
connection to the AIDS epidemic.[26] There is, furthermore, a growing literature on homosexual consciousness and behavior and the construction
of gay identity among Latinos.[27] In "Echoing Stonewall and other Dilemmas," Frances Negrón-Muntaner, for example, has presented the most
complete account of the development of an organized lesbian and gay
movement in Puerto Rico with the intent to "provoke a discussion regarding the past and future practice of Puerto Rican gay and lesbian
struggles."[28] Her effort is an attempt to analyze the "central issues that
shaped the public and private agendas of many groups."[29] She concen-
trates in telling the story and struggle to build two major organizations:
the Comunidad de Orgullo Gay (COG; Gay Pride Community), and
Mujer Intégrate Ahora (MIA; Woman, Integrate Now). Negrón argues
that the development of the gay movement in Puerto Rico in many ways
took as its model the organized U.S. gay movement. Thus "it is necessary
to recognize the COG not only as a local response to the oppression of
Puerto Rican gays and lesbians but as an articulated one in relationship
to the gay and lesbian movement which was already constituted in the
United States."[30] This differed a great deal from other accounts of the
development of organized liberation groups in Spain, Mexico, and Latin
America.[31] The way gays organized in the United States could not be repeated in Latin American societies. "Dictatorial military states characterized by violence, repression, torture, and institutionalized acts of dis-
appearance were the sociopolitical reality in most of Latin America in the
1970s."[32] Thus political organizing in Latin America took place around
human rights instead. However the word "gay" in Latin America, the Caribbean, and Spain—although still considered "foreign"—gained com-
monplace status in most countries.[33]

The linkages between gays in Puerto Rico and the United States are
in many ways part and parcel of the "circular migration" pattern of the
Puerto Rican diaspora. One area that remains unclear is the role, if any,
the gay bar and discotheque had in the construction of a gay culture in
Puerto Rico. The spaces and places created by Abbey, Bachelors, or Boc-
caccio, three bars that played dominant roles in shaping this bar-specific
gay culture in the seventies and eighties, for example, needs careful examination. This bar/discotheque culture emerges in part to supply "enter-
tainment" to local queers as well as to the increasingly important tourist
trade, which included North American gays in search of the "exotic" and

resulting in the "commodification of sexual desires."[34] It is arguable that with the "closing" of the Cuban tourist industry to U.S. gays, Puerto Rico became a choice port-of-call for gays in their quest for fun and excitement. It is ironic that while many of these bars were "Americanizing" Puerto Rican gay culture in Puerto Rico, in New York City the *BonSoir,* a gay bar in the Village, was "Puertoricanizing" New York gay culture in the 1970s.

Another contribution to the construction of gay identity in Puerto Rico is the recent book *Dime Capitán: Reflecciones sobre la masculinidad* by Rafael L Ramírez. In *Dime Capitán* the author examines the construction of masculinity in Puerto Rico and explores homosexuality in that context. Homosexuality in Puerto Rico is a crime, and depending on one's ideology, social class, and personal views, it is considered a sin, a sickness, or a sexual orientation. Its existence, according to Ramírez, is usually manifested in the binary opposition of the categories *hombres y no-hombres* (men and nonmen). Thus it is intrinsically linked to the construction of masculinity. The *maricón* is the total denial of masculinity, thus *maricones* are scorned and devalued; being called one is perhaps the worst insult for a Puerto Rican male.[35]

In Puerto Rico the homosexual world is centered around *el ambiente.* *El ambiente* is the place for an "imagined community" where both gay and straight spaces cross—since in Puerto Rico, very few homosexuals have the luxury of living in homosexual-centered communities. *El ambiente* is heterogenous. In it all mentalities crisscross, reproducing the class and cultural system of the society and its corresponding ideologies. There are bars, clubs, beaches, and other places exclusively homosexual. There are also "mixed" spaces, *interstitial spaces,* such as gyms, billiard halls, and even bars, where everyone keeps their masks on. Some of these places serve as pick-up centers for homosexuals and men who do not consider themselves homosexual but engage in sexual acts with other men.[36]

However these spaces, both inside/outside the *ambiente* have not been analyzed in a historical context. Beginning in the forties, for example, as Puerto Rican society changed from a preindustrial to an industrial society, rural-urban migration and rapid urbanization summoned new ways of socializing. These new urban or *pueblo* populations increasingly turned the town plaza into a major socializing space, for example, the talk after mass, the cultural events during the *fiestas patronales,* etc. It was also customary for young middle-class women to go to the plaza with friends and *chaperonas* to cruise and see who was in town. Being openly homosexual was not an option, particularly in the small towns where men's and women's behavior was subject to scrutiny. In many of these towns, the few openly gay figures, were cast, like in Cuba, in the "role of village queer."[37] Thus in small towns and even in cities like Ponce, Mayagüez, and Rio

Piedras, the town plaza turned "outlaw" after hours. Sometime in the late evening hours, when all "respectable citizens" had gone home, these plazas became liberated and local *patos* and *bugarrones* would meet and make contacts for their relationships. As the urban transformation continued with further suburbanization and concomitant loss of town life, however, many of these town plazas lost their lure, and new sexual geographies were created, including movie theaters, beaches, and cruising such places as Plaza de las Americas, the premiere shopping mall in Puerto Rico. Perhaps also, during this period homosexuality is transformed, and a multiple of spaces and places are generated specific to class, race, and other cultural factors that intersect the development of a homosexual identity.

Ramírez, furthermore, also identifies several categories in relationship to homosexual life in Puerto Rico. "Straight," he argues are those who have no relationship to the *ambiente*. *Entendido* includes heterosexual men who know *el ambiente,* share socially with gays, and are not homophobic. *Poncas* are those homosexuals who pretend to be heterosexual but those in the *ambiente* recognize their homosexuality. *Loca* is usually reserved by those in the *ambiente* to *pasivos,* or men that are penetrated either anally or orally, or who go both ways, although it may also include *activos,* or those who penetrate.[38]

CONTEXT: "We have been everywhere"

Todos los recien llegados estábamos muy bien vestidos . . . llevábamos nuestro ajuar dominguero. Debí haber llegado con un flamante reloj pulsera, pero un *compañero de viaje me aseguró que esta prenda la usaban sólo los afeminados en Nueva York.* Ya a la vista de la ciudad, cuando el barco penetraba en la bahía, *arrojé el reloj al mar* . . . ¡Y pensar que poco más tarde estos relojes-pulsera se hicieron moda y acabaron por imponerse! Llegué, pues, a Nueva York sin reloj (italics added).[39]

All of us new arrivals were well dressed . . . I mean, we had on our Sunday's best. I would have been sporting a shinny wristwatch too, if *a traveling companion hadn't warned me that in New York it was considered effeminate to wear things like that.* So, as soon as the city was in sight, and the boat was entering the harbor, *I tossed my watch into the sea.* . . . And to think that it wasn't long before those wristwatches came into fashion and ended up being the rage! And so, I arrived in New York, without a watch.

New York City has been home to Puerto Rican gay men (*afeminados* in Bernardo Vega's world) and lesbians ever since Puerto Ricans began living in the Big Apple. Most of the time living in the closet meant isolation from other queers in the community. The bars and clubs, and perhaps hustling strips like 42nd Street and elsewhere, were the only places many gays and lesbians could go to interact and share histories of survival. These bars and streets became interstitial spaces placed between the Puerto Rican barrio and the White gay community. Humor and oral tradition provided a major means of documenting queer journeys as oppressed people within an oppressed community.

The 1969 Stonewall rebellion in New York marked the beginning of the modern lesbian and gay rights movement. Puerto Rican gay men, lesbians, and transvestites (considered by some in the movement as "street people") were at the center of this rebellion. Initially the goal was to hold the police department and city hall accountable for the continuous harassment from the police department on gay and lesbian bars and for the increase of gay bashing. Puerto Rican activist Daisy de Jesus remembers: " . . . the cops would come in three times every night, pick up their money, circulate around, poke us with their night sticks and then leave, only to come back later." The year following Stonewall new voices began to be heard, such as that of Dr. Hilda Hidalgo, who came out as lesbian and began to provide a safe space for Latino and Latina gays and lesbians at Rutgers. In the spring of 1972 a group of gay men from Argentina, Cuba, and Puerto Rico published a literary magazine called *Afuera*. They hoped to raise the political consciousness of other Latino gay men in New York. The *Revista* was published entirely in Spanish. It contained poetry, original artwork, transcripts of oral histories, news and letters from Latin America and the Caribbean, and a political analysis of sexism, homophobia, and gay liberation. Around that same time a working-class, Vietnam veteran, Puerto Rican gay, and Stonewall witness, Danny Beauchamp, formed a group called Hispanos Unidos Gays Liberados (United Liberated Hispanic Gays). *Revista* and Hispanos Unidos Gays Liberados never crossed paths. The fact that the cultural workers did not connect or link to the working-class and poor Latinos of the barrios initiated a schism in organizing strategies that has continued to preoccupy the development of gay Latino institutions in New York. The question of building identity and forging a *movimiento* (movement), thus became entangled with class specificity. By the sixties and seventies the sons and daughters of the wave of immigrants from Puerto Rico began to search for their identities—an identity produced on the streets of New York and not in the parlors of Old San Juan or the boulevards of Buenos Aires.

During the early seventies in Boston, for example, and similarly to New York City, a good number of the core of the Puerto Rican agency leadership was queer. Key agencies were headed by Puerto Rican queers, most of whom had been born on the island and had arrived in Boston for their educations. They never "came out" and chose to "prioritize their struggle" by keeping their sexuality known only to a close group of intimates. However by 1977 other Puerto Ricans and Latinos began organizing a queer organization to "combat" the homophobia in radical parties, such as the Puerto Rican Socialist Party (PSP). In 1977 for example, under the leadership of Efraín Barradas, the Acción Socialista Pro Educación Gay (ASPEG; Socialist Action for Gay Education) was formed with the primary goal of developing a "gay platform" that would be accepted by the PSP. In a key passage of a resolution that was ultimately presented in New York City and adopted in 1978 in New York City, ASPEG called for the Congress to "strenuously condemn all acts of persecution and discrimination based on sexual preference of individuals."[40] In June 1979 the first meeting was called in Harriet Tubman House by the Comité Latino de Lesbianas y Homosexuales de Boston (CLLHB; Latino Lesbian and Homosexual Committee of Boston), the first Latino-centered general membership organization in Boston. There are no works relating the story of either group; presently the authors and others, including Barradas, are exploring ways of recovering this history.

The Comité Homosexual Latino Americano (COHLA; Homosexual Latin American Committee) was formed in New York City toward the end of 1977. As the first queer organization that in 1978 marched in the Puerto Rican Day Parade, they joined the People's Contingent in the parade and for two years attempted to march. Unfortunately the members of COHLA met with a lot of resistance (and high-flying bottles) from the people viewing the parade. They had to drop out before completing the entire route. As in the case of ASPEG and CLLHB, there are no works relating the story of COHLA. Francisco Domínguez, one of the founders of the organization, has complete records and is contemplating writing the story of the organization. In 1978 COHLA member Juanita Ramos (a Black, Puerto Rican, lesbian, feminist, and socialist) became an active member of the Coalition for Lesbian and Gay Rights. She was also one of the national organizers for the National March on Washington for Lesbian and Gay Rights that took place on October 14, 1979.

After the 1979 march on Washington, most of the Latino queer momentum in New York City changed direction. Domínguez argues that as a result of the march COHLA entered a very intense period of debate along several ideological issues that ultimately divided the group between the men and women in the organization, leading to the final demise of the group. Most of the efforts at building a collective movement for the affirmation of Latino gay and lesbian identity were diverted to the support of the struggle in the larger queer community. However as members joined other "mainstream" organizations they found that these groups were not interested in the issues raised by Latinos and were at best paternalistic toward them. The reality of being the oppressed within the oppressed became more evident with each attempt at collaborating with the queer "mainstream." In the mid-eighties a number of gay men found a space to explore their identities as Latinos in the Hispanic outreach committee of the Metropolitan Community Church (MCC) and in the catholic organization Dignity New York, the two leading gay and lesbian religious organizations at the time. Even such churches as MCC, which provided the only safe space in which Latinos had been able to openly explore their sexual identity, were "outside" the mainstream Puerto Rican churches. Some Puerto Rican lesbians continued their journey for empowerment by joining such organizations as Salsa Soul Sisters. Others (men and women) decided to continue the political work defined by the needs of the larger Puerto Rican community. Some joined the National Congress for Puerto Rican Rights, others worked in support of Puerto Rican Political Prisoners or joined the Puerto Rican Socialist or Independence Parties, and some just went back to the bars and the night scene.

By the early 1980s AIDS began to take its toll in the gay and lesbian community. Although slow in responding, by 1985 the Puerto Rican and Latino communities in New York engaged in full to fight what has become a monumental health problem. Because of the historical association of AIDS with gay men, Latino politicians rejected any dealings with the disease as part and parcel of their homophobic view of society. In 1985 the Hispanic AIDS Forum (HAF) was founded by a group of human-services and health professionals concerned over the inaction of Puerto Rican political leaders and the ominous impact the disease was having in the community. Unfortunately neither HAF nor any of the Latino AIDS organizations founded since then have been able to reach the funding streams necessary to deal with the epidemic effectively. Furthermore in many instances mainstream queer institutions ended up competing for and receiving funds to address the Latino community.

In 1986–87 three very different Latino lesbian and gay organizations were founded: Las Buenas Amigas toward the end of 1986, and in 1987 Boricua Gay and Lesbian Forum (Boricua) and Hispanics United Gays and Lesbians (HUGL). The birth of these three groups marked the beginning of a new era of activism for Latino gays and lesbians, opening the doors for a new generation of activists struggling to create a safe space both within the gay and lesbian community as well as in the Latino community in general. Based in New York and mostly led by Puerto Ricans, each of the organizations chose a different path in defining and carrying out its activism. Las Buenas Amigas was founded as an organization by

and for Latina women exclusively. The other two were cogender organizations; although the groups' constituencies consisted of Latino men
and women, their approach, politics, and style of work were completely
different. In 1991 another organization, Latino Gay Men of New York
(LGMNY) was founded by former Boricua and HUGL members as well
as a new breed of activists that emerged in the 1990s. LGMNY however
was organized by Latino men who believed that cogender Latino queer
organizations could not be sustained because of the differences between
queer men and women. As of this writing LGMNY remains the only Latino queer organization that caters to Latino queers of all nationalities as
well as New York Latinos.

THE GROUPS: "We Are Here"

Being outsiders to both the gay and Puerto Rican communities, institution-
building for Puerto Rican queers has been very difficult. First there have
been institutional barriers. Puerto Ricans and other Latinos have no historical connection with other homophile societies, which served as a base
for the modern lesbian and gay movement's institutional development, or
to those that developed after the sixties. There is also discontinuity between the development of Puerto Rican institutions and organizations that
had provided a home for the communities' general development and identity formation. Thus Puerto Ricans have had to start from scratch, with
the only models to emulate found in the human-services community organizations that developed in the sixties and seventies. Also there has been
a total absence of Puerto Rican lesbians and gay men heading major mainstream lesbian and/or gay organizations. Similarly there were very few
"role models" in the Latino community to emulate because those leaders
who headed the major Puerto Rican organizations and who were Lesbian
or gay elected to stay in the closet. Most individuals involved in inventing
the new gay organizations had limited experience organizing and struc-
turing organizations. Thus the new groups suffered from this experiential
deficit. Since there had been a tendency for Puerto Rican queers to move
out of their ethnic enclaves as part of their "liberation," organization
founders, many of whom had broken their ties to their ethnic community,
were severely limited in understanding the needs of those left behind and
who were either too poor to leave or chose other ways of dealing with
their sexualities utilizing alternate routes or support systems. There were
many, furthermore, who had spent long periods of their lives in a dual
Latino/gay self-hatred and had grown up rejecting their Latino heritage as
well as their gayness. Thus emerging organizations were asked to do emer-

gency repair work, something not one of them was capable of doing at the time. Building gay institutions in the age of AIDS has added to the difficulties.

Organizing dual-identity organizations posed complex organizational strategies. What is tackled first? Homophobia in the Latino community? Racism in the White gay community? Invisibility in the Latino and gay communities? The new organizations had difficulty prioritizing their struggle, thus conflicting agendas have troubled their history and added to their fragility. Finally these organizations suffered from the impact of the need to "supply" Latinos to fill the gaps generated by previous racism and neglect by major gay organizations. This led to the emerging leaders in Latino gay organizations being called to "represent" the interests of Latinos in these mainstream organizations, adding to the already stressful role of providing leadership to a young community. Unfortunately it also encouraged the emergence of a cadre of "leaders" analogous to Latino mainstream political leaders. In all, with a sense of mission during the last decade a group of dedicated men and women chose to "break the silence" and take on the responsibility of inventing organizations for themselves and those who would follow.

Boricua Gay and Lesbian Forum

"We have history, therefore we are. *Somos, pues tenemos historia.*"[41] Boricua Gay and Lesbian Forum (Boricua) was founded in 1987 after the historic Lesbian and Gay March on Washington that same year. Of the two cogender organizations founded in 1987, Boricua had the most clear and specific political agenda. The general aim of the organization was to educate the Latino community on issues concerning lesbian and gay people. Some of the issues Boricua concentrated on were the New York State gay rights bill, the antibias law, child custody issues, recognition of domestic partnerships, and funding advocacy for AIDS prevention and treatment in the Latino community.

The objectives drawn by Boricua were achieved in many different forms. The organization participated in two Latino legislative conferences (the *Somos Uno* Conference in 1989 and 1990) with a proposed agenda and letters of support on lesbian and gay issues. Boricua also organized and participated in many community workshops, panels, and advisory committees. Constant public testimony for Spanish-language radio and television was another of the forms in which the members of Boricua challenged homophobia in the Latino community. The thrust of Boricua's work was guided by a genuine hope for the Puerto Rican/Latino community to become more tolerant to the idea of accepting lesbian and gay issues as an intrinsic part of the community at large.

Civil rights activist Brunilda Vega, a founder of Boricua, had joined the National Congress for Puerto Rican Rights (El Congreso) earlier where she met Pedro Pérez, another of the founders of Boricua. There they worked together and would always argue about how far they should push the gay agenda in El Congreso. In retrospect, Brunilda says: "He felt introducing gay and lesbian issues was not going to work with El Congreso. He was right. He always suggested that we should do our own thing instead." [42] On October of 1987 Vega and Pérez officially requested that El Congreso support the Lesbian and Gay March in Washington by providing the organization's banner. They were not able to succeed. Fed up with their collaborators at El Congreso Pedro Pérez and Vega proceeded to "do our own thing." The main reason behind calling the new organization Boricua, as opposed to Latino, was a strategic one. At the time, the political structure in New York, as for Latino elected officials, was mostly Puerto Rican. Vega and Pérez felt that to organize people to put pressure on the establishment, the name Boricua would attract more attention. They thought the Puerto Rican political leaders would have to respond to a coalition of Boricuas.

At first Boricua support came from personal finances. Later they were able to get technical assistance from the Association of Puerto Rican Executive Directors (APRED), where flyers and mailings were done. Vega and Pérez made a list of all their friends and sent them a flyer with Boricua's logo and information on the organization. The logo consisted of a slightly altered Puerto Rican flag; the flag's star was replaced by a pink triangle. Boricua's logo provoked the first disapproving reaction from the general Puerto Rican community. Some felt Boricua was defaming the flag by substituting the star for a symbol of gay and lesbian liberation.

That same year New York governor Mario Cuomo declared November as Puerto Rican History Month and Comité Noviembre was established to coordinate all the events. Boricua took advantage of the celebratory atmosphere. In less than two weeks after the march on Washington, Boricua was officially recognized by the Comité Noviembre as a Puerto Rican organization, and its first general meeting was advertised in the APRED calendar as one of the events celebrating Puerto Rican Heritage. This was the first and only lesbian and gay event to be recognized by the Latino community for the November celebrations.

The first meeting of Boricua took place Tuesday, November 17, 1987, at the Lesbian and Gay Community Center. The evening began with a slide presentation by Vega entitled "In Search of Puerto Rican Gays and

Lesbians at the March on Washington." The slide presentation was followed by three speakers and artistic presentations. The speakers were Hector Muñoz, Dr. Hilda Hidalgo, and Pedro Pérez. Muñoz is an Argentinean gay man and the first Latino to organize a Spanish-speaking group for men with AIDS at the People With Aids Coalition (PWAC). Dr. Hilda Hidalgo paid tribute to three generations of Puerto Rican gays and lesbians who paved the way for the new voices. Pedro Pérez made a presentation on organizing within the Puerto Rican gay and lesbian community. The evening's presentations were rounded off with singer Sandra Roldán's "Commemoration of Puerto Rican History through Song."

Boricua's Leadership

The first to join Vega and Pérez were Beatrice Gutierrez, Pedro Velázquez, and Luis Nieves-Rosa. Gutierrez was a Puerto Rican lesbian mother from Brooklyn; Velázquez worked as a police officer for the New York City Transit Police Department; Nieves-Rosa was the first HIV-positive gay man to join the core group. Back in Puerto Rico, Nieves-Rosa had been a founding member of the Colectivo de Concientización Gay de Puerto Rico (Puerto Rico's Gay Consciousness Raising Collective). Other early members were Ramonita García and Jimmy López, both with lengthy backgrounds in activism. As the work and visibility grew (and some of the original members began to burn out), a new group of young activists shared the coordinating responsibilities. Some of them were Rafaella Billini (Ronnie), Manolo Guzmán, Marcos Rodríguez, Julio Discent, and Jorge Merced.

Boricua's Accomplishments

The bulk of the work during the first two years of Boricua's existence was in developing leadership within the organization. At first Boricua avoided establishing any type of structure for its operation. There were no membership requirements and no bylaws. Whoever wanted to do the work was welcomed to join the organization. The coordinating core group was slowly expanded and a few unsuccessful fund-raising events were organized. Time was spent in processing a plan of action regarding how to best carry out the goals of the organization. Out of a desire to take its gayness to *El Barrio,* the Bronx, and wherever Latinos moved, Boricua avoided conducting activities at the Gay and Lesbian Center. Most of the organization's meetings took place at the Centro de Estudios Puertorriqueños, in members' homes, and at centers in the Latino community.

In April of 1989 the *Somos Uno* Conference took place in Albany. Organized by Hector Díaz, Somos Uno was the Puerto Rican and Latino lobbying task-force event in Albany, New York. Boricua applied as an organization to host a workshop during the conference but was denied participation. Immediately they wrote a letter to Virginia Puzzo, the governor's liaison to the lesbian and gay community. After Ms. Puzzo put pressure on Hector Díaz, Boricua was included as one of the lobbying organizations on the task force. Ironically they had to go through a White woman to put pressure on a Puerto Rican via the governor. Using APRED's political agenda for the conference as a model, Boricua organized its own agenda. They drafted a petition, collected close to one hundred signatures, and published a booklet on lesbian and gay issues. Nevertheless, instead of calling it "*Somos Uno,*" Boricua called its agenda "*¡SOMOS OTROS!*" ("WE ARE OTHERS!") in response to the treatment they received from the event organizers.

The "*¡SOMOS OTROS!*" agenda took many people by surprise. The document presented to the New York State Assembly Puerto Rican/Hispanic Task Force was a very eloquent and well-researched agenda with very specific proposals on such issues as AIDS in the Latino community, gay and lesbian rights, bias-related violence, child custody and adoption, and domestic partnership. "*¡SOMOS OTROS!*" broke the silence that historically forced queer issues "to be taboo among family, friends and co-workers in the Puerto Rican/Latino community," as stated in the document's introduction. With a call for tolerance and acceptance, the agenda asked people to stop themselves from perpetrating against Latino gays and lesbians the same injustices that were committed against the larger Latino community because of the color of their skin, their accent, or their national origin. Further "*¡SOMOS OTROS!*" demanded a more responsible position from the Latino leaders.

Still many feared Boricua was an army of gang busters coming to destroy the work of the task force and "out" all the closeted Latino leaders. Threatened by Boricua's presence at *Somos Uno,* the worst reaction received by the organization came from closeted gay men, some of whom had a lot of political power and status up in Albany. Not rejecting Boricua's presence at the conference meant *leerse,* which was something they were not ready to do.[43]

The AIDS workshop where Boricua was *allowed* to participate consisted of a panel of elected officials. Boricua was represented by Luis Nieves-Rosa, the only person on the panel who was living with and struggling with the AIDS virus. In what became one of Boricua's most memorable and emotional moments, Nieves-Rosa's presentation became a celebration of his life as an HIV-positive, gay Puerto Rican man, and he challenged the victimization of people living with the AIDS virus. Boricua's call for action came from the heart and could not be challenged by any skepticism. The following year, Boricua was invited to participate in

Somos Uno and this time the organization was able to give a special work-shop on gay and lesbian issues. Boricua's agenda for the 1990 conference was titled *"Somos Uno Otravez"* ("We Are One Again").

After the events at the first *Somos Uno* Conference, Cable News Network and Telemundo approached the organization about participating in special programs dealing with gay and lesbian issues in the Latino community. For Telemundo the special featuring Boricua members was the station's first gay and lesbian exposé. Manuel Unánue, the former editor of *El Diario,* invited Boricua to do a show on Radio Hit, a popular Spanish-speaking radio station. The show was called *"Lo que los otros callan"* ("What the Others Conceal"). Luis Nieves-Rosa and Brunilda Vega were on the air for three hours. Although the topic of the show was domestic partnership, the evening turned into a circus. Calls flooded the radio station for three hours of what was mostly hate radio. Officials from the station's executive offices came down to the studio (calls were being made to the radio station's president). According to the producers, never in the history of Radio Hit had the station received so many calls. Nieves-Rosa and Vega tried to keep their calm, especially when Pentecostals called to say that all gays and lesbians were going to burn in hell.

After the show Boricua planned its next step: the Puerto Rican Day Parade. The organization formed the Latinos and Friends Coalition, inviting anyone in the larger gay and lesbian community to come celebrate the twentieth anniversary of Stonewall by marching with Boricua at the Puerto Rican Day Parade. Until 1989 no gay and lesbian organization had officially applied to march as a separate contingent. As was the case with the *Somos Uno* Conference, the parade organizers denied Boricua's initial application. Boricua proceeded to contact the lesbian and gay liaison for the New York City government to put pressure on Luis Miranda and the parade committee. After some struggle, permission was granted. Boricua's contingent grew to seventy-five people from such organizations as PFLAG (Parents and Friends of Lesbians and Gays), Hispanic United Gays and Lesbians, Las Buenas Amigas, several drag queens from the bar La Escue-lita, and a few dozen brave individuals who endured the entire march. Thanks to Boricua there has ever since been a queer contingent in the Puerto Rican Day Parade.[44]

One of the last major activities organized by Boricua was an event cele-brating the participation of the Latino queer community in the Puerto Rican Day Parade. The event took place Friday, June 22, 1990, at the Office of Puerto Rican Affairs on Park Avenue. Nydia Velázquez, the for-mer director, never agreed to meet with representatives from Boricua, passing on the request for the meeting from department to department. Phone calls were transferred to her subordinates who had no power in granting permission. Several faxes and letters were intercepted, altered, copied, and sent to staff with anonymous notes reading "Beware! Look who wants to come to the office!" Despite the obstacles the meeting took place and was well attended. An unedited version of a video taken that year at the parade was shown. The video was witness to both the rejection and acceptance of queers by the Puerto Rican community. Some of the interviewed parade observers provided evidence of their uneasiness of discussing queer issues openly.

During its last few months of activism, Boricua attempted to build a complex organizational structure aimed at formalizing leadership and accountability within the group as well as establishing Boricua as a non-profit organization. This process diverted the energy of the organization away from political activism and dismantled the "guerrilla" nature of Boricua's work. Members divided into several work committees including finance and fund raising, community action, publications, correspondence, political, cultural, and executive committees. As the overview process extended, membership began to decrease until each committee was headed by the same two or three people. The time that up until then had been dedicated to organizing and carrying out events was now devoted to endless meetings analyzing bylaws, mission statements, and marketing strategies. Boricua's last meeting of the executive committee took place Friday, October 19, 1990, at the Lesbian and Gay Center.

Boricua's Shortcomings

Boricua lacked the active and consistent participation of women. Although cofounded by a lesbian and although many Puerto Rican lesbians supported the work of Boricua and attended most of its major events, only one or two women would participate in the organization's general meetings. For some the reasons why were very clear: unless work centered around a very specific political issue, collaborations between men and women within the organization always ended up being monopolized by men. Boricua did not provide the separate spaces needed to deal with the internalized homophobia and sexism of its members. In many instances women grew tired of dealing with men's attitudes toward women and vice versa. Whenever the issue of misogyny was brought up, most men discarded it as a fantasy or insecurity on the part of lesbians. Another problem was the fact that the assumption that everyone was ready and willing to do only political work failed to address the needs of those new to political activism. The challenges of analyzing and redefining a Puerto Rican gay and lesbian identity were rarely addressed within the organization. Instead the energy was aggressively devoted to planning activities with great speed and urgency. Very often new members were not adequately informed or given sufficient background and time to process information already internalized by the core members. Because Boricua had neither the room nor time for consciousness-raising and bonding, many members new to activism felt left behind and without the emotional support needed to work within the Latino community. Educating both the Latino community and the larger gay and lesbian community took precedence over debating and sharing knowledge with new members within Boricua. As time went on Boricua's dances and social events were great successes while participation in the core of its political activism decreased dramatically. A third complication was simply leadership burnout. The organization's core leaders did not find a consistent enough membership to promote new leadership and delegate responsibilities. Additionally Boricua was not able to address the needs of all the different nationalities that found refuge in the organization. Once most of the founding members had left, the new membership became more Latino than Puerto Rican. Supporting events aimed mainly at the Puerto Rican community was not something that appealed to everyone. During the "restructuring process" several of these new members became very vocal about changing Boricua's name to Latino Gay and Lesbian Forum. At this point it was obvious that a new organization needed to be created. It could be argued also that the organization did not have the skills or energy to go through the incorporation process—a process that proved to be Boricua's doom. Many became frustrated with the formality of establishing a corporation without the necessary volume of people to support the work generated by the organization. Finally many saw Boricua as an issue-oriented effort where support was provided sporadically depending on the event. There was no prolonged commitment by a great number of supporters, most of whom divided their activism between Boricua and the work they had already been developing in the larger Puerto Rican community—work that did not necessarily center around a gay and lesbian agenda.

THE PRESENT: Challenges and Opportunities

The challenges and opportunities facing Puerto Rican and other Latino queers during the 1990s and beyond are immense. As the city becomes "colorized" fears among some city residents will increase. Many in the new generation of gays and lesbians will be left out and be pushed out of the communities they feel they must migrate to, such as Chelsea or the Village. Violence against lesbians and gays has increased significantly. The increased violence will deter many from coming out because the risks of violence may outweigh the "benefits" (i.e., living one's life openly and with pride). The impact of AIDS in the Latino gay community has been immense, and it appears that it will remain a major health problem in the future. As part of the backlash against gays and lesbians, the rejection of the Rainbow Curriculum and assorted multicultural agendas seem also to be tied to the fear of "aliens."[45] Finally, although there are some signs of progress being made in the political arena, it is still very easy for a Puerto Rican elected official, such as Israel Ruiz, to call former Human Rights Commissioner Dennis de León *pato* in a pejorative manner during a public forum and get away with it.

At last count there were at least eight different Latino gay organizations meeting regularly at the Lesbian and Gay Community Center and elsewhere. It also happens that some of these groups are no longer pan-Latino organizations. Some have a specific national orientation: Venezuelan, Dominican, Cuban, etc. Different nationalities are claiming their own identity and are willing to reinvent themselves in the New York lesbian and gay landscapes. A new organization, Puerto Rican Initiative to Develop Empowerment (PRIDE), has been formed. The good news also includes the organization of the Coalition of Latinas, Latinos, and Friends Against Homophobia, a united front of several lesbian and gay organizations that have come together to fight the homophobe Rubén Díaz. Rev. Luis Barrios has supported this coalition and continues to use his religious beliefs to support the liberation of all individuals. The good news also includes the emergence of such new organizations as Latinos Latinas de Ambiente Nueva York (LLANY; Latinos and Latinas of the New York Environment) and *"Homovisiones."* LLANY is another attempt at a cogender organization. *"Homovisiones"* is a weekly cable program providing air time for Latino gay voices. The moves made by the Puerto Rican Association of Community Agencies (PRACA) at *Muévte,* their youth conference in 1994 are a sign of hope. During *Muévte,* lesbian and gay Puerto Rican youth were provided a space and a place of dignity. For the first time, a Puerto Rican organization supported gay and lesbian issues with a major activity. The Puerto Rican Traveling Theater broke new ground by producing as part of their 1996 season "Bomber Jackets," a scathing analysis of homophobia in a New York City Latino barrio. Finally the emergence of Latina/o Lesbian and Gay Organization (LLEGO), a national Latino lesbian and gay organization based in Washington, D.C., is ready to speak for Latinos from all over, and its attempt to organize at a national level points toward a brighter future.

James Early

18   An African American–Puerto Rican Connection

An Auto-Bio-Memory Sketch
of Political Development and Activism

The Beginning: Melding Academic Aspirations and Social Activism

I am an African American whose ideological and political radicalization found organizational expression in the movement for Puerto Rican independence. Recently I was prompted to reflect in writing on my personal political history and by inference on some aspects of the Black–Puerto Rican social and political experience—a reflection prompted by a pointed and emotionally ladened plea made by a woman at the 1995 Puerto Rican Studies Association that Puerto Ricans emulate the development of African American activist leadership. Since my political development was influenced by the Puerto Rican independence movement, I thought it might be useful to recall what in the personal life of one African American led to participation in another ethnic group's struggle.

At this stage of my life (fifty-one), I think that all responsible activists should face the challenge of periodically summarizing their experiences in order to assess what to maintain and what to discard; such a process would no doubt assist their individual development. This process may also provide guidance and lessons for younger activists, which would assist them in making contributions to the achievement of the age-old goals of self-determination, democracy, social and economic justice, and human dignity. Despite many diversions into individualism, personality cults, ultraleftism, undemocratic centralism, and unpardonable support for transgressions on personal liberties and mass atrocities committed in the name of social progress, the great majority of Left social-change activists I have encountered began their active commitments as young people intensely earnest about making a contribution to progressive social change. And to some extent many did make and continue to make contributions. We are no longer recognizable by our youthful passions or bold actions, which once gave organization and visibility to our strivings to help construct a new society. Nor are we generally recognized as valuable resources or points of reference by today's younger activists.

This "auto-bio-memory sketch" of my experiences in the Puerto Rican movement—mostly with the Puerto Rico Solidarity Committee (PRSC)—is written in part for my own reflection and self-indulgence. And in part it is written as a belated sharing with my young-adult children and other young people who are trying to figure out how, or whether, to integrate personal goals with social agendas that require radical stands. The actual experiences herein described are probably less instructive and historically significant than the underlying ideological developments that led to those experiences.

I crossed the threshold from passion to theory to practice as a young adult struggling with the challenges and the dilemmas that arose as I was actively searching to meld academic training and interests with social and political activism. Much contemporary political activism by young people lacks systemic focus notwithstanding similar experiences of economic and social discrimination, alienation, and colonialism that motivated the political activism of their parent's generation. Through participation in the historical struggles of their own and other national and international communities, some older activists—frequently the parents of today's younger generation—can and should share experiences of how they wrestled with and resolved tensions between personal achievement promoted by family and societal values and the demands for social justice so evident in the world. The status of Puerto Rico as a U.S. colony became the first bridge where I tested myself to fully enjoin the two goals.

Puerto Rican Colonialism: From Racial Nationalism to Political Internationalism

Why I became organizationally involved with the Puerto Rican movement and not, for example, in one of the revolutionary Black Nationalist trends (an ideological perspective with which I identified myself), is, I think, ironically tied up with the Civil Rights–era slogan "Black and White Together." That slogan opened for me a sense of humanity bigger than Black or White without my having to abandon my primary Black identity. That "opening" to a broader identification with people in struggle allowed me to rather easily imagine linking academic and professional interests and facility in the Spanish language (the subject of my undergraduate degree at Morehouse College) and Latin American and Caribbean history to the social, cultural, and political realities of Blacks in Latin America and the Caribbean. The U.S.-based component of the Puerto Rican movement for independence centered principally around the Puerto Rican Socialist Party (PSP), and PRSC provided the platform. In later years I would identify work around Puerto Rico as the foundation upon which I later became active in progressive multiculturalism.

Prior to joining PRSC, my rather pristine moral sensibilities about right and wrong, just and unjust, had been up to that time shaped mostly by the clear-cut social morality I knew either indirectly or from experience of White racism against Black people in the United States and the world. The basic moral and material realities underlying the sharp dichotomies of U.S. White/Black race relations became for me the basic measurement for evaluating struggles and offering support to other oppressed and exploited peoples around the globe—particularly if they were non-White.

My entrance into the Puerto Rican movement through PRSC placed me for the first time in my life as an activist in a nationally and internationally organized political environment that included few Black activists—African American or Puerto Rican. My undergraduate student activism, which exclusively involved Black people, was intense but short-lived as I completed my degree shortly after I entered organized student political activity.

My two years of experience around activist scholars—such as Vincent Harding, Joyce Ladner, and William Strickland while I was working at the Martin Luther King Jr. Documentation Center and the Institute of the Black World (IBW)—spurred development of my political consciousness and in part influenced my political and cultural interests in international affairs. While at the IBW I began to seek a more encompassing explanation for the ills of U.S. society, the U.S. role in world affairs, and what I wanted the country to be and how to help get it there. Exposure to the thoughts and activities of people of the likes of C. L. R. James, Harry Hayward, Amiri Baraka, and numerous others who passed through the Institute of the Black World helped to consolidate my interests and activities toward applied academic pursuits and social activism.

But those years were short on direct-organizing experience.

GRADUATE SCHOOL: "*Las Dos Alas*" (The Two Wings)— *Puerto Rico y Cuba*

As a twenty-five-year-old African American graduate student at Howard University in Washington, D.C., in 1972, I had been radicalized in the ferment of the Black student/intellectual and Black Power movements of the 1960s, and I was hungry for an environment where I could apply my

feelings about social justice and the revolutionary theory that I was reading and discussing with professors and fellow students. I had not been
active in the Civil Rights movement, but I was deeply moved by the courage and actions of people of my generation who were active—such as
Bernice Johnson Reagon, with whom I attended college at the Atlanta
University Center and worked with at the Martin Luther King Jr. documentation project, and Phil Hutchins, former chair of the Student Non-
Violent Coordinating Committee (SNCC), who I met later on his return
to complete his undergraduate studies at Howard University. Phil was active in the Washington, D.C., PRSC chapter (he would later recommend
that I, rather than he, be the D.C. PRSC chapter representative to the First
International Conference in Solidarity with Puerto Rico held in Havana,
Cuba, in 1975).

My graduate studies inadvertently contributed to my interests in and
subsequent affiliation with the Puerto Rican independence movement. Dr.
Maria Brau, the granddaughter of Salvador Brau, known as the "father
of Puerto Rican history," was one of my professors. Dr. Brau was the
one who led me to discover and to research and write about Pedro Albizu Campos. With disapproving acknowledgment of activist and social-
change perspectives I expressed in response to her academic, but conservative, ideological approach to Puerto Rican history, she said to me in
front of other class members, "You should do your class paper on Pedro
Albizu Campos . . . he and his cohorts wore black shirts." I was confused
by her comment, wondering in my ignorance what significance the reference to black shirts may have had to issues of racial identity. At the time
I was not at all familiar with the negative inference to Mussolini's black-
shirted Fascists.

All that I encountered in and around the movement to free Puerto Rico
from colonial status was new and exciting. In many respects my affiliation
with the Puerto Rican movement literally altered the course of my personal and political life. I was attracted to the revolutionary romance and
intrigue surrounding the movement. Soon I was making ideological and
political decisions the consequences of which are still unfolding today.
I recall being impressed by the fiery, articulate, confident oratory of PSP
leader and spokesperson Alfredo López, who for a while traveled around
the country speaking. I probably saw in Alfredo some of my personal passion and aspirations for leadership and service to a just cause. Rev. Philip
Wheaton, a key member in the D.C. PRSC chapter and a major U.S.
contributor to overturning U.S. occupation of the island of Culebra,
was a model of moral dedication and active commitment to the cause. I
would eventually become more conscious of the significance of moral

perspectives in struggling with anger and the all-too-frequent self-righteousness among comrades in struggle against imperialism.

Participation in the PRSC had unexpectedly provided me an opportunity to pursue interests in Cuba. I was not yet familiar with the expression *"Puerto Rico y Cuba dos alas del mismo pajaro"* ("Puerto Rico and Cuba, two wings of the same bird.") The Cuban Revolution was a major feature of the excitement-packed 1960s, which were largely dominated in the United States by the Civil Rights movement, the Black Power movement, the antiwar movement, and student activism among other political activities. While in college I occasionally hung out with a few older activists in the Student Non-Violent Coordinating Committee. Some evenings several student buddies from Morehouse College (among them the acclaimed actor Samuel L. Jackson) and I would go with these activists and ramble around the then-closed SNCC office located in a warehouse on Nelson Street in Atlanta, Georgia. There I came across the first issue of *Pensamiento Crítico* (*Critical Thought*), a Cuban publication I found among the various books and foreign publications (one of which was on Ben Barka and the revolution in Algerian) scattered about the cavernous warehouse space. One article in *Pensamiento Crítico* was about confronting internal and external enemies of the Cuban Revolution—a framework I would later recall in discussions and debates about U.S. imperialism and Puerto Rican bourgeois forces on the island. Years later I would subscribe to another publication called *Pensamiento Crítico*. But this one was published in Puerto Rico, and I spent some time with editors and various activist-writers working with this publication.

Within a short span of less than a year after joining the Washington, D.C., chapter of the Puerto Rican Solidarity Committee, I was in transition, being propelled along an ideological course that would intersect with what became, or was at that time called, the New Communist Movement. Within a few months or so after joining PRSC, and a month or so before the birth of my and my wife, Miriam's, first child, there I was in Havana, Cuba, talking with Julián Rizo, a Cuban government official formerly stationed in New York. Rizo was the first person to ask me, "Are you a part of the New Communist Movement?" And thus he set an ideological reference, which I would reflect on a short time later.

I stood talking seriously with Rizo but frequently succumbing to my curiosity over porcelainlike pig figures mounted on corner tables in the reception room. The room slowly filled with conference delegates from around the world. I began to think about the broader and deeper dimensions to this solidarity movement that I had somewhat naively joined to give meaningful outlet to my fervor for social justice while I pursued academic and professional goals in the study of Latin American and Caribbean history at Howard University.

Rizo's question about the New Communist Movement did call to mind my experience of a few days before when I arrived as part of a U.S. delegation in New York City at a union hall (where we were greeted by PRSC board member Jim Haughton, a Black labor organizer) to prepare for our departure to Havana the following day. There was clear tension among the delegates, who I quickly discovered represented different and warring ideological perspectives and political lines. Some of them, such as Irwin Silber, were former members of the Communist Party and had different ideological and political views and positions than the component of "our" delegation, which was headed by Helen Winters, secretary of the Communist Party, and Grace Mora, head of the Puerto Rican Commission of the Communist Party. Dorian Weinberg (who at that time, I believe, was head of the National Lawyers Guild) became the uniting force that kept the U.S. delegation relatively intact.

Fidel Castro was to arrive soon. I was already stunned to meet Blas Roca (member of the old Cuban Communist Party) at the head of the receiving line as I entered the reception. I had written about Roca in a paper on Blacks in Cuba for the renowned, self-described "Negro" historian, Dr. Rayford W. Logan, one of my graduate professors in the history department of Howard University. Dr. Logan, in response to my statement that Blas Roca was "Black," wrote in the margins of my paper "Not when I met him in the forties." My affirmative response to Rizo's ideological/dietary question "Do you eat pork?" heightened the historic moment as we were soon served savory slices of glazed *lechon asado* stuffed with black beans and rice.

The Havana conference on Puerto Rico turned out to be my first real political experience with sectarianism. Much of the tension was centered in the Sino-Soviet debates, and thus (can you now imagine?) how to accurately frame the independence movement of the Caribbean island colony of Puerto Rico in a world context.

Because all this was new and titillating to my very active and eclectic mind, and honestly confusing, I maintained outward calm; inside I felt nervous and adrift about my lack of depth in the theories and political lines upon which the U.S. delegation and other delegations from across the world seemed to have life-defining positions. Although I did look to Frances Beal and Irwin Silber to try and discern what was really at stake and how I might position myself around the issues. All aspects of the Havana conference on Puerto Rican independence were not "politically heavy." I think I met for the first time on that trip delegation member

Margaret Burroughs, African American activist, artist, writer, and museum founder and director who sketched profiles of delegates on the plane to Havana.

THE PUERTO RICO SOLIDARITY COMMITTEE

Within a short time after joining the Washington, D.C., PRSC chapter, I became a fully active member, heading the local chapter two or three different times over three or so years as the interests or time capacities of others waned. As chapter chair I became a member of the PRSC National Board where I came to know such PSP members as Florencio Merced, Digna Sánchez, and Andy Torres. Frank Vergara, among other New York Puerto Ricans, struggled against the weight of revolutionary legitimacy accorded the island-based PSP to bring into PRSC a no-less fervent radical perspective based in working-class New York communities. I encountered seasoned activists, such as Annie Stein, a chain-smoker as I recall, who always had a friendly word or sincere inquiry about my life or family. Then there was Morton Sobell, who seemed slightly odd to me but to whom I respectfully listened because he had been imprisoned around the Rosenberg trials.

As an active national board member I was also engaged around the frequent internal political squabbles that sometimes led to irreconcilable differences. My first trip to California (my first trip west of Chicago in fact) came as a member of a PRSC team that was dispatched to suspend the Prairie Fire organization from PRSC. We stayed with PRSC board member Robert Chrisman, publisher of *Black Scholar Magazine* and poet whose renderings I sometimes recall as I think of the evening Irwin Silber, Fran Beal, and I sat into the late hours, before the next day's PRSC board meeting, drinking Johnny Walker Red and listening to Irwin read Carl Sandburg.

I always felt, and would continue to feel in later years, as I became involved with the U.S. Left (initially through association with PRSC) that there was a premium on Black participation. I was willing, enthusiastic, disciplined, a quick learner, and politically motivated ("young, gifted, and Black," Fran and Irwin would often jokingly say). Board members, such as Fran, Rosemary Mealey, and me among others, felt a particular responsibility to take the case of Puerto Rico to the Black community. The one discussion I recall about Afro–Puerto Ricans brought a quick, dampening response from someone in PSP, the main point of which seemed to indicate that conceptions of race in Puerto Rico, and by implication political attention to racial issues, were different there than in the United States—a topic that never received much attention. It is a topic about which, in hindsight,

I and others could have been and should have been more inquiring and proactive.

PRSC activities and PSP's central role for a while in the public activities of the U.S. Left brought me into close contact with many of the later-formed political trends of the New Communist Movement. Frequent trips to Puerto Rico while representing PRSC led me to a more politically developed internationalist perspective, which was grounded in the diversity of *independentista* organizations and the varied lives of individuals and community people in Puerto Rico who held strong convictions about the colonial status of the island. There I encountered perspectives rooted not just in theories about two-staged revolution, debatable theses about a "Divided Nation," or party squabbles in the Left, but perspectives intimately tied to problems and challenges posed by colonialism to the everyday lives of working-class people in organized political activity.

I remember visiting Puerto Rico with Rosa Borenstein, PRSC Executive Director, to meet representatives of different independence organizations. Rosa was a serious, competent, savvy, but low-key organization person who kept her cool. She kept the work of PRSC moving forward through the sometimes turbulent political developments in Puerto Rico and the United States and through the ideological and political wranglings and shifts in the board and chapter affiliates (I would think of her and her leadership qualities frequently in later years as I worked with various directors of the Nicaragua Network). In Puerto Rico we met with several veteran members of the Nationalist Party in an old, distinctive building. I felt that I had stepped into a heroic aspect of Puerto Rican history—the party of Don Pedro Albizu Campos. We also met with representatives of the Puerto Rican Communist Party (all five members someone would later joke). The Puerto Rican Independence Party refused to meet with us.

Noel Colón Martínez was gracious and took us to a Cuban restaurant for dinner. I was impressed with this husky-voiced lawyer and former head of the Puerto Rican Bar Association, who had sat on a tribunal in southern Africa. In my view, Martínez's public stature and professional demeanor was an example of committed activism connected to, but quite different from the activism of full-time revolutionary cadre. The latter image was encapsulated in someone like Juan Mari Brás, who I encountered on a few occasions when I either accompanied him and his staff or joined them and another PRSC representative in meetings on Capital Hill with one or another U.S. Congressmen to discuss Puerto Rico's colonial status. Most of the party and other organizational activists, university professors, trade unionists, and fishermen I met there, I never saw again. Some I maintained contact with, such as the late Maldonado Denis.

Because of PRSC's close association with PSP (some critics labeled it a PSP front) not all encounters with proindependence forces were comradely or civil. I once had an intense debate with Juan Antonio Corretjer, well-known poet, Nationalist, and leader of the Liga Socialista (Socialist League), about a political matter. Nevertheless I was moved by his deep passion and his willingness to seriously, though forcefully, engage a young, perhaps overconfident African American activist.

The "Rescate" (Rescue) campaign in Vieques was yet another occasion to meet a cross section of Puerto Rican people and well-formed political activists engaged in life-defining struggles that impacted everyday existence. I was asked to go to Vieques as an observer for the Quakers (the electronic media would refer to me and Bob Hindmark, the Quaker official who joined me on Vieques, as "*Los Quakeros*"). In Vieques I joined other U.S. activists (such as D.C. PRSC member Rev. Phillip Wheaton and his daughter Lisa, who worked with the fishermen on Vieques, and environmental activist and *independentista* Neftalí García) and numerous Puerto Rican organizations to challenge U.S. Navy's occupation of the island by entering "unauthorized" grounds, clearing a space and setting up tents where we stayed a few days.

The "Rescate" in Vieques also brought me into contact with security issues in the movement. I innocently went about taking photos as people cleared a space to put up tents. As dusk fell on the first day of our "occupation," I was approached by two or three Puerto Ricans who were concerned that their faces might be in the photographs; they firmly, but politely, requested that I turn over my film to them. Phil Wheaton wanted to discuss the matter, but I quickly agreed to relinquish the film thinking that they might have a point about security—an issue about which I was unaware, and I did not feel the need to question their motives. I gave them the film with the naive request that they develop the one role on which I had taken previous shots of my family back in Washington and that they send those photos to me. Guess what?

Visiting the houses of fishermen and hearing of their horrifying stories of children finding unexploded ordinances and of their plans to take to their small fishing crafts to directly confront the U.S. Navy was one of the many experiences with U.S. colonial occupation of Puerto Rico that provided a concrete outlet for my political idealism and structure for my political maturation. In a real sense such encounters broadened my personal experiences and my sense of humanity (I have not had *arrepas* and honey butter since I was introduced to both at a seafood restaurant on Vieques, nor have I had similar direct experience with the heroism of everyday, working people confronting the military might of imperial occupation). After vacating Vieques Bob Hindmark and I went to the Casita Episcopal in Rio Piedras where we drank gin and tonic, and I taped the singing *coqui.*

Activism and Family Life

In the midst of all this solidarity activity, I was in graduate school, was learning to be a husband and father, and was speaking and organizing around Puerto Rican independence. Puerto Rican trade-unionist lawyers from the Bufete Sindical (a law firm specializing in labor cases), PSP youth leaders, Trotskyists with whom I had political differences—all would visit Washington and stay at our apartment, eat, drink, and discuss Puerto Rican politics.

I always thought of Rafael Anglada's visits to our apartment as special. He stayed with us a few times. Rafi was then one of the chief assistants to Juan Mari Brás. Miriam and I felt close to Rafi. He was always jovial but serious and dedicated to his work, the process of which seemed well-thought out before he arrived in Washington. His interaction with us did not have the edge of official political business and one-dimensional political talk. For instance, he asked excitedly one morning (and commented to others later about what seemed for him a new cultural experience) what to call a typically large breakfast of bacon, eggs, sausage, pancakes, and a few other items prepared by Miriam. (I was reminded of such social exchanges that frequently took place in a letter from Andy Torres requesting that I contribute to this book. He recalls first hearing of the Afro-Cuban musician Cachao during a conversation with me in our Washington apartment. I met and came to know Cachao through another Puerto Rican cultural connection to Cuba, New York–based ethnomusicologist Rene López).

Once Rafi and I visited Saul Landau at the Washington, D.C., Institute for Policy Studies to talk with others about support for Puerto Rican independence. We were introduced to Orlando Letelier, exiled foreign minister of the Allende government in Chile. Letelier, well-dressed and neatly groomed, without hesitation offered to call Senator Kennedy to discuss the matter over drinks. I remember thinking, "Wow! . . . Can you really do political business of this type like that?" I was impressed by the quick and easy way he offered to be helpful.

I would go on radio programs and speak at various public events describing the Puerto Rican colonial reality: 33 percent of Puerto Rican women of child-bearing age have been sterilized; 5 percent of men have had vasectomies; other reflections on U.S. colonialism. I had memorized stats on pharmaceuticals, U.S. corporate investments and tax breaks, and many more details to vividly describe the colonial reality for different audiences. And I would tell people how they could get involved.

FBI visits to my apartment building in connection to my work around Puerto Rico had begun, as far as I know, November 11, 1975—the morning after our first child was born. I had returned from the Havana conference on Puerto Rico a short time earlier. The visits increased later and seemed to coincide with my weekend visits to New York to meet with PRSC member Author Kinoy and others to prepare testimony for the congressional hearings on the Compact of Permanent Union (a proposed amendment to the commonwealth status, which was opposed by independence forces) held before the Interior Committee headed by the late California congressman Philip Burton. I remember Jaime Benítez, resident commisioner from Puerto Rico, suited up and strutting like a bantam rooster around the hearing room of the Long Worth House Office Building preparing to defend colonialism against the intrepid PSP representatives and their PRSC cohorts. Puerto Rican activists and solidarity supporters would be outside with banners protesting.

My mother came to Washington a few times on the weekends. On two occasions while I was out, two FBI agents knocked on our apartment door, one polite and the other gruff (their "good cop–bad cop" roles) as they inquired of my mother about me—where I was, etc. Not intimidated my mother once talked one of the agents into giving his name. Later that afternoon when he called asking for me and wanting to know when I would return, my mother talked him into confirming the spelling of his last name. Sometime later as I introduced a film about the Weather Underground (which Haskell Wexler had loaned for a PRSC fund-raiser), I told the theater audience that I was being harassed by the FBI and gave the agent's name. The unannounced visits stopped all together, but phone calls dribbled in over the following years regarding other political activities in which I was involved.

In 1989 I requested under the Freedom of Information Act to receive any documents on me held by the FBI. A year or so later I received the file with the majority of every page blackened out except for a few references to Irwin Silber, my studies at Howard University, references of concern about potential links between the Black movement and the Puerto Rican movement, and a statement that infuriated Miriam—"nationality and race of Mrs. James Early unknown." A year later I received one page from the CIA, which was impossible to read because of markings that covered almost the entire page.

THE PARTY-BUILDING MOVEMENT

The exciting and productive times for me were eventually tempered by struggles on the PRSC board that intersected with developments in the party-building movement. Political work around Puerto Rico invariably involved systemic analyses of colonialism, imperialism, capitalism, socialism, and discussions of political line and strategy and tactics. These kinds of big-picture issues influenced my attraction to the predicates of the party-building movement: antinationalism and reformism and differences with the Communist Party U.S.A. over general political line and the pivotal importance of race in U.S. politics and political organizing. Transition toward party-building was hastened by the ebb of political motion in Puerto Rico, the gradual decline of the PSP, and consequently the decline in the political life of PRSC. "The revolution was not just around the corner," as the urgency of PSP had suggested. El Comité–MINP and other U.S.-based Puerto Rican organizations had, at least for me, brought forth some working-class perspectives and racial issues that added complexity to the revolutionary march I think many of us thought we were on.

I, like many PRSC members, had worked long and hard at great sacrifice to family life, educational endeavors, and professional aspirations to make a contribution to the Puerto Rican independence movement. The rewards had also been great. I think that all experienced solidarity activists will recall that the personal satisfaction one gains is tremendous—turning anger and disgust into focused activity, ideals of social justice into practice. And then there is the added value of learning adventures in another country and culture.

Political associations I had made on the PRSC board matured into ideological unity and later organizational affiliation. A growing circle of groups and individuals dialogued and struggled over how to construct a new Left movement: the Guardian Clubs, the Organizing Committee for an Ideological Center, the National Network of Marxist-Leninist Clubs, the National Committee for Independent Political Action, Arthur Kinoy, Ted Glick, Clay Newlin, Rosemary Mealey, Melinda Paras. These and others would become vectors on the seemingly ever-expanding party-building left of the period that I would relate to in various ways as I ventured into the broader arena of progressive and Left politics after the decline of PRSC.

I don't remember when exactly I phased out of PRSC—maybe the early 1980s. But for many years after, political associations I made through PRSC either blossomed into political comrades and friendships or spoiled through political confrontations in the party-building movement. Few purely social ties were maintained with the many people in the movement that I liked and related to socially in political activity. For many years after the demise of PRSC, organizational files, literature, buttons, banners, and posters cluttered my basement. I discarded all but a few things (which I promised Juan Flores I would give to the Center for Puerto Rican Studies at Hunter College). On hearing of what I had discarded, Howard Dodson, chief of the Schomburg Center for Research and Study of Black Culture, chided me for not properly valuing and caring for the culture of "our" movement—a value that I now urge all young activist to cultivate.

I must attribute much of what I have done and accomplished as a professional and as a political activist to positive experience with the Puerto Rican independence movement, which now dates back twenty-plus years. I also attribute to that experience much of the beginnings of the sectarianism, ignorance of the nature and practice of democracy, and overemphasis on ideology in relation to politics in which I have been mired at times over the years. Overall the positive has far outweighed the negative. In a general sense for me the most important development has been the day-to-day experience of trying to integrate deep-seated interests and commitment to social justice with deep-seated intellectual and professional career interests. Through experiences with Puerto Rican activists from all walks of life on the island and in the United States, I observed firsthand, and learned to craft for myself, a kind of workable unity of those two aspirations that is discouraged and undervalued in mainstream U.S. centers of education and professional life. Too few older activists have attempted to assist new generations of activists in being aware and in bridging the divide to the extent possible. To live exclusively on either side of the divide will not likely contribute to fundamental improvements in the quality of social life for the masses of the world's peoples, nor to the development of social individuals. One route frequently leads to dogmatism and justification of ends at any costs; the other route frequently leads to overly cautious, self-interested means and ends, if not vulgar pragmatism.

There are personal risks that will be encountered and potential career jeopardy for activists who try to connect up to all those worlds. However an improved future for humankind is a reward that requires contributions from all of us. The Puerto Rican independence struggle was for me the first crucible—and is an enduring reward.

Katherine McCaffrey

19   Forging Solidarity

Politics, Protest, and the Vieques Support Network

ON FEBRUARY 6, 1978, a flotilla of eighteen-foot fishing boats stopped NATO warships from firing off the coast of Vieques, Puerto Rico. The maneuvers, organized by the U.S. Navy, would have prevented local fishermen from fishing for thirty days during scheduled war games. The fishermen instead blocked the navy. The Vieques fishermen's blockade kicked off a direct-action campaign that was joined by other members of the community. Together with others from Vieques the fishermen mobilized to stop the bombing and military activity on their island. The Vieques movement against the U.S. Navy captured international attention. Demonstrations and blockades continued over roughly a five-year period, between 1978 and 1983.

The strength of the Vieques movement was built on two major factors: a well-organized, committed, and militant local movement and a network of equally well-organized and committed support groups spreading from Puerto Rico throughout the United States. This essay explores the development of U.S.-based support groups, their significance in sustaining the antinavy struggle in Vieques, and the importance of the antinavy struggle in Vieques in relation to Puerto Rican politics in the United States. The essay also considers the politics of solidarity work and efforts to forge a coalition despite differences in ideology between activists, the local movement in Vieques, and Puerto Ricans in the United States.

BACKGROUND: Vieques and the U.S. Navy

Vieques is an island municipality of Puerto Rico and part of the Roosevelt Roads Complex, the largest naval base in the world. In the 1940s the U.S. Navy expropriated three-quarters of Vieques Island in order to construct a massive military installation on the eastern shores of Puerto Rico. Usurping land used for sugarcane cultivation, the navy established two military installations in Vieques: an ammunition facility on the west of the island and a maneuver area on the east. With the military in control of

329

more than three-quarters of the island, residents were left sandwiched be-tween the two facilities on a narrow strip of land.

In the mid-seventies, the navy consolidated its training activities in Vieques, intensifying shelling, maneuvers, and amphibious assaults on the island. Previously the navy had transferred its bombing activities to Vieques in response to antinavy protests on the neighboring island of Culebra. The heightened maneuvers and environmental destruction came as a direct threat to Vieques fishers. Navy boats cut traps, costing fisher-men equipment and destroying marine life. Bombing destroyed coral reefs and killed fish. Maneuvers on the land destroyed mangroves and lagoons. New restrictions on the seas blocked fishermen from access to most of the island's waters during times of maneuvers. In response to the navy's grip on the island, fishermen spearheaded a direct-action campaign to halt military maneuvers.

While in the past there had been attempts in Vieques to develop a community-based movement against the military, most efforts dissolved. The fishermen's militant campaign gave substance and direction to a new organization. A local movement called the "Crusade to Rescue Vieques" was organized and engaged in a number of activities—demonstrations, blockades of military maneuvers, and pickets. Individuals with different political ideologies and from different social sectors—teachers, workers, local business owners—united to back the fishermen and oppose the mili-tary presence in Vieques. Yet the politics of the local movement were un-usual for Puerto Rico. Strong support for the crusade came from sectors of the statehood party Partido Nuevo Progresista (PNP; New Progressive Party) apparatus, which traditionally had been regarded as pro-American and promilitary. An unusual alliance was formed between statehood pro-ponents, many of whom were active in the local struggle, and *independen-tistas* in Puerto Rico and the United States, who provided crucial support for the Vieques movement. In Puerto Rico a national committee in sup-port of the Vieques movement was founded, and the National Lawyers' Guild's Puerto Rico Project and Puerto Rico Legal Aid assisted Vieques fishermen in filing suit against the navy.

THE VIEQUES SUPPORT NETWORK

The Vieques struggle against the U.S. Navy attracted the interest and com-mitment of activists in the United States working on Puerto Rican issues. The Vieques Support Network, a national organization, was founded in 1978 with the intent of fomenting and coordinating action in the United States in support of the Vieques struggle; of bringing about the withdrawal of the U.S. Navy and termination of military activity in Vieques; and of receiving restitution for the people of Vieques from all damages and losses resulting from the military presence on the island. The support network drew together a constellation of different support groups in various U.S. cities. Among the more important support groups were committees in New York, Philadelphia, and Washington, D.C. Each support group built upon the different politics, political formations, and social compositions of the cities that sustained them. People of diverse backgrounds and political ideologies united under a common goal: the support of the movement in Vieques as part of the struggle for human rights and social justice in Puerto Rico. The solidarity movement was strong and committed. As a forceful, intensive movement it lasted from 1978 to 1983, at which point the local movement in Vieques began to lose momentum.

Activists presented common explanations for why Vieques was attractive to people concerned with Puerto Rican issues. Ana Rosa Cuilan came from Puerto Rico to Washington, D.C., through a youth exchange program sponsored by the American Friends Service Committee (AFSC). In Washington, Cuilan became active in local support efforts for Vieques. She remembered that "[t]he Vieques movement was a very concrete example of relations between Puerto Rico and the United States. I think many people became aware of the colonial relationship because of the Vieques struggle. It was a very vivid example of this relationship. It was expressed in the way the rights of people were disrespected—even the established political and judicial process were disregarded. Human, environmental, and political rights were disregarded."

James Early shared a similar analysis. Early was also active in Vieques solidarity work in Washington, D.C. An African American activist, Early came to the Vieques issue through involvement with the Puerto Rico Solidarity Committee (PRSC) and the American Friends Service Committee, Latin American Board. Early commented that Vieques was " . . . one of the sharper expressions of Puerto Rico's lack of sovereignty. If you wanted to name it imperialism or colonialism you could. The way the people's lives were delimitated by the navy—and they were engaged in a fight back. They were out there. It's not that frequent that you see that graphic and vivid an example of the incursion against a people's everyday lives and their resistance against that incursion."

One of the strongest Vieques support groups was based in New York City. Solidarity efforts began there in 1978 when Carlos Zenón, the president of the Vieques Fishermen's Association, traveled to New York to meet with Gilberto Gerena Valentín, a New York City councilman from the South Bronx. Zenón requested that a support group be formed in New York to carry the message of the fishermen's struggle and to encourage politicians in Washington to act to stop the bombing in Vieques. Valentín's office helped organize a support group that drew its membership largely from several different political organizations: the Partido Socialista Puertorriqueño (PSP; Puerto Rican Socialist Party), El Comité–MINP (Movimiento Izquierda Nacional Puertorriqueño) and the Union Patriotica Puertorriqueño (UPP). The MLN (Movimiento de Liberación Nacional) was also involved, as were a variety of nonaffiliated individuals with links to Valentín and the independence movement. The solidarity effort in New York had a solid base in the city's large Puerto Rican community. Despite the different people involved in the Vieques movement in New York, its leadership was largely *independentista*.

Philadelphia also sponsored a Vieques support group that developed out of political formations particular to the city. The cause of Vieques was taken up by the Puerto Rican Socialist Party and the Alianza Puertorriqueña, an umbrella organization founded in Philadelphia that concentrated mainly on issues facing Puerto Ricans in the United States, such as housing, workers' rights, and police brutality. The only Puerto Rico–based issue that the Alianza took up was the Vieques struggle. Although people from the PSP had been working on Vieques earlier, a formal Vieques support committee was organized under the auspices of the Alianza and was linked to the national Vieques Support Network. The character of the Philadelphia support group was influenced by the expatriate Viequense population living in the city. Indeed Carlos Zenón lived for ten years in Philadelphia and had friends and family still residing in the city. These social and kin links facilitated political organization in Philadelphia on the Vieques issue.

In Washington, D.C., support for the Vieques struggle took a different form from that in New York and Philadelphia, not surprising given the social composition of the nation's capital. In 1978 the district's Latino population was small, and few Puerto Ricans were involved in support work in Washington. The Washington office of the Vieques Support Network became the national headquarters for the organization, linking the different support groups that already existed in different cities and focusing on coordinating events and fund-raising and education efforts. Support for the committee came from the local chapter of the Puerto Rico Solidarity Committee. The PRSC was composed mainly of North Americans from the Left and along with some Puerto Ricans, and it promoted solidarity with Puerto Rican progressive movements on the island and in the United States.

SOLIDARITY ACTIVITIES

In New York City the Vieques support group focused their organizing efforts on the Puerto Rican community, particularly in the South Bronx and

East Harlem. The group established a presence at cultural activities, such as the annual Puerto Rican Day Parade and several cultural festivals that were held in Central Park and on Randall's Island. The group marched, tabled, passed out literature, and collected signatures.

In Philadelphia support work focused on educating people in the Puerto Rican community and putting pressure on the U.S. military. The group held weekly pickets in front of the navy office in Philadelphia that were regularly attended by fifty to one hundred people. It put out a bilingual newsletter that was sent to members of the Alianza across the nation—about two thousand people. The group even organized a Vieques solidarity softball team, which served as a public-relations vehicle, building good will and raising awareness of the Vieques struggle.

In Washington, D.C., solidarity efforts were different in part because of the fact that the group was based in the nation's capital and did not emanate from a local Puerto Rican community. The national support network office coordinated, educated, and fund-raised. Activists spent time in the halls of Congress speaking on the behalf of Vieques and helped sponsor a congressional forum on Vieques. They forged links with other solidarity groups, such as the AFSC, Left organizations in D.C., and political groups from Central America. Though the core group of activists in the D.C. Vieques Support Network was small, the group was effective and could mobilize many allies in the D.C. area for demonstrations and other political actions.

All activists interviewed remembered the 1980 march on Washington as the most successful event organized by the Vieques Support Network. The march, which took place on May 17, 1980, demonstrated a coordinated national effort to build support for the struggle in Vieques. Four thousand people from fourteen different cities marched through downtown Washington, D.C., to protest the use of Vieques by the navy for target practice and amphibious exercises.

The Politics of Solidarity Work

One of the major achievements of the Vieques solidarity movement was that it brought together people from diverse political experiences and orientations to work collaboratively on a single issue. In a 1981 testimony before Congress, Ruth Reynolds, then cochair of the Vieques Support Network, argued that unity was forged among individuals and organizations of diverse backgrounds for three main reasons: "One, recognition of the abuses to which the people of Vieques have been subjected since the early 1940s. . . . Two, admiration for the intransigence and methodology of the struggle being waged by the Crusade to Rescue Vieques for the recovery of their land and their sea. . . . Three, revulsion at the repression with which this peaceful movement of protest has been answered."[1] A major reason, however, why unity was built on these three issues was that organizers made the tactical decision early on not to focus on Puerto Rico's political status in framing the political response to Vieques. Although the large majority of activists involved in the solidarity committees were *independentistas* of different persuasions, they chose not to emphasize the need for Puerto Rican independence in the case of Vieques. Ephrain Roche, formerly head of the Philadelphia Vieques Support Network, explained:

> We in the Alianza supported the self-determination of Puerto Rico. We supported the Dellums Bill, the UN report. Our line of thinking was that we have a very divided community. The issue of status divided us more. To improve the condition of the lives of the people, we needed to separate the issue. . . . We wanted a wide range of people fighting for Puerto Rico in the United States. We saw Vieques as raising issues of civil rights. The people have a right to live in peace, a right to their own land. . . . The conditions they were living under with the bombing and all were violating their rights, their civil rights. The Constitution of the United States says that people have a right to live in peace. And the fishermen didn't have the right to fish because of all the restricted areas that were established. We saw it as an issue of civil and human rights. We understood that this was happening because Puerto Rico is a colony, but we wanted to include more people. We saw this as part of the struggle of the people of Puerto Rico, not just *independentistas*. If we restricted the group to *independentistas,* people wouldn't come. For the great majority of people involved, the status issue didn't matter in the struggle of Vieques.

Sandra Trujillo, one of the coordinators of the New York Solidarity Committee, commented:

> There had always been tensions on the Left. This was one of the first successful efforts to put aside differences and develop an independent group. . . . Vieques gave us the opportunity to work together collaboratively. From the onset we presented it as an issue in which you didn't have to have a position on status. However, the case was a crass and blatant way of exposing the colonial relations between the United States and Puerto Rico. But we followed the cue of the fishermen and built a solid movement that we tailored to be broad-based. Our education project reflected this. For instance, we focused on the disregard for human life.

Organizers could shy away from emphasizing colonialism or imperialism and let the facts of the case speak for themselves. Angel Ortíz, a PSP party activist and member of the Philadelphia support group, explained, "Of course status is a divisive issue. But when you start looking at the situation it begins to be there. You don't have to raise the issue overtly. If you look at the very nature of the case—when you see how people were moved, relocated, how land was taken from them and how they were required to stay in a circumscribed area—when you see how they were not allowed to use the beaches, or have areas to graze their cattle, people always ask why. And things get answered, and as you answer, you develop a consciousness."

The political strategy proved wise given the politics of the Puerto Rican community and liberal sectors of the United States, but it was even more important because of local politics in Vieques. The local movement never envisioned itself as an anti-imperialist mobilization; rather it framed its struggle as one of social justice and human rights that was being waged for the right to work, to live in peace, to reclaim land, to exist as a community. It was a source of pride in the local movement that all four electoral parties were represented and that the struggle was not a partisan one, but one of the "whole people together." This ideology may have obscured some of the political differences that did exist within the community. It certainly failed to highlight the unusual presence of the PNP in the local movement. As mentioned above, the PNP had traditionally been considered the most pro-American and promilitary of the Puerto Rican political parties. To find PNP party activists in leadership positions of the antinavy struggle in Vieques was surprising to many people.

Zoilo Torres, a member of the PSP and a New York solidarity committee coordinator, was one of the people who found local Vieques politics "strange." Torres said that because of the political dynamics of the situation, it was important to develop a strategy that focused on civil and economic rights and steered away from status, even though many of the U.S. activists recognized Puerto Rico's colonial status as a key element to understanding the situation. "We knew that it was because of Puerto Rico's political status that this was happening—the bombing, etc. wouldn't happen in the United States. However Carlos Zenón was a statehooder and so was the mayor. They wanted the navy out, and they were statehooders. As a tactic we decided to focus on human rights and not on status, although it was a big debate. There were many clashes between different sectors of the independence movement." Asked whether he had any regrets about not taking a firmer stand on Puerto Rican independence in relation to Vieques, Torres was resolute: "I have no regrets. We took the right position." Torres pointed to the recent island plebiscite as indicating that Puerto Ricans are split on the issue of independence. Consequently, he concluded, activists have to focus on issues that are more immediately relevant to most people. "We fail if we focus only on independence. The United States has enforced dependency on Puerto Rico. For about ninety years we have been disoriented politically and culturally. We can't impose our agenda on movements that lend themselves to independence. It would be offensive to impose our agenda."

The Vieques Support Network forged an antimilitarism agenda that would appeal to a broad constituency in the United States. Torres explained: "Being from the Left, we knew the importance of the U.S. military in the Caribbean and Latin America." The group focused on how the multibillion-dollar military budget was built on the backs of the poor by cutting social services and funneling public monies into a bloated defense budget. "We were for 'human needs, not war.' We were among the first to bring this up, to make this connection," stressed Torres. Furthermore the group emphasized the way in which Puerto Rico and Vieques were used as a training ground for the U.S. military to establish control of Latin America and the world. They pointed out that a significant percentage of Puerto Rican territory was under the direct control of the U.S. military. Vieques itself was important for its use as a base, for munitions storage, and for training exercises. The island was even rented to other navies. "It was very connected to the Panama Base at the time they were trying to negotiate relocating the Southern Command to Puerto Rico. We saw the Southern Command treaty, then a new Reagan concept, and efforts to create military connections to apartheid South Africa. This small island was connected to a worldwide military complex," said Torres.

"We were antimilitarist, not antimilitary," Torres stressed. "We recognize that a country needs to be able to defend itself. But it doesn't need militarism and the moral degradation that that brings." The fact that the solidarity movement took an antimilitarist position opened avenues of support from the ecumenical Left in the United States. The sight of fishermen in small boats confronting battleships pulled at the heartstrings of pacifists who saw Vieques as a David-and-Goliath struggle. The American Friends Service Committee, among other religious groups, gave significant financial and social backing to the Vieques movement because it saw the movement as an antimilitarist battle for human rights. Churches across the United States passed resolutions in support of the people's struggle in Vieques.

Because of the manner in which it framed the Vieques struggle, the solidarity movement was able to draw support from sectors not previously involved in progressive Puerto Rican politics. For example, in Philadelphia Roche assessed that while most people who formally belonged to the committee were *independentista,* the committee was able to attract people to work with them who were not. As a result of working together, the non-*independentistas* "realized that all the stuff people had been telling them about us wasn't true . . . that we were communists, that we were bad people, that we ate children. We converted quite a few people!" Roche said with a smile.

Trujillo mentioned that she received much more positive feedback from the New York Puerto Rican community with her work with the Vieques Support Network than she had working for El Comité–MINP—a group clearly identified as a Left organization. When Trujillo handed out literature in support of freedom for the jailed Nationalists, people might comment to her that the Nationalists "deserved what they got . . . they were terrorists . . . they shot at the White House." The reaction to Vieques was entirely different. "Here we had a case of these poor fishermen trying to make a living. People who had been bulldozed out of their land. It was seen as an abuse of the Puerto Rican people."

Many activists felt that Vieques politicized people about Puerto Rico's relationship with the United States. Cuilan explained: "Vieques was a very vivid example of the nature of Puerto Rico's relationship with the United States. Many people became aware of the essence of this relationship. Many people became politicized because of this. Many people became very sophisticated because of this. The movement was able to reach sectors that were not reached before. We were able to make connections between what was going on in Puerto Rico and the rest of Latin America. And individuals in other struggles were educated."

Nonetheless it was not always easy to maintain a unified front and follow a middle-of-the-road position with so many diverse groups represented within the solidarity movement. Trujillo said she developed some good skills chairing "rancorous, constantly out-of-order discussions." The movement hit a hard spot after the suspicious death of Angel Rodríguez Cristóbal, a socialist activist from Ciales, Puerto Rico. Rodríguez was arrested for trespassing on military property during a ecumenical protest service in Vieques and was sentenced to serve a six-month prison term in the federal penitentiary in Tallahassee, Florida. When Rodríguez was found beaten and hanged in his cell on November 11, 1979, many on the Puerto Rican Left understood his death as a clear attack on *independentistas* and were enraged. In New York the MLN pushed the Vieques Support Network to take a stronger stand on the independence issue in response to the murder. The committee insisted on keeping its politics at the same level, supporting the fishermen based on issues of human and economic rights. As a result the MLN split from the group.

Assessments of the Movement

Vieques solidarity efforts lasted as long as there was a strong movement in Vieques. Though the movement in Vieques was impressive for its intensity, unity, and broad base, it succumbed to the pressures of time, forceful opposition from the navy, and the difficulties of maintaining unity among a diverse population. Some residents were frightened by the dirty-handed tactics of the navy, while others were tired and wanted only to see progress. When Gov. Romero Barceló interceded, signing an accord with the navy in 1983, many people saw this as the solution to the island's dilemmas. The navy agreed to be a good neighbor and bring industry to Vieques. Time proved the navy's promises to be empty, but in 1983 many Viequenses embraced the accord as the answer to a long, difficult struggle. The accord effectively defused the local movement.

Solidarity efforts, by nature, were predicated on the existence of a local movement, and when the struggle in Vieques dissipated so did the Vieques Support Network. Activists were asked to assess the solidarity efforts in light of the fact that the ultimate goals of the Vieques movement—the removal of the U.S. Navy from Vieques, the cessation of military activity, and restitution to the Viequenses—had not been achieved. All activists made positive assessments of the movement. Roche commented: "We worked together for a long time and educated a lot of people. We kept the issue alive in Philadelphia. The committee was really active. It wasn't just a name. We did something at least every two weeks. We had no staff, no money; it was all volunteer work. We had a good relationship with the people of Vieques." Ortíz believed that the solidarity efforts made a lasting impression on the Puerto Rican community in Philadelphia:

> We created consciousness in the Puerto Rican community about Vieques. We had good attendance at our activities. I believe the greatest victories are those that stay with you. We raised consciousness among people about what being a colony really means. . . . The thing we were left with was a consciousness, an understanding that Puerto Rico was used in a way in which we had no say; we had no decision-making power. Our people were being abused. The fishermen were not allowed to fish and earn a living. If nothing else is left after all the demonstrations and pickets, it is that if you go into the Puerto Rican community and ask people what they think about what's happening in Vieques, the large majority will tell you that what the navy is doing is bad.

Torres felt that the Vieques Solidarity movement provided important lessons to political activists: "We infused the Puerto Rican movement with a spirit toward coalition-building. We were able to do this by addressing the immediate needs of the fishermen and by focusing on winnable goals. We were able to respect people's differences. Before it was all infighting. By focusing on limited goals, we could reach significant numbers of people. It was a significant political achievement. Now perhaps we have lost sight of that. We were able to sit down with statehooders. We needed to start with a minimal agreement and be clear on objectives." Trujillo believed that the Vieques movement laid the groundwork for new political organizations: "We provided information and concrete support for a case that was needing support. We succeeded in getting the word out to the Puerto Rican community. We worked in a unifying way that hasn't happened in a long time, and in a sustained way. This effort was the basis for groups afterward. The National Congress for Puerto Rican Rights was built on this momentum, on the need for union and coalition. The same people from the Vieques movement came together to form the National Congress."

The National Congress for Puerto Rican Rights emerged on the heels of the Vieques movement as a national organization with four thousand to five thousand members. Following the approach of the Vieques solidarity movement, it focused on issues of human rights. In an effort to maintain unity, the group supported the Dellums Bill, which called for Puerto Rico's right to self-determination and a plebiscite on Puerto Rico's status. In this way people with different positions on Puerto Rico's political status might be brought together to concentrate on the common goal of civil rights for all Puerto Ricans. In New York many of the people who participated in the Vieques Support Network formed the backbone of the campaign to elect New York City's first African American mayor, David Dinkins. Indeed the Puerto Rican Left proved instrumental in his electoral victory. Thus the Vieques movement not only provided crucial support for a hard-fought campaign against the U.S. Navy and raised consciousness among many people of Puerto Rico's political dilemmas; it also provided important lessons in coalition-building that would translate into other areas of political activity among Puerto Ricans and their allies in the United States. The Vieques solidarity movement's strength lay in its ability to set and maintain clear goals and to sustain a commitment to both unity and diversity among its membership.

Notes

CHAPTER ONE

Thanks to Esperanza Martell, Iris Morales, Carmen V. Rivera, and José E. Velázquez for their feedback on an early draft. I am especially grateful to Doris Braendel, José Cruz, Jill Hamberg, and José M. Navarro for their detailed comments. This chapter draws on various pieces included in the present anthology. Neither the authors or the above-mentioned persons are responsible for any errors of fact or interpretation that remain.

1. "*Boricua*" is a popular term for Puerto Rican; it is derived from "*Boríken*," the name given the island by the indigenous Tainos.

2. U.S. Commission on Civil Rights, *Puerto Ricans in the Continental United States: An Uncertain Future* (Washington, D.C.: Government Printing Office, 1976), 5.

3. U.S. Commission on Civil Rights, 145.

4. Since the time of Columbus until 1898, Puerto Rico was a colony of Spain. After the Spanish-American War the island became a possession of the United States. As a U.S. territory its residents share most of the benefits and obligations of U.S. citizenship, including service in the U.S. military. However they do not vote in federal elections—including presidential elections, neither do they pay federal income taxes. Independence advocates argue that because the United States wrested control over the island from Spain, Puerto Ricans have never had sovereignty and continue to exist as a colonized people. Since 1974 the United Nations has defined Puerto Rico as a U.S. territory that has yet to be decolonized. For expositions of Puerto Rico's colonial status see, Ronald Fernández, *The Disenchanted Island: Puerto Rico and the United States in the Twentieth Century* (Westport, Conn.: Praeger, 1996), Alfredo López, *Doña Licha's Island* (Boston: South End Press, 1987), Edwin Meléndez and Edgardo Meléndez, eds., *Colonial Dilemma* (Boston: South End Press, 1993).

5. Founded in 1922, the Nationalist Party of Puerto Rico became the militant standard bearer of independence for decades. Its president for many years was Pedro Albizu Campos, who spent years in prison on charges of sedition.

6. U.S. Commission on Civil Rights, 36.

7. Piri Thomas, *Down These Mean Streets* (New York: Vintage, 1991), 330.

8. Jesús Colón, *A Puerto Rican in New York* (New York: Mainstream Publishers, 1961); Jesús Colón, Edna Acosta-Belén, and Virginia E. Sánchez Korrol, eds., *The Way It Was and Other Writings* (Houston, Tex.: Arte Público Press, 1993); Roberto P. Rodríguez-Morazzani, "Linking a Fractured Past: The World of the Puerto Rican Old Left," *Centro* 7, no. 1: 20–30.

9. There is a sizeable literature on the evolution of the Puerto Rican migration. Recent examples include Clara Rodríguez, *Puerto Ricans: Born in the U.S.A.* (Boston: Unwin Hyman, 1989), Virginia E. Sánchez Korrol, *From Colonial to Community* (Berkeley: University of California, 1994), and Andrés Torres, *Between Melting Pot and Mosaic* (Philadelphia: Temple University, 1995).

10. As groups developed over time they sometimes modified their ideological stance and programmatic priorities. These alterations were sometimes accompanied by changes in their names. Thus the Young Lords started out as the Young Lords Organization (YLO), changed to the Young Lords Party (YLP), and eventually became the Puerto Rican Revolutionary Workers Organization (PRRWO). The same was true of the MPI-PSP, which began as the Movement for Independence and evolved into the Puerto Rican Socialist Party, and El Comité–MINP, which eventually became the Movimiento de Izquierda Nacional Puertorriqueño (Puerto Rican National Left Movement). In this book, the specific name used will depend on the chronological context. In some discussions, the name used will be the one that the organization was known by during its period of greatest influence (e.g., Young Lords, PSP, El Comité).

11. Important organizations, such as the Nationalist Party and the Puerto Rican Independence Party, maintained a following in U.S. communities but were not preoccupied with organizing around issues affecting Puerto Ricans as a racial/ethnic minority. Within several groups of the U.S. Left, Puerto Ricans were active, often forming a caucus or commission with responsibility for representing their respective organizations on Puerto Rican issues. In effect, they were Puerto Rican leftists participating within multinational groups. The clandestine Armed Forces for National Liberation claimed responsibility for numerous bombings of mostly military and corporate facilities during the 1970s. In one of their earliest actions (January 1975), the bombing of New York City's Fraunces Tavern, four people were killed. This was done in reprisal for a right-wing bombing two weeks earlier in Puerto Rico, in which two *independentistas* were killed. Several members are currently serving long sentences in federal prisons. Ronald Fernández, *Prisoners of Colonialism* (Monroe, Maine: Common Courage Press, 1994).

12. Examples, taken just from among New York groups, are Resistencia Puertorriqueña, Unión Latina, Justicia Latina, Third World Revelationists, Puerto Ricans for Self-Determination, and the Health Revolutionary Unity Movement. PRISA, a leader in the struggle for open admissions at the City University of New York, was one of numerous student organizations at the time.

13. The PSP continued until 1995, when it became a broader political coalition, the New Independence Movement (NMI). The MLN still exists, as do the Nationalist Party and the Puerto Rican Independence Party (PIP). The PIP continues to participate in commonwealth elections and has maintained a representation in the legislature.

14. In this regard the PSP was similar to the Nationalist Party and the PIP but was much more successful in expanding throughout U.S. communities.

15. The Young Lords trace their beginnings to 1968 in Chicago, when a Puerto Rican street gang transformed itself into a radical political group under the leadership of Cha Cha Jiménez. After the New York–based Young Lords

Party changed to the PRRWO in 1972, the group continued to function until 1976.

16. Juan González, *Roll Down Your Window: Stories From a Forgotten America* (New York: Verso, 1995), xiii.

17. José Martí, an exiled Cuban revolutionary in the nineteenth century, spent years in New York organizing opposition to Spanish rule over Cuba and Puerto Rico. He was also a poet and journalist, writing "from the belly of the beast" (*desde las entrañas*) about U.S. events and institutions. An ardent fighter for liberation from Spain, he also warned against U.S. ambitions in Latin America and the Caribbean.

18. Victor M. Rodríguez, "Boricuas, African Americans, and Chicanos in the 'Far West': Notes on the Puerto Rican Pro-Independence Movement in California, 1960s–1980s" (Irvine, Calif.: Concordia University, Sociology Department, 1997).

19. Four of the five prisoners—Lolita Lebrón, Rafael Cancel Miranda, Andrés Figueroa Cordero, and Irving Flores—had been imprisoned since 1954 for their attack on the U.S. Congress. The other, Oscar Collazo, had been jailed since 1950 for participating in the attack on Blair House, the temporary residence of President Truman.

20. The PSP formed the University Federation of Socialist Puerto Ricans (FUSP) and El Comité–MINP set up the Puerto Rican Student Front (FEP).

21. Interview with José López Rivera, spokesperson for the MLN, *Claridad*, May 6–12, 1988, p. 9.

22. Notwithstanding its militant nationalism the MLN proclaimed itself open to socialists, socialist democrats, and communists. It also adopted a Marxist-Leninist framework for analyzing the social and political reality. *Program and Ideology of the MLN: First Congress of the Movimiento de Liberación Nacional (MLN)* (Chicago, Ill.: MLN, 1987), 8, 58.

23. See the chapters by Gil and Susler in this book on the history of the FALN. Also, see Ronald Fernández, *Prisoners of Colonialism* (Monroe, Maine: Common Courage Press, 1994).

24. Disputes between Puerto Rican Left organizations rarely escalated into violent encounters. There were isolated incidents of confrontations with sectarian U.S. leftist groups. These conflicts were assumed by most Puerto Rican radicals to have been instigated by provocateurs who had infiltrated the latter.

25. This wasn't an open-ended recommendation. The PSP exhorted *Boricuas* specifically to join the U.S. branch of the PSP (La Seccional), as the best vehicle for carrying out the dual functions. The organization argued against Puerto Rican radicals dissolving themselves into the U.S. left but recognized their right to do so. PSP, U.S. Branch, *Desde Las Entrañas* (New York: Casa Puerto Rico, 1973); PSP, U.S. Branch, *One Nation, One Party* (New York: Casa Puerto Rico, 1974).

26. *Program and Ideology of the MLN: First Congress of the Movimiento de Liberación Nacional (MLN)* (Chicago, Ill.: MLN, 1987), 19.

27. In probably the sharpest self-critique to appear in this volume, José Cruz argues that the Left's successes had little to do with its official ideology and strategic vision (i.e., independence and socialism). He argues the PSP's influence and

support (in Hartford) was because of its ability to use activist pressure on city hall, following the time-honored principle that the "squeaky wheel gets the grease." In her chapter, Carmen Teresa Whalen identifies a similar phenomenon in the case of the Young Lords (in Philadelphia). Much of the respect grudgingly accorded to the Lords was because of their spiritually tinged social populism.

28. The lack of a chapter on labor organizing is one of the principal gaps in this anthology. There was extensive activity in this area, covering the agricultural, industrial, and service sectors. Also within a number of unions Puerto Rican/Latino members formed rank and file caucuses that operated as a base for political organizing.

29. Angelo Falcón, "The Puerto Rican Activist Stratum in New York City, 1978" (New York: Institute For Puerto Rican Policy, 1994).

30. As of this writing some of these institutions are facing severe challenges to their existence. For example, Hostos Community College has been attacked by the conservative-dominated City University of New York Board of Trustees for the performance of its bilingual education programs. Some institutions have been targeted with severe budget cuts; some have had difficulty redefining their mission in the new political and social climate; others have yet to pass control onto a new generation of leaders and managers.

31. "Defiant Act Questions Puerto Rico Ties to U.S.," *New York Times*, December 17, 1995, p. 31. Juan Mari Brás, "El Proyecto Young," *Claridad*, July 26, 1996, p. 6.

32. On the new wave of social movements in Puerto Rico, see part 3 in Edwin Meléndez and Edgardo Meléndez, eds., *Colonial Dilemma,* (Boston: South End Press, 1993). Jorge Duany presents an incisive review of the Spanish-language literature touching on this issue in "Imagining the Puerto Rican Nation: Recent Works on Cultural Identity," *Latin American Research Review* 31, no.3 (1996): 248–67.

33. Francisco L. Rivera-Batiz and Carlos Santiago, *Puerto Ricans in the United States: A Changing Reality* (Washington, D.C.: National Puerto Rican Coalition, 1994), vi–vii.

34. Among elected officials perhaps none is more emblematic of the theme of this book as José Rivera, New York City councilman from the Bronx. Rivera, an *independentista* and community and labor organizer in New York since the early sixties, symbolizes the melding of "patriotic" and "democratic-rights" concerns.

35. Richard Flacks and Jack Whalen make a similar point with regard to the U.S. Left in general. Richard Flacks and Jack Whalen, *Beyond the Barricades: The Sixties Generation Grows Up* (Philadelphia: Temple University Press, 1989).

36. For evidence of this, see the special issue entitled "Youth Culture in the 1990s" in *Centro 5*, no. 1 (winter 1992–93): 10–93.

Chapter Two

This chapter is a condensed version of a longer unpublished paper (available from the author), which covers a wider range of factors influencing the rise of the generation of Puerto Rican radicals. Much of this work is based on interviews with participants in that movement. In the interests of brevity, direct quotes have been omitted from this version. The author is grateful to the following persons for participating in interviews and discussions: José Alfaro, Alkil Al-Jundi, José Braconey, Juan Flores, Miriam González, Esperanza Martell, David Montgomery, Jorge "Che" Nieves, Kathy Ochoa, José "GI" Paris, Richie Pérez, Hector Rivera, Carlos Rodríguez, Edgar Rodríguez, Oscar Santiago, and Ben Walker.

1. Perry Anderson, *Arguments Within English Marxism* (London: Verso, 1980), 87.

2. A recent example of this in the political life of Puerto Ricans in the United States is the emergence over the past years of the cult of Albizu Campos. The late leader of the Puerto Rican Nationalist Party has been resurrected and conferred the status of sainthood; and the struggle for independence, in keeping with the tradition of the Nationalist Party, has been transformed into a quasi-religious millenarian quest. The center of this Nationalist revival is among independence activists and supporters in Chicago and New York.

3. Herbert Marcuse's concept of "institutionalized desublimation" offers a paradigm for this process, and is found in *One Dimensional Man* (Boston: Beacon Press, 1964), 74.

4. Karl Marx, *The Eighteenth Brumaire of Louis Bonaparte* (New York: International Publishers, 1977), 15.

5. Fred Greenstein, "Political Socialization," in *International Encyclopedia of the Social Sciences,* vol. 14 (New York: MacMillan, 1968). See also Richard E. Dawson and Kenneth Prewitt, *Political Socialization* (Boston: Beacon Press, 1969).

6. During the turn of the century Puerto Rican migrant workers brought with them a rich working-class political and cultural tradition. The institution of the *lector* (reader) to the tobacco workshops in such cities as New York, Tampa, and Chicago is just one of the contributions that Puerto Rican and other Latin American workers brought to the labor movement in the United States. For a fascinating description of the world of Puerto Rican working-class political culture, see Bernardo Vega, *Memoirs of Bernardo Vega* (New York: Monthly Review Press, 1984).

7. Paul Buhl, "Italian Radicals and Labor in Rhode Island, 1905–1930," in *Radical History Review* 17 (spring 1978): 122.

8. See Albert E. Kahn, "Canceling Workers' Insurance Policies," in Ann Gagen Ginger and David Christiano, eds., *The Cold War Against Labor* (Berkeley, Calif.: Meiklejohn Civil Liberties Institute, 1987); Roger Keeran, "The International Workers Order and the Origins of the CIO," in *Labor History* (Fall 1989).

9. Augustín Laó, "La Raza Latina: Racialized Jíbaros, Proletarianized Urban Maroons, and New Mestizos," lecture presented at the University of California at Los Angeles, July 7, 1993.

10. Joel Kovel, *Red Hunting in the Promised Land: Anticommunism and the Making of America* (New York: Basic Books, 1994).

11. Robert L. Allen, *Reluctant Reformers: Racism and Reform Movements in the United States* (Washington, D.C.: Howard University Press, 1974): 175–76.

12. Van Gosse, *Where the Boys Are: Cuba, Cold War America, and the Making of the New Left* (New York: Verso, 1993).

13. For a history of Maoism in the United States, see A. Belden Fields, *Trotsky-ism and Maoism: Theory and Practice in France and the United States* (New York: Autonomedia, 1988).

14. The Progressive Labor Party (PLP) emerged from a split in the Communist Party in 1960. Comprised of members who sided with the Chinese in the Sino-Soviet split, they left the CPUSA believing the organization had lost its revolutionary character. During the early sixties the PLP participated in a number of struggles that brought them into contact with Puerto Ricans. These included efforts to gain better housing for Puerto Ricans in the Lower East Side of Manhattan and support for Puerto Rican independence.

15. Maurice Isserman, *Which Side Were You On: The American Communist Party During the Second World War* (Chicago: University of Illinois Press, 1982); Michael E. Brown et al., eds., *New Studies in the Politics and Culture of U.S. Communism* (New York: Monthly Review Press, 1993).

16. Frank Pierce, *Crimes of the Powerful* (London: Pluto Press, 1978); Tony Platt and Paul Takagi, eds., *Crime and Social Justice* (Totawa, N.J.: Barnes and Noble, 1981).

CHAPTER THREE

1. Unless otherwise noted, this work refers to the PSP branch in the United States. Structurally, the U.S. branch of the PSP (La Seccional) was subordinated to the national Central Committee in Puerto Rico, which had authority over the entire organization in both Puerto Rico and the United States. In turn, the members of the U.S. branch elected a central committee (El Comité Seccional) to direct its work. A political commission (Comisión Política) and secretariat (Secretariado) was in charge of day-to-day operations. The political commission and secretariat were elected by the Central Committee of the U.S. branch.

2. This chapter is excerpted from a work in progress about the PSP, U.S. Branch. The author has relied on extensive personal files, interviews with former members, and personal recollection. He was a member of the Central Committee of the U.S. branch from 1971 to 1983.

The author was also part of a group of former members who, during the early 1980s, conducted a historical study and evaluation of the PSP experience. The present work has benefitted from the discussions and analysis carried out by this group. Thanks to the following individuals who participated in that process: Maritza Arrastía, Denis Berger, Manuel Caballero, Emeterio Díaz, Juan R. Duchesne, Ramón Feliciano, Haydee García, Milton García, Luzgardo González, Iván Gutierrez, Shelley Karliner, Alfredo López, Graciano Matos, Melba Maldonado, Palmira Ríos, Carmen V. Rivera, Aurea Rodríguez, Alberto Salas, Eduardo Santiago, Alice Simon Berger, Andrés Torres, Carmen Vázquez, and the late Dennis Urrútia. The opinions expressed in this chapter are the author's alone, and are not intended to represent the views of this group, either collectively or as individuals. Thanks also to Marta Bahamón, Sigfredo Carrión, Rita Mañas, Norma Ortega, and Andrés Torres for their contributions to this chapter.

3. This perception is clear in interviews with former members of the PSP. The

concept of *lumpen proletariat* was traditionally used in Marxist theory to refer to society's outcasts: criminals, beggars, even the long-term unemployed. Originally the *lumpen proletariat* were viewed as a potential source of recruits for fascism. Certain sectors within the sixties New Left saw this stratum as having a potentially radical/progressive role. It is clear, however, that as a whole, the Young Lords did not endorse this viewpoint.

4. Puerto Rican Socialist Party, U.S. Branch, *Desde Las Entrañas* (New York: Puerto Rican Socialist Party, 1973), part 2, 3.

5. Ibid., part 2, 3. Other important English-language documents and writings relating to this phase of the organization's history are Juan Mari Brás, "Interview with Juan Mari Brás," *NACLA's Latin America and Empire Report* 6, no. 5 (May–June 1972): 11–17; Florencio Merced, *One Nation, One Party* (Rio Piedras, P.R.: Ediciones Puerto Rico, 1975); Puerto Rican Socialist Party, *The Socialist Alternative: Political Thesis of the Puerto Rican Socialist Party* (New York: North American Congress on Latin America, 1975; "The PSP in the United States," *NACLA's Latin America and Empire Report* 6, no. 5 (May–June 1972): 20–22.

6. Puerto Rican Socialist Party, U.S. Branch, *Informe Comité Seccional, Primavera 1975*, U.S. Central Committee minutes, February 1975, 6–10.

7. COINTELPRO, the name given to the counter intelligence program directed by the FBI against radical movements in the United States, was one such program that sought to establish this connection.

The hearings were published in Senate Subcommittee to Investigate the Administration of the Internal Security Act, Committee on the Judiciary, *Terroristic Activity: The Cuban Connection in Puerto Rico; Castro's Hand in Puerto Rican and U.S. Terrorism*, U.S. Senate, 1st sess., 1975, part 6.

The clandestine Armed Forces for National Liberation (FALN; Fuerzas Armadas de Liberación Nacional) between 1974 and 1981 claimed responsibility for 120 bombings, mostly at military and corporate sites. One of its earliest—and most remembered—actions took place at the Fraunces Tavern in Manhattan's Wall Street area, in which four people were killed. This bombing was in retaliation for a right-wing bombing that took place in Mayaguez, Puerto Rico, two weeks earlier as crowds were gathering for an annual proindependence rally sponsored by the PSP. At Mayaguez two people were killed. Ronald Fernández, *Prisoners of Colonialism* (Monroe, Maine: Common Courage Press, 1994), 209–11. The PSP, as did most of the Puerto Rican Left, condemned the bombing at Fraunces Tavern.

8. Eventually all these charges were dropped.

9. Puerto Rican Socialist Party, U.S. Branch, *Ante Proyecto de Tesis Seccional*, internal discussion document, spring 1978, 44–63.

10. The five Nationalist prisoners were Oscar Collazo, Lolita Lebrón, Andrés Figueroa Cordero, Rafael Cancel Miranda, and Irving Flores. Oscar Collazo received the death penalty for his attack on the Blair House, President Truman's residence, on November 1, 1950, which resulted in the death of a Secret Service agent. President Truman commuted the death sentence to life imprisonment in 1952. The remaining four Nationalists received maximum prison sentences of fifty to seventy-five years for their armed attack of the U.S. Congress on March 1, 1954.

11. The electoral question had always been something of an awkward issue

for the PSP in the United States. In its international work, the PSP for many years had relied on stalwart Democratic congressional supporters of Puerto Rican independence, such as Ronald Dellums of California.

CHAPTER FOUR

1. This chapter is based on a much longer piece in which all radical groups in Hartford are examined in detail. I am deeply grateful to the individuals who agreed to share their knowledge and views of the Puerto Rican radical experience in the city. I also thank those who read parts of or the entire manuscript and provided comments: the editors of this volume, Peter Breiner, Melinda Lawson, Louise Simmons, Charles Tarlton, Stephen Valocchi, Edwin Vargas Jr., and Sylvia Vargas. Needless to say they are not responsible for my errors. For research and editorial assistance my thanks go to Vilma E. Cruz and Elizabeth K. Allen, respectively. I owe a special thank you to Louise Simmons for sharing documents from her personal files, for graciously answering my numerous E-mail queries and for helping me contact Aida Claudio.

2. For reasons of space I have abbreviated the complex dialectic that underlies migratory processes. For good theoretical and empirical treatments of the subject, the reader may consult Centro de Estudios Puertorriqueños, ed., *Labor Migration Under Capitalism: The Puerto Rican Experience* (New York: Monthly Review Press, 1979), and Francisco L. Rivera Batiz and Carlos Santiago, *Puerto Ricans in the United States: A Changing Reality* (Washington, D.C.: National Puerto Rican Coalition, 1994).

3. "Puerto Rican Relations in Community Vary," *Hartford Times*, May 10, 1957, p. 7.

4. Interview with James Kinsella, July 19, 1994.

5. Connecticut Department of Labor, statistics assembled by Louise Simmons; Department of Planning, Hartford, Conn. *Hartford: The State of the City*, September 1983.

6. Janet Anderson, "Ethnic Need: Political Muscle," *Hartford Courant*, March 19, 1970, p. 1. Kernstock offers an estimate of about 18,000 by multiplying the Puerto Rican school population in 1969 (4,441 children) by 4, the size of an average Puerto Rican family. Elwyn Nicholas Kernstock, *How New Migrants Behave Politically: The Puerto Rican in Hartford, 1970* (New York: Arno Press, 1980), 106.

7. María Sánchez, video recording of forum held at Immaculate Conception Church, Park Street, Hartford, Conn., January 7, 1979. All quotes from sources in Spanish have been translated by the author. Spanish names and surnames have been transcribed from documents as originally printed.

8. *"Vecinos Denuncian Desalojan Puertorriqueños,"* p. 1; *"Inseguridad Para los Puertorriqueños,"* p. 3; and *"La Destrucción de Las Areas Hispanas,"* *Qué Pasa* (Hartford, Conn.), September 1978, p. 5.

9. "Here We Stand," *Claridad*, March 19, 1972, p. 2-S. Unless otherwise noted, all *Claridad* articles came from the New York edition.

10. *Desde Las Entrañas, Political Declaration of the United States Branch of the Puerto Rican Socialist Party* (photocopy), April 1, 1973, app. A, p. 27.

11. The characterization and pattern of activities were confirmed in separate interviews on September 29, 1995, by former PSP members Aida Claudio, Edwin Vargas Jr., and Sylvia Vargas. The following articles are representative examples of how *Claridad* was used: José La Luz, "Model Cities Is Not for the Poor," *Claridad,* April 2, 1972, p. 4-S; José La Luz, *"Policía Atropella Anciano Trabajador,"* *Claridad,* April 9, 1972, p. 3-S; Manuel Blanco, "Pressure Stops Fencing In," *Claridad,* December 1, 1974, p. 3-S.

12. MPI Hartford, *Mete Mano* 1: 1; Department of Puerto Rican Community Affairs, Commonwealth of Puerto Rico, New York City, Archival Collection, box 10, Centro de Estudios Puertorriqueños, Hunter College, City University of New York.

13. Interview with José La Luz, July 6, 1989.

14. "Ponce Massacre Rally Examines Present Struggle," *Claridad,* March 26, 1972, p. 3-S; Shelley Karliner, "Situation of Migrant Workers Examined," *Claridad,* April 2, 1972, p. 7-S.

15. Angel M. Agosto, *"Lucha Obrera Puertorriqueña en EU," Claridad,* April 2, 1972, p. 6

16. José La Luz, "On the Need for Popular Campaigns," *Claridad,* June 18, 1972, p. 2-S; Victor E. Sasson, "Puerto Ricans Picket to Protest Editorial," *Hartford Courant,* September 13, 1972, p. 8; Elissa Papirno, "Socialists Picket Labor Unit, Paper," *Hartford Courant,* July 10, 1973, p. 11

17. "Puerto Rican Socialists Agree to Stop Painting Illegal Signs," *Hartford Courant,* March 13, 1973, p. 27; Bill Grava, "Group to Protest Grant Remark," *Hartford Courant,* October 23, 1973, p. 27.

18. Ruth Glasser, interview with Juan Fuentes, July 2, 1992.

19. Interview with Aida Claudio, September 29, 1995; Ricardo Brown, *"Alcalde Cree Debe Haber Representación Hispana en Gobierno Municipal," La Prensa Gráfica* (Hartford, Conn.), December 8, 1974, p. 1; John Zeaman, "Support Demonstration Held," *Hartford Times,* December 5, 1974, p. 18; "PSP Protesta Arresto," *La Prensa Gráfica* (Hartford, Conn.), December 19, 1974, p. 1; Enilda Rosas, "Más de 15 Mil Asisten Día de Solidaridad," *La Prensa Gráfica* (Hartford, Conn.), November 17, 1974, p. 1.

20. Walter Gray Markham, "Chromatic Justice: Color as an Element of the Offense," paper presented at the 1974 annual meeting of the American Political Science Association, August 29–September 2, pp. 5, 15; *"Protestan Proyecto de Verjas," La Prensa Gráfica* (Hartford, Conn.), November 24, 1974, p. 1.

21. José La Luz, "Racism, Hartford Process, *La Historia de Una Conspiración," La Prensa Gráfica* (Hartford, Conn.), February 17, 1975, p. 2.

22. Between 1977 and 1979 there is not one word in the mainland edition of *Claridad* about the postelection crisis in the U.S. branch of the PSP, with the exception of one reference to "radical changes in leadership," which intimated that something serious was taking place. Only an examination of statements by party leaders years after the 1976 election provides a sense of what the postelection

situation in the U.S. branch was like. See *"La Renovación de la Dirección," Claridad,* June 2–8, 1978, p. 10; Olga Sanabria, *"Asamblea Zona Chicago: 'Palante',"* *Claridad,* July 14–20, 1978, p. 8; Miñi Seijo Bruno, *"El independentismo 'desde las entrañas,'" Claridad,* September 18–24, 1981, p. 5; José Alberto Alvarez, *"¡A Organizar!," Claridad,* April 30–May 6, 1982, p. 10.

23. Interview with Aida Claudio, September 29, 1995.

24. Herbert F. Janick Jr., *A Diverse People: Connecticut 1914 to the Present* (Chester, Conn.: Pequot Press, 1975), 94; interview with Aida Claudio, September 29, 1995.

25. *Freedom-Libertad* (newsletter of the Connecticut Defense Coalition) 1 (June 1974): 1; *Freedom-Libertad* 1 (January 1975): 5; letter of Sister Mary Beth Johnson, Sister Kathleen St. John, and Henry Huavitz to WTIC-TV, October 12, 1973; letter of Louise Simmons and Isabel Carrasquillo to Alfredo Lopez and Ben Chavis, October 16, 1973; bulletin announcing march in support of Pepe Torres and Rubén Vargas, John Stanford, and Jim Grant, (copy), n.d., collection of Louise Simmons; interview with Louise Simmons, August 28, 1995.

26. Carol Giacomo, "Puerto Ricans Seeking Role in Politics," *Hartford Courant,* August 3, 1977, p. 35.

27. Letter of Andrés Torres to Edwin Vargas, September 25, 1977, collection of Edwin Vargas Jr.

28. An example of this attitude can be found in Alfredo Lopez, *The Puerto Rican Papers: Notes on the Re-emergence of a Nation* (New York: Bobbs-Merrill, 1973), 263–64.

29. Letter of Oscar Nieves, et al., to José Garay, December 7, 1978, Department of Puerto Rican Community Affairs, Commonwealth of Puerto Rico, New York City, Archival Collection, box 372, Centro de Estudios Puertorriqueños, Hunter College, City University of New York.

30. "PSP Begins U.S. Voters' Registration Drive," *Claridad,* July 20, 1975, p. 8-S; Milton García, "In the Elections in P.R., You Can Be a Volunteer for PSP," *Claridad,* October 10, 1976, p. 10-S; "Favor Independent PR Action," *Claridad,* October 31, 1976, p. 3-S; interview with Wilfredo Matos, January 29, 1993.

31. See José E. Cruz, *Identity and Power: Puerto Rican Politics and the Challenge of Ethnicity* (Philadelphia: Temple University Press, 1998).

32. Ismael Barreto, "ATA's Assembly," *Claridad,* August 4, 1974, p. 5-S; letter of tobacco workers to the governor of Puerto Rico, June 3, 1973, collection of the New England Farmworkers Council, Hartford, Connecticut.

33. Milga Nadal, "Explains U.S. Branch Role in PSP's Electoral Campaign," *Claridad,* August 22, 1976, p. 3-S; James Jennings, "Introduction: The Emergence of Puerto Rican Electoral Activism in Urban America," in James Jennings and Monte Rivera, eds., *Puerto Rican Politics in Urban America* (Westport, Conn.: Greenwood Press, 1984), 10.

For ample documentation of this point, see José E. Cruz, *Consequences of Interest Group Political Mobilization: A Case Study of the Puerto Rican Political Action Committee (PRPAC) of Connecticut,* Ph.D. diss., City University of New York, 1994.

34. Ken Cruickshank, "Grant's Remarks Irk Puerto Rican Group," *Hartford Courant*, October 20, 1973, p. 17; Grava, "Group to Protest," p. 27.

35. In 1974 in order to generate momentum toward a national mobilization, Ramón Arbona, editor of *Claridad* in the United States, claimed that "our country is menaced as never before with total destruction." See "The Impact of October 27," *Claridad*, July 7, 1974, p. 4-S.

36. See Peter Kivisto, "The Decline of the Finnish American Left, 1925–1945," *International Migration Review* 17, no. 1 (spring 1983): 65–94, and Charles Leinenweber, "The Class and Ethnic Bases of New York City Socialism, 1905–1915," *Labor History* 22, no. 1 (winter 1981): 31–56, reprinted in George E. Pozzetta, ed., *Immigrant Radicals: The View From the Left* (New York: Garland, 1991), 263–92, 293–318.

37. *"No Seamos Socialistas Anti-Sociales,"* letter of Wilfredo Cárdenas, Bronx, N.Y., to *Claridad*, March 12–19, 1982, p. 17.

38. *"Difícil Ingreso al PSP,"* letter of Marcelino Carrión, Hartford, Connecticut, to *Claridad*, January 15–21, 1982, p. 18.

39. José Alberto Alvarez, "Two Great Campaigns," *Claridad*, July 25, 1976, p. 9-S. According to Alfredo Lopez, only the following description of life in the PSP is universally accepted: "a frenzied existence of constant tension and endless activity." In Lopez, *Doña Licha's Island: Modern Colonialism in Puerto Rico* (Boston: South End Press, 1987), 162.

40. Joseph R. Conlin, ed., *The American Radical Press, 1880–1960*, vol. 1 (Westport, Conn.: Greenwood Press, 1974), 7, 11–12, 15.

41. An egregious example of the PSP's flair for unfounded claims is Juan Mari Brás's 1978 charge that Frank Bonilla and the Centro de Estudios Puertorriqueños staff at Hunter College were CIA agents. The Centro, as was the case with many other research and academic institutions, received funding from the Ford Foundation. As was wont among left organizations at the time, the PSP leadership equated this with being a "tool" of the CIA. It was an outlandish accusation used to discredit the Centro's intellectual work, which was at odds with the PSP political line. A letter signed by thirty-nine Puerto Rican intellectuals and community leaders demanded a retraction but Mari Brás, officially speaking for the party, did not budge. See Juan Mari Brás, *"La Patria Socialista,"* *Claridad*, June 23–29, 1978, p. 11, and "Open Letter to the Compatriots of the Center for PR Studies," *Claridad*, August 11–17, 1978, p. 17.

42. For examples of repression against party members in Hartford, see "Supreme Court Denies Appeal to Hartford Migrant Workers," *Claridad*, May 21, 1972, p. 1-S; José Antonio Bizarro, *"Manifestación Inicia Campaña Pro Presos Políticos Hartford,"* *Claridad*, May 28, 1972, p. 3-S; "Biased Jury Finds Pepe and Rubén Guilty," *Claridad*, April 8, 1973, p. 1-S; Isabel Carrasquillo, "PSP Member Fired for Organizing, Forces Company to Reinstate Him," *Claridad*, April 28, 1974, p. 6-S; Isabel Carrasquillo, "Despite Threats, Socialist Couple Firm," *Claridad*, May 19, 1974, p. 6-S; "To Support Arrested Leaders, Demo Called for Monday," *Claridad*, September 19, 1976, p. 10-S. For cases of threats and intimidation of party-supported organizations, see Isabel Carrasquillo, "ATA Ready to Fight

Threats From Growers," *Claridad,* April 28, 1974, p. 3-S; José La Luz, "A Campaign to Intimidate ATA," *Claridad,* August 11, 1974, p. 6-S. In 1973 the offices of the party were burglarized twice. See "Attacks on PSP," *Claridad,* June 17, 1973, p. 3-S.

43. José La Luz, "The Most Participatory Way, Prospects for Radical Democracy in the Americas: An Interview with José La Luz," *Democratic Left* (January–February 1993): 3–6; Vargas, author's participant observation, forum on community politics at Trinity College, Hartford, Connecticut, December 5, 1994.

44. Carmelo Ruiz, *"PSP Hartford Traza Objetivos,"* *Claridad,* January 15–21, 1982, p. 9; *"Derechos Democráticos y la Independencia de P.R.,"* *Qué Pasa* (Hartford, Conn.), June 24, 1982, p. 5; Víctor Meléndez, *"Desatan Debate Sobre Derechos Democráticos,"* *Claridad,* November 26–December 2, 1982, p. 5.

45. The first Young bill, H.R. 3024, was introduced on March 6, 1996. The 1997 bill, H.R. 856, was introduced on February 27.

46. Kwame Ture (formerly known as Stokely Carmichael) and Charles V. Hamilton, *Black Power: The Politics of Liberation in America* (New York: Vintage Books, 1992), 28, 79, 199; citation on p. 15. Another important difference is that for Ture and Hamilton change is the result of the clash between the forces of modernization and moderation; see 180–81. In the Puerto Rican case, it was the result of the *convergence* between outsider and insider strategies.

I do not know whether to acknowledge my concurrence with Anthony Giddens on this point with chagrin or delight. All I can say is that the thought occurred to me before reading his book *Beyond Left and Right: The Future of Radical Politics* (Cambridge, U.K.: Polity Press, 1994), 10, 246–53.

47. In a press release dated October 1977, José Garay, a Republican candidate for a city council seat, accused Vargas of being anti-American and chastised Sánchez for supporting a socialist.

48. Karl Marx and Friedrich Engels, "Manifesto of the Communist Party," in Robert C. Tucker, ed., *The Marx-Engels Reader* (New York: W. W. Norton, 1972), 352, 361.

49. See, for example, Agustín Lao, "Resources of Hope: Imagining the Young Lords and the Politics of Memory," *Centro* 8, no. 1 (1995): 34–49, and Ruth Glasser, *"En Casa en Connecticut:* Towards a Historiography of Puerto Ricans Outside New York," *Centro* 8, no. 1 (1995): 50–59.

50. Conlin, *American Radical Press,* 1:8.

51. Lopez, *Doña Licha's Island,* 153.

CHAPTER SIX

The author wishes to thank Rafaela Colón, Angel Ortíz, Juan Ramos, and Wilfredo Rojas, without whom this paper would not have been possible, and Andrés Torres for his helpful comments on earlier drafts of this paper.

1. Thomas Madden, "Young Lords Come to City: Ask Food, Shun Strife, Dope," *Philadelphia Inquirer,* August 10, 1970, clipping, Urban Archives, Temple University, Philadelphia, Pennsylvania (hereafter cited as UA).

2. While this generational and political confrontation occurred in other Puerto Rican communities, in Philadelphia this activism realigned Puerto Rican politics. See Roberto P. Rodríguez-Morazzani, "Puerto Rican Political Generations in New York: Pioneros, Young Turks, and Radicals," *Centro de Estudios Puertorriqueños Bulletin* 4 (winter 1991–92): 96–116, and Felix Padilla, *Puerto Rican Chicago* (Notre Dame, Ind.: University of Notre Dame Press, 1987).

3. Interview with Wilfredo Rojas and Juan Ramos and interview with Rafaela Colón, January 3, 1996, Philadelphia, Pennsylvania. References to these individuals are from these interviews unless otherwise cited.

4. "Drive Started to Develop Puerto Rican Leaders," *Philadelphia Inquirer,* November 21, 1969, clipping, UA.

5. "Young Lords in Philadelphia," *Palante,* August 28, 1970, p. 10; and Young Lords Party and Michael Abramson, eds., *Palante: Young Lords Party* (New York: McGraw-Hill Book Company, 1971), 5.

6. "People's Church in Philadelphia," *Palante,* November 20, 1970, n.p.

7. "Young Lords Party: Thirteen-Point Program and Platform," in YLP and Abramson, eds., *Palante: Young Lords Party,* 150.

8. Michael Kimmel, "You've Come a Long Way, Bebe!," *Philadelphia Magazine* (August 1971): 91, 95.

9. "Thirteen-Point Program" in YLP and Abramson, eds., *Palante,* 150; Juan D. González, "The Turbulent Progress of Puerto Ricans in Philadelphia," *Centro de Estudios Puertorriqueños Bulletin* 2 (winter 1987–88): 37; and Kimmel, "You've Come a Long Way," 91.

10. "Puerto Ricans to Demand Full Voice at Lighthouse," *Philadelphia Inquirer,* June 20, 1971, clipping, UA.

11. "Young Lords Declare War on Dope Pushers," *Philadelphia Inquirer,* November 5, 1970, clipping, UA; and Kimmel, "You've Come a Long Way," 165.

12. "Unarmed Young Lords Seek to Boost Image of Puerto Ricans Here," *Philadelphia Inquirer,* October 5, 1970; Kimmel, "You've Come a Long Way," 180; and "100 Puerto Ricans and Blacks Join in Candlelight March with Crosses," *Philadelphia Inquirer,* April 10, 1971, clipping, UA.

13. "People's Church in Philadelphia," *Palante,* November 20, 1970, n.p., and Kimmel, "You've Come a Long Way," 88, 174–75.

14. "Young Lords Blamed by Police for Unrest," *Philadelphia Inquirer,* August 13, 1970, clipping, UA; and Kimmel, "You've Come a Long Way," 168.

15. "Young Lords Blamed," clipping, UA; "Residents Charge Police Brutality; Captain Describes Rock Barrage," *Philadelphia Inquirer,* August 14, 1970, clipping, UA; and Kimmel, "You've Come a Long Way," 168.

16. YLP and Abramson, eds., *Palante,* 13. On earlier relations between the police and the Puerto Rican community, see Philadelphia Commission on Human Relations, *Bulletin* (February 1961): 3, and Puerto Rico, Department of Labor, Migration Division, "Puerto Ricans in Philadelphia: A Report Prepared by the Migration Division, Department of Labor, Commonwealth of Puerto Rico for the Council of Spanish speaking Organizations" (1963): 27–30, 35–40.

17. YLP and Abramson, eds., *Palante,* 13. See also U.S. Senate, Committee of the Judiciary, Subcommittee to Investigate the Administration of the Internal

Security Act and Other Internal Security Laws, "The Puerto Rican Revolutionary Workers Organization: A Staff Study" (March 1976).

18. "Faction Leaves Young Lords Party," *Palante,* June 6, 1972.

19. "Puerto Ricans Feel New Wave of Pride," "Job Picture is Bleak for Puerto Ricans Here," and "Language is Great Obstacle," *Evening Bulletin,* June 13 and 19, 1971.

20. *Palante,* November 20, 1970, p. 22; and "Thirteen-Point Program," in YLP and Abramson, eds., *Palante,* p. 150. On nationalism and gender, see Edna Acosta-Belén, "Puerto Rican Women in Culture, History, and Society," and "Ideology and Images of Women in Contemporary Puerto Rican Literature," *The Puerto Rican Woman: Perspectives on Culture, History, and Society,* 2d ed. (New York: Praeger Publishers, 1986), 1–29 and 120–46.

21. "Restaurant Is a Strategy Center for New Spanish Council Leader," *Evening Bulletin,* June 15, 1971, clipping, UA; "Puerto Rican Leadership Split By Bickering and In-Fighting," *Evening Bulletin,* June 15, 1971, clipping, UA; and interview with Angel Ortíz, December 27, 1995, Philadelphia, Pennsylvania.

22. González, "Turbulent Progress," 38.

23. González, "Turbulent Progress," 41; and Pablo "Yoruba" Guzmán, "Puerto Rico Barrio Politics in the United States," in Clara Rodríguez, Virginia Sánchez Korrol, and José Oscar Algers, eds., *The Puerto Rican Struggle: Essays on Survival in the U.S.* (Maplewood, N.J.: Praeger Publishers, 1988), 122.

CHAPTER SEVEN

1. The *maceta* is a mallet or pestle used in grinding substances in a mortar. This was a popular slogan in Puerto Rico and Latin America during the sixties and seventies: a warning that an oppressed people will resort to any means to receive its due respect.

This history is largely based on personal recollection, organizational documents, and conversations and interviews with former activists of the student movement. In particular, I wish to thank George Colón, Eduardo "Pancho" Cruz, and Anthony and Elena Román for their interviews and conversations.

2. Richie Pérez, "Unión Estudiantil Boricua—Puerto Rican Student Union," *Palante: Latin Revolutionary News Service* 3, no. 3 (1971): 6–7. Puerto Rican Student Union, *La Historia de la Unión Estudiantil Boricua: Movimiento Estudiantil Revolucionario* (Bronx, N.Y.: PRSU, 1970), 1.

3. "But then came the break; the Young Lords and Isaac Hayes, the Puerto Rican Student Union and the new 'Retha Franklin, Melvin Van Peebles and Eddie Palmieri. This was the new modus operandi for survival." Felipe Luciano, *New York Times,* June 25, 1972, p. D26.

4. U.S. Commission on Civil Rights, *Puerto Ricans in the Continental United States: An Uncertain Future.* (Washington, D.C.: Government Printing Office, 1976), 119.

5. Rick Martínez, "The Chicano Community Sorely Misses Its 'Willies.'" *Hispanic Link Weekly Reporter,* October 9, 1995, p. 3.

6. Bart Meyers. "Radical Struggle for Open Admissions at CUNY," *The Kingsman* 2, no. 3 (February 27, 1976): 11, 13.

7. Interview with Eduardo "Pancho" Cruz, December 1995.

8. "Student Strike at BCC," (Bronx Community College) *The Communicator* 21, no. 7 (May 22, 1969): 1.

9. Bart Meyers, "The Political History of BC: Justice Will Die Without Activism," *The Kingsman* (December 13, 1974): 7.

10. Fred Miller and Gil Friend, "The Week That Was," (City College of New York) *Observation Post* 45, no. 10 (1969): 4.

11. Meyers, "Radical Struggle," 11, 13.

12. Juan Mari Brás, *"El MPI Ante el Pueblo de Puerto Rico,"* *Claridad* 13, no. 298 (1971): 3.

13. *"Estudiantes de la FUPI Luchan Contra La Fuerza de Choque,"* (Puerto Rican Student Union) *Maceta* 1, no. 2 (1971): 1, 4.

14. PRSU, *La Historia.*

15. Puerto Rican Student Union. *History of the Puerto Rican Student Movement.* New York: 1973.

16. Pérez, *"Unión Estudiantil Boricua,"* 1.

17. PRSU, *La Historia,* 4.

18. PRSU, *La Historia,* 6–7.

19. *Claridad* 12, no. 278 (October 18, 1970), p. 5.

20. Iris Morales. *"¡PALANTE, SIEMPRE PALANTE!": The Young Lords.* Documentary film circular, New York (1995); Puerto Rican Student Union. *National Conference of Puerto Rican and Latino Students.* Conference circular, Bronx (1970).

21. PRSU, *History,* 6.

22. The following discussion of chapter experiences is based on interviews with former members and my own recollections and records. It does not pretend to provide complete coverage of all the activities or sites.

23. "A spokesman for the students, who declined to identify herself, said that last November Dr. Marshak (the CCNY president) received a letter from the Puerto Rican Student Union 'exposing the conditions of Puerto Rican studies and the existing discrimination against Puerto Rican students, professors and workers at City College,'" C. Gerald Fraser, *New York Times,* February 19, 1971, 10.

24. I was part of a PRSU collective that was living and working with the YLP in El Caño.

25. *Palante: Puerto Rican Revolutionary Workers Organization* 4, no. 15 (July 21–August 4, 1972): 9.

26. Pablo Guzmán, *"La Vida Pura: A Lord of the Barrio,"* *Village Voice* 40, no. 15 (March 21, 1995): 30.

27. Several of the original founders of the Young Lords in New York were enrollees in a special college program of SUNY–Old Westbury in the late 1960s.

CHAPTER EIGHT

1. Frederic Soll and James Jackson, "The Tuley thing . . . it gave people a chance to win," *Chicago Tribune,* February 18, 1973, sec. 1, p. 43.

2. Frederic Soll and Edith Herman, "Tuley Protesters Battle Police," *Chicago Tribune,* February 1, 1973, sec. 1, p. 3.

3. U.S. District Judge Thomas R. McMillen (who in 1981 sentenced the FALN members), in Gary Marx, "Terrorism on Trial: Justice and the FALN," *Chicago Tribune Magazine* (October 22, 1995): 26.

4. *Toward People's War for Independence and Socialism in Puerto Rico: In Defense of Armed Struggle: Documents and Communiques from the Revolutionary Independence Movement and the Armed Clandestine Movement,* 1979, pp. 97, 70, and 67.

5. Interview with Eddie Negrón, Chicago, Illinois, February 11, 1996.

6. "Prisoner of War: Oscar López Rivera is a pepiniano and Puerto Rican prisoner of war," *El Progreso,* November 27, 1995, p. 22.

7. Oscar López Rivera, written interview, postmarked May 16, 1991, from USP Marion.

8. Arthur Liebman, "The Puerto Rican Independence Movement," in John R. Howard, *Awakening Minorities: American Indians, Mexican Americans, Puerto Ricans* (Chicago: Aldine Publishing Company, 1970), 162–63.

9. Thirteen of the fifteen prisoners were part of the FALN. Two, Antonio Camacho Negrón and Juan Segarra Palmer, were part of the *Macheteros* (machete wielders), an armed clandestine group that operated in Puerto Rico, and also sought independence. (In February 1998 Negrón was released from prison after serving eleven years.)

10. See General Assembly Resolution 1514 (XV), December 12, 1960; General Assembly Resolution 2621 (XXV), October 12, 1970; and General Assembly Resolution 3103, December 12, 1973. On prisoner of war status, see General Assembly Resolution 2621 (XXV), October 12, 1970; Geneva Conventions of 1949 and the Additional Protocols (I and II), June 8, 1977; and General Assembly Resolution 3103, December 12, 1973.

11. In spite of Amnesty International's normal policy of distancing itself from political prisoners alleged to have participated in armed actions, the board of Amnesty International U.S.A. passed a resolution asking its international headquarters to conduct an investigation about the situation of the Puerto Rican political prisoners in U.S. custody, along with a companion statement seeking inquiry into human rights violations in Puerto Rico.

12. "Terrorists without a Cause," *Chicago Tribune,* March 18, 1980, sec. 2, p. 2.

13. Alice Vachss, "Megan's Law Won't Reduce Sex Crime," *New York Times,* July 31, 1995, p. A9. This article cites a recent report by the U.S. Bureau of Justice.

14. U.S. Department of Justice, Office of Justice Programs, Bureau of Justice Statistics, *Sourcebook of Criminal Justice Statistics 1993* (Washington, D.C.: Government Printing Office, 1994), 495, table 5.23.

15. *"Acuerdo esclarecería Caso Muñiz Varela,"* Claridad, August 4–10, 1995, p. 3; Márilyn Pérez Cotto, *"Justicia no puede descansar en testimonio Alejo,"* Claridad, August 11–17, 1995, p. 3.

16. Ortíz Luquis, "Ignacio Rivera: Un agente encubierto de abogado," *Claridad,* November 29–December 5, 1991, p. 5. According to *United States v. Moreno Morales et al.,* 815 F.2d 725 (1st Cir. 1987), the commander was indicted in 1984 and tried in 1985. He was given a sentence of twenty years and released on parole in 1991, immediately upon becoming eligible.

17. Benjamin Torres Gotay, *"Sin aclarar aún muerte hijo Mari Brás,"* El *Vocero,* April 1, 1996, p. 11.

18. See, for example, "Ex-Detroit Officers Will Go to Prison for Beating Death," *New York Times,* October 13, 1993, p. A1; "Border Shootings," *USA Today,* September 9, 1994, p. 3A.

19. James Ridgeway, "Hard Time: Why the Left Goes to Jail and the Right Goes Home," *Village Voice* (December 11, 1990); Mark Starr, "Violence on the Right." *Newsweek,* March 4, 1985, p. 25; "Guilty Plea Expected in Fires at Clinics," *New York Times,* June 4, 1995, p. Y16; Sue Anne Pressley, "From Prison Back to P.G. Pulpit," *Washington Post,* July 26, 1989.

20. *Sourcebook of Criminal Justice Statistics 1993,* 652, table 6.92 (federal); U.S. Department of Justice, Office of Justice Programs, Bureau of Justice Statistics, *National Corrections Reporting Program 1992,* p. 34 (state).

21. In 1993 70 percent of applicants were granted parole. *Sourcebook of Criminal Justice Statistics,* 658.

22. Howard Jordan, "The Puerto Rican Political Prisoners: Criminals or National Symbols?" *Critica* nos. 19–20 (December 1995–January 1996): 15.

23. See, for example, Warren Christopher, "The United Nations at Fifty: Renewing the Vision," *U.S. Department of State Dispatch,* July 3, 1995, vol. 6, no. 27, p. 535. (Address of the U.S. Secretary of State at an event in San Francisco marking the fiftieth anniversary of the UN Charter).

24. U.S. House Resources Committee, *Attorney Fernando Martín, Vice President, Puerto Rican Independence Party, Testimony before the Resources Committee of the U.S. Congress Public Hearings Regarding H.R. 856,* April 19, 1997.

25. Julia Alvarez, *In the Time of the Butterflies* (New York: Plume/Penguin Group, 1995), 313.

26. Persons wishing to support the petition for the prisoners' release can write a letter to: President William J. Clinton, 1600 Pennsylvania Avenue, Washington, D.C. 20500. E-mail to President@WhiteHouse.gov. For other information about the prisoners, contact the following sources: National Committee to Free Puerto Rican Prisoners of War and Political Prisoners, 2067 W. Division, Chicago, IL, 60622 (773-278-0885; ncprpowpp@aol.com); Human Rights Committee, Calle 8 Rodríguez Serra, #2B, San Juan PR, 00907 (787-723-9829); and ProLibertad, P.O. Box 477, New York NY 10149 (718-601-4751).

Chapter Fourteen

1. Ann Kirchheimer and Walter V. Robinson, "Second Night of Trouble in Boston's South End," *Boston Globe,* July 18, 1972.

2. Paul Corsetti, "Riots Hit South End for Third Night," *Record American and Boston Herald Traveler,* July 19, 1972.

3. Kirchheimer and Robinson, "Second Night."

4. Ibid.

5. Peter Cowen, Walter Haynes, and Ann Kirchheimer, "A Look Back at the South End Disturbance," *Boston Globe,* July 23, 1972.

6. *Record American and Boston Herald Traveler,* July 20, 1972 (no author, title, or page number available).

7. Ibid.

8. Howard Marks, "Kevin White Discovers 'His' Puerto Ricans." *Boston After Dark,* August 1, 1972, n.p.

9. Editorial, *Boston Globe* July 21, 1972.

10. I am deeply grateful to the following for agreeing to be interviewed for this history: Annette Díaz, Victor López Tosado, Roberto Marrero, Tito Mesa, María Morrison, Pablo Navarro, Nelly Rivera, and Jaime Rodríguez. The interviews were conducted during March, July, and August 1995.

11. For a description of Villa Victoria and its significance to the Boston Latino community, see Carol Hardy-Fanta, *Latina Politics, Latino Politics* (Philadelphia: Temple University Press, 1993).

12. Discussions of the busing crisis are contained in James Green and Allen Hunter, "Racism and Busing in Boston," in William K. Tabb and Larry Sawyers, eds., *Marxism and the Metropolis* (New York: Oxford University Press, 1978); Mel King, *Chain of Change: Struggles for Black Community Development* (Boston: South End Press, 1981); and Hardy-Fanta, *Latina Politics, Latino Politics.*

13. Inquilinos Boricuas En Acción (Boricua Residents in Action), the agency that administers the Villa Victoria Housing Complex, located in the South End of Boston.

14. The late Mauricio Gastón was very active in Boston's PSP during the mid-1970s as well as a key leader of the Antonio Maceo Brigade, a Cuban Solidarity group. In his memory the Mauricio Gastón Institute for Latino Community Development and Public Policy was created in 1989 at the University of Massachusetts, Boston. Carol Hardy-Fanta, *The Life and Writings of Mauricio Gastón* (Boston: Gastón Institute, UMASS-Boston, forthcoming); Marie Kennedy, Mauricio Gastón, and Chris Tilly, "Roxbury: Capital Investment or Community Development?" in Mike Davis et al., eds., *Fire in the Hearth: The Radical Politics of Place in America* (London: Verso, 1990).

CHAPTER SEVENTEEN

We would like to thank the many persons who provided us with their stories and their insights into the development of Latino-centered gay organizations. Special thanks to Brunilda Vega, Louis Ortiz, Jimmy López-Acosta, José Olmo, Francisco Domínguez, and Efraín Barradas. The views expressed in this article are those of the authors and do not represent views of the organizations mentioned herein. We write this essay from personal experiences—both of us are founding members of one or more of the organizations. We conducted interviews with key members of the organizations and consulted records of the organizations, including flyers, newsletters, minutes of meetings, and other materials. Our attempt here is to present a critical view of the organizations; we do not claim to provide the definitive history of the Latino gay organizations under study. We only hope that others fill the blanks left open.

1. Antonio Martorell, *"Nominación, dominación, y desafío,"* *Piso 13 Edición Gay* 2, no. 2. (1993): 13.

2. COHLA "opened" the first gay space in the Puerto Rican Day Parade as early as 1978. During this same period, four Latino gay men, Pedro Velázquez, Antonio Pagán, Richard Irizarry, and Joe Franco, ran for political office. Only Irizarry and Franco ran as openly gay candidates. Irizarry, who died recently, ran as an openly gay, HIV-positive candidate for state Senate in East Harlem and Washington Heights. It is important to note that aside from the "liberal" White press, that is, *The New York Times,* Irizarry was also endorsed by *El Diario/La Prensa,* the Latino news daily not necessarily known for its liberal stands on gay issues. Joe Franco ran for the U.S. Senate in 1994 as an openly gay and HIV-positive candidate.

3. Toby Marotta, *The Politics of Homosexuality* (Boston: Houghton Mifflin Company, 1981), 28.

4. Hilda Hidalgo and Elia Hidalgo Christensen, "The Puerto Rican Lesbian and the Puerto Rican Community," *Journal of Homosexuality* 2, no. 2 (1976–77).

5. Martin Duberman, *Stonewall* (New York: Plume Books, 1994), 66. Ray (Sylvia) Rivera is one of six individuals whose life story is highlighted by Martin Duberman to "ground the symbolic Stonewall in empirical reality and placing the events of 1969 in historical context" (xvii). Through these pages one can begin to reconstruct what it was like to be gay, Latino, and poor and growing up in the Lower East Side in the early sixties. Although Ray may not represent the totality of the Latino gay experience previous to Stonewall, his story is emblematic of the limited opportunities for self-development that Latino gays had during this period. Not all Latinos prostituted themselves to survive and gain independence from oppressive environments, but far too many did.

6. During the 1970s and 1980s all radical political parties in Puerto Rico were blatantly homophobic. In fact being revolutionary was very *macho,* thus any hint at being a *maricón* or *marimacha* was grounds for discipline or even dismissal.

7. Manuel Castells, *The City and the Grassroots: A Cross-Cultural Theory of Urban Social Movements* (Berkeley: University of California Press, 1983).

8. Marotta, *Politics,* 64. Italics added by authors.

9. Terence Kissack, "Freaking Fag Revolutionaries: New York City's Gay Liberation Front," *Radical History Review* 62 (1995): 108. Bruce Bawer, *A Place at the Table* (New York: Poseidon Press).

10. Ibid.

11. Duberman, *Stonewall,* 234.

12. Joseph Beam, ed., *In the Life* (Boston: Alyson Publications: 1986), 14.

13. Warmer, Michael, introduction to *Fear of a Queer Planet: Queer Politics and Social Theory* (Minneapolis: University of Minnesota Press, 1993), xvi–xvii.

14. Ibid, xvii.

15. Charles Fernández, "Undocumented Aliens in Queer Nation: Reflections on Race and Ethnicity in the Lesbian and Gay Movement," *Democratic Left* (May–June 1991): 9.

16. Kissack, "Freaking Fag Revolutionaries," 115.

17. Fernández, "Undocumented Aliens," 9.

18. Ibid., 9.

19. Perhaps the most extreme case in the White gay world was portrayed January 9, 1995, in an ad placed in *Homo Xtra Magazine (HX)*, a gay publication, which announced a contest called "Sucking Off Puerto Rican Drug Dealers in the Bathroom" to be held at Webster Hall, a major ballroom in Manhattan.

20. The authors are working on an expanded essay that will examine other salient and associated issues. Please see "Latino Gay Organizations and Identity Formation in New York City: 1978–1995" where we explore the development of Latino gay identity and the role of other organizations in its development.

21. Gloria Anzaldúa, *Borderlands, La Frontera: The New Mestiza* (San Francisco: Aunt Lute Books, 1987), 20.

22. Rodolfo de la Garza, et al., *Latino Voices: Mexican, Puerto Rican, and Cuban Perspectives on American Politics* (Boulder, Co.: Westview Press, 1992).

23. Ibid., 81.

24. Ibid., 84.

25. Hidalgo and Christensen, "The Puerto Rican Lesbian"; Juanita Ramos, ed., *Compañeras: Latina Lesbians* (New York: Routledge, 1994); Victor de la Cancela, "A Critical Analysis of Puerto Rican Machismo: Implications for Clinical Practice," *Psychotherapy* 23, no. 2 (1986): 291–96.

26. N. Burgos and P. Díaz, "An Exploration of Human Sexuality in the Puerto Rican Culture," *Journal of Social Work and Human Sexuality* 4 (1986): 135–51; Joseph Carrier, *De Los Otros: Intimacy and Homosexuality Among Mexican Men* (New York: Columbia University Press, 1995); A. Carballo-Dieguez and C. Dolezal, "Contrasting Types of Puerto Rican Men Who Have Sex with Men," *Journal of Psychology and Human Sexuality* 6, no. 4 (1993).

27. Tomás Almaguer, "Chicano Men: A Cartography of Homosexual Identity and Behavior," *Differences: A Journal of Feminist Studies* 1 (1991): 75–100; Fernández, "Undocumented Aliens," 9–10; Clark L. Taylor, "Mexican Male Homosexual Interaction in Public Contexts," *Journal of Homosexuality* 11, no. 3–4 (1985): 117–35.

28. Frances Negrón-Muntaner, "Echoing Stonewall and Other Dilemmas: The Organizational Beginning of Gay and Lesbian Agenda in Puerto Rico, 1972–1977," *Centro* 6, nos. 1–2 (1992): 77.

29. Ibid., 79.

30. Ibid., 80.

31. Lillian Manzur-Coats, introduction to David William Foster and Emmanuel S. Nelson, eds., *Latin American Writers on Gay and Lesbian Themes: A Bio-Critical Sourcebook* (Westport, Conn.: Greenwood Press, 1994).

32. Ibid., xviii.

33. Ibid., xxv.

34. Lourdes Argüelles and B. Ruby Rich, "Homosexuality, Homophobia, and Revolution," *Journal of Women in Culture and Society* 9, no. 4 (1984): 687.

35. Rafael L. Ramírez, *Dime Capitán: Reflexiones sobre la masculinidad* (Rio Piedras, P.R.: Ediciones Huracán, 1993), 111.

36. Ibid., 112.

37. Argüelles and Rich, "Homosexuality, Homophobia, and Revolution," 386.

38. Ramírez, *Dime Capitán. Entendido* is a term increasingly used by Spanish-speaking lesbians and gays to denote gayness.

39. Bernardo Vega, "Memorias de Bernado Vega," in Juan Flores, *Divided Arrival: Narratives of the Puerto Rican Migration, 1920–1950* (New York: Centro de Estudios Puertorriqueños, Hunter College, 1984), 9. This excerpt was reprinted by permission of Monthly Review Press, © 1984.

40. *"Resolución sobre los derechos de los homosexuales,"* Partido Socialista Puertorriqueño, Seccional de E.E.U.U. Nueva York, 1978.

41. From logo design by Jorge Merced and Marcos Rodríguez, 1989.

42. Interview with Brunilda Vega, April 1995.

43. *Leerse* is a Spanish word used to indicate being outed with or without one's consent. When one fails to pass the *macho* test, one is *leido*.

44. In the 1991 through 1993 parade organizers coupled the queer organizations with the AIDS contingent, which included such organizations as Hispanic AIDS Forum. In the 1992 parade tension arose between the leadership of HAF and the lesbian and gay organizations, which included contingents from other non-Latino organizations. After this dispute both contingents wanted separate identities in the parade—for example, AIDS groups were not necessarily gay groups, and gay groups were not necessarily part of the AIDS organizations. During the past two years parade organizers have insisted that the gay and lesbian organizations be part of a larger "radical" contingent, (i.e., political prisoners, Puerto Rican independence supporters, etc.). In 1994 we marched together without incident. In the 1995 parade the queer contingent, as usual, was one of the last to appear in the procession, although this time parade organizers allowed the addition of two newcomers to the radical contingent: the Latin Kings and Queens and the Ñetas.

45. An example of this challenge was a "town meeting" that took place at the Lesbian and Gay Community Services Center in the Village in 1992. At that meeting the underlying issue was the then-hot topic of "Children of the Rainbow" curriculum. That curriculum was supported by then Chancellor Fernández, a Puerto Rican, as well as Luis Reyes, the Manhattan representative to the board, who was also Puerto Rican. On the opposite side of the fight was Ninfa Segarra, the Bronx representative, who sided with the "gang of four," the conservative majority that expelled Fernández.

CHAPTER NINETEEN

My thanks to Ana Rosa Cuilan, Cam Duncan, James Early, Angel Ortíz, Sandra Trujillo, Zoilo Torres, Ephrain Roche, and Lisa Wheaton, whose comments and insights formed the basis of this chapter. All conclusions, of course, are my own. Special thanks to Antonio Lauria Perricelli and the Intercambio, the City University of New York–University of Puerto Rico Exchange program at Hunter College for continued support of my work on Vieques. This chapter builds on fieldwork conducted in Vieques, Puerto Rico, with a doctoral dissertation grant from the Intercambio program. Additional support was provided by Intercambio to write this paper. Final thanks to Howard Fischer for his editorial comments and insights.

1. *Naval Training Activities on the Island of Vieques, Puerto Rico,* Hearings before the Panel to Review the Status of Navy Training Activities on the Island of Vieques, Committee on Armed Services, House of Representatives, 96th Cong., 2d sess., May 28, 29, July 10, 11, September 24, 1980, p. 122.

Selected Bibliography

Aponte-Parés, Luis. "What's Yellow and White and Has Land All Around It?" *Centro* 7, no.1 (winter 1994): 8–19.

Berríos, Rubén. "Independence for Puerto Rico: The Only Solution." *Foreign Affairs* (April 1977): 100–114.

Blaught, James M. *The National Question: Decolonizing the Theory of Nationalism.* London: Zed Books, 1987.

———. "Are Puerto Ricans a National Minority?" *Monthly Review* 29, no. 1 (1977): 35–55.

Bonilla, Frank. "Beyond Survival: Porqué seguiremos siendo Puertorriqueños." In Iris M. Zavala and Rafael Rodríguez, eds., *The Intellectual Roots of Independence: An Anthology of Puerto Rican Political Essays.* New York: Monthly Review Press, 1980.

Brown, Elaine. *A Taste of Power.* New York: Pantheon, 1993.

Carr, Raymond. *Puerto Rico: A Colonial Experiment.* New York: Vintage Books, 1984.

Castañeda, Jorge G. *Utopia Unarmed: The Latin American Left after the Cold War.* New York: Vintage, 1993.

Colón, Jesús. *The Way It Was and Other Writings.* Edna Acosta Belén and Virginia Sánchez Korrol, eds. Houston, Tex.: Arte Público Press, 1993.

———. *A Puerto Rican in New York.* New York: Mainstream Publishers, 1961.

Corretjer, Juan Antonio. *Albizu Campos and the Ponce Massacre.* New York: World View Publishers, 1965.

Cruz, José E. *Identity and Power: Puerto Rican Politics and the Challenge of Ethnicity.* Philadelphia: Temple University Press, 1998.

Darnovsky, Marcy, Barbara Epstein, and Richard Flacks, eds. *Cultural Politics and Social Movements.* Philadelphia: Temple University Press, 1995.

Diggins, John P. *The Rise and Fall of the American Left.* New York: Norton, 1992.

Duany, Jorge. "Imagining the Puerto Rican Nation: Recent Works on Cultural Identity." *Latin American Research Review* 31, no. 3 (1996): 248–67.

Escobar, Elizam. "The Heuristic Power of Art." In Carol Becker, ed., *The Subversive Imagination.* New York: Routledge, 1994.

———. "Art of Liberation: A Vision of Freedom." In Mark O'Brien and Craig Little, eds., *Reimaging America.* Philadelphia: New Society Publishers, 1990.

Falcón, Angelo. *The Puerto Rican Activist Stratum in New York City, 1978.* New York: Institute for Puerto Rican Policy, 1994.

Fernández, Ronald. *The Disenchanted Island: Puerto Rico and the United States in the Twentieth Century.* Westport, Conn.: Praeger, 1996.

———. *Prisoners of Colonialism*. Monroe, Maine: Common Courage Press, 1994.

———. *Los Macheteros*. New York: Prentice-Hall, 1987.

Richard Flacks and Jack Whalen. *Beyond the Barricades: The Sixties Generation Grows Up*. Philadelphia: Temple University Press, 1989.

Flores, Juan. *Divided Borders: Essays on Puerto Rican Identity*. Houston, Tex.: Arte Público Press, 1993.

Foner, Philip S. *The Black Panthers Speak*. 2d ed. New York: Da Capo Press, 1995.

Garza, Catarino. *Puerto Ricans in the United States: The Struggle for Freedom*. New York: Pathfinder Press, 1977.

González, José Luis. *Puerto Rico: The Four Storeyed Country*. Princeton: Marcus Wiener Publishing, 1993.

González, Juan. *Roll Down Your Window: Stories About a Forgotten America*. New York: Verso, 1995.

Hidalgo, Hilda, and Elia Hidalgo Christensen. "The Puerto Rican Lesbian and the Puerto Rican Community." *Journal of Homosexuality* 2, no. 2 (winter 1976–77).

Hilliard, David, and Lewis Cole. *This Side of Glory*. Boston: Little, Brown, 1993.

History Task Force, Centro de Estudios Puertorriqueños. *Labor Migration Under Capitalism*. New York: Monthly Review Press, 1979.

James, Winston. "Afro-Puerto Rican Radicalism in the United States: Reflections on the Political Trajectories of Arturo Schomburg and Jesús Colón." 8, no. 1–2 (1996): 92–127.

Jiménez, Lillian. "From the Margin to the Center: Puerto Rican Cinema in the United States." *Centro* 2, no. 8 (1990): 28–43.

Jiménez de Waghenheim, Olga. *Puerto Rico's Revolt for Independence: El Grito de Lares*. Princeton: Markus Wiener Publishing, 1993.

Jordan, Howard. "The Puerto Rican Political Prisoners: Criminals or National Symbols?" *Crítica* no. 19–20 (December 1995–January 1996).

Katz, George. *The Imagination of the New Left*. Philadelphia: Temple University Press, 1987.

Liebman, Arthur. "The Puerto Rican Independence Movement." In John R. Howard, ed., *Awakening Minorities*. Chicago: Aldine, 1970.

López, Adalberto, ed. *The Puerto Ricans: Their History, Culture and Society*. Cambridge, Mass.: Schenkman, 1980.

López, Alfredo. *Doña Licha's Island*. Boston: South End Press, 1987.

———. *The Puerto Rican Papers*. New York: Bobbs-Merrill, 1973.

Maldonado-Denis, Manuel. *The Emigration Dialectic: Puerto Rico and the USA*. New York: International Publishers, 1980.

Mari Brás, Juan. "Albizu Campos: His Historical Significance." In Iris M. Zavala and Rafael Rodríguez, eds., *The Intellectual Roots of Independence: An Anthology of Puerto Rican Political Essays*. New York: Monthly Review Press, 1980.

———. "Toward Independence and Socialism: An interview with Juan Marí Brás." *NACLA's Latin America and Empire Report* 6, no.5 (May–June 1972): 11–17.

Meléndez, Edwin and Edgardo Meléndez. *Colonial Dilemma*. Boston: South End Press, 1993.

Mendel-Reyes. *Reclaiming Democracy: The Sixties in Politics and Memory.* New York: Routledge, 1995.

Meyer, Gerald. *Vito Marcantonio, Radical Politician 1902–1954.* Albany: State University of New York Press, 1989.

Morales Carrión, Arturo. *Puerto Rico: A Political and Cultural History.* New York: W. W. Norton, 1983.

Muñoz, Carlos. *Youth, Identity, Power: The Chicano Movement.* New York: Verso, 1989.

Negrón-Muntaner, Frances. "Echoing Stonewall and Other Dilemmas: The Organizational Beginnings of a Gay and Lesbian Agenda in Puerto Rico" (pts. 1 and 2). *Centro* 4, no. 1 (winter 1991–1992): 76–95; 4, no. 2 (spring 1992): 98–115.

Negrón-Muntaner, Frances, and Ramón Grosfoguel, eds. *Puerto Rican Jam: Rethinking Colonialism and Nationalism.* Minneapolis: University of Minnesota Press, 1997.

Ojeda Reyes, Félix. "Vito Marcantonio and the Independence Movement." *Centro* 4, no. 2 (1992): 58–63.

Padilla, Felix M. *Puerto Rican Chicago.* Notre Dame: University of Notre Dame Press, 1987.

Pearson, Hugh. *The Shadow of the Panther.* Addison-Wesley, 1994.

Pérez, Richie. "From Assimilation to Annihilation: Puerto Rican Images in U.S. Films."*Centro* 2, no. 8 (1990): 8–27.

Puerto Rican Socialist Party. *The Socialist Alternative: Political Thesis of the Puerto Rican Socialist Party.* New York: North American Congress on Latin America, 1975. Original Spanish-language edition, Rio Piedras, P.R.: Ediciones Puerto Rico, 1974.

Puerto Rican Socialist Party, U.S. Branch. *Desde Las Entrañas* New York: Puerto Rican Socialist Party, 1973.

Reynolds, Ruth M. *Campus in Bondage.* Carlos Rodríguez-Fraticelli and Blanca Vázquez, eds. New York: Center for Puerto Rican Studies, CUNY, 1989.

Rivera-Batiz, Francisco, and Carlos Santiago. *Puerto Ricans in the United States: A Changing Reality.* Washington, D.C.: National Puerto Rican Coalition, 1994.

Rivera Correa, R. R. *The Shadow of Don Pedro.* New York: Vantage Press, 1970.

Rodríguez-Fraticelli, Carlos. "U.S. Solidarity with Puerto Rico: Rockwell Kent, 1937." In Edwin Meléndez and Edgardo Meléndez, eds., *Colonial Dilemma.* Boston: South End Press, 1993

———. "Pedro Albizu Campos: Strategies of Struggle and Strategic Struggles." *Centro* 4, no. 1 (winter 1991–1992): 24–33.

Rodríguez, Clara E. *Puerto Ricans: Born in the U.S.A.* Boston: Unwin Hyman, 1989.

Rodríguez, Clara E., Virginia Sánchez Korrol, and José Oscar Alers, eds. *The Puerto Rican Struggle: Essays on Survival in the U.S.* Maplewood, N.J.: Waterfront Press, 1984.

Rodríguez-Morazzani, Roberto. "Puerto Rican Political Generations in New York:

Pioneros, Young Turks, and Radicals." *Centro* 4, no.1 (winter 1991–1992): 96–116.

Rodríguez, Victor M. "Boricuas, African Americans, and Chicanos in the 'Far West': Notes on the Puerto Rican Pro-Independence Movement in California, 1960s–1980s." Irvine, Calif.: Dept. Of Sociology, Concordia University, 1997.

Sánchez Korrol, Virginia E. *From Colonia to Community*. Berkeley: University of California, 1994.

Santiago, Roberto. *Boricuas: Influential Puerto Rican Writings*. New York: Ballantine, 1995.

Silén, Juan Angel. *We, the Puerto Rican People: A Story of Oppression and Resistance*. New York: Monthly Review Press, 1971.

Thomas, Piri. *Down These Mean Streets*. New York: Vintage, 1991.

———. "Puerto Ricans in the Promised Land" *Civil Rights Digest* 6, no. 2 (n.d.): 5–39.

Torre, Carlos Antonio, Hugo Rodríguez Vecchini, and William Burgos, eds. *The Commuter Nation: Perspectives on Puerto Rican Migration*. Rio Piedras, P.R.: University of Puerto Rico Press, 1994.

Torres, Andrés. *Between Melting Pot and Mosaic: African Americans and Puerto Ricans in the New York Political Economy*. Philadelphia: Temple University Press, 1995.

Wagenheim, Kal, and Olga Jiménez de Wagenheim, eds. *The Puerto Ricans: A Documentary History*. Princeton: Markus Wiener Publishing, 1994.

William Wei. *The Asian American Movement*. Philadelphia: Temple University Press, 1994.

Young Lords Party and Michael Abramson. *Pa'lante: The Young Lords Party*. New York: McGraw-Hill, 1971.

Zavala, Iris M., and Rafael Rodríguez. *The Intellectual Roots of Independence: An Anthology of Puerto Rican Political Essays*. New York: Monthly Review Press, 1980.

Contributors

ANGEL A. AMY MORENO DE TORO, born in Santurce, Puerto Rico, is an oral historian, photographer, writer, and educator. Currently he is Professor of Social Sciences at Roxbury Community College in Boston. He has received two fellowships in history from the National Endowment for the Humanities. A member of the editorial board of *El Carillón*, a Spanish-language newspaper based in Boston, he is also working on an oral history of the city's Puerto Rican community and an oral history of Puerto Rican veterans of the war in Vietnam.

LUIS APONTE-PARÉS is Associate Professor of Community Planning at the University of Massachusetts–Boston. His work focuses on the Puerto Rican struggle against urban "renewal" programs and the building of *casitas* in New York City. He is also doing research on Latino gay men, identity, and the institutions they have built during the last decade. A cofounder of the Latino Gay Men's History Project, he is carrying out several projects documenting the history of Latino gays in New York City.

FRANCISCO CHAPMAN is Assistant Professor of Education at Western Illinois University. He received a Ph.D. in education from the University of Massachusetts–Amherst and has directed programs in bilingual education, curriculum development, and teacher training. He has worked in higher education and with community-based organizations. His published articles deal with Dominican and Puerto Rican culture, Latino political unity, and Caribbean cultural migration.

HUMBERTO (PANCHO) CINTRÓN was an organizer, trainer, and advocate in *El Barrio* during the 50s, 60s, and 70s. His *No Orphans for Tía* (1971) won silver in the New York Film and TV Festival. He published *Frankie Christo* in 1972, wrote for and produced the TV series *Realidades* (WNET) from 1972 to 1977, and produced scripts from *Villa Alegre* (1977) and *Oye Willie* (1979). Today he lives in San Francisco where he continues his advocacy work.

JOSÉ E. CRUZ is Assistant Professor of Political Science at the University of Albany, State University of New York. His research interests include the role ethnicity plays in the political mobilization of Latinos, and racial and ethnic relations in urban settings. He is the author of *Identity and Power: Puerto Rican Politics and the Challenge of Ethnicity* (Temple University Press, 1998).

JAMES EARLY is the Director of Cultural Studies and Communication at the Center for Folklife Programs and Cultural Studies at the Smithsonian Institution,

Washington, D.C. Over the course of his professional career spanning three decades, Mr. Early has promoted the values and traditions of African American,
Latino, Native American, and Pacific American communities. He has lectured
widely and written extensively on the politics of culture.

CARLOS GIL is a political and social philosopher. He is coeditor of the Puerto
Rican journal *Postdata*. His published works include *Ensayos críticos: Apuntes
para una filosofía crítica puertorriqueña* (1986) and *El orden del tiempo* (1994).
Soon to be published is a book analyzing the work of Louis Althusser.

JAMES JENNINGS is Professor of Political Science and Director of the William
Monroe Trotter Institute at the University of Massachusetts–Boston. He has pub-
lished several books based on both his own activism and scholarship focusing on
Black and Latino urban affairs including, *The Politics of Black Empowerment*
(Wayne State University Press, 1992), *Blacks, Latinos, and Asians: Status and
Prospects for Activism* (Praeger, 1994), and *Race and Politics* (Verso Press, 1997).

ESPERANZA MARTELL, CSW, is an educator, a community organizer, and a life-
skills counselor. She specializes in organizational development, conflict resolution,
and diversity training. She has a self-healing practice, adjuncts at City University
of New York colleges, and is one of the coordinators of ProLibertad, the amnesty
campaign to free the Puerto Rican political prisoners and prisoners of war. She
lives in New York City with her compañero José Alfaro and son, Amilcar.

KATHERINE McCAFFREY is a doctoral candidate in the Anthropology Program of
the City University of New York Graduate School. She conducted her field research in Vieques, Puerto Rico, focusing on social change and conflict caused by
the U.S. Naval presence. She is currently completing her dissertation and teaches
in the Thematic Studies Program at John Jay College of Criminal Justice.

JORGE B. MERCED is a member of the Boricua Gay and Lesbian Forum and a
founding member of Latino Gay Men of New York. He is Associate Director of
Pregones Theater in the Bronx and has adapted several short stories for the stage,
including *The Wedding March, El Apagón, Translated Woman,* and *El bolero fue
mi ruina,* based on Manuel Ramos Otero's *Loca la de la locura.*

IRIS MORALES was Deputy Minister of Education of the Young Lords Party. She
is an educator, a community activist, a lawyer, and the producer of *¡PALANTE,
SIEMPRE PALANTE!,* a video documentary about the Young Lords. Currently
Ms. Morales works as an educator and is the president of Latino/a Education
Network Service (LENS). She continues to work with Latino/a youth and com-
munities and the media arts. She lives in New York City with her teenage son.

CARMEN VIVIAN RIVERA moved from her native New York City to Boston in 1991
with her husband and son. In 1994 she cofounded Community Assessment and
Development Associates (CADA), an organizational development consultancy

group. Carmen continues to be an advocate for women's rights and social and political justice. She is Board Chairperson of Casa Myrna Vázquez, New England's largest shelter for battered women.

ROBERTO P. RODRÍGUEZ-MORAZZANI was Director of Research in History at the Center for Puerto Rican Studies, Hunter College, City University of New York. He has published articles on the Puerto Rican diaspora, the labor movement, race, and education as well as in the area of critical theory. Currently he is writing a critique of North American and Puerto Rican historiographical traditions.

BASILIO SERRANO is Associate Professor of Education at SUNY–Old Westbury. He was born in San Sebastian, Puerto Rico, and raised in New York City. His professional career began as a public school teacher and he has been active for many years in the development and evaluation of special education and bilingual education programs. He has also taught at Brooklyn College, New York City and LaGuardia Community Colleges, and Jersey City State College.

JAN SUSLER is a lawyer and partner in the People's Law Office, Chicago. She is an attorney for the Puerto Rican Political Prisoners and legal consultant with the campaign for their release. She has authored many articles about their case, including "*Palomas voladoras por los cielos de libertad*," and is currently working on a book about the prisoners.

ANDRÉS TORRES is on the faculty of the College of Public and Community Service at the University of Massachusetts–Boston. He became politically active in the late 1960s and joined the Puerto Rican Socialist Party (PSP) in 1971. He was with the PSP until the early 1980s. He has published articles on Latino labor market experiences, workforce development issues, Latino public policy agendas, and is the author of *Between Melting Pot and Mosaic* (Temple University Press, 1995).

JOSÉ (CHÉ) VELÁZQUEZ was active in the SNCC/Black Panther Party youth groups, Third World Revelationists, and the antiwar movement. From 1971 until 1982 he was an organizer with the Puerto Rican Socialist Party (PSP). In 1976 he received a pardon, along with other resisters, for his opposition to the military draft during the Vietnam War. Velázquez has a B.A. in History from Columbia University. Presently he teaches U.S. history in the Newark public schools. He has lectured at several universities on the African heritage of Puerto Rico.

CARMEN TERESA WHALEN is Assistant Professor in the Puerto Rican and Hispanic Caribbean Studies Department and the History Department at Rutgers University in New Brunswick, New Jersey. She is currently working on a book about Puerto Rican migration to Philadelphia in the post–World War II era.

Index